FAMILY PLANNING AND MODERN PROBLEMS

A Catholic Analysis

FAMILY PLANNING AND MODERN PROBLEMS

A Catholic Analysis

by
STANISLAS DE LESTAPIS, S.J.

With a Preface by
MICHEL RIQUET, S.J.

LONDON
BURNS & OATES

This translation of La Limitation des Naissances, *second and revised edition (Editions Spes, Paris), was made by* Reginald F. Trevett.

NIHIL OBSTAT: HUBERTUS RICHARDS, S. T. L., L. S. S.
CENSOR DEPUTATUS
IMPRIMATUR: E. MORROGH BERNARD
VICARIUS GENERALIS
WESTMONASTERII: DIE XXVI NOVEMBRIS MCMLX

PRINTED AND BOUND IN ENGLAND BY
HAZELL WATSON AND VINEY LTD
AYLESBURY AND SLOUGH
FOR BURNS AND OATES LIMITED
28 ASHLEY PLACE, LONDON, S.W.1

PREFACE

THOSE who attend the *Semaines Sociales*, the active members of family organizations or pre-marriage centres, the doctors of the Guild of St Luke, Catholic nurses and midwives, already know Fr de Lestapis, S.J. They know how able he is and, above all, how zealous and devoted he is in the cause of the family and of married life based on the teaching of the Gospel.

In his book *Family Planning and Modern Problems* we shall find this teaching once again but, to no less an extent, the historical, sociological, demographic and statistical data concerning this burning question.

We must pay our tribute to the care which our friend has constantly taken to present objectively all the elements of the problem of world overpopulation and that of the underdeveloped countries. We can confidently say that his legitimate interests as priest and moralist have never led him to underestimate difficulties or to disregard any fact. Yet this conscientious and scientific objectivity has not prevented him from remaining from the beginning to the end of his book within an authentic Christian frame of reference. Here, as elsewhere, there is no salvation save in Jesus Christ. Everything in fact is all of a piece. All the problems of married life and sexual mastery which everyone has to face in relation to the growth of world population and the need to ensure a corresponding increase of food resources, cannot be separated from the supernatural destiny of man and the ways in which his Redemption by Jesus Christ offers solutions. Fr Lestapis has had the courage to say this and to write it in a book which is intended to be as much a scientific as a theological work. As soon as our concern is man, man in his totality, his future and his destiny, there is no genuinely human solution other than that which considers man in his entirety, in all his dimensions.

Here lies the explanation of the failure and the disappointment that follow all efforts made to solve a problem of this type by some technical trick or procedure which is applied to one fragmentary or secondary aspect of so complex a reality. It is childish to think that a contraceptive or an Ogino method that has at last been made absolutely foolproof would suffice to make the number of mouths to be fed exactly equivalent to the resources of the world's agricultural production. As though it is enough to put the brake on human fertility in order to bring about an increase in the fertility of the soil or even to keep it automatically at its present level! The two are linked together and it is a fact that a diminishing or ageing population resulting from an improper form of birth control means, more often than not, that the soil itself loses its fruitfulness.

When we are dealing with the mystery of man, we never know where the repercussions of a violation of his nature and of his soul will stop. Since he is endowed with intelligence and liberty, we cannot foresee the results of forcing him to take a wrong direction. in the same way as we are able to calculate the deflection of a billiard ball. The sorcerer's apprentice is always left behind by the event.

This does not mean there is nothing we can do, but only that we must refuse facile solutions, mechanisms which are astute but deceptive and only too often degrade the mind. We have to combine an all-embracing effort to exploit the resources of the planet in a more rational way, with an increased awareness in man of his potentialities and responsibilities, and at the same time with a more perfect control by man over his instincts and energies. We have therefore not only to equip and to organize, but still more to educate or even to convert. For Christians this is a magnificent task and in line with their Christianity itself, but on condition that no Christian principles are denied or compromised.

This is the clear and convincing teaching of Fr Lestapis's book.

He begins by giving us a statement of the points of view and the arguments that favour contraceptive birth planning throughout the world, starting with Malthus and ending with the India of Gandhi and Nehru and including on the way Marx and his modern disciples, Stalin, Khrushchev and Mao Tse-Tung; the reformed Churches and Islam. No doubt this survey is not exhaustive. It could be carried further, particularly in regard to birth limitation and contraception before Malthus, and something might have been said about the Jewish attitude. But it was not so much a question of writing the history of contraceptive methods as of dealing with the more recent idea of planning births on a national or even world-wide scale.

In any case the chapter in question ends as follows: "The only population groups in which an *élite* still offers some deliberate resistance to the waves of family planning, are the Catholic peoples of the Latin tradition—Spain, Italy, France, Canada (Quebec), South

America, as well as the Catholic sectors in the Anglo-Saxon (Great Britain and the U.S.A.), German and Flemish nations" (p. 44).

The second part of the book shows what are the observable results of this widespread control of fertility by contraceptive techniques, and of its official dissemination.

To those who think the dissemination of contraceptive methods would at least have the very desirable effect of decreasing the number of abortions, the facts provide the answer—where contraceptive techniques have become most common and with official sanction, the abortion figures have risen considerably even when those for pregnancy are taken into account. In 1939 it was possible for Dr Pearl to write, in regard to the United States—"for three-quarters of the abortionist's business . . . he can thank the 'birth controllers' ". In Sweden in 1951 the number of legal abortion operations was eight times greater than in 1943—6,328 as against 703. In England, the Royal Commission on Population notes that in 1949 the proportion of procured abortions was 8·7 times greater among couples who habitually practise contraception than among the others. In Japan, the figures rise from 246,104 in 1949 to 1,068,066 in 1953 and to 1,170,143 in 1955. This means that the percentage of abortions to births is 67·64. The fact is that those who adopt the Malthusian view and are lured into avoiding at all costs a birth which they consider undesirable have no hesitation in resorting to abortion when contraceptive methods fail. Further, especially in Japan, we see an increasing number of couples resorting no longer to abortion or contraceptive methods but to sterilization; 258,205 in 1957–58 as against 55,812 in 1952–53 and 5,752 in 1949.

Obviously, the more general use of contraception, in addition to that of abortion and sterilization, does succeed in putting the brake on fertility. In Sweden it has fallen from 22·1% to 13·7% in twenty years. In the United States from 1910 to 1940, the birth rate per thousand married women decreased by 30·3%. In Japan, the decrease is still more spectacular. But these are cases of highly civilized countries. The problem remains unsolved in underdeveloped populations which are precisely those most unwilling to accept contraceptive methods either because they suspect on principle all methods imported from the West, or because they are inept at using them efficiently. This is more particularly the conclusion reached by those who have studied the problem in India.

On the other hand, it remains to be seen whether the results of this sharp fall in the birth rate are in keeping with our idea of what is in the best interests of the countries which have achieved it, whether we consider their collective prosperity, economic and demographic stability or the happiness of the individual and the married couple.

The answer to this question is provided principally in the chapter entitled "Contraceptive Civilization". It suggests, by establishing a series of converging pieces of evidence, that the general spread of contraceptive practices and the contraceptive mentality:

(1) does not diminish the number of abortions and only succeeds in lowering the birth rate in sufficiently advanced population groups, and this means a dangerous widening of the gap between the latter and the underdeveloped populations which continue to be prolific;

(2) brings into being a disturbing amount of social and psychological unbalance;

—the gradual disappearance of the group of families which choose to have a large number of children and who are responsible for three-quarters of the number of births needed to maintain the population of our nations at its present level;

—premature ageing of the mind and mental sclerosis among peoples and families, leading to the atrophy of the adventurous creative spirit;

—the increase of sexual licence, due to the fact that the sexual function, once it is separated from its procreative purposes, finds itself reduced to the status of a sterile erotic game;

—a serious deterioration in the unitive character of love, due to the inversion of the purposes of sexuality and its fixation at a very adolescent stage;

—the willed sterilization of the maternal instinct, brought about by the repression of the desire for children which is innate in woman. This gives rise to a sullen hostility towards life and its primary manifestations—pregnancies, maternity, babies and young children. There is also the divorce of female sexuality from marriage;

—a new concept of sex which, since it is cut off from its essential relationship to procreation, becomes a mere capacity for erotic play and leads to an increasing confusion between the two sexes and a decreased resistance to sexual perversions: men become less virile and women less feminine;

—an increasing toleration of homosexuality as erotic play expressing the intimacy of friendship, etc. . . . (pp. 69–94). Freud himself wrote in his *General Introduction to Psychoanalysis*:

The common characteristic of all perversions, on the other hand, is that they have abandoned reproduction as their aim. We term sexual activity perverse when it has renounced the aim of reproduction and follows the pursuit of pleasure as an independent goal. And so you realize that the turning point in the development of sexual life lies in its subjugation to the purpose of reproduction. Everything this side of the turning-point, everything that has given up this purpose and serves the pursuit of pleasure alone must carry the term "perverse" and as such be regarded with contempt.[1]

It is obviously difficult to bring forward conclusive proofs in this sphere of sexual psychology and its aberrations. But when we read the pages Fr Lestapis has devoted to the question, we cannot dispute the fact that the abuses listed above have their logical roots in the attitude arbitrarily adopted by the contraception experts in regard to nature, the sexual function and married relationships. We shall understand this still better when, in the third part of the book, we have considered the Catholic position.

There are those, Christians among them, who judge this Catholic position to be excessively intransigent, out of touch with the conditions of life today, not sufficiently aware of the often tragic difficulties that beset large families and force husbands and wives either to practise a day-to-day heroism or to despair of their salvation. And these same difficulties drive prolific populations to a state of mediocrity or of abject poverty.

Yet both Pius XI and Pius XII have not failed to insist upon the sympathy and understanding of the Church in regard to these couples whose grave difficulties she certainly does not underestimate since they have to overcome them if they are to remain entirely faithful to their married obligations.

But, and Fr de Lestapis strongly emphasizes this point, the position of the Church as regards contraception must not be put forward in isolation but linked to a complete and coherent theory of married life taking its stand firmly within the supernatural framework of the Christian life.

The demands of Christianity in this sphere, as in many others, cannot be fully and normally met except in a social order which is itself sufficiently Christian and, above all, in a supernatural climate

[1] *A General Introduction to Psychoanalysis*, Preface by G. Stanley Hall, New York, 1920, p. 273.

of faith, hope and charity. It is not at all surprising that these demands seem superhuman and impossible to carry out for those who
live in a state of spiritual mediocrity and tepidity, under the law of
egoism rather than that of charity, in a soulless world, where, at
one and the same time, living conditions, conditions of work and
housing are clearly incompatible with a healthy and normal family
life. Meanwhile our erotic civilization over-excites us in every kind
of way, in the promiscuity and solicitations of the streets, the workshop and public transport services, as well as by the hallucinatory
suggestions of cinema, radio and a literature obsessed by sexuality.

This is why Fr de Lestapis has not failed to present the Christian
demands in the matter of married chastity, within their true framework with their preliminaries and consequences where grace must
constantly correct and uplift nature. For these demands to be understood and carried out, it is indispensable that young couples should
be prepared long before marriage and that, in all their married and
family life, they should be supported by the teaching and the hundred
and one helps and comforts of a Christian community that creates
and maintains conditions of life and an atmosphere conducive to the
virtues which make the integral fulfilling of duty relatively easy. An
early education in chastity and mastery over sexuality, preparation
for marriage, for motherhood, for the educative task of parenthood,
all this should be presupposed as should also social reforms en-
suring for the family, even when it is a large one, "genuine human
living and housing conditions".

This is certainly a vast and difficult undertaking but it is directed
towards the advancement of mankind. For this intransigence of the
Church in maintaining her condemnation of contraceptive methods,
of abortion (even when therapeutic) and of divorce finally proves to
be a safeguard for human values which would otherwise become debased and perish. Among these values are: the equal dignity of each
of the partners in their mutual married love; the creative will of love;
the sense of fatherhood and motherhood; the sacred and religious
sense of the family. From a merely human point of view, Messrs
Robert Debré and A. Sauvy have had no hesitation in writing: "Malthusianism is a pattern of thought, feeling and reacting; a concept of
existence but a doubtful concept dominated by destructive forces
within itself. It is really a deliberate movement towards death"
(*Des Français pour la France*).

Yet the safeguarding of these human values which are of supreme
importance for the preservation and progress of the society of man-

kind is not for the Christian the only nor, above all, the chief reason why he refuses to accept contraceptive practices and the Malthusian mentality. He is concerned first and foremost with fidelity to the love the Holy Spirit pours into his heart and which bids him develop, even in his sexual life and through it, the likeness in himself to the divine Trinity which is a community of persons in perfect and intimate union. And this he is to do by that generosity in giving and taking from which issues creative fertility. St Paul never mentions marriage without setting it in close relationship with the mystery of the Church and the mystical body of Christ. It is here that the sexual morality of the Christian finds its foundation and its supreme law. It is through this mystery that the Christian's attitude to the problems of population as they arise today, is made clear.

"At the level of the individual conscience of the married couple," as Fr Lestapis writes, "it cannot be doubted that, since the natural and primordial end of the marriage act is the procreation of children, we are not allowed to do away with it in any arbitrary or absolute fashion" (pp. 124–32). Does it then follow that "fertility delivered over to the caprices of instinct" is the sort of "fertility which the Creator has willed should be normal in the human race"? In this connection, Fr de Lestapis very rightly notes: "Instinctual action has never been given any kind of regulating task in the sphere of human acts by the Catholic tradition. On the contrary, this tradition has always assigned this regulative role to reason illuminated by faith and inspired by love and prudence" (p. 132). Thus, he concludes, "in the realm of mankind, the practical regulation of sexuality and fertility depends on liberty or in other words on a decision taken after due deliberation by responsible husbands and wives, a decision inspired by the supreme law of all human activity—justice and love towards God and our neighbour" (*ibid.*).

It cannot be denied that husbands and wives have a duty in justice and charity to provide for the continuation of the human race. But, whilst reminding us of this essential duty of the married, Pope Pius XII did not fail at the same time to point out that "serious reasons" could dispense from it. Fr de Lestapis here lists as "motives which should inspire love and prudence in determining the degree of regulation desirable; the mother's health, the health of the future child, financial and housing problems, education, domestic harmony" (p. 134).

In regard to the means of spacing or limiting births, the express teaching of Pius XI and Pius XII and indeed of the whole Catholic tradition, admits only one: chastity either complete or merely limited to the woman's fertile periods as these can be determined more or less reliably by the use of Ogino's data or the method of variations in temperature, or again by that of vaginal secretions.

It is precisely because chastity and chastity alone whether before or during marriage, makes it possible to limit or at least to space births, that it is obvious that sexual mastery, the fruit of grace and disciplinary effort, is the essential condition for a genuinely moral birth regulation. And is it not also the condition required for happiness in marriage? Chastity and discipline are the manly virtues which enable men to make the forces of nature the instruments of his freedom.

This is very forcefully proved in Chapter XII, "Birth Control or Birth Regulation" (pp. 180–94). These pages, the most original and the most penetrating in the whole book, make us aware of the profound difference between—on the one hand—birth control which tends to satisfy and to encourage the excessive growth of the appetite for pleasure by suppressing the balancing factors of generosity and responsibility which ennobled it, and—on the other hand—birth regulation which calls for self-mastery out of respect for the nature and the vocation of the husband and wife, called as they are to glorify God in their bodies either by raising their love to the level of a perfect virginal chastity or else by courageously and generously accepting all the consequences of their physical fertility. In these pages we have genuine and moving statements from Christian couples who have in this way achieved harmony and unity by means of wholesome and judicious birth regulation.

But, as we have said, this type of regulation, which presupposes a fairly advanced degree of sexual mastery, cannot be improvised. It must be prepared for and lived out in an atmosphere of faith, hope and charity. As Pius XII pointed out: "Lack of understanding, callousness, ill-will on the part of others, make life hard and all but unbearable for the heroes who do their duty in marriage. In fact, only a genuine heroism sustained by Divine Grace can preserve in the hearts of husbands and wives the desire to know the joys of a large family." Chapter XIII deals with this preparation for the heroism of a fully Christian married life (pp. 198–214). But this type of regulation, when prepared for and lived out within the framework of a progressive transfiguration of human love into supernatural and virginal charity, finally leads to the stage at which humanity is mistress of its instincts and energies and so can enrich the earth with

peoples who are adult. It is to this noble conclusion that Fr de
Lestapis comes: "Where contraceptive techniques only succeeded in
covering up examples of bogus stability, the practice of continence,
when foreseen and prepared for by suitable training, leads to an
authentic stabilization of the sexual function.

"Birth regulation makes men and women adults. Contraception
keeps them adolescent. Regulation ennobles human effort. Contraception declares it redundant and eventually deprives it of all value"
(p. 213).

It is certainly true that in a world which derides continence and
turns its back on fertility, Christians are bound, considering the
solution they have to offer, to look like out-of-date slaves of a
bygone tradition, and Utopians whose ingenuousness is unshakable.

Not that this matters if the Christian solution is justified not only
from the point of view of the married couple and the values that are
essential for them, but also from the point of view of the whole
human race and, more particularly, of the underdeveloped countries
whose economic and demographic problem is in fact one of the most
urgent in our century.

Is it not true that Catholicism, more than any other ideology,
leads those it inspires towards a cosmic effort which—*a priori* and
as a matter of principle—envisages an expanding creation, an
"economy of the whole human race", something diametrically
opposed to the petty calculations of "the greed of nations"?

And does not this vision also, more than any other, underwrite
the courageous views of those who are the most convinced advocates
of the social evolution of the masses and the gradual emergence of
élites?

And finally, does not this cosmic and supernatural vision of
history imply a trust in human beings and in human personality
which no naturalistic ideology can surpass?

"Human beings are plentiful, but there are far too few men", we
have written elsewhere. "With the energy and technical skill of determined men, Israel is succeeding in making the desert bloom again.
The adjustment of food production in relation to the increase in the
number of human beings is first and foremost a problem of men.
What makes a man is the power to master his destiny, to make
natural forces the instruments of his own freedom, progress and
fulfilment. But we must insist that the sluggard's solutions and the
facile methods offered by neo-Malthusian propaganda, far from
increasing man's mastery over his instincts, eventually make him,

in practice, more of a slave to his impulses and erotic obsessions and too cowardly to make an effort. In so doing, it radically undermines that effort towards humanization which conditions the whole problem of harmonizing an increase in the number of human beings with the increase in the means whereby they are to be assured of a genuinely human standard of living."

And so, as Fr de Lestapis writes: "The world, in its uncertainty, waits for Catholics to show it a more vital faith in the values of existence, a more spiritual mastery of fertility through continence, an ardent search for the help that a deeper science of man could provide, and finally a struggle for a more just distribution of wealth and of men upon this planet" (p. 228).

"The agonizing problems of the underdeveloped countries and of married couples in difficulties, it will only solve . . . by a *'forward, transcendent* movement'. It will not *turn back*, as fear and egoism would have it do, or be satisfied with a *limited objective*.

"In a word, at the level of the race, the problem of hunger in the world or, to call it by its other name, the problem of the underdeveloped countries, is fundamentally the problem of a more universal, more authentic charity, a charity which is better able to develop and to organize the common life of the nations. Once the better equipped and wealthier nations put themselves at the service of the others, the latter will in their turn become conscious of their own responsibilities and their own destiny. They will acquire a more adult, more moral and more spiritual will to master their own fertility.

"In the same way, at the level of the married couple, the problem of fertility is fundamentally the same as that of married chastity which is sensed from the outset and is then gradually experienced as the very purpose of love and the explanation of its power to attract.

"In practice, at each of these levels, these problems are soluble only through Christ the divine model of universal charity and virginal chastity; only soluble too in the communitarian spirit of hope and love which the Church spreads abroad through her sacraments and her *magisterium*" (p. 286).

This outlook obviously goes far beyond the horizons within which many men confine their ambitions and their hopes. It most certainly goes beyond the point of view of those sciences which endeavour to be purely positive. The question is whether they could ever be adequate to resolve all man's problems, in particular those that concern his happiness and his destiny.

But Fr de Lestapis is speaking above all as a Christian to Christians. There can be no doubt that for the Christian the solution lies in the direction which he indicates. To the extent that Christians resolutely and generously set their feet upon this path, they will know the joy of suffering and of fighting for the world's salvation.

Fr MICHEL RIQUET, S.J.,
Chaplain General to the Société Médicale Saint-Luc

CONTENTS

xviii   *Contents*

INTRODUCTION

A NEW addition to "The Rights of Man and of the Citizen" has apparently come to the surface of human consciousness—the right to limit births, the right, that is, of the individual to limit the number of his children by all the means placed at his disposal by modern science.

Four-fifths of the human race, we are told, enthusiastically approve of this new right. Only the Catholic section, it seems, remains anxious and perplexed at the prospect and hesitates between the desire to do as everyone else does and the fear that, if it does, it will find itself at variance with the declarations of its own *magisterium*.

The following pages are addressed principally to Catholics experiencing this kind of anxiety and uneasiness. They are addressed also to all men of good-will who have doubts and misgivings. We shall merely try to examine the problem intelligently, discerningly, reflectively and so come to the point at which we must commit ourselves to a definite position.

Intelligently—we wish to examine as impartially as possible the various positions in regard to birth limitation and to assess the validity of the arguments put forward.

Discerningly—we must inform ourselves of the results achieved where contraceptive family planning has been made legal. Above all, we must estimate the value of these results. We must assess, that is, the value of the new concept of man implanted by every "contraceptive civilization".

Reflectively—finally, we have to grasp once again the full significance of the Catholic position, the values it safeguards, the conditions it presupposes.

Commitment—nevertheless, all this must lead to a definite commitment. Catholics must be "a sign to the world". Their attitude must be a witness and a rallying cry.

The four sections of this book correspond to these four ways of approach—

1. A statement of the positions and arguments that favour contraceptive family planning throughout the world.

2. A critical assessment of the results and implications of contraception where it is officially accepted.

3. The true meaning of the Catholic position.

4. The mission of Catholicism and the part it must play when faced with world-wide anxiety concerning increases in population.

Part One

Statement of the Positions and Arguments
in Favour of Family Planning
Throughout the World

HISTORICAL NOTE

WE are well aware how difficult it is to make anything like an exhaustive survey of the various positions adopted by the great ideologies and the various human societies in regard to the essential rights of man and woman in the sphere of sexuality and the rational control of the procreative function.

Although there has never been a religion which has not dealt with sexuality and procreation, if only from the standpoint of moral obligations, nor any common law civilization without its taboos, yet the fact remains that, until very recently, silence was the rule in these matters which were almost forbidden territory even to the thinker. If a problem of birth control existed, it was never put into words.

It is not until the beginning of the nineteenth century and the spread of Malthus's theories that we find public opinion first concerning itself with this problem.[1]

The notion of a deliberate control of fertility makes its appearance with Malthus and his *Essay on the Principle of Population*. It is put forward principally as a demographic and economic measure.

Later, towards the second half of the nineteenth century, with Francis Plate in London, Dr Knowlton in Boston, Dr Drysdale, Charles Bradlaugh and Annie Besant, "birth control" becomes, in the mind of the popularizers of these authors, the way to restrict fertility while allowing man to continue the free exercise of his sexuality. Neo-Malthusianism is to be a doctrine of sexual liberty.

In France, with Paul Robin and the *Ligue Française pour la régéneration humaine*, founded by him in 1896, the "refusal to bear children" (*la grève des ventres*) is an integral element in certain forms of socialism and the class struggle or, on the contrary, in certain forms of bourgeois individualist liberalism.

In the Anglo-Saxon and Scandinavian world during and after the

[1] For more details on the history of this problem see Dr Jean Sutter, *L'Eugénique*, P.U.F. (I.N.E.D.), 1950, Chapter 5—"La prévention des naissances et la planification des familles"; M. Chachuat, *Le mouvement du "birth control" dans les pays anglo-saxons*, Bibliothèque le l'Institut de droit comparé de Lyon, Paris, Giard, 1934, 553 pp.; *Family Limitation and its Influence on Human Fertility during the past fifty years*, Papers of the Royal Commission on Population, London, 1949; Dr J. Sutter, "Va-t-on diffuser les méthodes contraceptives en France?" in *Concours médical*, 9 and 24 March 1957.

First World War, "birth control" appears as an essentially "feminist" demand. The movement was started in New York by Mrs Margaret Sanger in 1910 and in London, Marie Stopes founded the first "birth control" clinic in 1923. In the same year, the Church of England made its first pronouncement in favour of contraception. The House of Lords followed suit by passing a law to authorize the teaching of "Birth Control" at Welfare Centres, by 57 votes to 44 (1926).

The year 1930 is especially noteworthy for the famous Lambeth Declaration of the Anglican bishops. Contraceptive methods may be used by the faithful of their communion "provided that this is done in the light of Christian principles".

In the following year, Pope Pius XI's Encyclical *Casti Connubii* (1931) sets against this Declaration the uncompromising character of these same Christian principles.

France, bruised and bled white by the Great War (1914–18) felt the need to recover her strength. Therefore by the law of 31 July 1920 she prohibited all contraceptive propaganda and the sale of contraceptive products and even the propagation of information concerning methods of preventing pregnancy.

After the Second World War, men suddenly seemed to discover the limits of their living-space or at least the disastrous results of squandering their resources. Authors such as William Vogt and Fairfield Osborne sounded the alarm when faced with the growth of certain sectors of the world's population, a growth with which no expanding economy seemed able to keep pace. Panic swept like a whirlwind across part of the globe. Japan introduced eugenic birth control legislation, Nehru's India at first hesitated and finally committed herself officially to a policy of contraceptive family planning. Other countries were still wondering what to do. Laboratory research was undertaken in the service of the cause of assisting humanity to restrict its fertility.

For a short time the Socialist Soviet republics took up this same cause. Whereas, until 1954, the U.S.S.R. had always shown itself resolutely hostile to any policy of contraceptive family planning, at first China then other satellite countries reversed their opinions. For a few years the "general line" officially sanctioned a slowing down of the birth rate, legalized abortion once again, provided instruction in contraceptive techniques, while still remaining strictly opposed to Malthusianism.

Such then, it seems, is the progress made in less than two centuries by the idea of birth control. We must now return to some of its former stages in order to discover its meaning. It has in fact been possible in passing to sense that the planning of the birth rate has not the same connotation in the context of economic Malthusianism, Marxist rationalism, Protestant ideology, or the perplexities of traditional religions with their customary laws.

We shall therefore review in turn the position of these several doctrines, all of which ultimately favour contraceptive family planning and, with this end in view, the adoption of contraceptive practices.

Chapter I

IN THE WAKE OF MALTHUS

I T cannot be too often repeated that the Malthusian view of the organization of human society was originally above all an economic one. The curate of Albury's first concern was to make it possible for the human race to raise the standard of its economic life. As a founder member of the Political Economy Club and the Statistical Society, Malthus approached demography and arrived at his own personal views on sex from this angle alone.[1]

Among the data of the problem, the first in his opinion is the obvious fact that increase of wealth and of the supply of goods can only be achieved on a world-wide scale at the slow rhythm of arithmetical progression, which is determined by laws over which man has little control.

The second obvious fact, still in the category of data, is the species of sexual frenzy imposed on man by nature. Without deliberate control, the reproduction of the race would unquestionably proceed at a more rapid rate of which geometrical progression can give us some idea.

On both counts the Anglican curate as moralist and philosopher was to erect a kind of positive religion of control, a rational philosophy of planning. We may question whether he realized that in so doing he was in practice confining man's horizon within the limits of his temporal life and well-being.

Although he rejected the idyllic picture, painted by such men as Godwin and Condorcet, of a future human race replete with goods and pleasures and exempt from sacrifice—Malthus, in contrast to these optimists, feared that the number of those invited to nature's banquet would be excessive—nevertheless the worthy cleric conducted the whole of his argument on the same plane as the analyses of his opponents, the plane of well-being, the plane upon which "having" alone is envisaged.[2]

[1] Research work on Malthus has been done in recent years. Two books have thrown some new light on his work—T. R. Malthus, *An Essay on Population*, with an introduction by Michael P. Fogarty, two volumes, J. M. Dent, London, 1958; J. Stassard, *Malthus et la Population*, preface by Paul Lambert, Faculté de Droit, Liège, 1957, 343 pp.

[2] Cf. Gabriel Marcel, *Etre et Avoir*, Aubier, 1935 (Translator's note).

His ethical system to which he gave this ultimate direction in fact if not in intention—for Malthus remained a sincere believer—was bound to be indebted to another theory, that of mechanical determinism erroneously attributed to nature and to economics. As Vialatoux has well said,[3] this ethical system is a "social physics" enjoying the prestige of a moral system based on grounds that appear to be rational and scientific. This doubtless accounts for the incredible success of the Malthusian Myth and for its influence on some of the "great minds" of the nineteenth century, Darwin, Say, Sismondi, S. Mill, etc., for the nineteenth century prided itself on its unbelief.

Naturalism and determinism under cover of a puritan moralism were all that was needed to delight an intelligentsia which was beginning to conceive a passion for objectivity, whilst man and the meaning of human life were to become for a time "the unknown".[4]

Hence the success of Malthusian ethics was and still is due to the fact that it was able to justify in the eyes of its supporters the unconscious egoism of acquisitive man, the avaricious owner of the good things of this world.

This precautious and avaricious man reaches the point at which, in all good faith, he parodies the words of the Gospel and says to himself: "Whenever a man is rich, gifts will be made to him, and his riches will abound; if he is poor, even what he accounts his own will be taken from him." Let the rich then consider their wealth as a blessing and a reward from Heaven due to their forethought and their prudent stewardship. Let the poor for their part blame nobody but themselves for their misfortunes which they have deserved because of their lack of foresight and their improvidence.

It is doubtless true that, at the time Malthus was writing, philanthropic movements were attempting to provide education for the masses rather than poor relief. This is sufficient to soften the unhappy impression left by the words of the economist on the poor laws.[5]

---

[3] J. Vialatoux, *Philosophie économique*, Ch. 4, "Economie et Population. Essai sur le principe malthusien," Desclée, 1933, pp. 205–8.

[4] There is an illusion here to Alexis Carel's book *Man the Unknown* (Translator's note).

[5] In a London newspaper (1766), Benjamin Franklin wrote—"In my youth I travelled much, and I observed in the different countries that the more public relief is provided for the poor, the less do they seek to help themselves and the more do they go from bad to worse. And, on the contrary, the less that is done for them, the more do they do for themselves and so become rich."

Malthus remarked:

> We are bound ... to disclaim the right of the poor to support (*An Essay on Population*, ed. by Prof. M. Fogarty, Everyman's Library, vol. II, p. 201).

> If this clause were really and *bona fide* put into execution, and the shame attending the receiving of parish assistance worn off, every labouring man might marry as early as he pleased, under the certain prospect of having all his children properly provided for (*ibid.*, pp. 51, 52).

> All parish assistance should be denied him and he should be left to the uncertain support of private charity.

> He should be taught to know that the laws of nature, which are the laws of God, had doomed him and his family to suffer for disobeying their repeated conditions (i.e. by having too many children).

In whatever way Malthus's intentions are explained or excused, it remains none the less true that he wrote these words and that they are responsible for the economic liberalism of the nineteenth century.

MALTHUSIANISM TODAY

These basic passages from the *Essay on Population* were written 150 years ago. Followers of Malthus such as Sismondi have smoothed off the angles and planed away the rough edges. The workers are no longer denied a place at the feast nor even access to higher incomes. But among the Malthusians of today, the fundamental attitude still remains the same—men are to cut down their expenses, to cut down the number of their children, at least to begin with, in order that they may be able to grow rich. When wealth is acquired and a man is no longer a charge on public funds and the taxpayer, he can then allow himself a larger number of children. But everybody knows that once this aim is achieved, those who have acquired wealth no longer want to have children.

Such then is the social ethics of Malthusianism and it always appeals to the propertied classes. In our times we find it again in the language used towards the poor and underdeveloped nations of the Far and Near East by peoples with great possessions who are benevolent apostles of the international struggle against fertility.

In his *Théorie générale de la Population*, Sauvy presents the two aspects of this social ethic, the altruistic and the egoistic:

The Altruist—These poor people will never succeed in emerging from their poverty as long as they produce children so thoughtlessly. If we did as they do, we should inevitably go down to the lowest rung of the ladder, in spite of our wealth. Our duty is to teach them how to reduce their animal-like fertility. This is the best way to raise them up towards our level. It is in *their own* interests that we are giving them this advice.

The Egoist—We might certainly abandon these poor wretches to their poverty and their thoughtless fecundity, but sooner or later they will become our responsibility. A world-wide solidarity is gradually coming into being as a result either of a genuine moral evolution or of the mere fact that distances are growing smaller. We shall therefore be obliged to do something for them since it is easier to leave people to die who live a long way off and are not well known, than it is those who are fairly near and about whom we hear every day. There is an even greater risk. Some international Council with a passion for justice and equality may have in mind and suggest a more even distribution of population throughout the world. It is in *our own* interests to urge these peoples to reduce their birth-rate.

So we find a curious blend of real philanthropic concern and thinly disguised selfishness in this denunciation of the uncontrolled fertility of the human race as enemy number one.[6]

THE BIRTH CONTROL CRUSADE

And so Malthusian ideology is in practice embodied in a vast propaganda crusade in favour of severe birth restriction among the underdeveloped peoples and a general lowering of the birth rate throughout the world. Two Anglo-Saxon organizations are the king-pins of this crusade. In the United States, the Planned Parenthood Federation of America, formerly known as the American League for Birth Control and founded in 1921 by Margaret Sanger; in Great Britain, the Family Planning Association, the successor of the National Birth Control Council founded in 1930. An International Federation for Planned Parenthood ensures the coordination on the

[6] A. Sauvy, *Théorie générale de la Population*, t. II, pp. 156-7.

international plane of contraceptive movements throughout the world.[7]

The Birth Control propagandists of yesterday and those of Planned Parenthood today consider their beliefs as a veritable gospel. A few quotations will be sufficient to make this clear. For instance, Sir Russell Brain, President of the F.P.A., declares: "It seems to me that there can be few associations in existence which have such opportunities of contributing to human happiness as this."[8]

And Bertrand Russell writes:

> Nothing is more likely to lead to an H-bomb war than the threat of universal destitution through over-population . . . (*The Human Sum*, p. 63). The leading Powers of the world spend enormous sums and devote their best brains to the production of methods of killing each other. Eminent moral leaders give their blessing to such efforts, and at the same time tell us that it is wicked to prevent the births which, by their excessive number, drive the nations on to the invention of H-bombs. I could wish to see it generally recognized in the West, as it is coming to be recognized in the East, that the problem of over-population could probably be painlessly solved by the devotion to birth control of one-hundredth or even one-thousandth of the sum at present devoted to armament. The most urgent practical need is research into some method of birth control which could be easily and cheaply used by even very poor populations (*ibid.*, p. 71).

The propaganda pamphlet *Breaking the Vicious Circle* published by the "Planned Parenthood Federation of America", 501 Madison Av., New York 22, N.Y., maintains that many American politicians are convinced that "Planned Parenthood" is an actual necessity to call a halt to Communism and to preserve peace. The accompanying illustration shows the large family as doomed to poverty and an unwilling prey to Communism. If, the pamphlet continues, family assistance as an eventual antidote to pauperism and Communism is expensive—2,400 dollars a year, so we are told, would be demanded

---

[7] For information on the International Planned Parenthood Federation and the Family Planning Association of Great Britain, see a special number of the review *Gynécologie pratique* devoted to birth control, 1955, t. VI, No. 6, pp. 391-6.

The International Planned Parenthood Federation publishes a monthly bulletin in several languages: *News of Population and Birth Control* (69 Eccleston Square, London, S.W.1) which reports all the efforts of this organization to spread knowledge of contraception throughout the world.

[8] *The Human Sum*, edited by C. H. Rolph, London, Heinemann, 1957, p. 3.

of the taxpayers for each family so assisted—the upkeep of a contraception clinic, on the other hand, requires only ten dollars a year for each family to be educated.

VOLUNTARY MATERNITY AND THE EMANCIPATION OF WOMEN

Other well-meaning considerations and arguments are urged in addition to this philanthropic world-view. Contraceptive techniques are for women a genuine psychological emancipation from all fear of an unwanted pregnancy.

So from this angle, the birth control crusade offers itself as a crusade for "voluntary motherhood", and this means that there will no longer be a stronger and a weaker sex, no more domination of one over the other, no more mothers burdened with undesired or undesirable pregnancies.

This in fact seems to be the aspect of motherhood most emphasized by Malthusianism and the only one about which it has anything to say. Thus Miss Jacquetta Hawkes writes:

> If the suffering of each woman who has known the fear and horror of unwanted pregnancies could generate a cloud only the size of a man's hand, then I believe that what has already been suffered would blacken out the sun over the whole world. It has been a most terrible thing, this, and perhaps more terrible because it has been so largely stifled, battened under the hatches of respectability, of prudery and—more admirably, perhaps,—of pride. That it has already been so greatly reduced by our new mastery of birth control is surely one of the really great advances of our modern world.[9]

According to such views as these, it is a duty to persuade the world's women to relegate to a past epoch the traditional and old-fashioned idea of "woman in the service of motherhood" and to replace it by the new notion of "motherhood in the service of woman". Further, motherhood, once it becomes voluntary, offers new possibilities of healthier, fuller and happier childhood.

"Planned parenthood is able to ensure that each child enjoys its natural right to health, care and warm affection" (Harry Emerson Fosdick, 1953). For these children will be looked after and cherished; they will be all the more and all the better educated in that there will

[9] *The Human Sum*, p. 112.

be fewer of them in the cradles of modern nurseries and on the benches of experimental schools. And so, we are told, "planned parenthood is a genuine godsend".

To sum up: what is the essence of the Malthusian ideology, especially when it is linked with the birth control crusade? It is one way of seeking to protect human love, its security, its survival, its pleasures in the interests of those who have chosen one another as partners and companions for life. It is one way of protecting women against the mishaps, fears and countless annoyances of motherhood, by reducing the latter to a minimum and above all by preventing it from catching women unawares and contrary to all expectation. It is one way of providing the child with a comfortable, rationally organized world, with an environment from which effort, sacrifice and dependence will be excluded as far as is possible, so that there will be room only for the child's spontaneous development, active inventiveness and its own good pleasure.

Finally, it is one way of delivering the human race from the obscurantism of the ages of mystery and of faith and of putting in its place the realism of sociological foresight and practical planning. When this is done, humanity will be able to go forward, legitimately proud of itself, and victorious over such irrational phenomena as the class struggle, Communism and war.[1]

[1] In French, the book most representative of this mentality is that of the journalist J. Derogy, *Des enfants malgré nous*, 1956. See also Mme Dr Weill-Hallé's articles in *Gynécologie pratique*, 1955, No. 6, pp. 429–33, and 1957, No. 3, pp. 185–202, and by the same authoress: *Le "Planning Familial"*, with a preface by Simone de Beauvoir, Ed. Maloine, 1959.

Chapter II

UNDER THE BANNER OF MARX

MARX'S OPTIMISM

"ONCE Malthus had asserted that the poverty of the common people was due to its numbers, Marx was bound to go in the opposite direction and consider apparent over-population as due entirely to private property." [1]

In other words, while Malthusianism tends to see the solution of demographic and economic problems solely in a restrictive policy favouring the privileges acquired by the propertied classes, the Marxist attitude, on the contrary, offers itself as a search for the solution in economic expansionism and the ideal system of a politics of plenty. Every man will receive according to his needs because all work for one another.

The fact is, as we are told by Marx's disciples, that once the privileges of those in possession and the rights of private property are abolished, there is nothing to prevent a system of distributed wealth and full employment of labour. There will no longer be any reason to fear that labour will exceed requirements; the contrary will be the case.

The explanation is simple. Capitalism is by definition an economy based on the misuse of profits and cannot fail to produce bottlenecks in the flow of capital at regular intervals. Hence periodical slumps in the labour market and constant under-employment. This under-employment gives rise in its turn to increasing pauperism. Eventually increasing proletarianization causes artificial growths in population, impossible to absorb.

Socialism, on the other hand, is by definition the continual provision of new employment since it automatically distributes accrued profits justly and wisely. Hence it is, in theory, able constantly to absorb any eventual surplus over-population and, through this in-

[1] P. Vincent, "La liberté de la contraception, opinion d'un démographe," in *Les Temps modernes*, April 1957; A. Sauvy, *Théorie générale de la Population*, t. II, p. 358. See also L. Ronald Meek, *Marx and Engels on Malthus*, London, Laurence and Wishart, 1953; Sydney H. Coontz, *Population Theories and Economic Interpretation*, Routledge and Kegan Paul, London, 1957.

creased number of workers, to create new wealth that, in its turn, will create new employment.

Briefly, in what Malthus considered the gravest threat to private property, namely over-population among the working classes and the poorer nations, Marx found reason for hope and optimism.

BEFORE 1956

Mr Khrushchev still held this view when he addressed an audience of young people on 7 February 1955. He said:

> Our country will become stronger in proportion as its population increases. The bourgeois ideologists have adopted cannibalistic theories, among them the theory of over-population. They ask one another how the birth-rate can be reduced and the increase in population restricted. With us, comrades, the situation is entirely different. Even 200 millions added to the 200 millions we now number would be very little.[2]

At the 1954 World Population Conference in Rome, the Soviet delegates said the same thing. Mr Riabouchkin in his statement of the "Marx-Leninist theory of population" and his criticism of current neo-Malthusian doctrines, roundly declared that "demographic phenomena depend on the nature of the social system and that, beyond the historical process, there is no universal law regulating fluctuations in population".

Thus the rational use of natural resources and national wealth for the benefit of the world's population could, in his view, ensure, with the help of modern techniques, a normal standard of living for a population two or three times greater than that of the whole world at the present time. Therefore Mr Riabouchkin denounced the neo-Malthusian doctrine of limitation of population increase as "anti-scientific" and "reactionary". He quoted the experience of the U.S.S.R. as giving the lie to it.[3]

In fact, until 1956, the U.S.S.R. found conditions highly favourable for the preaching of its Marxist doctrines. Having at its dis-

[2] Quoted by A. Sauvy, "La population de l'Union soviétique, situation, croissance et problèmes actuels," in *Population*, 1956, No. 3, p. 475.

[3] *Proceedings of the World Population Conference 1954, General Report of the United Nations Department of Economic and Social Affairs*, 1956, p. 131 and p. 167.

posal immense and under-populated areas, enormous natural wealth and above all a totalitarian system of government, it did not scruple to demand of its peoples, suffering from a shortage of consumer goods, superhuman efforts in the manufacture of producer goods from which there could be no returns for a long time to come. What did it matter if, in these economic struggles, whole populations died out? In time of war, the end justifies the means and nobody therefore has any right to complain.[4]

A CHANGE OF FRONT?

However, things seem to have changed for the time being. First in the Chinese People's Republic and then in Soviet territory, legal measures have been decreed authorizing birth control in China and abortion in Russia.

Modifications of this kind should not surprise us. They are not uncommon under the Marxist regime. In spite of Lenin, who in 1913 came out so strongly against birth control and the refusal to bear children (*grève des ventres*),[5] there had to be a toning-down in 1936 and it was made permissible to quote certain statements of Engel's who was in favour of birth control under certain circumstances.[6]

We are told that this has nothing to do with Malthusianism. If abortion has in fact again become legal, it is with a view to preventing clandestine abortion, which is still practised and is the cause of too many deaths and too much injury to the health of the female population. If the Academy of Medicine's current Five Year Plan of medical research (1956–1960) puts forward a programme for the manufacture of contraceptives, this, we are informed, is in order to stop women from having too frequent recourse to surgical operations.

However that may be, the population development Plan has come to a temporary halt. This may indicate the need of a breathing space for a nation which, from 1928 till 1955, has seen its basic industries increase producer goods by thirty-nine times their previous total whilst its own consumer goods have only increased by nine times their former figure. It may be a precautionary measure since the

[4] A. Sauvy, *Théorie générale de la Population*, t. II, p. 365.
[5] *Pravda*, No. 137, 16 June 1913, *Sochinenia*, 4th edition, 1948, Moscow, vol. 19.
[6] Smulevich Boleslav, *Théories bourgeoises de population à la lumière de la critique marxiste-léniniste* (in Russian), 1936, p. 109.

same policy is to continue and the present plan will demand an increase of 66% in producer goods as against only 14% in consumer goods. It may be an admission of the considerable gap between the achievements of the building programme and the annual housing requirements.[7]

In fact, even if the present high Soviet birth-rate of 26.6 per thousand were to fall to 20 per thousand, the population would still continue to increase at an annual rate of 1%. Under any social system whether capitalist or communist, such an annual growth requires a correspondingly high rate of investment in non-profit-making concerns such as schools, hospitals, cheap housing, etc. These investments absorb from 4 to 7% of the annual national income without any reward in the way of improvement of the standard of living for the individual.

Doubtless the overall total of goods, especially producer goods, is always on the increase. Doubtless the Soviet citizen can wax enthusiastic over the triumphs of his socialist economy and the world records of his technical research. All the same, it seems it is tacitly admitted for the first time in the U.S.S.R. that an increase of the population both in numbers and in age may mean a larger proportion of inactive citizens (pensioners) who nevertheless will have to be looked after.

Hence a type of policy which checks population without adversely affecting the opposition to Malthusianism. The ideology still remains openly hostile to the privileges of the propertied classes and to the possibilities of encroachments on the part of private ownership.

In China, from 1954 till 1958, this same policy was even more marked. The men in power did not seem unduly concerned about the amazement this may have caused in the non-Communist world. The official sources of information have, for the sake of appearances, given it an interpretation which is nevertheless anti-Malthusian.

However that may be, it was on 18 September 1954 at the National People's Congress that a member of Parliament, Shao Li Tsu, tackled for the first time the question of birth limitation by contra-

---

[7] Myron K. Gordon, "Notes on recent Soviet Population Statistics and Research," *Population Index*, Jan. 1957, p. 13, and A. Sauvy, *Population*, 1956, No. 3, p. 477, Institut National d'Etudes démographiques, special number devoted to the Population of the U.S.S.R. (1958); Georges Davidoff, *De la médecine et de la sécurité sociale en Chine*; A. Sauvy, "La population de la Chine, Nouvelles données et nouvelle politique," in *Population*, 1957, No. 4, and in his book, *De Malthus à Mao-Tse-Toung*, Denoël, 1958, pp. 242-6.

ceptive means. In August 1956, the Minister of Health ordered the launching of a vast birth control campaign. The basis of abortion and sterilization legislation has been broadened. Officially this has nothing to do with the question of over-population.[8] All that is desired is to ease the burden of mothers and to allow them more opportunity to fulfil their other civic tasks, and this by seeing that the undertakings employing them are not forced to accept too much absenteeism.[9]

But once more, in January 1958, there is a return to the official doctrine. Neither radio nor press will have the right to mention birth control, contraceptive methods, birth limitation. The author of "the new theory of population", Wa Yiu Chu, is the object of vigorous criticism. His views are declared "incompatible with the materialist concept of history". Birth control is in no sense the essential factor determining social progress.

In August 1958, Radio Pekin, announcing that there would be 700 million Chinese in 1962 and probably 800 million in 1968, made this comment on these forecasts—"Here, under a Marxist regime, there will never be too many people."[1]

Do these statements mean that the positions adopted between 1954 and 1958 have been abandoned? As far as appearances go, yes. The Chinese people are not to have the least idea that there are or might be too many of them. Although contraceptives are still on sale, no propaganda on their behalf is allowed. Congestion in the towns will be relieved not so much by countering the birth rate as by removing inactive sectors of the population into the country districts, where they will find work to do in the people's communes.

[8] At Shanghai, in the No. 9 Cloth Mill, the attention of the female personnel was drawn in 1959 to the need for fewer pregnancies in the interests of increased production. "As a matter of fact," it was explained, "out of the 4,500 workwomen, there were on the average 1,112 each year who had a baby, which meant that absenteeism among women as the result of indisposition due to pregnancy, amounted to 11,220 days per year." When to this was added absenteeism due to miscarriages, time off for confinements, etc., the total number of working days lost was 62,832, the equivalent of 260 wage-earners receiving their pay and yet remaining out of work for the whole year. "It is high time," the article concluded, "that women should be taught how to control births and should have at their disposal the necessary contraceptive facilities, including surgical sterilization."

[9] See *Extracts from China Mainland Magazines* (Hong-Kong), No. 128, 12 May 1958; "Criticism and Appraisal of the 'New Theory of Population'," by Wang Tsao and Tai Yuan-chen (Ching Chi Yen Chiu), pp. 5-16, and "Refutation of Wu Ching-chao's slanderous Remarks against the Chinese People on the Population Issue," by Chu Pao-yi (Tsai Ching Yen Chiu).

[1] See our article, "Crise de surpopulation mondiale? Prévisions et opinions," in *Revue de l'Action Populaire*, No. 127, April 1959.

The increased amount of work to be found there will not encourage a higher birth-rate. The exact opposite is true. To those families who might complain about this, the official newspapers reply: "The type of family life which grew up with the system of private property during the last few thousand years, has given the people a narrower point of view and cultivated egoistic tendencies in their minds. This sort of life not only produces a wastage of labour and hence is a hindrance to the development of socialist ideology, but it also is an obstacle to the building up of the socialist and communist community." "It is obvious that if husband and wife are both out at work and the children live in a crèche, a kindergarten or a school, there cannot be much time for family life. But we should alter the point of view which makes us think of the family as the centre of our lives, and considers family life the foundation of personal happiness. We should change our individualist ideas which drive us to order everything for the good of our family life. For us, child care and child education is a public affair. Does this mean the destruction of the family?"[2]

But in fact the fundamental objectives have not changed. Today the dominant idea in Soviet population policy is, as it was yesterday, the advancement of socialism. The adoption of contraceptive techniques, even if it is essential, should not deceive us or give us the impression that there is a compromise with bourgeois liberalism. The best thing is to say nothing about it and look for other ways of reducing family fertility.

[2] The review *Hung Ch'i* (The Red Flag), 1 Sept. 1958, and *Chung-kuo Fu-nu* (Women of China), 22 Dec. 1958.

Chapter III

THE REFORMED CHURCHES

VARIOUS DECLARATIONS BY THE REFORMED CHURCHES

BEFORE the *Declaration of the 1930 Lambeth Conference* which was attended by 260 bishops of the Anglican Church, the teaching of the various Protestant Churches remained uncertain. It would be easy to quote many official Protestant statements hostile to birth control from the first quarter of the 20th century.[1]

Since 1930, on the contrary, the hesitations of the various reformed Churches of Europe and America, especially evident during the twenties, have ceased to exist. Birth control or, to use the current terminology, "planned parenthood" is now considered lawful although only under certain conditions which may moreover vary from church to church. For instance in 1930 the Lambeth Conference voted by a majority of 193 to 67 its fifteenth resolution:

> Where there is a clearly felt moral obligation to limit or avoid parenthood, the method must be decided on Christian principles. The primary and obvious method is complete abstinence from intercourse (as far as may be necessary) in a life of discipline and self-control lived in the power of the Holy Spirit. Nevertheless in those cases where there is such a clearly felt moral obligation to limit or avoid parenthood, and where there is a morally sound reason for avoiding complete abstinence, the Conference agrees that other methods may be used, provided that this is done in the light of the same Christian principles. The Conference records its strong condemnation of the use of any methods of contraception-control from motives of selfishness, luxury or mere convenience.[2]

---

[1] Lambeth 1908, resolutions 41 and 43. Lambeth 1920, resolution 68.

[2] *The Threshold of Marriage,* A practical Guide for all who intend to be married in Church, published for the Church of England Moral Welfare Council by the Church Information Board, Church House, Dean's Yard, Westminster, S.W.1, 1949, Appendix I, Family Planning and Birth Control, pp. 26-7.

In 1943 the British Council of Churches echoes this declaration and specifically states:

> This granted, the question whether any particular method of avoiding contraception is appropriate to the marital relation would then be a question of real, but *lesser* importance to be judged on its own merits.[3]

The essential thing is the *intention,* the habitual conduct of the couple who are to admit that

> the use of a contraceptive method can only be justified if the marriage bond and married love are thereby truly honoured and . . . if family life is enriched . . . and if increase and not diminution of good comes to society.

In its general report the preparatory committee of the ninth Lambeth Conference (July 1958) would willingly have gone further. It wanted the Conference to recognize as a point common to the various opinions put forward that "there are cases where a conscientious decision to use contraceptives is justified".

In actual fact it does not appear that the Conference, in which 310 Anglican bishops took part, agreed to make as clear a pronouncement as the preparatory committee requested. The resolution on Family Planning remains vague and obviously avoids any kind of definite statement on the *objective morality* of the use of contraceptives.

> 115. The Conference believes that the responsibility for deciding upon the number and frequency of children has been laid by God upon the consciences of parents everywhere; that this planning, in such ways as are mutually acceptable to husband and wife in Christian family life, is a right and should be the result of positive choice before God. Such responsible parenthood, built on obedience to all the duties of marriage, requires a wise stewardship of all the resources and abilities of the family as well as a thoughtful consideration of the varying population needs and problems of society and the claims of future generations.[4]

The Conference is bound by this resolution alone. On the other hand, the much more definite commentaries made by the Committee

---

[3] *Home and Family Life,* published for the British Council of Churches, S.C.M. Press Ltd., 56 Bloomsbury St., London, W.C.1, 1943.
[4] *The Lambeth Conference,* S.P.C.K. and Seabury Press, 1958, pp. 1 and 57.

appointed to study "the Family in contemporary society" during the Conference, bind this Committee alone. Here are a few extracts:

> Techniques and devices for controlled conception now make it generally and easily possible to plan for parenthood at will. Thus the old direct relationship between sexual intercourse and the procreation of children has been largely broken. The fear which has so often dominated sexual intercourse has largely disappeared, and with it many of the accustomed disciplines of sexual conduct. And, in this new situation, there appear new problems for conscientious choice, and new possibilities for the marital relationship. . . .
>
> It must be emphasized once again that family planning ought to be the result of thoughtful and prayerful Christian decision. Where it is, Christian husbands and wives need feel no hesitation in offering their decision to God and following it with a clear conscience. The *means* of family planning are in large measure matters of clinical and aesthetic choice, subject to the requirement that they be admissible to the Christian conscience.[5]

The National Council of the Churches of America also declares that the need for a certain type of effective control over the number of children and the spacing of their births cannot be questioned. The prudent and limited use of contraceptives by married couples is normal. This position has been adopted because it seems important to space births, to ensure that mother and child are protected and because sexual relations between husband and wife are legitimate when they are the expression of their spiritual union and their mutual affection.[6]

The World Council of Churches in its turn published in 1959 a report on "responsible Parenthood and the Population Problem". Its tone is the same as that of Lambeth, but it is more definite in regard to methods:

[5] *The Lambeth Conference, op. cit.,* pp. 2, 145 and 147.

[6] Quoted in *Réforme,* 10 Nov. 1956, p. 6. See also the Declaration of the Methodist Church (1939); Declaration of the 95th Synod of the Augustana Lutheran Church (Los Angeles, 1954), published by the Planned Parenthood Federation of America; L. F. Delcombe, O.P., Letter of the Lutheran Bishops of Sweden on sexual questions in *Nouvelle Revue Théologique,* Nov. 1951, pp. 926–37. Finally, see the Report prepared by a group formed at the request of the Archbishop of Canterbury, by the Church of England Moral Welfare Council, for discussion at the Lambeth Conference in July 1958 and entitled *The Family in Contemporary Society,* London, S.P.C.K., 1958.

"Life", however, does not begin until the sperm has fertilized the ovum and conception has taken place. Knowing this, what means may Christians properly employ to prevent an individual act of intercourse from resulting in conception? Granted that the attempt may rightfully be made, there appears to be no moral distinction between the means now known and practised, by the use whether of estimated periods of infertility, or of artificial barriers to the meeting of sperm and ovum—or, indeed, of drugs which would, if made effective and safe, inhibit or control ovulation in a calculable way. It remains that the means employed be acceptable to both husband and wife in Christian conscience, and that, on the best evidence available, they do neither physical or emotional harm.[7]

As regards the populations of underdeveloped countries considered, as the report says, incapable of "such deliberation and such estimation of human, spiritual and social values, as has been outlined above", and therefore incapable of responsible procreation, we are not told what methods for the control of fertility will be justifiable. The question seems to be left open.

The National Council of the Reformed Church of France admits that a certain degree of control over births is lawful:

> The medical Committee points out that contraceptive methods are not always successful nor, in the long run, free from danger. Further, although the problem of birth control is a general one, its solutions are bound to be particular, since they depend on the circumstances which cause cases of conscience to arise. It is advisable therefore to recommend married people to seek the advice of a spiritual guide and a doctor's opinion.[8]

To sum up, it clearly appears from all these declarations both "that a certain control of births is lawful", and also that the method used to achieve this objective is a matter of indifference. The reasons put forward to justify this control of births come under two headings which are distinct though constantly associated—the particular welfare of married couples and the collective welfare of the various peoples of the globe. There is a third additional reason originating principally in the Anglo-Saxon and Scandinavian countries, namely

---

[7] The *Ecumenical Review*, Geneva, Oct. 1959. (A report on responsible Parenthood and the Population Problem, pp. 85–92.)
[8] "Le contrôle des naissances," *Réforme*, 10 Nov. 1956, p. 6.

the welfare of the woman and her dignity as a "responsible mother" which is compromised by too frequent and, above all, unwanted pregnancies.

OPINIONS OF PROTESTANT THEOLOGIANS

These official positions adopted by the reformed Churches have been followed by relatively new theological thought which has certainly introduced profound changes in the traditional view of the meaning of sexuality.[9]

Although in this sphere there is no single doctrine common to all the bodies in question, we can nevertheless detect a general movement of ideas in the case of such men as Leslie Weatherhead who represents liberal Protestantism, Otto Piper, a biblical theologian, Emil Brunner, neo-orthodox, Reinhold Niebuhr and Sherwin Bailey.[9a]

The fundamental idea underlying contemporary Protestant thought is that procreation is not the principal end of marriage.

Calvin himself is known to have held this view. He seems to have valued marriage chiefly for the mutual aid man and woman afford each other. As the Scriptural phrase expresses it—"It is not good for man to be alone". God's purpose in creating woman was "that there might be human beings on earth capable of combining with one another to form a society". Sexuality is not excluded from this relationship but, in the mind of the Genevan reformer, it takes second place after the *community principle*. The underlying explanation of the existence of the other sex is not in fact sexual but social. Woman is primarily man's companion and only secondarily a procreative agent.

[9] See the chapter devoted to contemporary Protestantism by Prof. William Graham Cole in his book *Sex in Christianity and Psychoanalysis*, London, George Allen and Unwin, 1956.

[9a] These theologians have been selected as particularly representative of the contemporary tendencies in Protestantism. Leslie Weatherhead represents the so-called "liberal" school. In the course of his work as a pastor he has long exercised the functions of counsellor and psychotherapist. Otto Piper, professor at the Princeton theological seminary, is quoted as a biblical theologian. Reinhold Niebuhr is one of the best theologians of American Protestantism. He has attempted a synthesis of American liberal Protestantism and Continental orthodoxy, a synthesis of the Reformation traditions and the social interpretation of the Gospel. Finally, Sherwin Bailey is a Church of England clergyman who is attempting to lay the foundations of a pastoral theology of the family. He is chaplain to the Church of England Moral Welfare Council.

This is precisely the idea revived by contemporary Protestantism. For instance, according to Weatherhead:

> Protestantism, freed from the dictum that procreation is the primary purpose of sex, with sex for love or pleasure in a secondary and subsidiary role, is forced into no such position. Modern Protestants recognize the two functions of sex as at least equal. Both have been ordained by God and no venial sin is involved in married persons expressing their love sexually even if they do so in such a way as to provide for the proper spacing of children with economic considerations in mind. Therefore, contraceptives are accepted and widely used in Protestant circles without guilt or sin, which marks an advance of naturalism over the old dualistic attitudes.[1]

Similarly, Otto Piper asserts that, according to the Bible—and this is the second principle governing sexuality that he detects in Holy Scripture—sexuality is not justified by procreation but derives its essential meaning from the personal relations it establishes. The fundamental purpose of sexuality is the creation of *"one flesh"* between a man and a woman. The children only come later as an added blessing, a kind of *"bonus"*.[2]

The Anglican Canon H. C. Warner is still more explicit:

> . . . the act of coitus . . . in its natural functioning has one "object" in uniting (or deepening the union of) man and woman, and an *occasional* end . . . of fertilizing the ovum. Hence moral reasons of a general character indicate the following conclusion: it is a bad thing to attempt to separate coitus from its "object"— mutual union, but it may legitimately be separated, for adequate reasons, from its procreative end.

And so men may use the techniques which help them—even at the material level—to achieve this separation between the two

---

[1] Leslie Weatherhead, *The Mastery of Sex through Psychology and Religion*, New York, 1932. W. G. Cole, *op. cit.*, p. 169.

[2] Otto Piper, *The Christian Interpretation of Sex*, New York, 1941, and W. G. Cole, *op. cit.*, p. 173. Otto Piper, *L'Evangile et la vie sexuelle*, adapted from the German by Francis Baudraz, Ed. Delachaux et Niestlé, 1955, pp. 26–32. "We have already insisted on the fact that the immediate end of marriage is not the handing on of life but the establishment of a fellowship between husband and wife. Yet children are a blessing which God grants to those who are married. This is why a sexual union in which there is absolutely no desire to have children is not a true marriage even if it has been blessed in church" (p. 126).

objectives, for the Canon continues: ". . . it is morally legitimate to use a material agent in order to make it easy for a human organ to achieve its 'objects' " (spectacles and dentures are examples). Coitus has two "objects": the union of husband and wife and procreation. If there are moral reasons for achieving union through coitus without achieving the (occasional) end—procreation—there is nothing wrong in using a material agent, since the latter helps to achieve the "object" of mutual union which could not be realized otherwise (for instance by *coitus reservatus*).[3]

Emil Brunner also says: "The Christian ethic must stand for the independent meaning . . . of the sex element within marriage as an expression of love, not merely as a means of procreation." [4]

The same author asserts that planned families are essential in our industrial era in which children are more of a liability than an asset and housing conditions are deplorable. Artificial contraception is in no way contrary to the divine will. "Birth control" through self-control" (continence) considered as a form of asceticism, is in no sense a virtue, it even contradicts the teaching of the Bible. Not that this practice is to be condemned. If some people prefer it to the use of contraceptives, that is their own affair. But in so doing, they should not think they are following a more perfect way which is more pleasing to God.

Dr S. Bailey, an Anglican clergyman and successor of Canon Warner as chaplain to the *Church of England Moral Welfare Council*, adopts a less rigid view. He is more conscious of the spiritual values implicit in human sexuality.[5]

As he sees it, the methods used to space and limit births are by no means all on the same footing. He absolutely condemns *coitus interruptus* as diametrically opposed to the two ends of marriage and the married union. He praises complete abstinence and reminds us that Lambeth considers it "the primary and obvious means" of limiting one's family. He admits the lawfulness of birth regulation

[3] H. C. Warner, *Theological Issues of Contraception*, 56 Bloomsbury St., London, 1954. By the same author: "La limitation des naissances," in *Christianisme social*, 1954, Nos. 7-8, pp. 552 and 554.

[4] Emil Brunner, *The Divine Imperative*, The Lutterworth Press, London, 1937, pp. 367-72.

[5] Sherwin Bailey, "Marriage and the Family, Some Theological Considerations," in *The Human Sum*, pp. 201-24. For a more detailed study of these theological considerations, see the preparatory Report drawn up for the Lambeth Conference 1958 and entitled *The Family in Contemporary Society*, London, S.P.C.K., 1958, pp. 137-48. See also pp. 159 and 162 below.

based on periodic continence and the use of the infertile periods. It appears that he only accepts the use of contraceptives with reservations and under special conditions, and so, in this respect, he does not adopt the opinion so commonly "endorsed" in England, as he says, and according to which contraception is morally justified, whatever the circumstances.

He is aware that a human act derives its moral value not only from the right *"intention"* of the agent but also from its conformity with its own immediate specific *object*. This is so in the case of the organs of taste and the digestive system, the proper objects of which are deglutition and the assimilation of food, and not the pleasures of the table. Nor does he hesitate to call the act that fulfils these two conditions regarding both intention and object, a natural one.

But having come so far, Dr Bailey does hesitate to adopt in its entirety the view which he recognizes as traditional in moral theology, namely that the proper *object* of the sexual function is procreation. He wonders whether recent developments in psychological awareness where sexuality is concerned, may not have broadened the meaning of the traditional *object* of the sexual function by giving it a "more than genital" extension. Therefore when faced with the allegations of those who claim "that contraception . . . so alters not merely the biological effect but also the entire character of coitus that it is no more what God intended it to be", Dr Bailey puts this question: ought we not to ask ourselves "whether it is possible any longer to accept a definition of the 'object' of coitus which was framed before its relational meaning was properly appreciated, and which concerns only one of its aspects?"

It is this doubt apparently which moves the Anglican theologian to go further and consider himself free to justify contraception under certain circumstances. He writes:

> Contraception, used responsibly and conscientiously within marriage, does not exploit or abuse human sexual nature, but rather enables it better to achieve its generative and relational ends.

FRENCH PROTESTANT OPINION

Positions similar to those just analysed are found among French Protestants. In an article in *Réforme,* M. Reguilhem writes:

It is true to say that marriage is justified independently of procreation. It is a partnership in living founded on the union of husband and wife. This partnership gives their union visible expression and includes its physical sign—the sexual relationship.[6]

And M. J. Ellul, professor in the Faculty of Law at Bordeaux, in an article entitled *"Position des Eglises protestantes à l'égard de la Famille"* asserts:[7]

Marriage is essentially a new state to which God calls man, not so that he may serve natural needs but the deepest needs of all, those that arise from his share in the Redemption. This state is permanent and marriage is revealed as a "work" on which husband and wife are continually engaged. The purpose of this work is to give glory to God. Consequently, procreation is neither the end nor an essential element of marriage. The children who are born may add something to it, but marriage is complete in itself without them, since its mainspring is its spiritual purpose.

His position with regard to birth control follows logically from this. He defines it as follows:

In regard to birth control, we first of all refuse to make any distinction between the means used (chastity, the woman's infertile periods, *coitus interruptus*, chemical or mechanical methods). In general, we hold that the problem is one of personal decision and not one of means. We most certainly do not recognize the superiority of the first method on the grounds that it is natural.

The fundamental reason for this attitude is given later:

Whereas the Roman Church has written its theological decisions into ethical systems and hence imposes obligations and duties, the Protestant churches have, for the most part, avoided taking this step. Even Calvin's moral intransigence never produced a moral system. The basic rule of Protestantism is that we pass directly from faith to act and so by-pass the Law. But this translation of faith into act necessarily remains on the plane of the individual and in the sphere of a constantly renewed judgment and choice. The ethics of the Reformation is the ethics of freedom.

[6] *Réforme*, 10 Nov. 1956, p. 6.
[7] Jacques Ellul, professor in the Faculty of Law at Bordeaux, "Position des Eglises protestantes à l'égard de la Famille," in *Renouveau des idées sur la Famille*, I.N.E.D. 1954, pp. 270-1.

This is a very clear statement and characteristic of a fundamental tendency in Protestantism: "We pass directly from faith to act and so by-pass the Law." Karl Barth, according to M. Reguilhem who quotes him, says the same thing: "*The law of nature* cannot always be identified with the will of God, and it may be admitted in theory that there are cases where birth limitation is possible." [8]

THE CONCEPT OF NATURE, THE POINT AT ISSUE BETWEEN CATHOLICS AND PROTESTANTS

For a follower of Luther or Calvin, the law of nature no longer has very much meaning since nature was radically corrupted by the Fall and by original sin. As Emil Brunner suggests, we have no common criteria to apply to the "orders of creation" whose norms can be determined by scientific observations, and to the transcendent order of God which faith alone reveals.

W. Graham Cole comments in his book *Sex in Christianity and Psychoanalysis*:

> The outer, objective, static law, even if it be the divine law, must not be confused with the personal, dynamic will of God. This is always the mistake of legalism, whatever guise it may assume, Pharisaic, Roman Catholic, or Puritan. It fails to recognize that God may actually command a man to sin *against* the law, as for example, when the dissolution of a marriage might be a positive duty. The legalist sees only the law against divorce and regards the question as closed, while the evangelical sees the overarching fact of the divine love and grace which can, in concrete situations, break through a general law. . . .
>
> The difference between Roman Catholic and Protestant ethics is strikingly illustrated by this whole discussion. The former is characterized by a more generally optimistic anthropology which issues in legalism. [The author doubtless applies this word to Catholicism's recognition of nature and its fundamental laws as a primary datum with a valid and genuine meaning.] The results of the Fall are considered as comparatively slight: man has lost none of his natural powers.[9] . . . (Thus) his reason is able to

[8] K. Barth, *Die Kirchliche Dogmatik*, III, pp. 300–11.
[9] The view of Catholic Theology is rather that "man has lost nothing *essential* to his natural powers". There is a shade of meaning here which is not without importance.

discern the divine will in the natural law, and for the most part, he can obey. Whatever gaps there may be in his knowledge or weakness in his will are filled and overcome by the grace supplied by the Church. Protestantism, on the other hand, at least in its traditional aspects,[1] has a much more pessimistic anthropology, regarding man as totally depraved, his reason corrupted so that he rationalizes and his will weakened so that in Augustine's terms he is not able not to sin. . . . The only hope is to be found in the divine mercy, in freedom from the bondage of the law, in the direct, personal encounter with God. . . . Protestantism sets the relative character of all legislation, even the so-called orders of creation, over against Rome's absolute and immutable natural law. For Protestantism, the individual stands before God in a unique situation, where the divine law can dispense with all rules. For Rome, all mankind stands before the divine law, and the regulations cannot be set aside for individual exceptions. The ethic of Protestantism is "Christian liberty", where the ethic of Rome is natural law.

It will not therefore be surprising if, as a result of these principles, there are always, according to the reformed Churches, allowances to be made in cases that are considered as exceptional. Thus Pastor de Pury, in his discussion on induced abortion, declares:

> Dr Schlemmer says: "It is always a crime". I shall not say absolutely always, but almost always. . . . We ought certainly to *tend* towards intransigence and not be too readily moved to pity. Yet I find it hard to be patient with Churches and people who too easily wash their hands of problems by acting automatically in accordance with a set of regulations. . . . God's Law is not given to automatons.[2]

Hence, when faced with the possibility that man has a right to plan births, Protestant thinkers proclaim an ethic of individual freedom in Christ. The believer as he faces his God is the only judge in conscience, not only of the intentions which lead him to desire to

[1] There is, in fact, a Protestant "naturalism" which seems to take no account of the wound inflicted on nature by original sin, and which considers any assertion that human nature has been thrown off its balance in consequence of its sin, as "Manichean dualism".

[2] Statement by Pastor R. de Pury on the married couple and birth limitation in *Jeunes Femmes* (Bulletin) of the "Groupes Jeunes Femmes", May–June 1956, p. 13.

limit births, but also of the validity of the means he employs for the purpose.

This ethic moreover claims to find in conjugal sexuality an explicit meaning which, in practice, is independent of all reference to procreation. This point of view, characteristic of Protestantism, seems to the latter a surer way of safeguarding the values of partnership and companionship in the relation of man and wife, since it places these values higher in the psychological scale than those of procreation, fatherhood and motherhood. These latter values are, of course, still retained, but one often has the impression that they are looked upon as rather questionable.

Taking everything into account, it is the personal and relatively egocentric good of the individual as revealed to him by his conscience that takes precedence. It is the particular good of the couple as it appears to both of them that prevails over all natural universal law. The *objective* boundary, between the norm provided by nature and what the individual feels is an exception to it, disappears to make way for the *subjective* judgment of conscience. The latter, if it considers itself guided by the Spirit and by faith, prevails absolutely and immediately.

Chapter IV

ISLAM

TRADITIONAL AND COMMON LAW CIVILIZATIONS

B Y definition, or at least by contrast with modern Western civilizations, the ancient common law and traditional civilizations of the East have scarcely any of the intellectual characteristics of the former. Not that reflective thought is lacking in Hinduism, Buddhism and Islam, but in these civilizations it has never reached the point at which a thorough study is made of the problem of the relations between Revelation and History, Revelation and Science, Faith and Reason, Spirit and Technics. For these oriental religions, ethics is not what it is for Christianity—a distinct though integral chapter in a whole body of doctrine.

Buddhist, Hindu, Confucian, Mohammedan ethics are inextricably interwoven with sacred traditions. It is useless to try to find logically consistent attitudes in them, still less solutions decreed by the authority of a *magisterium* which normally does not exist.

It is therefore only to be expected that civilizations whose spirit is derived from these religions should not yet have put forward definite opinions regarding man's rights in the matter of sexuality and procreation.

THE SEXUAL ETHICS OF THE KORAN

There can be no doubt that the psychology of Islam tends to uphold the male sex, under the influence of the powerful instinctual drive that urges men to beget children and rule over their families. There can be no denying that the Mohammedan family is patriarchal and strongly characterized by male domination.[1]

In any case, there has been little evidence over the centuries of any

[1] L. Millot, *Introduction à l'étude du droit musulman,* Sirey, 1953, Ch. IV, "La famille musulmane," pp. 324–30; René Schaefer, "La femme et la famille musulmanes," *Pour la Vie,* No. 51, Oct.–Dec. 1952; Joanny Ray, "Facteurs d'évolution de la famille musulmane," in *Renouveau des idées sur la famille,* pp. 282–8, I.N.E.D., 1954.

dissociation of sexuality from procreation. A large family was a sign of wealth and of God's blessing on the father.

"Your wives are your field," says the Koran, "go to your field as you please, but first do something for the good of your souls" (IV, 3).

It is true that the Prophet allows as many as four lawful wives. He merely recommends that a man should treat his wives fairly.

> You will never be able to treat all your wives in the same way, even though you may ardently desire to do so. Take care then not to give full rein to your inclinations. Take care not to leave one of your wives as it were in suspense . . . (IV, 228). If you still fear that you may be unjust, marry only one or a slave (IV, 3).[2]

The husband must show love and affection towards his wives:

> It is one of the signs of God's power . . . that he has given you wives created from yourselves so that you may live with them. He has established love and affection between you. Herein are signs for those who reflect (XXX, 20).

In spite of this, the natural inclination of the religion of the Koran favours the man and only too rarely reminds him of his duties and obligations towards the woman; it even gives him frequent occasion to consider himself superior to the female sex. "Men make decisions for women, since God has shewn his preference for men rather than for women" (IV, 34).

We must not therefore be surprised that, in practice, the birth of female children has not been celebrated as on a par with that of male children in Islam, nor that female infanticide was a temptation which the Prophet was obliged to condemn:

> If the birth of a daughter is announced to any one of you, his face darkens and he becomes as it were choked with grief. Because of this disastrous news he hides himself from his relatives. Should he keep the child and suffer shame on her account or bury her in the dust? How foolish are their judgments! (XLVIII, 5–6).

A man must accept life and the child, every child, as a gift from God.

---

[2] Polygamy is tending to disappear in the Moslem world. In Egypt in 1947, only 3·8% of married men had more than one wife, in Iraq 9%, at Baghdad 5·3%. See E.S.N.A. *Cahiers Nord-Africains*, Dec. 1957, Jan. 1958: Polygamie et promotion de la femme, Appendix I, pp. 1–24; "La condition de la femme dans le Moyen-Orient Arabe," in *La Documentation Française*, 13.10.1956.

Do not slay your children out of fear of poverty. We shall give them their food just as we shall to you. The murders you commit will be foul sins (XVII, 33. See also V, 141–31 and 32).

In fact abortion, since it is murder, is in principle forbidden by Islam. Exceptions have only been introduced quite recently in the name of therapeutic abortion, when the latter is presumed to be the only means of saving the mother's life.

In short, Islam is a civilization which looks favourably on the male sexual instinct, encourages fatherhood and motherhood, protects the life of the embryo and that of the child once it is born, and yet fails to give the recognition it deserves to the dignity of woman. All this is due to its veneration for Allah, the sovereign master of heaven and earth. Islam through the centuries has therefore been scarcely aware of any problem concerning deliberate birth limitation. The idea of restraining or containing the sexual instinct, especially with the aim of subjecting the body to the spirit, did not even enter the mind of the Prophet nor those of his disciples. Celibacy has always been looked at askance, so too has sterility for that matter. As for consecrated virginity, it is absolutely unthinkable in the context of the Koran. It is only within the past fifteen years that the lawyers and doctors of Islam have searched the sacred texts and traditions for indications which may justify arguments in favour of voluntary birth restriction, and they have come across a few historical references to the practice of continence among the founders of Islam.

MODERN DEVELOPMENTS OF ISLAM IN EGYPT[3]

Thus Doctor Al Bah Al Khouli, Religious Inspector in the Wafd Ministry, invokes the testimony of certain of the Prophet's companions such as Amr Ibn Al As who said "Take care not to have too many children. They prove difficult to bring up."

M. Yousef Husayn Tahir, a Cairo jurist, also refers to two verses of the Koran in an attempt to undermine the belief according to which the Moslem religion is said to be opposed to birth limitation. It is a fact that in these two verses, a large family is compared by the Prophet to abundance of riches which may sometimes bring a well-deserved punishment in the other world.

[3] Mohammedans discuss the limitation of birth in E.S.N.A. *Cahiers Nord-Africains*, March–April 1956, Appendix II, pp. 1–12.

Finally, H.E. the Sheik Sayid Sabeq, Director of the Cultural Department in the Wafd Ministry, quotes cases in which—still according to the Prophet and, after him, the *"Shariyat"*—birth limitation—may be lawful, when, for instance, the woman is too weak to withstand the fatigue of childbirth, or when the man is too poor to support his family, or again, even when the woman is afraid she may lose her beauty. Moreover, according to Djaber Ibn Abd Allah, some of the Prophet's companions did not have sexual relations with their wives and the Prophet did not blame them on that account.

And so in contemporary Islam, an opinion is gradually gaining ground, without, however, being officially approved as yet by a *fetwa*—according to which for good reasons, some new and proper to our own times, man has the right to limit the number of his children.

The Sheik Radwan Ahmad Radwan, departmental head in the Wafd Ministry, declares, for example:

I most certainly think there is no single animal on the earth to which God does not give the means of subsistence. Yet, if my means do not permit me to bring up a being who will be perfect— and it is not merely a matter of feeding an animal—birth limitation becomes lawful, since our aim is to give our society and our children a human standard of life.

We ought to leave each individual [says the Sheik Mansour Ragab, professor in the Faculty of the Principles of Religion— Usul-Al-Din] the right to procreate within the limits possible to him and after we have enlightened him on the issues involved. In any case, birth limitation cannot be laid down by law or by given individuals.

But other opinions go further. M. Mariette Ghali observes:

In the past, limitation did not aim of course at limiting the number of citizens but at protecting the family from fatigue and threats to its health and finances when it had too many children to bring up and births followed one another without any respite.

But he adds:

Now it may well be that we too (in Egypt) are experiencing the evolution which, by improving the standards of living, finally leads to the limitation of births. In any case, I think that the organization (the planning?) of births is indispensable for our country from the social point of view.

Yousef Husayn Tahir whom we have already quoted comments:

The people must understand the danger of our situation, the misfortunes that are in store for us unless birth control is introduced. We used to number 15 million, today there are 25 million of us and the territory we possess has not increased.

"Birth control is a social action (duty?)."
How is it to be achieved?
"The first method of birth limitation is for individuals to remain unmarried," observes Sheik Radwan Ahmad Radwan, perhaps with his tongue in his cheek.
This is obvious enough, but what are prolific couples to do?
The semi-official Government daily *Al Goumhuriyya* states:

Religious opinion on this point is represented by the true Islamic principle which holds that the end justifies the means. . . . Our social and economic life must be given solid foundations if we are to benefit by the great projects on which the Revolution is now engaged in its efforts to improve our own standard of living and that of our children. This cannot be done while we have this threat hanging over us, the threat, that is, of an ever increasing over-population continually raising new problems and undermining all the beneficial results of our efforts. Hence birth limitation is the only course of action, the only *speedy* and *obvious* solution.

Although the word "contraceptive" is not used with the term "birth limitation" to make its precise meaning perfectly clear, nevertheless it clearly must be understood if a "speedy and obvious" solution is envisaged.

In any case, a Ruling by the Grand Mufti of Egypt, issued on 25 January 1937, is sufficient to dispel all doubts on the point, since it deals with contraceptive practices and admits that they are lawful when there is good reason for limiting births.[4]

According moreover to certain doctors of the Law, there is a kind of oral tradition justifying the practice of the *'Azl* (*coitus interruptus*)

[4] *Journal of the Egyptian Medical Association*, July 1937; *News of Population and Birth Control*, New York, May 1952.

which was already prevalent among the ancient Arabs and yet was not forbidden by the Prophet. It is true that other interpreters of the Law question the lawfulness of this practice when a free woman is involved. However that may be, it seems that while it is often blame-worthy, especially when invalid motives are adduced to justify it, the practice of the *'Azl* is not absolutely unlawful for the followers of Islam.[5]

It is towards this position that, in practice, the most progressive portion at least, if not the whole of Islam, is now moving. . . . It is true that we find less advanced positions in Islamic countries with smaller populations than that of Egypt, Iraq [6] for instance and Afghanistan. It cannot be doubted that this view finds support among small avant-garde groups, of women especially, who find it hard to bear the yoke of male sexuality as the latter's pattern has been organized in practice by the traditions of Islam for centuries. Already in North Africa, in the Near East and among the Moslems of Pakistan and Indonesia there are premonitory signs of the un-easiness whose existence in Egypt we have already noted above.

[5] G. H. Bousquet, "L'Islam et la limitation volontaire des naissances," in *Population*, 1950, No. 1, pp. 121–8. By the same author: "De la nécessité d'une politique anticonceptionelle en Algérie," in *Le Développement Africain*, Oct. 1958, para. vi. La religion musulmane admet formellement les pratiques anticonceptionelles, pp. 14–16.

[6] M. K. Nahas, "Married Life in Iraq," in *Recherches sur la Famille*, Ed. J. B. Mohr, Tübingen, 1956, and by the same author: "La famille dans le monde arabe," in *Familles dans le monde*, July–Dec. 1955, p. 160.

Chapter V

GANDHI'S AND NEHRU'S INDIA

FERTILITY A SACRED THING IN INDIA

WHEN we pass from Islam to Hinduism, our first impression is one of greater freedom. The personal rights of women in particular seem better safeguarded. Even though the family is still patriarchal and the authority of its head beyond dispute, the religious climate seems both more mystical and more humane with a greater emphasis on love and kindness.

The source of Hinduism is the Vedas (XIII–VIII centuries B.C.), texts in which the wisdom inspired by Brahma in Indian antiquity finds its expression. In the course of time, laws and customs became established and, since they ensured the permanence and the growth of the caste system, were of great ethical importance for the Hindus who observed them. To these two sources of their religion was added the ancestral belief in Karma and in the reincarnation of souls. For the Hindu masses, every action done in this life has its retribution in another life. Therefore Good and Evil exist and there is a chain of births and rebirths linked with the development of good and evil throughout the course of any given individual's existence. There is one more factor, Yoga, an ascetic technique which underlies the whole religious impulse of India. Although Yogis are becoming rare, their technique of *"en-stasis"* reveals man's constant desire to escape from his condition and from time, both of which are illusory, and to enter the Paradise of the divine immutability.

With or without this ascesis, we cannot say that traditionalist India has a moral code in the same exact sense of the word as it is used in monotheistic religions with their belief in a personal God.[1]

A man is only holy in relation to himself and in so far as he loves others. Not to be holy is an error by which a man injures himself

---

[1] "The Hindu dharma gives us a programme of rules and regulations and permits their constant change. The rules of dharma are the mortal flesh of immortal ideas, and so are mutable." S. Radhakrishnan, *Religion and Society*, London, 1948, p. 108. See also Swami Abhishikteswarananda, "L'Hindouisme est-il toujours vivant?" in *Vitalité actuelle des religions non chrétiennes*, Ed. du Cerf, collection Rencontres, No. 48, 1957.

and the order of the world, rather than a sin which genuinely offends the Deity. Indeed the Deity seems to be relatively indifferent to perfection in his creatures. In such an atmosphere of undefined ethical principles resulting from belief in Karma, it is easy to see that it is evil to attack life. Births and rebirths are sacred moments and to interfere with the mysterious rhythm of the *"avatars"* might well be the most heinous form of sacrilege. As the laws of Manu say: "women were created to bring children into the world and men to perpetuate the species. That is why the fulfilment of religious duties by man and wife together is commanded by the Vedas." [2]

Fertility is always, in fact, a value so steeped in "sacred meaning" that it is even forbidden to interfere with the lives of certain sacred animals such as the cow and the monkey. It obviously cannot be permitted to do so in the process of human life whether by means of abortion or contraception.

And since it is good to ensure that one has male descendants to continue praying for one's ancestors, there is all the more reason to avoid such deliberate interventions. The Vedas often stress the need for this: "May a son be born to us to continue our line for a hundred winters" (*Rig Veda*, 1, 64, 14), sons which in another passage are called "our everlasting dwelling-place". It is the son's mission to deliver his parents after their death from the sufferings of the Beyond.[3] Hence infanticide is always condemned. Therapeutic abortion alone is authorized under certain circumstances.[4]

Nevertheless, in spite of such a background of vitalist belief, the Parsee community has not scrupled for many years past to limit deliberately the number of births on eugenic grounds. This *élite*, descended from immigrants who came from Iran three thousand years before our era, has remained outside Hinduism and played a very important part in the emancipation of India. From the outset birth control found a ready welcome among these highly cultured people. Their growth was therefore slowed down to such an extent that between 1900 and 1940 their birth-rate fell from 30·5 per thousand in 1901 to 16·6 per thousand in 1940. In 1941 there were

---

[2] *Code de Manou* (revised version of a previous work: *Manava Dharma*, 600–250 B.C.); G. Strehly, "Les lois de Manou," *Annales du Musée Guimet*, Ed. E. Leroux, 1893, IX, p. 96.

[3] Hence the name *Putra* given to the son because of his mission to deliver his parents from *Pu* (Hell). P. Thomas, *Hindu Religion, Customs and Manners*, Tarapovedala and Sons, Bombay, 1947, p. 87.

[4] It is true that the Kamasutras (fourth century A.D.) contain prescriptions for the prevention of pregnancy.

only 115,000 Parsees or 1 to every 3,000 Indians. S. Chandrasekhar, their historian, predicts a still greater decrease by 1980.[5]

Thus in spite of their culture and their sense of forming a privileged caste within the nation, the Malthusian "wisdom" of the Parsees has outstripped the bounds of "Reason" and this community is doomed to disappear in the near future.

It is true that the Parsees are a special case. The reactions of the Hindu masses have remained more in line with their traditional wisdom. If nevertheless we have quoted the example of the Parsees, it is because it shows how an *élite*, called to lead a whole people in its movement towards emancipation, has yet lost its way on the fatal road of neo-Malthusianism.

GANDHI'S VIEW

It cannot be denied that Gandhi, on the authority of the Vedic texts,[6] attempted on many occasions to hold the advocates of birth control in check by setting before them the ideal of *brahmacharya*, that is, chastity.

The Mahatma believed much more than is commonly supposed in a Hinduism capable of evolving with the times, and in real progress at the level of institutions and morals, but he wanted at all costs to safeguard certain matrimonial and family values which India had inherited from her past.[7] He even wished to set a still higher ideal. Thus he would have liked married couples to lead a life of self-control and recommended that their union from the sexual point of view should be limited to procreation. He considered it "disgusting" for them to act otherwise, so strongly did he feel that "any abuse in this direction threatens with very grave consequences not only the individual but also society". The only purpose of sexual relations, he said, should be the desire to procreate and never the satisfaction of carnal instincts. Once this ideal of marriage is accepted, any activity

[5] S. Chandrasekhar, "Some Aspects of Parsee Demography," in *Human Biology*, 1948, pp. 47–89.

[6] The *Dharmasastra* frequently mentions, as deserving of punishment and demanding expiation, the unnatural crime of a man in his relations with a woman, which the Bible attributed to Onan (Genesis 38.9–10). This sin is placed on the same footing as the unnatural relations of homosexuality (*Vishnu Dharmasastra*, XXXVIII.35). See A. Nevett, S.J., *Too many of us?*, Poona, 1952, p. 180.

[7] "Must births be limited? What Gandhi thought," by N. Krishnaswamy, in *Way Forum*, June 1957, pp. 19 and 51.

which deviates from it is lustful. Relationships whose sole object is the satisfaction of sexual needs, he wrote, are a return to bestiality.

Arguing from principles such as these, it was only to be expected that Gandhi vigorously opposed birth restriction by contraceptive means. He held that these procedures were immoral and harmful to mankind from both the individual and the social point of view.

In the paper *Harijan* (Young India), 5 May 1946, the Mahatma wrote an article in which he said that contraceptives are an insult to womanhood. The difference between a prostitute and a woman who uses contraceptives is merely that whilst the former sells her body to many men, the latter when using contraceptive methods, sells it to one man only.[8]

He wrote that the greatest reproach that can be levelled against contraceptive propaganda is that it rejects the ancient ideal and substitutes in its stead another which, if it becomes a reality, must lead to the physical and moral annihilation of the race. The horror with which our forefathers considered the infertile use of the vital seed was not the result of superstition born of ignorance. What should we ourselves think of a husband who sowed the best grain in his possession on a stony soil, or of a landowner who would stand by and see his field (whose soil is good) sown with grain that was certainly beyond all criticism, but under conditions which would make it impossible for it to germinate? God in his goodness has endowed man with a seed that is specially fruitful and woman with a "field" richer than the most fertile soil in the whole world. It is undeniably criminal folly on man's part to allow the most precious thing he has at his disposal to be wasted and lost. In the same way, the woman is also guilty when she receives this precious thing with the firm determination that she will waste it. Sexual desire is not without beauty and nobility, there is nothing in it to be ashamed of. But it must be at the service of procreation alone. Any other view is a sin against God and against humanity. There have always been and there always will be contraceptive procedures, but in the past, to use them was considered an offence against God. It has been left for our generation to glorify vice by calling it virtue.[9]

In the course of a conversation with Mrs Margaret Sanger who

[8] Quoted by Nevett, *op. cit.*, p. 120. See also M. K. Gandhi, *Self-Restraint versus Self-Indulgence* (Ahnedad, 1947); Gandhi and Margaret Sanger, "Debates on Birth Control," *Asia*, Nov. 1936. Cf. *Cahiers d'action religieuse et sociale*, No. 236 (1.6.1957), pp. 343–4.
[9] N. Krishnaswamy, *op. cit.*, p. 51.

asked his opinion of the so-called "Safe Period" as a method of birth limitation, Gandhi is said to have replied: "I do not find it so objectionable as the other." [1]

But in spite of all this, he insisted on the need to practise and to preach self-restraint and continence.

MODERN INDIA

But the leaders and demographers of modern India override these objections on Gandhi's part. Dr S. Chandrasekhar in his opening speech at the *"All India Conference of Family Planning"* in November 1951, considered himself justified in asserting: "Fortunately all the great Hindu reformers have been in favour of planned parenthood." A dubious statement, since the *Dharmasastra* frequently mentions as deserving of punishment and demanding expiation, the unnatural act attributed by the Bible to Onan. This act is even classed with the crime of homosexuality. [2]

Whatever may be the truth concerning these traditions and teachings, Chandrasekhar preferred to base his opinion on interviews and inquiries carried out in a large number of centres of population in the States of Mysore and Uttar Pradesh, where from 60 to 78% of the fathers and mothers of families stated that they wished to learn how to limit their offspring. Chandrasekhar considers it a duty to instruct these unfortunate people in the use of contraception. This, he says, is a public health measure and would reduce infantile mortality. Later, the spacing of births would ease the burdens of motherhood and save the lives of a considerable number of young mothers. In short, birth control is a public welfare measure which the Government must adopt. Hence the first Five-Year Plan made it an important part of its programme and set aside £485,000 for its implementation.

On 5 January 1957, at the third congress of the *"All India Conference of Family Planning,"* Colonel Barket Narain, social Counsellor in the Ministry for the Expansion of Communities, declared

---

[1] *Cahiers d'action religieuse et sociale*, p. 344.
[2] J. C. Gosch, "Family Planning of India," *Journal of Family Welfare*, Bombay, May 1956, pp. 130-4 (a summary of family policy since 1941); A. B. Wadia, "Planned Parenthood in East Asia," *Journal of Family Welfare*, Bombay, Jan. 1956. For S. Chandrasekhar's ideas see his books, *Hungry People in Empty Lands* (1952) and *Population and Planned Parenthood in India*, Ed. George Allen and Unwin, London, 1955, p. 116.

that it was the Government's intention to equip 2,000 rural clinics for instruction in planned parenthood.[3] The future will show how successful a resistance traditional ideas will be able to offer to the contagion of this new mentality.

Nevertheless it is very probable that, with the decline of moral and religious traditions, the official interpreters of these traditions will come to terms with it, in the supposed interests of eugenics and the common good. Ancestral beliefs, even the belief in the reincarnation of souls, may well be gradually superseded. That contraception has hitherto made little impact on India is due far less to consciously held spiritual convictions than to lack of culture and to inertia among the masses, the women especially, who are scarcely yet aware of the meaning of personal autonomy.[4]

CONCLUSION

It is clear from this rapid survey of the principal ideologies and the principal ethical systems into which the world is divided, that there is an increasing interest shewn by those in authority, if not by those they govern and by the masses, in the *planning of births* and the control of fertility by modern contraceptive methods. This interest, it is true, is not a universal phenomenon of spontaneous generation. It originated a century and a half ago in the West. It was systematically propagated in the Anglo-Saxon and Scandinavian countries, where it eventually won over the reformed Churches and, through their good offices, was officially accepted by the public authorities.

Experimental legislation which today authorizes and sanctions the use,[5] popularizing, publicizing and sale of contraceptives exists in Great Britain (1926), in 46 States of the U.S.A. (1936), in Denmark (1937) and in Sweden (1938).

Contraception has apparently become so much a part of the American way of life that it is practised by 90% of the married couples in towns such as Indianapolis. In Sweden the League for

---

[3] *News of Population and Birth Control*, March 1957.

[4] W. A. Morrison, "Attitudes of Males and Females toward Family Planning in a Western Indian Village," in the *Milbank Memorial Fund Quarterly*, July 1956, pp. 262-86 and Jan. 1957, pp. 67-82.

[5] Tibor Mende, *L'Inde devant l'orage*, pp. 95-6. See also earlier works: L. K. T. Merchant, "Changing Views on Marriage and Family," in *Hindu Month*, Madras, 1935; J. J. Meyer, *Sexual Life in ancient India*, two volumes, Routledge, 1930.

Sexual Education and Birth Control has more than 100,000 members. In Great Britain the Family Planning Association, after twenty-five years of intensive propaganda, had, in 1957, more than 200 clinics in which the use of contraceptives was taught. The Royal Commission on Marriage and Divorce is generous in its encouragement of this work.[6]

But, as we have seen, the birth planning movement now extends beyond the frontiers of the Western nations. Under the vigorous stimulus of a genuine Anglo-Saxon crusade it is beginning to penetrate peoples which have a traditional religious respect for fertility.

An international organization, *The International Planned Parenthood Federation* (I.P.P.F.), is responsible for fostering and coordinating this vast movement. In 1957, it numbered fourteen fully active member bodies (national Associations) and four associate member bodies. It has its headquarters in London and three regional offices —in New York for the Western hemisphere, in London for Europe, and in Bombay for the Indian Ocean. A fourth office for the Far East is provisionally established in Singapore. Private and government foundations contribute regularly to the propaganda fund and support the practical schemes of this vast organization.[7]

We may note that in recent years, a special effort has been made among island populations—Fiji, Tonga, Samoa, Mauritius, the Caribbean islands (Puerto Rico, Jamaica, Barbados, Trinidad, Bermuda). But propaganda is also seeping into Africa (Rhodesia, Kenya, Tanganyika, Uganda, Zanzibar) and into Asia (Singapore, Malaya, Ceylon, Hong Kong). All these countries are under British influence.

The principal area for pilot schemes nevertheless remains Japan. Millions of copies of women's magazines and 30,000 primary school teachers are constantly initiating women in contraceptive methods. New birth control clinics are continually being opened. Progress reports are impressive, to judge at least by their figures. The birth rate —32·8 per thousand in 1949, the year in which the eugenic legisla-

---

[6] J. Sutter, "Le mouvement dans le monde en faveur de la limitation des naissances," in *Population,* 1955, No. 2. Hope T. Eldridge, *Population Policies,* A Survey of recent Developments, the International Union for the Scientific Study of Population, 1954.

[7] P.E.P., *World Population and Resources,* 16 Queen Anne's Gate, London, 1955. See especially Part II: "Regions and Islands". This book clearly shows the dilemmas confronting a certain number of countries, in particular archipelagos, but its point of view is unconsciously profoundly Malthusian. "Birth control" is the one great source of hope.

tion was promulgated—fell to 21·5 per thousand in 1953 and to 20·3 in 1955. The government plans to reach a figure of 13 per thousand. The population increase in 1957 was only 0·91% or 820,000 for a total of 91·1 million inhabitants. If this tendency continues, it may well be, according to some authors, that the Japanese population will become stationary at a figure of approximately 110 million after 1990.

China, together with Japan, is the great unknown quantity. Will China, under the banner of Marxism, carry out the scheme of family planning which seems to be a success in a Japan under American influence? Will the 600 million Chinese of today, conditioned by the "psychological techniques" of Communism, manage to avoid passing the 1,000 million mark within the next forty years? Or will the regime fail because of the inertia of the masses?

The only population groups in which an *élite* still offers some deliberate resistance to the waves of family planning are the Catholic peoples of the Latin tradition: Spain, Italy, France, Canada (Quebec), South America, as well as the Catholic sectors in the Anglo-Saxon (Great Britain and the U.S.A.), German and Flemish nations. The crusade for the planning of human fertility seems to them incompatible with the humanism which their Christian faith instils in them. We do not deny that the Catholic groups are becoming increasingly aware of the world-wide influence of a new phenomenon, to which is due a growth in human population on a scale hitherto unknown. Nevertheless, they remain sceptical of the value of the proposed solution: birth control.

This is especially true of France, an old Catholic nation, ravaged, it may well be, by almost two centuries of rationalism and naturalism, but whose *élites* cannot bring themselves to disown the values of the spirit.

Hence, according to a public opinion poll undertaken in 1956,[8] by the Institut National d'Etudes Démographiques, Frenchmen remain profoundly divided over the policy of birth planning. While 43% declared they were in favour of it, 43% were definitely hostile and 14% were unwilling to give an answer either way. Practising Catholics gave a 76% vote against such a venture.

But are these Catholics quite certain of what it is they believe? Are they capable of supporting it with decisive arguments? Are

[8] A. Girard et R. Samuel, "Une enquête sur l'opinion publique à l'égard de la limitation des naissances," in *Population*, 1956, No. 3, pp. 481–506.

they able to face the dilemmas with which contraceptive propaganda presents them? [9]

Which is preferable:
—600,000 abortions or birth control?
—a starving or a planned human race?
—unwanted pregnancies or fertility control?

These highly complex questions need clear and penetrating answers and these we must now provide.

[9] J. P. Dubois-Dumée, *Va-t-on contrôler les naissances?*, 49 rue du Faubourg Poissonière, 1956. *Population: An international Dilemma*, A Summary of the Proceedings of the Conference Committee on Population Problems, 1956–7, by Frederick Osborn, The Population Council, 230 Park Ave., New York, 1958.

Part Two

A Critical Assessment of the Results and Implications of Contraception in Countries where it is Officially Authorized

INTRODUCTORY NOTE

THE statement drawn up in the first part of this book has led us to the conclusion that, to many of our contemporaries, birth planning appears to be a necessity and contraception a boon.

But is this really so?

The answer to this question must be approached in two different ways. In the first place, we must inquire what results have in fact been obtained where birth planning and contraception are systematically and officially recognized by law. Above all, we must compare the real results with those which the out-and-out supporters of these techniques claim we have a right to expect. If we may be allowed the expression, this will give us the *answer provided by the facts*. We shall deal with it in the first chapter of this section (Ch. VI).

But this answer is not sufficient in itself. We need to go further and, in the light of the results that have been obtained, assess the values of the new Humanism, the new concept of Man and Society which are bound up with and implied by the introduction of birth planning and its techniques.

For, whether we like it or not, contraceptive techniques as they become more generally practised and especially as they become recognized by law, establish new cultural values (as has already been the case with divorce and prostitution) when they are given legal status and come under the control of the civil authorities.

If we bring to light the new humanism implied in the legalized introduction of contraception, we shall provide the true and only adequate answer to the question—what are the ultimate benefits of contraception? This we attempt to do in Chapter VII.

Chapter VI

THE "ANSWER OF THE FACTS" TO CONTRACEPTION AS OFFICIALLY RECOGNIZED

DOES CONTRACEPTION PREVENT ABORTION?

A BILL "to prevent the increase of criminal abortion by contraceptive prophylaxis" was tabled in the French National Assembly on 23 February 1956.[1]

The arguments in favour of the measure contained the following points—

"The preventive measures instituted by the law against criminal abortion do not appear to have reduced either its incidence or its dangers. As statistics of this social scourge cannot be obtained because of its intimate nature and clandestine character, and as it is only partly affected by scientific and medical progress, one out of every two pregnancies, according to the specialists, will be wilfully and prematurely terminated and the operation performed in two cases out of three, on married women and, in many instances women with children."

But "other countries have not scrupled to submit their legislation to a thorough revision in this field. They fight abortion by instructing their people in a rational control of births and by providing women especially with the means of preventing a pregnancy they dread."

"Is it not time," the text continues, "that doctors in France should be allowed to prescribe contraceptives, as are the majority of their colleagues abroad, when their professional conscience directs them to take precautions for the future by advising their women patients against an undesirable pregnancy?"

"Former objections against authorizing the use of contraceptive products and apparatus no longer exist. . . . Within the framework of

[1] Bill No. 715, Appendix to the report on the session of 25 Feb. 1956, for the prevention of the increase of criminal abortion by contraceptive prophylaxis, moved by MM. d'Astier de la Vigerie, Dreyfus-Schmidt and P. Ferrand. Three other bills followed: 15 March, No. 1252 (Hernu etc., group), 25 May, No. 1945 (Communist group), 25 May, No. 1963 (socialist group).

present-day legislation, it seems possible to prevent a large number of abortions by contraceptive prophylaxis."

"A possible fall in the number of births would be of less importance than the loss of human lives—of women and future children—caused every year by these abortions."

Many articles in support of this argument have appeared in the national press. They all quote the evidence of experiments made in other countries but fail to provide statistics since these in any case are non-existent.

We shall therefore attempt to rebut these assertions by stating the facts.

THE FACTS

In the first place, clandestine abortion has not disappeared from countries which have officially recognized and recommended birth planning. This is certainly the case in the U.S.A.[2] and no less so in Sweden which, as we have said, was among the first to experiment with contraceptive prophylaxis. A Swedish doctor, Axel Westman, admitted the fact as far as his country was concerned, at the Fifth International Conference on Planned Parenthood held at Tokyo in October 1955.[3] He said:

The promoters of the Law of 17 June 1938 officially recognizing contraception had hoped that this law would be successful in putting a stop to criminal abortion. However, it has not been so effective as they had hoped. The statistics available on the incidence of criminal abortions are as yet far from reliable, but it seems that no noticeable decrease in their number has been observed. It has even been admitted that the number of criminal abortions has shown a steady increase since the law came into

[2] Dr A. J. Rongy, *Abortion: Legal and Illegal*, New York, 1942; J. G. Mears, "In Fear and in Secret they do damnable Deeds." *America*, vol. 67 (1942) pp. 96–7; C. S. Mihanovich, G. J. Schnepp, J. L. Thomas, *A Guide to Catholic Marriage* (Milwaukee, Bruce, 1955), pp. 351–4. The Indianapolis inquiry has shown that 1·8% of married couples admitted procured abortions, i.e., 2·3% of pregnancies recorded. Cf. Whelpton and Kiser, *Social and Psychological Factors affecting Fertility*, vol. II, Part VI, p. 211 (1950). These figures are subject to reservations since the problem of abortion is one of those which the interested parties are most likely to keep secret.
[3] Quoted by Dr Jean Sutter, *Concours médical*, 16 March 1957, p. 1312 and in "Limitation des naissances," in *Population* 1956, No. 2, p. 218. The Fifth International Conference on Planned Parenthood, Report of the Proceedings, 1955, p. 236.

force. This increase is due to the fact that the possibility of terminating pregnancy has become a common topic of conversation with the result that the idea of abortion is generally accepted among our people.

Although this idea has not ceased to exist, perhaps clandestine procured abortion at least is on the decrease wherever prophylactic contraception is allowed. It is difficult to say. Dr J. Sutter, of the *Institut d'Etudes Démographiques*, writes:

> The figures available for the number of abortions are entirely without foundation. On what basis could they be tabulated? All genuine specialists who have tried to determine scientifically, even if only approximately, the number of procured abortions *in any country whatsoever*, have been honest enough to give up the attempt. . . . Any conclusions or any hypothesis that might be put forward in connection with the decrease in the number of procured abortions are based on shifting sands.[4]

We are entirely without data to show how far the spread of contraceptive methods makes a decrease in the number of procured abortions possible. The principal argument of the Neo-Malthusians has never received the slightest statistical confirmation.[5]

In her account of a Congress on abortion held at Arden House (U.S.A.) in 1955, and on the authority of Dr Shanoltz, Dr Lagroua Weill-Hallé stated: "A superficial glance might allow us to claim that contraception counteracts abortion, since it does away with unwanted pregnancies. A more detailed examination of the real situation leaves us in some doubt as to whether this is true." [6]

On the other hand, there is a real fall in the birth rate resulting from the spread of contraceptive methods when the latter are given practical encouragement by the civil authorities.

A case in point is the U.S.A. The first birth control clinic opened by Margaret Sanger dates from 1916 and the American Birth Control League was founded in 1921. Two States, New York and Connecticut, gave legal recognition to instruction in contraception in 1923.

[4] Quoted by Professors Rivière and Dr Traissac, "A propos du Birth Control," in *Gynécologie pratique* 1957, No. 1, p. 29.
[5] J. Sutter, *Concours médical,* 16 March 1956, p. 1311.
[6] Dr Lagroua Weill-Hallé, *Le "Planning" familial,* Preface by Simone de Beauvoir, Maloine 1959, p. 45.

The birth rate soon began to fall. The sectors most affected by this decrease between 1910 and 1940 were the upper classes (31·5% decrease), the white collar workers (28·2%) and the lower classes (28%).[7]

Contraceptive propaganda also spread in Norway between the two world wars. Whereas in 1910, 1,000 women who had married at the age of 25 had given birth during their period of fertility to 3,420 children, in 1920, 1,000 married women, under the same conditions, gave birth to no more than 2,540 and in 1930 to 1,980. This represents a fall of 25·7% during the first ten years, and a fall of 42·1% during the second.[8]

In Sweden there is a similar drop in the population curve. It too has been accelerated by the spread of birth control, which was finally made legal in 1938, the first bills having been laid before Parliament in 1918 and 1921.[9]

Sweden	Birth rate
1911–21	22.1 %
1933	13.7 %
1950	16.4 %
1955	14.8 %

It may be that this fall in the birth rate is accompanied by *a corresponding fall in the number of abortions*, but, we repeat, there is no proof that this is so.

On the contrary, there now exists proof that the rise in the abortion rate coincides with the wider use of contraceptive methods. This is the case among the Japanese of Iwasaki specially studied by Dr Koya.[1] This doctor went to this mining town to give instruction on birth control. But before beginning this instruction, he wanted for reference purposes to draw up statistics of pregnancies, births and abortions among the 716 married couples of the locality for the year preceding his arrival. During the period in which con-

[7] See Appendix III, p. 294.
[8] "La fécondité des mariages en Norvège, d'après les recensements," in *Population*, 1958, No. 1, p. 137.
[9] *The United Nations Demographic Yearbook*, 1956, p. 619 and A. Myrdal, *Nation and Family*, Kegan Paul, London, 1940.
[1] Yoshio Koya, and others, "Preliminary Report of a Survey of Health" and "Demographic Aspects of induced Abortion in Japan," *Archives of the Population Association of Japan*, II (1953), pp. 8–9; and "A Study of Family Planning of Coal-Miners," quoted in *Comptes rendus du Congrès mondial de la Population*, 1954, vol. I, p. 923; and by the same author, "Five-year Experiment on Family Planning among Coal-Miners at Joban, Japan," in *Population Studies*, Nov. 1959, pp. 157–63. See below, Appendix IX, p. 303.

traceptive methods were popularized, he made similar inquiries each year, and here is a comparison between the results:

Fertility Changes among 716 Japanese Couples (1952) reduced to 590 in 1958.

Year	Pregnancies	Births	Abortions
1952–3	208	130	63
1953–4	177	77	91
1954–5	105	53	49
1955–6	88	32	46
1956–7	78	32	37
1957–8	53	17	28

The raw figures for the number of abortions show a decrease of 35 in 6 years, but we must note that the decrease in the number of families during the same period was 126. The abortion rate there-fore (the ratio of the annual number of abortions to that of natural pregnancies) rose from 30% to 52·8%.

Another inquiry very carefully conducted in 1952 among 3,500 families by the Demographic Research Committee of *Mainichi*, a Japanese daily, provides further evidence to show that couples who use contraceptives are those who most frequently have recourse to abortion—6 times more than couples who do not practise birth control.[2] The Royal Commission on Population (Great Britain) had already noted this fact in 1949. The proportion of induced abortions in Great Britain was 8·7 times greater among couples who were in the habit of using contraceptives than among the others.[3]

The explanation of this strange fact, which directly contradicts the theory that contraception is a preventive prophylaxis against abortion, is not difficult to discover. When a couple has agreed to introduce an artificial technique into the most intimate and sacred relations of married life, it is less able than the couples who have deliberately rejected contraceptive methods, to resist the temptation to resort—in the event of an unexpected pregnancy—to another tech-nique, the only one they have left, if they want *at all costs* to avoid a birth, and that is the technique of abortion.

Dr Popenoe, an American marriage guidance counsellor, wrote the following in 1934 and it was still true twenty years later:

[2] Tatsuo Honda, "Extent of Diffusion of Fertility Control in Japan," a report presented to the World Population Conference held at Rome in Sept. 1954, E/13/129 Meeting 8 in *Papers for the World Population Conference,* vol. 1, p. 884. Quoted in Thomas Burch, "Patterns of Induced Abortion and their Socio-moral Implications in Postwar Japan," in *Social Compass,* vol. III, No. 4.

[3] *Papers of the Royal Commission on Population,* vol. I. "Family Limita-tion and its Influence on Human Fertility," Ch. IX, p. 173.

Advocates of the companionate always begin with the brave assumption that "Modern Medical Knowledge" makes it possible wholly to dissociate the reproductive from the erotic aspect of the marriage. It does, but only through the abortionist, and not through the contraceptive as the writers infer. Every married person knows there is no foolproof contraceptive yet in existence.[4]

In 1932, Dr Pearl in his well-known book *The Natural History of Population*, wrote: "The number of induced abortions . . . are from three to four or more times greater, generally speaking, among contraceptors than among non-contraceptors. . . ." He explained this by adding: ". . . criminal abortion is the last desperate remedy to correct the failures of contraceptive techniques . . . for something like three-quarters of the . . . abortionist's business he can thank the birth controllers. . . ."[5]

It may be objected that contraceptive techniques have been improved during the last few years and that the "sterilizing pill" will make possible successful results hitherto unknown. This may be the case. Yet everyone will admit that no method is absolutely infallible and that some of those using it will be absent-minded or careless, at least at the beginning of their experiments. In 1939 Dr Pearl pointed out that on the average 15% of pregnancies were unexpected even with the best contraceptive methods available at the time. For certain couples whose sexual activities had been given a stimulus by the false promises of propaganda, this meant an increase of 4·5 unexpected pregnancies as compared with the figures for the period

[4] Paul Popenoe, "Family or Companionate," *Journal of Social Hygiene*, vol. IX, No. 3, quoted by Carl C. Zimmerman and Lucius F. Cervantes, *Marriage and the Family*, Regnery, Chicago, 1956, p. 632.

[5] R. Pearl, *The Natural History of Population*, 1939, pp. 222 and 240. The March report of the *Milbank Memorial Quarterly* declared that there were at that time ten times more induced abortions among contraceptive couples than among the others.

In the New York clinics founded by Margaret Sanger's Planned Parenthood Association movement, the proportion of successes generally recorded is 75%, see J. K. Folson, *The Family and Democratic Society*, J. Willey, New York, 1943, p. 259. Even as contraception progresses (?) no method is put forward as absolutely certain. Cf. Abraham Stone, *The pre-marital Consultation, A Manual for Physicians*, Grune and Stratton, 1956, pp 36-7. In any case even if there were (and there is not) a method which would ensure 100% successes, there would still be the risks involved in its use which may comply to a greater or lesser extent with the instructions given. There would not be so many millions of dollars spent on laboratory research if "certain, efficient and harmless" (some add "not unpleasant") methods were available. Cf. Dr Lagroua Weill-Hallé, *La liberté de la conception à l'étranger*, Librairie Maloine, 1958.

when they kept less of a check over themselves. And how did these pregnancies terminate? In the same way, we hope, as unexpected Safe Period pregnancies (and the Ogino method is, we are told, responsible for a great many births) and not at the hands of the professional or legalized abortionist.[6]

FROM LEGALIZED CONTRACEPTION TO
LEGALIZED ABORTION

It is all but impossible not to feel that one has been cheated when an unexpected pregnancy arrives in spite of the prophylactic methods authorized by law. One naturally turns to the legislator who is indirectly guilty of having approved an imperfect and defective technique whose results are unexpected and disappointing. He must be asked to supplement such dubious legislation by allowing abortion to those whose belief in the effectiveness of a contraceptive technique has proved unfounded.

In fact, this is precisely what we see happening in countries which have legalized contraception. Their legislation inevitably leads the way to so-called therapeutic, eugenic and social laws whose purpose it is to correct the errors and deficiencies of the prophylactic measures.[7]

This has been the case in Denmark and Sweden. Their contraceptive legislation (1937–8) had soon to be supplemented by more liberal abortion laws. Thus in Sweden the State Insurance began to pay the cost of abortion after the sixth child. Since then, abortions have increased to such an extent that there were eight times more legal abortions (6,326) in Sweden in 1952 than in 1943 (703). This means an abortion rate of 57·5 as against 5·6 per thousand women.

There is also the temptation to resort to sterilization. Here too we see another type of "amendment" to defective contraceptive measures—legalized sterilization. Thus in Japan, there were

[6] R. Pearl, *op. cit.*, pp. 94 and 232. See also Warren Thompson, *Population Problems,* New York, 1942, p. 195, and Raymond W. Murray and Frank T. Flynn, *Social Problems,* New York, pp. 264–5.

[7] J. Sutter, *L'Eugénique,* 1950, pp. 136–7 and 154. J. Varangot, "Pratiques anticonceptionnelles, interruptions de grossesses et stérilisation," in *La Progénèse,* facteurs préconceptionnels du développement de l'enfant, ouvrage collectif sous la direction du Prof. Turpin, Maison, 1955—See Appendix I, p. 289.

1,170,000 legal abortions in 1955 whilst the number of women legally sterilized in the same year was 42,000.[8] At the Sixth Congress of the International Planned Parenthood Federation held at New Delhi in February 1959, the 587 Indian representatives and the 163 delegates from the other nations were for the most part ready to vote for a motion approving sterilization as the most effective means of limiting population increase. The resolution was referred back by Lady Rama Rao, President of the I.P.P.F., as requiring further study . . . but for how long?

DOES CONTRACEPTION REDUCE THE NUMBER OF THE UNDERFED THROUGHOUT THE WORLD?

Another argument advanced by the advocates of birth control is that it alone can effect an immediate reduction in the number of the underfed throughout the world. They quote the case of a nation prevented by insuperable obstacles from increasing its food supplies whilst its population is growing at an alarming rate. One example is Mexico whose annual rate of population increase was 0·63% in 1920–4, 2·32% in 1940 and 2·91% in 1953. Another case is Ceylon whose annual increase has rapidly risen from 1·34% in 1921–30 to 2·7% in 1953–5. Solutions to this state of affairs must be found at once, it is argued.

It is true that the Caribbean Islands, Mauritius, Formosa, North Africa, India, Egypt cannot remain any longer in their present state of chronic undernourishment and poverty. Everybody knows that India cannot provide 1,700 calories per head per day, whereas 2,500 are needed if men are to live by European standards. Egypt cannot offer her people 12 grammes of animal protein (meat, milk, eggs, cheese, fish, etc.) per day, whilst a Frenchman consumes 46 and an American 61.

Has it not been proved that in 1957 the human race was eating less than thirty years ago? The F.A.O. has calculated that if the 70

[8] *Nippon Times*, 13–12–55. In March 1947, the Minister of National Insurance and the Family Planning Association Federation of Japan held a ten-day conference whose object was to work out a better scheme for co-ordinating birth control activities throughout the country. The conference noted that although there was a decrease in the number of abortions in Japan, the figure for sterilization was increasing at an alarming rate. The official number for 1956 was 45,000, whilst the abortion figures still remained at the level of 1,200,000 per year. See Appendix II, p. 291.

countries in which it conducted its inquiry are to eat enough to satisfy their hunger, the world must increase its pre-war production of cereals by 23%, of fats by 34%, of dried vegetables by 80%, of fruit and green vegetables by 163%, and of milk by 100%. In terms of the economy of the underdeveloped countries, this would mean in India—to take one example—an increase of 305% in its meat production, of 113% in its production of fats and 330% in its production of fruit and vegetables. It is surely high time to intervene and check this catastrophic fertility before it is too late. If the human race does not want to founder in an anarchy of famine and war, it is high time to instruct all the nations, or those at least which are most prolific and least developed, in birth limitation by the only technical means effective within a short period of time, namely contraceptive techniques. We surely cannot be so naïve as to expect absolute continence from these nations.[9]

This is obviously a trenchant argument. The threat of world over-population is imminent. Action must be rapid and effective. Contraception alone meets these requirements. The Japanese experiment is sufficient proof as is shown by the record time (40 years; 1949–90) in which her demographic growth will have been completely halted.[1]

THE ANSWER PROVIDED BY THE FACTS

In fact the reality is more complex. Even if the Japanese experiment is a success (?) [2] merely from the Malthusian point of view and solely from a quantitative standpoint—and by this is meant that the development of human fertility has been checked—we may question whether this success is not due rather to abortion than to contraception. Already legalized abortions almost equal the number of births. In 1955 there were 1,170,143 legalized abortions as against 1,727,040 births.

---

[9] *Population Bulletin,* The Population Reference Bureau, 1507 M. Street N.W., Washington 5, D.C. e.g. "The West Indies, New Bottle, Old Wine." This periodical, although well known for its reliable statistics, insists exclusively on the Malthusian view of a world with far too large a population.

[1] A. Sauvy, *De Malthus à Mao-Tse-Toung,* Ed. Denoël ,1958, p. 239.

[2] We agree that Japan's situation immediately after her defeat was tragic. The population figures rose from 55,400,000 in 1920 to 73,300,000 in 1943. Then the repatriation of Japanese combined with a high fertility rate produced an annual increase—1,500,000 to 1,800,000—during the period 1945–50.

But above all, in 1948 Japan provided the ideal social and cultural conditions for an experiment in contraception. The country had long ceased to be one of the so-called underdeveloped nations. Although its national income per person was still between 200 and 300 dollars—which placed it on an income level comparable with that of Bulgaria, Brazil and Spain, whilst that of India and Burma is still only 100 dollars per person—nevertheless, the Japanese enjoyed a far higher standard of comfort than the Italians and the Spaniards and were not far behind the Argentine and Czechoslovakia in this respect. For every thousand inhabitants, there were in Japan 2·5 times more pupils at secondary, technical and higher grade schools than in France.

Under such conditions of culture and comfort, the spread of contraceptive techniques was not likely to meet with the same obstacles as it does among the illiterate populations of predominantly agricultural and rural nations. For it is a characteristic of such peoples that they are unable to use modern techniques nor do they even desire to do so. Hence, the use of contraceptives, far from being, as the advocates of birth control would like us to believe, a condition of social progress, is a result and a corollary of such progress.[3]

The case of India is instructive in this respect. In spite of hard work among the rural populations, the Family Planning leagues obtain only very meagre results. A recent sample taken in one of the small villages of Bombay State, Badlapur—there are almost 500,000 of these communities in India—with approximately 3,000 inhabitants, 45 castes and 4 religions, has proved beyond all doubt that these people are not impervious to birth control propaganda. Among the men 28·2% and among the women 38·1% stated that they wanted no more children, but only 25·8% of the men and 40·5% of the women had any intention of using contraceptives.[4]

However, even supposing that 2,000 birth control clinics could be

[3] A. Sauvy, *Théorie générale de la Population*, t. II. Intérêts particuliers et bien public, p. 147. "Existe-t-il une volonté collective?" p. 151. "Finally, contraceptive advice has its effect on families which already have an eye to the future rather than on those that are large and ill-cared for. Its quantitative effect is therefore very debatable" (p. 79, p. 231, p. 217). See below, p. 61, note 1.

[4] W. A. Morrison, "Attitudes of Males and Females towards Family Planning in a Western Indian Village," in the *Milbank Memorial Fund Quarterly*, July 1956 and Jan. 1957.

opened at great expense in 2,000 villages including within their radius 10,000 smaller population groups, what sort of *immediate result* would this give in comparison with the 500,000 villages to be won to the cause?

In actual practice the spread of birth control among an under-developed population only succeeds in accentuating the difference between fertility in the towns and fertility in the country districts. The more advanced *élites* in the towns do in fact adopt the Malthusian behaviour of the Western nations and so reduce their birth rate, although a higher number of births among these *élites* would be in the interests of the nation. The rural masses, on the other hand, either remain indifferent to the town way of life, stay where they are and continue to increase, or else begin to take an interest in the fortunes of the large centres of population within which they hope to find employment, and so move rapidly into the cities. There they congregate into "shanty towns" and their fertility remains high whilst there is no improvement in their cultural level. On all counts, contraceptive policy meets with failure. The inertia of the masses defeats it[5] unless the State assumes dictatorial powers, has no hesitation in imposing heavy penalties and sets up a system of police control over the family. Contraceptive legislation is then

[5] The situation is not the same if we are dealing with a population living in a confined space such as an island, where the public authorities use all the modern methods of persuasion (propaganda?), conduct sociological inquiries to prove their point, and so in practice force families to limit the number of their children. But is not the net result of this a disguised form of "genocide", especially where there is a cultural distinction between the dominant and the dominated sectors? In Puerto Rico, for instance, after a preliminary failure of the birth control campaign in 1925 and 1935, a more carefully prepared plan was put into operation in 1939. A network of 160 Family Planning clinics was established. Facilities were offered to women who preferred to be sterilized after maternity. Hence 19·3% of the confinements in hospital were followed by a sterilization operation. Cf. J. Mayone Stycos and Reuben Hill, "The Prospects of Birth Control in Puerto Rico," in *The Annals of the American Academy of Political and Social Science*, Jan. 1953. The Puerto-Ricans, who are Spanish by culture and tradition although citizens of the U.S.A., only migrated in small numbers to the American mainland before 1945—about 4,000 a year (between 1908 and 1945). The rate of emigration definitely increased after the second world war and reached an annual total of 59,132 in 1952 and 69,124 in 1953. It is even estimated that the number of migrants between 1942 and 1951 amounted to 249,918. In an article in the *Population Bulletin*, April 1955, the author points out—with a sigh of relief? —that if the fertility rate had not decreased, as it actually has done, since 1940, there would have been 320,000 Puerto-Rican migrants on U.S.A. terri-tory instead of 249,918 (p. 28). In this connection, see also Kurt W. Back, Reuben Hill and J. Mayone Stycos, "The Dynamics of Family Planning," in *Marriage and Family Living*, Aug. 1956, pp. 195-200.

no more than a pretext[6] since a nation under such a regime is in fact adopting a eugenic policy under the complete control of the public authorities. Will this soon be the case in China? This surely constitutes a permanent temptation in the people's democracies and is the natural tendency of every contraceptive policy. On the pretext of "educating the people" the official or private bodies responsible for implementing this policy are constantly tempted to bring a certain "pressure" to bear, or even a form of compulsion which threatens the liberty and the rights of the human person.[7]

Finally, even where there is no such "discreet pressure", human nature will shoulder the task itself. The most modern contraceptive methods are in the long run difficult and costly. They demand a standard of personal hygiene beyond the reach of many. So the easy way out is to abandon all restraint . . . and, when all has been said and done, to have recourse to abortion, unless the interested parties decide "to finish with the business once and for all" and opt for sterilization.

This is probably the best explanation for the wave of abortions and also the present recrudescence of sterilization in Japan. 45,000

---

[6] A recent study by J. Mayone Stycos is very revealing in this connection: "Some directions for Research on Fertility Control," in *The Milbank Memorial Fund Quarterly*, April 1958, pp. 126–148. In this article the author deals with the evaluation of the obstacles raised by religion among the lower classes, and suggests how to avoid giving the impression that a white minority is attempting to reduce the numbers of the coloured masses. He is aware of the resistances arising from the class structures among populations in an underdeveloped state. And the most curious thing is that he admits that the sociologist hesitates between the most perfected contraceptives, the most effective from the scientific point of view but which it is difficult to persuade simple people to adopt, and the old "methods in vogue" (*coitus interruptus* and vaginal douches), whose effectiveness is only moderate. He says:

To those who would complain of the intrinsic ineffectiveness of the latter two methods, it can only be said that a relatively inefficient method which is used will prove more valuable than an efficient one which is not (p. 146). The author also raises the following objection: May not the failure resulting from intrinsically ineffective methods lead to a refusal of all forms of birth control?

On the other hand [he replies] the most important step is getting families to practise any method of birth control. For [he adds] though failure may occur, the pattern of use is established, and more effective methods will be sought out. In this connection, it is interesting that in Japan resort to abortion typically occurs after failure of contraception; in Puerto Rico, sterilization. (Note 11, p. 22.)

It is an odd sociology that ventures to make this kind of value judgment, especially after it has stated that scientific contraception was to replace abortion.

[7] See above, p. 60, note 5.

cases were openly admitted in 1956. The true figure is likely to be four times that number.[8]

Therefore we conclude with A. Sauvy: "Birth control produces results that are the exact opposite of those it sets out to achieve, since the spread of contraceptive methods affects especially the more advanced strata of society and it is in these that children usually stand a better chance of receiving the care and the education they need."[9]

VOLUNTARY CHILDBIRTH=HAPPY CHILDBIRTH

The third point in the argument of the advocates of birth control is that contraception clearly guarantees the emancipation of women and happy motherhood.

When contraceptives are freely used, we are told, there will be no more mothers in despair over too frequent pregnancies, no more ill-kept homes, child martyrs or juvenile delinquents. There will be no more—and this is said in a lower tone of voice—unmarried mothers, mothers that is, left to struggle alone and condemned to poverty or prostitution.[1]

On the contrary, as a result of a better spacing of births, there will be healthier children and healthier mothers. Women will be freer and more aware that they are approaching a status of equality with their husbands and are not merely the object of their whims or the victims of their instincts. This being the case, there will be happier homes, a more tranquil married life, couples who are better balanced

---

[8] See above, p. 57, note 8, and for other results: an ageing population, etc., see below, p. 79, note 1.

[9] A. Sauvy, "Le Malthusianisme anglo-saxon," in *Population*, No. 3, p. 221. See also Jacob Oser, *Must Men Starve? The Malthusian Controversy*, Jonathan Cape, London, 1956. Although the author approves of birth control, he has no illusions about the myth the Malthusian mentality has evolved around it. "Birth control is therefore one facet in a many-sided attack on the problem of adequate food for all people. The mistake of the Malthusians is that they make this the central theme, and sometimes the only one, in their proposed solution to the problem" (p. 285).

[1] See the case of Mr and Mrs B., which gave Dr Lagroua Weill-Hallé the chance to bring the problem of contraception before the Académie des Sciences morales et politiques: *Gynécologie pratique*, 1955, No. 6, p. 429: "Du conflit entre la loi et la conscience professionnelle du médecin," by Mme le Dr L. Weill-Hallé. See also the sad cases quoted by the review *Maternité Heureuse* and in the social novels of G. Cesbron, Van der Meersch, G. Duhamel, etc., etc.

psychologically and who more nearly approach the ideal of a family life of peace and intimacy.

In short, the interests of individuals and of society will be reconciled, since by giving birth only to the children they want to have, poor families will no longer become those heart-rending "social cases" where children are abandoned and husbands and wives deserted by their partners.

The argument then is as follows: contraceptively controlled childbirth = voluntary childbirth = happy childbirth = happy children. In support of this view, evidence provided by individuals and the results of inquiries are quoted.

One report, for instance, depicts for us the transformation of East London (the dockers' quarter and formerly that of the London proletariat), since contraception has succeeded in establishing itself there. Women, we are told, no longer break down under the burden of repeated pregnancies. This is proved by the spectacular fall, during a period of less than twenty years, in the number of children in each family when the mother has finished her child-bearing.[2]

In 1911, one in every three persons lived more than two to a room. In 1931 the proportion was already down to one in four. By 1951, it had fallen to 1 in 33. There has been a reduction in the hours of work. As people now live longer, homes are not broken up by the early death of the father. But, above all, the husband is no longer the tyrannical brute who used to spend his time at the public house spending his money recklessly, whilst at home, there was a swarming mass of children and his unfortunate wife worked, shouted and thrashed her offspring. The East Londoner has become a companion, a husband, a father. The children are loved for their own sakes and their parents think carefully about their future. Of 43 couples questioned, 25 stated they were doing their utmost to send their children to secondary or technical schools.

According to this picture, there have been obvious positive gains. It is therefore understandable that the advocates of birth control are proud of such results and wish to see them extended over as wide an area as possible. The irresponsible large family of the past has become the restricted and far-sighted family of today. The "social cases"—homes in which 6 to 10 children were huddled into

[2] Michael Young and Peter Willmott, "The Changing Families of East London," in *The Human Sum, op. cit.,* pp. 120–42. The inquiry notes that 28 families out of 43 stated that they had planned the arrival of their first child. Some said that two children were all they wanted, others three.

one or two rooms—are now non-existent or at least extremely rare in East London.

Surely then we may subscribe to the equation—voluntary child-birth=happy childbirth? And all the more so because in support of this argument, there are figures provided by American sociologists who have made inquiries in which "married happiness" has been correlated with contraceptive practices. Thus, in his Indianapolis inquiry, Dr Reed chose 1,444 couples whom he attempted to classify on the basis of their answers to the following questionnaire:

All things considered is your marriage:
—very unhappy indeed?
—genuinely less happy than the average marriage?
—a little less happy than the average marriage?
—more or less like everybody else's?
—genuinely happier than the average marriage?
—very happy indeed?

These same couples were also classified on the basis of the number of children they had had.

The review which quotes this inquiry remarks[3]: "A list of these couples based on the size of their families compared with another based on their 'happiness as a family' shows that the proportion of 'happy' husbands, wives and couples decreases as the number of children grows greater. The curve is absolutely constant. (There is only one exception. Childless women say they are 'less satisfied with their husbands' than those with one child). But this rather too simple and discouraging point of view was not considered enough, and a much more thorough investigation of the fertility of married couples than the mere enumeration of pregnancies, was to modify the above conclusions. A re-classification of these couples no longer in relation to the size of their families but in relation to the method they used to limit them, i.e. the way in which they had controlled the number of births and its complete or only partial success in preventing these, revealed that as preventive control decreased (i.e. the less successful it had been in preventing unwanted pregnancies), the smaller became the number of happy couples. Thus 45·2% of the couples who had always been able to avoid unwanted pregnancies were in the category 'happy', whereas only 17% of those who had had unwanted children were included in this group. If the category of those who

[3] *Maternité Heureuse*, No. 3, pp. 23–6.

had had two or more pregnancies in excess of what they had wanted is taken into account, the proportion of 'happy' couples fell to 14·7%." Dr Reed, we are told, concluded: "Thus, it appears that among these couples the major problem of family planning was the prevention of excess pregnancies and that success in solving this problem was associated with achieving a happy marriage".[4]

Such, it appears, are the facts.

.... BUT THE FACTS THEMSELVES REPLY:

. . . other facts, that is, answer that happiness or no happiness, the fertility of Protestant couples was shown by this celebrated Indianapolis inquiry to be below replacement level.

H. V. Musham and Clyde V. Kiser, well known for their systematic utilization of the Indianapolis data[5] admit that the group of families involved in the inquiry—and who agreed that they had decided to plan their fertility from the outset of their married life— had produced, by the end of their fertility period, an average number of children per family lower than that for which, taken as a whole, they had originally opted. In other words, the number of children actually born was smaller than had been desired.

Nor is this fact unusual or confined to Indianapolis. It reappears in two inquiries undertaken in the United States at different periods. The first, Gutman's, carried out in 1925 in a College of 445 young men, collected information on the number of children these young men wished to have during their married life, it being understood that births would be planned. The average figure was 2·6. Twenty-five years later in 1950, the same investigator renewed contact with 89 of these former students and found that the average number of their children was 1·9 per family.

[4] Robert Reed, "The Inter-relationship of Marital Adjustment, Fertility Control, and Size of the Family," in the *Milbank Memorial Fund Quarterly,* XXV, Oct. 1947, pp. 383–425, quoted in P. K. Whelpton and C. V. Kiser, *Social and Psychological Factors affecting Fertility,* New York, Milbank Memorial Fund, 1950, pp. 268 and 278. See also Christensen and Philbrick, "Family Size as a Factor in Marital Adjustment of College Couples," in *American Sociological Review,* XVIII (1952), pp. 306–12.

[5] H. V. Musham and Clyde V. Kiser, "Social and Psychological Factors affecting Fertility, The Number of Children desired at the Time of Marriage," in *The Milbank Memorial Fund Quarterly,* July 1956, pp. 1304, 1310; Robert Gutman: "College Men and the Birth Rate—25 Years After," in *Journal of Heredity,* XIII, No. 6, Nov.–Dec. 1951, pp. 285–7; Robert Gutman and Irving Bender, "Some Sources of Variation in the Family Size of College Graduates," in *The Milbank Memorial Fund Quarterly,* July 1957, p. 299.

The same sociologist conducted a similar inquiry among 95 old members of an American college who had gone up in 1939–1940. The number of children per family desired by the men of that year, 1939–40, was 3·14. The number actually born fifteen years later in 1955 was in fact 2·43 per family.

This proves that in the United States this effort towards "happy childbirth" through "voluntary childbirth", held up to us as an example, ultimately leads to a weakening of the maternal impulse itself. As A. Sauvy puts it: "Birth control, however praiseworthy its intentions (?), suffers from its inability to limit the sphere in which it operates . . . The struggle against too much life runs the risk of turning into a struggle against life itself."[5]

If some turn this struggle against life to account and find happiness in it, we now see what this "happiness" and this voluntary and happy motherhood mean. The latter is, in reality, a semi-sterility, an unconsciously sought, unconsciously desired sterility. What has been desired and worked for, is a reduction in the eventual number of children. If one or two children have been born, they have been accepted as a kind of tribute to the demands of nature and married love. The others, who might have been born, have been carefully avoided and their conception prevented by the use of a technique. The expression "voluntary motherhood", seeing that it implies above all an attitude of refusal, is very odd indeed. Does happiness consist above all in refusing, in being unprepared, to give life?

At this point, we go beyond the mere factual categories and enter the sphere of value judgments. These are the secret possession of every family and cannot in practice be classified and translated into statistics by any investigator. Yet here lies the question—were these births refused for love of the children already born so that these might have an easier, freer and more comfortable life? Was it because the parents wanted to provide them with better educational opportunities and devote themselves more fully to their welfare? Or, on the contrary, was it so that they might have peace and quiet? Was it because they wished to be in the fashion and have their television set, their car, their refrigerator, like everybody else?

It is impossible to say, and above all to claim the right to label "happy" the families where there are two children and every modern comfort rather than those with three or four children but less comfort and more worry.

[6] A. Sauvy, "Le Malthusianisme anglo-saxon," in *Population*, 1947, No. 3, p. 221.

What is happiness? Denis de Rougemont writes:

> It is hard enough to give a general definition of happiness, but the problem becomes insoluble as soon as we include in it the modern desire to be master of one's own happiness or, what comes perhaps to the same thing, to sense what happiness is, to analyse it, to enjoy it and so be able to improve it by successive and well-calculated adjustments. All happiness which we wish to feel and control—instead of experiencing it as a free gift—is immediately transformed into an intolerable sense that something is missing.[7]

Thus a calculated ease, foreseen and measured out so that it may increase and develop, is not happiness. It may, up to a point, be one of its conditions. That is why we do not dispute the fact that life in East London has been transformed. The changes there are happy ones from many points of view. But they are not enough, they do not really take us to the heart of true happiness, for, in spite of all appearances, happiness does not consist principally in enjoyment. Happiness is the fruit of self-giving, of self-forgetfulness and a will to work for the good of somebody else, of other people rather than one's own. Happiness is the fruit of love and devotion, the victory of altruism over egoism.

To sum up:

To the arguments which attempt to show that in birth planning and its contraceptive techniques we have a phophylaxis against abortion, an immediate solution to the problem of under-nourishment in the so-called underdeveloped countries, and a guarantee of happy motherhood, the facts themselves provide the following answer:

Where contraception is introduced and officially recognized and diffused:

—Clandestine abortion does not disappear.

—In general the fertility of married couples tends automatically to decrease.

—Married couples faced with an unexpected pregnancy, and tempted to go further by resorting to abortion, show a correspondingly weaker resistance to this temptation.

—Sooner or later, in view of the increasing number of disappointments due to failures in contraceptive practice, the public authorities are asked to introduce still more liberal laws by instituting what, under cover of abortion and sterilization on eugenic

---

[7] Denis de Rougemont, "L'idée moderne de Bonheur," in *Esprit*, Sept. 1938, p. 658.

and social grounds, are other additional ways of terminating or preventing pregnancy.

—In underdeveloped agrarian areas, the variation between the fertility rate of the countryside and the towns, and between the *élite* and the masses, far from showing a decrease, in fact grows greater, at least for so long as the social and cultural life of the masses fails to reach a higher level.

—The attempt to achieve "happy childbirth" by means of "controlled childbirth"—the so-called "voluntary motherhood"—in reality disguises an unconscious search for a type of motherhood which is restricted by deliberate sterility.

This, we repeat, is the answer given by the facts themselves.

It remains for us to discover the new concept of man, the new Humanism which these facts imply, and which they tend to implant in our patterns of behaviour and our institutions.

Chapter VII

CONTRACEPTIVE CIVILIZATION

TECHNICAL INVENTIONS AND CIVILIZATION

An inventor is rarely clear-sighted and shrewd enough to foresee at a glance all the changes his invention will produce in the habits of his fellow-men, all the transformations it will effect in customs and attitudes of the mind, all the alterations in the secret motivations of individuals, the perturbations it may cause in the conscious ideals of a society. Yet each invention is, in its own way, an explosive force. Each invention is like a sudden, rapid and powerful fire which either amplifies, though it does not deform, the image and concept of his own nature which man has acquired, or else reshapes this image in another pattern by changing its lines and contours.[1]

Among those who continually ask for birth planning and contraception to be established in France, there are some who seem aware of the eventual *mutation in our civilization* which this would involve. Thus the *Ligue des Droits de l'Homme* stated:

> If the abrogation of the Law of 1920 makes it possible to attenuate the torments, crises and anxieties which fear of an inopportune pregnancy brings to thousands of men and above all to women, it will be a great achievement. In the propagation of the human race, nature has placed the greater burden upon women. Men should make it a point of honour to compensate as far as they are able for this *natural injustice*.[2]

The expression "natural injustice" is significant. It makes abundantly clear what are the intentions of one sector of public opinion. It is not merely concerned to find a suitable remedy for a temporary

[1] On the transformation of man and the family by technics see *Encyclopédie Française*, t. XIV, "La civilization quotidienne," especially Section C. "L'organisation de l'espace et l'urbanisme, D. Se mieux loger, E. Se mieux nourrir, F. Se mieux vêtir, etc." The bibliography is large and well chosen, 1955; see also H. Migeon, *Le monde après 150 ans de Technique*, 1958; E. Girardeau, *Le progrès technique et la personne humaine*, Plon, 1955.

[2] "La ligue des Droits de l'Homme demande l'introduction en France du birth control," *Le Monde*, 16 Nov. 1957.

though tragic situation—inadequate housing and wages—even if this situation is that of a large part of the working-class population. Some are asking for far more than that. They claim that the very conditions nature has provided for human propagation and repro-duction should be altered.

In other words, a *new*, contraceptive *civilization* must compensate for and rectify the misdeeds and errors of nature. Twentieth century man puts right the damage done by temperature and weather. He changes the seasons and the days in order to double his crops. He breaks the sound barrier in order to reach his destination more rapidly. He equips satellites to enlarge the space in which he is con-fined by nature, etc. Why should he not alter as he pleases, the condi-tions surrounding, and the values attaching to, the process of genera-tion by restricting it to a strict and necessary minimum? And all the more so because the sexual function, mastered at last by the intellect and by science, could then bring man those benefits and values of which past centuries have taken insufficient advantage. And so we should find ourselves on the threshold of a new Humanism whose characteristics, though still uncertain and ill-defined, it would be in our interests with the aid of sociology to decipher in advance.

PREDICTION PROBLEMS

Let us frankly admit at the outset that the art of prediction is hardly that of the sociologist, although the latter knows well enough from experience that since new techniques bring new conditions, they sometimes also produce profound changes in a civilization's way of life.[3] Hence there are very few sociologists who would ven-ture to claim that in 1910 they would have been able to predict the effects of the general use of the *motor-car* on the stability and cohe-sion of family life, on its choice of residence and its home life.[4] Could they have foretold the traffic congestion in the towns, the rapid development of the kind of garden suburbs that now surround the great American cities, together with all the new problems raised by these "haunts of wealth"? Could they have foreseen the competition between road and rail, the increasing symbolism of town and country, the latter's psychological transformation, the disappearance of the small business? Could they have given advance notice of the

---

[3] J. Fourastié, *La civilisation de 1970*, P.U.F., 1954.
[4] J. Desforges, *Le divorce en France*, Ed., Familiales de France, 1946.

changed uses of leisure which we owe to the car, could they have
estimated the extent to which the middle-class woman is tempted
to break away from home life or her efforts to combine housework
with paid professional employment?

Even today, the "civilization of the car" has not really revealed
all the sociological changes which it is still capable of producing,
and of these the least desirable are not necessarily the most obvious.
Yet the advent of the car is a very superficial phenomenon by comparison with the inner nature of man.

It should surely be generally admitted that the introduction of
contraception into a given society must inevitably produce, to say
the least, equally profound changes. We need only glance at the
results of the introduction into France in 1884 of the legal procedure
of *divorce*. Those who introduced it flattered themselves at the time
that they were making possible only the achievement of the results
they considered to be favourable to their point of view—the suppression of free love and concubinage, the gradual elimination of
moral hypocrisy, etc. Some, like M. de Marcère in the Senate itself,
went so far as to say:

> Far from attacking the institution of marriage, divorce on the
> contrary can help to increase its moral value by making it possible
> to prepare for it more seriously. Today, unfortunately, people
> marry for reasons, some of which certainly are no credit to the
> state of public morals. We may be allowed to hope that when
> young people realize that the union into which they are about to
> enter, the family they are about to found, the whole of the future
> of which they have dreamed, may be broken and brought to
> nothing because there is such a thing as divorce, this thought will
> make preparation for marriage a rather more serious and more
> adult affair, and people will think twice before venturing on a
> career which can be so soon and so tragically interrupted.[5]

Today such optimism makes us smile. Doubtless M. de Marcère
was not a sociologist, but even had he been, would he have been able
to foresee how the trickle of divorce in French legislation would
become a great torrent? Whereas in all countries such as Italy, Spain
and Portugal, where the law authorizes separation alone, the annual
number of applications for such separations remains constant, in
those where divorce has been adopted, on the contrary, the latter is

[5] "La contagion du divorce," in *Cahiers d'Action Religieuse et sociale*, No.
88, 1 Jan. 1950, p. 515, note 2; *Débats au Sénat*, 20 June 1884, p. 1116.

constantly on the increase and so much so that sociologists classify it among epidemic phenomena and deal with its infectious character from the standpoint of epidemiology.

Could the French legislators of 1884 have possibily estimated the increase in the numbers of unhappy children or of those in moral danger because of the "third party in the home"? Could they possibly have predicted that Parliament would be persuaded to authorize the legitimation by subsequent marriage of a child born of an adulterous union? And this is a most serious affront to married fidelity. Could they have foreseen the devaluation of the marriage contract and the practical difficulty of distinguishing between the natural institution and trial marriage?

What would be the effect of *euthanasia* on our morals and our legislation if ever its techniques were authorized? There would no doubt be people to plead in its favour. And why should an individual who can only look forward to suffering days and nights of useless anguish not be put painlessly out of his misery? Should we not be helping mankind to solve one of its most terrible problems, should we not be acknowledging that one of society's most noble functions is to bring relief to the victim of an evil fate beyond the power of reason to explain? And, we might add, above all at a time when there exist techniques to ensure painless death and suicide without suffering. Should we not be demonstrating the perfect mastery man has acquired over life? Why not sanction this mastery by allowing scientific suicide and so satisfy both heart and mind? Yet some obscure reason prevents men from adopting this view and stops society from making up its mind to translate it into action. Is this obscure refusal a mere parasitical survival of a civilization which had an inadequate technical equipment? Or, under the guise of mysterious prohibitions, is it anything more than a projection of the gaps in our scientific knowledge? If so, is it not the duty of mankind today to brush aside these old-fashioned scruples? As some authors have recently written in regard to contraception: "Is it not right that the experiment should be tried? If only one of the predictions of our adversaries proves true . . . there will still be time to turn to other solutions or, if necessary, to retrace our steps."[6]

We agree that at this point we are approaching the area into which medical experiment may justifiably venture. As is well known, this

[6] J. Vincent, "La liberté de la conception," in *Science et Vie,* Nov. 1957, p. 97.

simple question of the rights and limits of medical experiment has given rise to considerable controversy.[7]

Why should there not be similar justification for the introduction of a new sociological experiment among the world's population groups? Why should no attention be paid to the warnings and recommendations of sociologists? Must we insist, in this age of sociology, that a measure which apparently will not harm the individual nor even the married couple, may—once it has become general throughout a whole society and above all, once it has been made legal—produce results which, though scarcely noticeable at the level of the individual, are of the greatest importance to society as a whole? A few moments ago, we referred to the surprises which divorce legislation had in store for us. May it not be that the "sorcerer's apprentices" of Family Planning and contraceptive legislation run the risk of falling into similar errors?

Social and legal experts are well aware of what ensues when *prostitution* in countries with a parliamentary regime is officially regulated and also considered to represent a certain *value* in our *civilization*. In practice there is no means of combating the white-slave traffic.[8] The traffic in women no longer raises any general protest. Political circles, even Governments at times, become mysteriously infected by the favourable treatment accorded to the most depraved members of our society—those who traffic in women. It is impossible or very difficult for this state of affairs to exist when regulation of prostitution has been abolished. The reason is easy to understand. In the latter case, there is a mere passive tolerance of prostitution. No attempt is made to justify it and hence it remains clandestine. In the former case, on the contrary, the State sets a "value" on the traffic in women.

It seems to us that an analogous problem arises when it is suggested that a "value" be set on contraception in that the State is asked to make it legal and authorize its diffusion. It is our considered opinion—and we do not hesitate to state it quite frankly—that "to set a value" on contraception will lead to profound changes in our civilization. We have only to look at those already taking place among nations which, for the past generation or two, have officially permitted contraceptive practices.

[7] *Cahiers Laënnec*, "L'expérimentation humaine en médecine," 1952, No. 1 (March) and No. 2 (June).

[8] O. Philippon, *Le trafic des femmes, La propagande et les appuis,* Téqui, 1956, pp. 26–42. By the same author: *L'esclavage de la femme dans le monde moderne ou la prostitution sans masque,* Téqui, 1954.

CHANGES IMPLIED BY A CONTRACEPTIVE CIVILIZATION

—The gradual disappearance of the group of families which deliberately have several children. This is a result of the tendency to consider the large family as an unnatural monstrosity.

—A decline into spiritual old age and a premature sclerosis among populations and families which have deliberately chosen to curb their creative powers.

—A debasement of the idea and the ideal of family happiness, which is reduced to a so-called "right to happiness" and what are considered its "techniques".

—A lowering of moral standards among young people, an increase of licentiousness among the unmarried, the severance of the link between female sexuality and marriage.

—A serious deterioration in the love relationship due to the reversal of the true order of values in the use of the sexual function and from its fixation at a very "adolescent" stage. The development of society arrested at this "transitional" stage.

—A deliberate "sterilization" of the maternal instinct due to the repression of the innate desire of women for children. A veiled hostility towards life and its primary manifestations—pregnancy, childbirth, sometimes even towards infants and very young children.

—A new concept of sex, the essence of which is now to be defined as "a capacity for erotic activity in the service of the couple". The link with procreation is only accidental.

—An increasing confusion between the sexes and a decreased resistance to "sexual inversion". A decline of masculinity among men and femininity among women.

—A growing toleration of homosexuality now considered as an erotic activity and even held to be an expression of personal relationship between friends.

—Finally, because of the hopes to which it gives rise but is unable to fulfil, contraception, with the many frustrations and profound disappointments it causes, is also partly responsible for:

—The prevalence of divorce and the lack of stability in marriages today.

—The decline in the level of mental health and the increase of aphrodisia in women. See the Kinsey Report.

—The failure of parents to face up to their tasks as educators.

—The boredom emanating from a civilization entirely preoccupied with a culture based on comfort and sexual satisfaction.

We may be accused of painting too dark a picture. We cannot be reproached with having failed to speak our mind. It now remains for us to justify these predictions, and we said at the outset that it is only too difficult to provide them with a statistical basis.

THE LARGE FAMILY IN DISREPUTE

Industrial civilization as such does not favour large families. All the inquiries undertaken among married couples for the purpose of discovering what, in their view, is the ideal number of children per family, reveal a sharp difference between townsmen and countryfolk, who usually contemplate a larger family than couples living in towns.

But once this point has been made, it is still true that the Malthusian climate created by propaganda in favour of contraceptive procedures weakens the home's creative urge. The artificial contrasts drawn by such propaganda between "happy" and "large" families, succeed in making the latter appear an unnatural monstrosity.

In this respect, contraceptive countries head the list for the constant decrease from census to census in the number of families with five children. Whereas in France this class of family has remained stable[9], in the United States the family with five or more children,

[9] If we consider the final number of children in the French and American family—the family, that is, in which the mother has reached the end of her childbearing period (at about 47) we note the following trends:
Married women between 45 and 49 years of age according to the number of live births:—

| Countries | Year | Total | Number of Children | | | | | |
			0	1	2	3	4	5 +
France	1931	100	17.4	21.7	22.1	14.6	8.9	15.3
	1946	100	17.8	25.5	13.7	7.8	11.9	11.9
U.S.A.	1940	100	15.0	16.2	19.8	15.7	10.0	20.1
	1952	100	19.4	20.7	23.3	14.7	7.5	13.1

We note therefore that over a period of twelve years large families (5 or more children) have decreased by 7·0% in America. In France there has been a fall of 3·4% over a period of fifteen years (cf. *Résultats statistiques du recensement général de la Population Française de 1946*, t. IV. *Familles*, pp. LXIV–LXVII; cf. *Current Population Reports, Population Characteristics*, Bureau of the Census, Series P-20, No. 46, 31 Dec. 1953, p. 11). We also note that the French women in question were born between 1884 and 1899 so that Family Allowances have had little influence in their case. The American women were born between 1893 and 1905 and were from 20 to 25 years old between 1925 and 1930, that is, at the time when contraceptive propaganda was in full spate in the U.S.A. See Appendix III, p. 294 for the fertility coefficient in the U.S.A. between 1910 and 1950, and Appendix X, p. 311, for the evolution of family fertility in France.

which in 1940 still accounted for 20·1% of families where no more pregnancies were possible, only reached the figure of 13·1% in 1952.

As it is also an established fact that those who have grown up in a large family generally have a proportionately larger number of children themselves, the reduction in the number of large families during the present generations shows that there is a break with tradition.[1] This can only be accounted for by the discrediting of the large family, an attitude either expressed openly or implied by the mere fact that there exists no policy of aid to large families. This is still the case in the United States whilst the opposite is true in France.

Unfortunately national catastrophes are needed to open the eyes of those who despise the large family. It is only at times of crisis that policies are formulated and draw the attention of public opinion to those large families without which the population figures would in fact fall below replacement level.[2]

Dr Sutter writes:

Demographic statistics show that the behaviour patterns of French couples who married after 1940 are eventually responsible for 2,200–2,300 live births per 1,000 marriages. These include

[1] On the handing on of a code of demographic conduct in large families, see the very apposite remarks of Fr Desqueyrat in "L'arche de Noé," *Revue de l'Action Populaire,* No. 41, June 1950, p. 426. "In the past the French family was Catholic and large by custom and tradition. When it encountered contemporary civilization, custom and tradition were swept away by the winds of positivism and rationalism. The family then lost its faith and became small. . . . *Today, those French families which have remained (or again become) Catholic and large, are what they are by free choice and conviction.* They have a message, they genuinely believe that love takes precedence over money and social conventions. They have an enthusiastic faith in woman's good qualities, etc." These pages are quoted again in A. Desqueyrat, *La crise religieuse des temps nouveaux,* Spes, 1955, pp. 314–35.
[2] P. Vincent ("Le rôle des familles nombreuses dans le renouvellement des générations," *Population,* 1946, No. 1) has studied a large group of 500,000 women born in 1881. Of their number, 140,000 died before the age of 15, 90,000 remained unmarried and 270,000 founded a family. Fifty years later, in 1931, 16·5% of these homes were childless; 44·6% had a family restricted to one or two children; in 14·7% there were 3 children; in 9%, 4; and finally, 15·2% had large families of 5 or more children. "This table shows," says the author, "that families with no children or one or two—and they account for more than half of the whole sample—only provide one quarter of a generation's descendants. On the other hand, families with a minimum of 7 children —they account for much less than one-tenth of the sample—give birth to a similar number. Families of 10 children or more—they are very few indeed— provide by themselves almost as many children as the aggregate of families with only one child. Families with at least 4 children account by themselves for more than half of a generation's descendants, whilst more than half of the families have only 2 children or less" (p. 152). Families with 5 children or more (15·2% of the families in the sample) provide 39·2% of the descendants.

people of every age and class. It is estimated that to maintain the French population at replacement level (taking into account the present marriage and mortality rates) the number of live births must not fall below 2,050. But *if there were no families with more than three children,* the number of children per thousand marriages would only amount to 1,750. The future generations would only be sure of an 84% replacement. *If there were no families with more than four children,* there would still only be 1,950 live births and the population replacement would still not be guaranteed.[3]

Families which are large deliberately (and we insist on this expression, for it can be proved that family allowances are not responsible for families of five and more children) and have five (or more) surviving children below the age of 21, were in 1946 only 2·8% of those with such children still living. Yet this very small group of families is responsible for a quarter of the numbers required for replacement, that is, for 24·6% of the children under 21.[4]

In a period of well-being, such as America is now experiencing, there is no concern for large families since all that is needed if the level of the birth rate is to be maintained here and now, is for the childless family to agree to have one child, the one-child family two and the two-child family three. But when a crisis arises in the shape of unemployment or a "depression" (a word which has still a sinister meaning in the United States) then the purely fortuitous fertility of the limited family immediately vanishes. The maintenance of the indispensable birth-rate level is no longer assured except by the family which is large of set purpose . . . if it still exists!

As Dr Sutter declares:

> The repercussions which an increase in the effectiveness of contraceptive methods might have in our country are therefore obvious. The I.N.E.D. quite rightly reminds us that family legislation has had no *direct* effect upon the fertility of large families: it is the three-child and above all the two-child family which has become more frequent in France than before 1939.[5] We may well

[3] Dr J. Sutter, "Va-t-on diffuser les méthodes contraceptives en France?" in *Concours Médical,* 24 March 1957, p. 1313.

[4] *Résultats statistiques du recensement général de la population* (1946), t. IV. *Familles,* P.U.F., 1953, pp. CVIII–CX.

[5] M. Febvay, *Niveau et évolution de la fécondité par catégorie socio-professionnelle en France.* Congrès de la Population, Vienna, 1959. See Appendix X, p. 311.

feel somewhat anxious about the immediate demographic effects upon France of a more general use of contraceptive methods.[6]

DECLINE INTO SPIRITUAL OLD AGE AND
PREMATURE SCLEROSIS

A kind of equation can be established between contraception and sterility, between the contraceptive mentality and the ageing of the spirit. For a long time it was possible to think that an ageing population was the result of the lengthening of the span of life.[7] Mortara and Bourgeois-Pichat have now proved that it is the outcome of the decline in fertility.[8] "The close link between an ageing population and deliberate sterility," writes Sauvy, "is of great sociological importance. The refusal to give life, whether justified or not, reduces the vitality of a population."

By causing such a natural phenomenon as the birth of a child to be dreaded as though the baby were an intruder and a nuisance, the contraceptive mentality imprisons the mind in a fear of the future and a dread of taking risks. When this mentality becomes characteristic of a whole community, we can predict that in such a country there are certain events which will cease to take place. An excessive love of comfort and material well-being draws the mind back to an excessive love of the past. Political protection for those who are already securely placed becomes increasingly powerful. New solutions to old problems are impossible. There is no imaginative view of the future. An "investor's" mentality becomes the rule and it sees no assets other than those of capitalization. Public opinion has more confidence in income derived from consumer production rather than from undertakings producing capital goods. A panic-like fear of unemployment crushes initiative. Capital is valued more highly than men. The desire to create, to pioneer, no longer haunts men's minds. Why should we inconvenience ourselves for the sake of future generations if we always consider these as the mere minimum necessary and who "will cost nothing" and disturb nobody? An

[6] Dr J. Sutter, *op. cit.*, p. 1313.
[7] See A. Sauvy, *Théorie générale de la Population*, t. II, Ch. IV, "Le vieillissement démographique," pp. 50–75; J. Daric, *Vieillissement de la population et prolongation de la vie active*, P.U.F., 1948.
[8] *Journal de la Société de Statistique de Paris*, March–April 1950, A. Sauvy, "Viellissement des populations et allongement de la vie," in *Population*, 1954, No. 4.

unhealthy lethargy then takes possession of a community, even though it may not be aware of it. A false perspective prevents a real diagnosis of the evil that is secretly undermining the nation. On the contrary, men believe they are on the right road and yet they are slowly moving in the direction of death.

Demographers have attempted to calculate the proportion of old people in a "happy" population, one, that is, which human ingenuity and science have succeeded in completely insulating from every epidemic, accident, catastrophe, etc., and in which they can maintain a birth rate just sufficient and necessary for replacement. The figure is 24% of people over 60 years of age. The point of saturation is then reached and sclerosis of the social organism sets in. Beyond this point there is scarcely any hope humanly speaking of economic, social and political revival or resurgence.[9]

Certain Western nations, asleep in their congenital sterility, are moving in this direction like genuine somnambulists. France whose population in 1950 had a sexagenarian rate of 16·2% will reach the figure of 17·1% in 1980. During the same period the figure for Western Germany will rise from 13·8% to 18·9%, for Belgium from 16% to 18·6%, for Great Britain from 15·7% to 21%.[1]

What then will become of these sclerotic nations when they face young, vigorous and creative peoples? There is only one way for them to recover their youth, they must launch an appeal to the nations' families and ask them for more births and greater fertility.[2]

But how can such an appeal elicit a response from those who have been weakened by habitual sterility? Will propaganda have to move in reverse and start again but in the cause of a higher birth rate? If so, it would surely have been wiser never to have set out to jeopardize both the birth rate and fertility in that sterile spirit that has been spread abroad by contraception campaigns.

[9] J. Bourgeois-Pichat, "Essai sur la mortalité biologique de l'homme," *Population*, July–Sept. 1952.

[1] A. Sauvy, *op. cit.*, p. 55, and *De Malthus à Mao-Tse-Toung*, "sur le vieillissement futur du Japon," p. 240. On the problem of the ageing population in Belgium, see C. Mertens, "Problèmes de population: 'croître ou vieillir," in *La Revue Nouvelle*, 15 April, 1959.

[2] "Le renouveau démographique français et l'avenir des jeunes. Journées nationales d'études organisées par l'Alliance Nationale 'Pour la Vitalité Française,'" Alliance Nationale, 217 Faubourg Saint-Honoré, Paris VIIIe, 1956, especially Paul Haury, "Le retournement d'une situation (1896-1956)," p. 17, "And so Malthusianism by its fear of excess leads in practice to a policy of the least effort—a pillow of idleness, if I may call it so, on which a great nation falls asleep and slips into an abyss that we were able to measure in 1940 but from which we have not yet emerged," and A. Sauvy, *La montée des jeunes*, Calmann-Levy, 1959.

DEBASEMENT OF THE IDEAL OF "FAMILY HAPPINESS"

By pretending to be unaware of the values of ascetism, continence and self-control, by turning their attention entirely to the relatively soulless techniques of contraception, the contraceptive legislators contribute, more than we think, to the debasement of their peoples. Let the reader judge for himself from the following page taken from a manual of preparation for marriage enjoying a considerable reputation in the United States. It expresses clearly enough the mentality of the Malthusian circles:

There is no longer any question as to whether we shall or shall not have, practise or permit contraception. It is already here on a large scale. The problem is one of improving use and eliminating abuse. Contraception is very widespread among the educated and upper economic classes and is extending among all classes. Its continued advance depends upon deep-set economic forces. Once a people have discovered how to raise their standard of living by regulating the number of offspring, the extension of that knowledge is inevitable and irresistible. It can be slowed down by law and prejudice, but it cannot be halted. . . . In all states except Massachusetts and Connecticut physicians may give contraceptive advice to their patients. But we still have far to go before we become a nation that regulates the production of human babies as efficiently as it regulates the production and improvement of its livestock.[3]

So there we are! We are to plan births as though we were so much livestock. What could be more rational, more logical, more normal? It is as necessary as the expanding use of the techniques of restriction and exploitation in the modern world.

Gabriel Marcel has written:

The Malthusian couple who go to the cinema twice a week and treat themselves to an expensive meal every Sunday at Pontoise or at Bourgival can no doubt claim that they love life, and it is precisely in order not to spoil it for themselves that they take such care, and if necessary efface the consequences of their amorous frolics without a scruple. But nothing brings out better how hopelessly ambiguous the words "life" and "loving life" are. ("Those

[3] H. A. Bowman, *Marriage for Moderns*, New York, 1954, p. 483.

were the good old days; life was worth living then," exclaim innumerable French people of both sexes as they sigh for the era of the tandem and the Simca 8.) It would be possible to say that they nursed in the depths of their being, and stored up for the time to come, the pretension of acquiring life as one puts electricity or central heating into a house. Life really seems to them like an element to be used in order to obtain a few patent satisfactions, without which the world would be nothing but a prison.[4]

It must be realized that contraceptive civilization is a form of rationalism that devalues personality and for which the expression "to place oneself at life's disposal"[5] quite literally has no longer any spiritual meaning. The technical mind is entrusted with the task of reducing life to this level. Life is now to be told to take its place in the categories of utilities. It loses its halo of mystery and grandeur, the sacredness and dignity it acquired because of its inherent virtualities in which lay the potential origins of new human persons. By means of contraceptive techniques it is requested to enter the category of commercialized leisure occupations. It is forced to undergo a kind of electrolysis which sterilizes its creative effects and retains only those which give sensual pleasure.

When society officially authorizes such techniques, does it genuinely realize the nature of the revolution it is bringing about or the reversal of values it is causing? Happiness is no longer to be sought in the realm of free giving and creativity but only in that of possessions and financial reward.

THE FALL IN THE STANDARD OF MORALS.
YOUNG PEOPLE. THE SINGLE LIFE.

This climate of opinion cannot fail to influence the younger generations and they too claim their share in the "right to happiness". If the social environment lets it be understood that happiness consists above all in sexual experience—and sterile sexual experience at that—and if, moreover, society provides this experience in married life with technical guarantees, why should young men and women deprive themselves of it outside marriage? Surely logic is on the side of these boys and girls.

[4] *Homo Viator*, translated by Emma Craufford, London, 1951, Chapter IV, "The Creative Vow as Essence of Fatherhood," p. 114.
[5] G. Marcel, *op. cit.*, p. 115.

And all the evidence converges in a remarkable way to show that societies in which contraception is the rule are those in which there is the largest increase in the incidence of pre-marital sexual experience.[6]

We do not thereby imply that outside these societies there is complete abstinence before marriage, particularly among men. We are only too well aware that prostitution on the one hand and on the other, marriages where the bride is already pregnant, have always existed.

In any case, it is clear that as a result of the increasing eroticism induced by contraceptive practices, young women are much more ready to indulge in extra-marital sexual experiences—at their own risk and peril let it be said (for these have not been abolished whatever the propagandists may say). Thus it is no secret that in Sweden people marry at a relatively more advanced age than elsewhere since the wedding marks the termination of a kind of trial marriage which, in the towns at least, lasts for two, three or four years.

The statistics of illegitimate births which are very numerous in Sweden—9·9% of the total number in 1952 (France = 6·7% and Italy = 3·4% in 1951)—give only an imperfect picture of the phenomenon of pre-marital relations.[7] At the time when the use of contraceptives began to spread (1911–1920), the illegitimate births among town populations in Sweden were 22·01% of the total. It is highly improbable that the fall to the present rate of 10% is due to an improvement in moral standards. Far from it! The fact is that the contraceptive education of the young people in the towns has been relatively effective . . . and abortion accounts for the rest. Further, among married couples in 26% of cases the first child is born 8 months after the parents' marriage. This means that (in the case of first-born children) *one child out of four* is conceived during pre-marital relations. We may well wonder what the picture would be had we statistics of the number of young women who are still virgins on their wedding day.

In the United States, sociologists such as Ogburn and Nimkoff

[6] Lewis M. Terman and others, *Psychological Factors in Marital Happiness*, New York, 1938. Following a study of 793 couples the author admits that among the men, virginity before marriage has fallen from 50·6% (in a group of men born before 1890), to 13·6% (in a group of men born after 1910). Similarly among the women, virginity at the time of marriage has fallen from 86·5% to 31·7%. The same conclusions are reached by A. C. Kinsey, *Sexual Behaviour in the Human Male* (pp. 411–13) and *Sexual Behaviour in the Human Female* (pp. 298, etc.).

[7] A. Myrdal, *Nation and Family*, London, Kegan Paul, 1945, pp. 39–47.

make no secret of the fact that the rapid fall in moral standards among young people is due to the diffusion of contraceptive methods.[8]

THE FIXATION OF SEXUALITY AT AN "ADOLESCENT" STAGE

Since an increasing number of couples deliberately obstruct the vital purposes of the marriage act and are no longer willing to experience in it the creative mystery which it is destined to be, this mystery itself loses its value for them. How could it be otherwise? Even if it is assumed that contraceptive intercourse is still based on mutual self-giving and a reciprocal desire to promote the growth of personality, such results are not achieved without an inner feeling that nature's fundamental impulse must be checked. The couple then commits itself to the search for a false stability which is not the one nature intended, a stability that is no more than a juxtaposition of two egoisms instead of the inclusion of the sexual instinct in the complex of those inter-personal relational phenomena which constitute a community.

This maladjustment is characteristic of an "adolescent" sexuality which haunts the mind and may even be a compulsive obsession. The well-being the couple experience merely disguises a deep-seated sense of insecurity. Instead of the stability resulting from the progress of the instinct towards maturity, the couple only experiences the unstable equilibrium of a transitional stage of development. Even though they close their eyes to this fact, they are not entirely unaware of it. Irritability, emotional disturbances, changes of mood raise the alarm sufficiently often to suggest that something is wrong. The dubious sense of well-being induced by their compulsive sexuality, far from compensating for the frustration such immature partners experience, only increases it. The most common result of this false stability is divorce.

In this connection the passage from Freud quoted above on p. ix —it would be interesting to determine its precise relation to the general teaching of the founder of pyscho-analysis—is relevant.

It is strange that psycho-analysis has not attempted to follow this trail opened up by the master and that, however expert it may be in

---

[8] W. F. Ogburn and M. F. Nimkoff, *Technology and the Changing Family*, New York, 1955, pp. 50-3.

uncovering the complexes which produce conflicts in the depths of the psyche, it should not have made a more extended study of this particular one. Surely we are aware that nature always ends by producing a disturbance when force is used to make it achieve a result contrary to what its own structure demands and seeks.

Of course sexuality being, unlike the alimentary instinct, a function directly ordered to the preservation of the species and not of the individual, the disturbances introduced into the working of this function may exist unnoticed by the individual or the couple who have in fact been responsible for them. Yet, as Abbé Oraison writes: "But if the sexual instinct is exercised in defiance of normal physiological standards or of the end for which it was naturally intended, the sanctions will be pressed not on the individual but on the species, because the function of the sexual instinct is directly oriented to the species itself." [9]

And so by authorizing false forms of stability and adolescent fixations through the legalization of contraceptive practices, a nation creates a serious handicap for individuals and couples who find themselves in difficulties.[1] It encloses them in a vicious circle, instead of persuading them to escape from it as it would do if it authorized only a sexuality directed to fertility, that is, a sexuality directed towards genuine maturity. It is always in a nation's interest to sanction a climate of opinion which does not permit dereliction of duty nor tolerate immaturity.

THE ATTACK ON MOTHERHOOD

Fr Henry writes:

There is talk of voluntary, free motherhood. Contraception is powerless to strengthen the will, to encourage increased freedom of soul, to develop our awareness of what we are doing, and

[9] Marc Oraison, *Man and Wife*, translated by André Humbert with an introduction by John Marshall, London, Longmans, 1958, pp. 8–9. Published in the U.S.A. under the title *Union in Marital Love*.

[1] M. Oraison, "L'avortement, aspect théologique, L'avortement et la limitation des naissances," in *Problèmes de déontologie*, Pages documentaires de l'U.C.C.S., 1957, pp. 50–2; J. P. Dubois-Dumée, "Le bonheur style magazine," in *l'Entente conjugale*, Semaine sociale de Bordeaux, 1957, pp. 321–4. On emotional and sexual immaturity and its disastrous effects once marriage has taken place, see *Ecole des Parents*, Nov. 1953, "La préparation au mariage"; on the encouragement given to this immaturity by women's magazines see M.L., "Coup de sonde à travers quelques magazines féminins," in *Fiches Rurales*, No. 143, Feb. 1958, pp. 37–48.

these are essential conditions of genuine happiness. Contraception is intended to give us a breathing-space and inhibit for a time our power to accept our obligations. We shall do this at a later date. It is rather like the man who says to his soul—"Come, enjoy yourself, leave conversion till the last days of your life." But can we be certain of the power of our will? The formation of a fervent, free, shared will requires effort and the grace of God. Deliberate, systematic contraception far from helping free will to progress towards maturity, thwarts it, corrupts it from within, corrodes it.[2]

It is useless to object that this must be equally true of periodic continence, when systematically organized for the spacing of births. Continence *practised in a spirit of chastity*, on the contrary, imposes on the will a generous effort towards spiritual mastery. Any contraceptive technique that is supposed to act automatically is bound of its very nature to dispense from this task. Where continence and chastity are the rule, motherhood preserves the creative impulse of which it is ultimately deprived by contraceptive sterilization. The love of the "contraceptive" mother for her child is not of the same order as the love of the "continent" mother.

One of the propaganda publications of the Family Planning Association provides enlightening reading in this respect. We sense in it a kind of secret hostility—always implied and occasionally present on the surface—towards procreation and life, towards the creative impulse and above all towards the large family. The baby's birth is no longer a joyful event, a blessing from God. On the contrary, the child seems always to be a kind of cunning enemy, a nuisance, an intruder, an absurdity. The illustrations in this book express, unwittingly no doubt, this unconscious aggressive spirit by giving to children in arms the vacant faces of grotesque old men. How many delightful photos of mischievous, jolly babies tell a very different story![3]

Not that among the nations which have opted for this authorized contraceptive civilization babies are no longer loved, infants attended to and children cared for. They are, thank heaven! But if we may be allowed to give our personal impression, love, attention and care are there but they are carefully watched, controlled, measured out,

[2] A. M. Henry, O.P., *Morale et vie conjugale*. This passage is quoted from an article: "Maternité volontaire," in *Supplément à la Vie Spirituelle*, 1956, No. 3.
[3] C. H. Rolph, *The Human Sum*, illustrations designed by A. G. Wurmser, London, Heinemann, 1957.

F.P.M.P.—4*

packed like fine wrapped fruit in the shop windows rather than
fruit in the orchard. Whether we like it or not, an atmosphere
of distrust towards nature is prevalent in these nations. Her prodi-
gality offends, her spontaneity is a nuisance, and the public authorities approve of this view.

In this respect, contraception is like an army on the defensive. It
gives an unquestionable priority to the *egocentric* direction of
married sexuality, and it does so against the creative demands of
nature.[4] Nature clearly shows, as we have said, that the obvious
orientation of the whole sexual complex is towards relationship.
Physically, physiologically and psychologically, sexual relations
between two persons of different sex are the expression of a creative
communion opening outwards to welcome others, and not of a
duality enclosed upon itself.

A NEW CONCEPT OF SEX

When, on the contrary, sexuality in marriage becomes, through
the use of contraceptives "a duality closed in on itself", the whole
concept of its nature undergoes a transformation. Sexuality figures
as *"a capacity for erotic activity in the service of the couple"*. Its
connection with procreation is no longer anything but accidental
and sex is *first and foremost* for pleasure and essentially so. This fact
may be hidden by the use of the term "communion". It is none the
less there. We are dealing with a communion that is essentially
narcissist, a juxtaposition of two egocentric individualities, as we
have said above.

We are surely right therefore to insist that when sexuality thus
becomes an end in itself, when a civilization officially adopts the
view that it is no more than this capacity for erotic activity provided
by nature for the couple, a genuine mutation and a complete reversal
of the order of values take place. Are we wrong in this case to talk
of a "contraceptive civilization"? Are we not facing a new Humanism, no longer centred first and foremost on personal and spiritual
creativity but on hedoism?[5]

[4] Oraison, *Man and Wife, op. cit.*, p. 47; M. Mertens de Wilmars, *Psychopathologie de l'Anticonception,* Lethielleux, 1955.
[5] Bergson in his *Deux sources de la Morale et de la Religion* described our
civilization as "aphrodisiac", Alcan, 1932, p. 326.

THE ATTACK ON MAN'S VIRILITY AND WOMAN'S FEMININITY

Since it wishes to improve on nature by relegating the creative meaning of sexuality to the background of consciousness and value, neo-Malthusian ideology blurs the distinction between the sexes. Whether we like it or not, the difference between the sexes is in fact defined in relation to their creative work, to the "work of the flesh". Man and woman are distinguished from one another by the part each plays in bringing a child into the world. One begets, the other gives birth.

But if we deprive the sexes of their different functions in regard to the "work of the flesh", or even if these are merely kept out of sight, how are men and women to be distinguished one from the other? Will they not acquire the indeterminate character of the adolescent? We are all aware of the type of ambivalence of which adolescents of both sexes are capable. When adults shows signs of what are called "intersexual" states, it is precisely because they are suffering from physiological or psychological fixations at this adolescent stage.[6]

The sign of maturity in young men and women is their arrival at genuine manhood and womanhood. In both cases, the normal road to this maturity is parenthood. In the case of the bachelor and spinster who have not succeeded in compensating for their unmarried state through spiritual fatherhood or motherhood, something adolescent or even infantile persists and the community generally makes it the butt of its witticisms.

The erotic civilization of contraception by devaluing fatherhood and motherhood is more responsible than is generally believed for the state of confusion between the sexes so characteristic of the contemporary world and so prejudicial—as all child psychologists agree—to the sound education of children.[7]

---

[6] *Cahiers Laënnec,* "Les états intersexuels," 1947, No. 1, p. 2. Dr Marañon, *The Evolution of Sex and Intersexual Conditions,* English translation by W. B. Wells, Allen and Unwin, 1932.

[7] "I am inclined to think that sociologists who, in the not too distant future, study the reasons for the disturbing increase in homosexuality, will plead for a return to increased authority vested in the husband. Husbands who abandon their tasks as heads of the family and wives who take advantage of their position produce abnormal sons. . . . The emotional stability of the child is governed by the emotional stability of those among whom it is reared. Mothers who are always insisting on their rights and fathers who act like dictators run the risk of eventually and irretrievably ruining the emotional life of their children." Dr M. Eck, "Autorité et liberté entre époux," in *Etudes,* May 1957, p. 190.

INCREASING TOLERATION SHOWN TOWARDS
HOMOSEXUALITY

In so far as human sexuality is said to exhaust its meaning *independently* of its reference to procreation, what is there to prevent a diversion in the direction of homosexuality? If in fact erotic activity between two persons has a complete meaning in itself, if its purpose is purely psychological and solely concerned with the service of the couple, if the reference to the "work of the flesh" is only incidental, why should we wish at all costs to limit mutual erotic activity to heterosexuality? Why should society continue to refuse to homosexuality the freedom it claims? If, as has been said, the primary function of sexuality is "to establish the couple in a state of 'enosis' (one flesh) by making it possible for the two partners to communicate to one another the ineffable meaning of their love," why should this union not exist between two men or two women? By constantly allowing the procreative function either directly or indirectly to be devalued in favour of an erotic activity supposed to be more in keeping with the nature of personality, married couples surely run the risk of creating in their environment—that of their limited number of children to begin with—a dubious and pernicious atmosphere which encourages sexual fixations. Sexuality instead of moving as it should towards self-giving and altruism, takes the opposite path leading to the regressive fixation which causes homosexuality, i.e. the desire to find one's own personality in that of the partner.[8]

We do not deny that we should show the same pity towards homosexuals as we do towards those who are ill, and find a remedy for their sickness rather than condemn them. But that is no reason for condoning the climate, literature, habits of thought and life which those suffering from homosexuality try to spread around themselves as a kind of protective covering. It is not for the civil authorities to interfere in the private lives of individuals but they should nevertheless protect the public against such individuals. The disease of homosexuality, like many others, is epidemic in character. There is no advantage to be gained by allowing it to profit by delays in applying the appropriate prophylactic methods of treatment. Among the latter we consider one of the most important is the reinstatement of *the*

---

[8] Dr M. Eck, *Ce que les parents doivent savoir de l'homosexualité*, Centre Catholique d'Education Familiale, 1960.

creative purpose of love and its finest work—the bringing of children into the world who are destined for a noble and generous life. Society and civilization will fulfil their mission to encourage the growth of personality only if they safeguard the basis of the order of nature. Otherwise, with the best will in the world, we shall be initiating a process leading to the ruin of human personality and to the desecration of society.[9]

CONTRACEPTION AS A CONTRIBUTING FACTOR
IN THE INSTABILITY OF MARRIAGES

We pointed out above that marriages whose stability was doubtful, and maintained by contraceptive methods between partners still sexually and emotionally immature, most frequently ended in divorce. This was all the more likely since they had been lured on by the mirage of contraception as a miraculous solution. Truth does not pardon her enemies.

Hence although contraception cannot be held wholly responsible for the great increase in the number of divorces in countries where such habits have been officially authorized, nevertheless we are justified in drawing attention to this coincidence.

Thus in four countries which are considered to be pioneers of contraception and where the use and diffusion of "scientific" methods have been adopted, namely Denmark since 1937, Sweden since 1938, the United States since 1936 and Switzerland, it is a fact that the incidence of divorce has continued to increase until it is now the highest in the world.[1]

[9] Paul Chauchard, *La Vie Sexuelle*, Collection Que sais-je?, P.U.F., 1957, "La vie sexuelle et la conscience sexuelle," pp. 89–99.

[1] J. L. Thomas, S.J., in his book *The American Catholic Family*, gives as one cause of broken marriages the will to sterility encouraged by contraceptive propaganda, pp. 289–300. In France, Dr P. Le Moal's inquiry has also brought to light the same correlation between infidelity and contraceptive habits. Question No. 43 was: "Have you since your marriage had sexual relations with any woman other than your wife?" The corresponding question was put to the women. It is clearly evident from the replies received, says the author, that adultery is more common in category A.P.A. (contraception practised) and especially among the women. "The habit of eliminating the child from her sexual life makes her less able to resist the solicitations of other

INCIDENCE OF DIVORCE
(Annual figure for divorces among 10,000 married couples)

Year	Denmark	Sweden	U.S.A.	Switzerland
1934–41	43	27	89	36 (1940–2)
1944–46	67	42	—	—
1951	68	49	104	42 (1949–51)

Compared with these pioneer nations, Holland, France and Belgium, where contraceptive propaganda is not authorized by law, do not show a parallel increase and their existing rate is itself lower.[2]

INCIDENCE OF DIVORCE
(Annual figure for divorces among 10,000 married couples)

Year	Holland	France	Belgium
1935–37	23	23	—
1945–47	49	49	30
1950–51	25	30	15

FURTHER CONSEQUENCES FOR WHICH
CONTRACEPTION IS RESPONSIBLE

Contraceptive habits, especially when officially sanctioned by law, are certainly responsible for further difficulties and disorders such as the threat to mental health represented by the increase of morbid anxiety among married couples, frigidity among women, a phenomenon clearly indicated by the Kinsey Report and so often caused by fear of pregnancy, and the evading by "adolescent" parents of their educative tasks.

However, it is much more difficult to prove responsibility in this connection since other difficulties and influences arising from modern urban civilization are also partly to blame. Be that as it may, the sociologist may at least note that the predictions of contraceptive propaganda cannot be shewn to be accurate. It was believed that the widespread diffusion of contraceptive methods and the general practice of "voluntary motherhood" were bound to favour adaptability and harmony in the home, to counteract family disasters attri-

men." The categories N.L. (number of births not limited) and O.C. (Ogino and continence) offer far fewer cases of infidelity.

Cases where infidelity was admitted

	OC	APA	NL
Men:	15 % (24 cases)	62 % (52 cases)	22 % (22 cases)
Women:	20 % (26 cases)	70 % (50 cases)	10 % (23 cases)

(Dr P. Le Moal, "Continence conjugale et morale sexuelle," in *Supplément à La Vie Spirituelle*, 1958, No. 1, pp. 60–1).

[2] *United Nations Demographic Year Books* 1954, p. 620, and 1958. *Supplément au Bulletin de la Statistique générale de la France* I.N.S.E.E., Oct.–Dec. 1957, p. 11.

butable to excessive fertility, and to prevent the increasing prevalence of conditions threatening children with moral danger and delinquency.

But it is well known that there are bitter complaints in Denmark of a considerable increase in personality disturbances among adolescents, and that Sweden has to stand by powerless before an ominous lowering of its moral standards. The United States do not report any spectacular improvement in mental health in spite of the use of contraceptives by 90% of its married population and hundreds of thousands of consultations provided each year in 800 birth control clinics. If contraceptive clinics and techniques were determining factors in producing domestic happiness we should surely witness at least an obvious strengthening of married unity and a higher standard of well-being among families living in cities.[3]

We repeat that we do not wish to imply that contraception is alone responsible for the existence or even for the growth of such social evils as mental diseases, juvenile delinquency, instability among married couples, nor that these evils exist only in countries which have officially authorized contraception. We are well aware that other factors are involved. We merely draw attention to the fact that nothing whatever proves that contraceptive control of births is a genuine remedy, still less the universal panacea extolled by so many publicists who are far too ignorant of the real nature of man and the complex character of society.

It is time to summarize our conclusions. From the point of view of anthropology and especially of sociology, *contraception and still more its official authorization are mistakes.*

It is a grave error indeed to claim to remould human nature, a grave error to think we can with impunity disturb extremely delicate mechanisms and processes in their essential functioning. Spurious stunts are always dangerous especially if we intend to set them up as norms. "The human race is clearly not intended to walk on its hands," writes Dr Rattner with a touch of humour. Nor is the human race intended to reduce its sexual function to mutual erotic activity.

Some people laud this century in which man is becoming the master of nature and fashioning the world in his own image. This

---

[3] S. A. Avestad and M. McGovern, "Hospital Service in U.S.," in *Journal of American Medical Association*, May 1952, v. CXLIX, No. 2, pp. 149–67. This article notes the ever-increasing number of persons receiving hospital treatment for mental illnesses. The increase is in the order of 2,500 per year. The figures for such hospital patients increased from 83,000 in 1942 to 110,000 in 1951.

praise is legitimate if man, whose being is not his own property, can realize what he should be, can know the Image in which he has been fashioned and which he must reproduce.

But nothing could be more unfortunate than that man, whilst claiming to fashion the world in his image, should distort his nature and drift towards a caricature of himself, for then the world would not only be disfigured but, in its turn, it would contribute to the increasing disfigurement of its model.

IN SWEDEN

Emmanuel Mounier's travels in Sweden a few months before his death and the Scandinavian Notes he left us in *Esprit* (February 1950) are not likely to reassure us concerning the "happiness" with which technical and contraceptive civilization threatens us. We do not wish on this account to identify one particular country with contraception, as France has sometimes been identified in the past with atheism and rationalism, yet we are bound to face up to the evils so characteristic of certain European nations.

Equipped with a body of information which does not arouse in him a passion for knowledge, firmly established in a form of religion which successfully complements the system of social security, does the individual (in Sweden) cherish within him some hidden fire which might rekindle the spiritual flame of the nation? At a first glance, one would not think so. Like many others before us we have referred to the impression of inflexibility, formalism, cheerful or ceremonious vacuity which the Swede usually produces on the Latins. But perhaps the emancipated Swedish woman is without this tendency to inflexibility. At home and abroad she is generally said to be free and happy—she works outside the home far more than her opposite number in France and, as Simone de Beauvoir would say, is also winning her "transcendence" . . . As a result of the 1920 legislation the man is no longer head and breadwinner of the family. Husband and wife both have a duty to provide for the needs of the home . . . The Swedish man (who, as we will remember, learns at school to cook, mend and do housework) shares the domestic chores far more than is the case with us. He may even be responsible for most of them. . . . The most obvious fact is that this professional evolution of women is accompanied by a fall in the birth rate, especially during the years 1930–40. There has even been talk of a "strike against mother-hood" . . . And since the child tends to spend the greater part of the day outside the home in the attractive centres provided for him, the relations between family and child are very loose. In Latin countries they tend to stifle him, yet the psychologists, those priests of the Scandinavian conscience, are beginning to be worried by the results, unhappy as they often are, of this emotional situation on the child's development.

Are the women satisfied with their position? They sometimes say they are. But the inquiry must be extended to relations be-tween husband and wife. In the main the Swede does not suffer from repressions. At least every precaution is taken to prevent him from doing so. Sexual education is provided in the schools and is in three stages: at the age of twelve, at puberty, on the eve of marriage in the "schools for engaged couples". The explana-tions given which, in accordance with the general and universal custom, are very detailed and concentrate chiefly on the study of functions and "precautions", succeed in transforming sexuality into an object, especially in the case of the men and so consoli-date their natural frigidity. The erotic character of certain films, the scanty clothing worn for sporting activities tend to give us a false view. These films are exhibited or tolerated precisely be-cause average erotic sensibility is slow to act and is only com-pletely aroused with the help of alcohol. I spoke to educationalists and many of them told me that the way itself in which sexual instruction is given in the schools, since it presents sexuality as a functional mechanism to this nation of mechanics, induces a kind of "cold" repression, evidence of which is provided by the endless discussions between the pupils or in the mass outbreak of fainting fits (girls and boys) caused by a recent very crude film on child-birth.

Whatever may be the truth concerning the root causes, the Swede in general is inhibited in his sexuality. He does not know what to say or do in his relations with women. He compensates for this sexual isolationism by indifference bolstered up by the attitude of the community at large. From early childhood the boy is the centre of attention. The a-sexual comradeship which is very soon established between boys and girls—the universal use of the familiar "du", complete freedom yet without refinement of feeling —is indicative of escapism rather than a stable relationship. For the Swedish male, woman is not a world to be discovered, a divine and disturbing force which is deserving of man's attention and at times transcends him. Except for a few organic peculiarities she is a person like himself. She comes into his life accompanied by the fumes of alcohol or for certain precise and intermittent biological purposes. On all other occasions, life is a serious and all-male affair. I was told by a man "An intelligent woman would take an hour to tell me what I could learn in three minutes' conversation with an average man." The Swedish woman, as the most acute observers have noted, has remained more sensitive than her partner, is more lonely and unhappy than she often admits. Many young Swedish women are obsessed with the idea of marrying a foreigner and as a general rule such marriages are more successful than those of Latin women with Swedish men. In the movement which has led so many Swedish women to take up a profession, there is an urge to escape and to find some kind of compensation. It is obvious that it is an over-simplification to state the problem of women in terms of the dilemma—purdah or the market place? Yet there may be a form of emancipation which does not bring true freedom.[4]

A civilization of "happiness through technics" may well be a delusion . . . and contraceptive civilization an unavowed and un-unavowable illusion.

[4] E. Mounier, "Notes scandinaves," *Esprit*, Feb. 1950, pp. 281–3.

Part Three

The True Meaning of the Catholic Position

INTRODUCTORY NOTE

BEFORE we state the position of the Catholic Church in regard to family planning and contraception, it is essential to have clearly in mind the level at which her teaching is situated in its relation to that adopted by Malthusian ideology.

"The advocates of birth control," notes Fr Tesson, "seem to limit themselves to the plane of sociological morality. Nothing in their statements implies that human conduct is under any obligations other than those necessary for the establishment of a better social order." [1]

Their principal concern is the standard of living and of well-being to be made available for the greatest possible number. Their ideal is that of nations abundantly provided with material goods, enjoying robust health and reaching a high level of education and culture, all this easily and in comfort.

The Catholic position does not of course refuse to make this concern its own, at least to a certain extent. The Church also wants her children and all mankind to have an adequate standard of creature comforts, as high a social and cultural level as possible, health, education, etc. But this does not mean that it is her foremost and principal concern, for this is the "Kingdom of God", not to be confused with the common temporal good of humanity. When Christ and the Church tell us: "How is a man the better for it, if he gains the whole world at the cost of losing his own soul?" (Matt. 16. 26) or "For a man's soul, what price is high enough?" (*ibid.*), they want us to understand that there is no common measure between this temporal world and the other, supernatural world.

"Make it your first care to find the Kingdom of God, and his approval," the Kingdom of God and its values "and all these things —temporal goods—shall be yours without the asking" (Matt. 6. 33). For the Church to whom this injunction is addressed, this means that she must attempt to make humanity live *first and foremost* by faith, hope and charity, in terms of which the various problems of temporal existence will find their solutions.

[1] E. Tesson, S.J., professor at the Institut Catholique de Paris, "L'Eglise et la fécondité dirigée," in *La Croix*, 27 April 1956. By the same author: "L'Eglise et la régulation des naissances," in *Etudes*, Dec. 1956, pp. 375-85.

St Paul expressed this same truth in another way: "Everything is for you, whether it be Paul, or Apollo, or Cephas, or the world, or life, or death, or the present, or the future; it is all for you, and you for Christ, and Christ for God" (1 Cor. 3. 21–3). This is one way of asserting that this world is for man to use, is at his disposal but for the one single purpose of helping him to establish a Christian Humanity, a Humanity living by the very life of Christ, according to the high priestly prayer of Jesus: "That they too may be one in us, as thou Father, art in me, and I in thee" (John 17. 22–3).

No misunderstanding is therefore possible. The sociological good and the supernatural good of humanity are not on the same plane nor do they have the same value. If a crucial choice has to be made between the two planes, the Church's decision is already taken and is dictated by her Saviour's words: "If thy hand or thy foot is an occasion of falling to thee, cut it off and cast it away from thee, better for thee to enter into life crippled or lame, than to have two hands or two feet when thou art cast into eternal fire" (Matt. 18. 8).

Therefore the Church takes her place on the plane of supernatural "life" and at this level of the soul, when she reveals her attitude towards *human fertility* and its *regulation*. She adopts this position as a result of the knowledge her Lord has given her of the "mysteries of the Kingdom" (Luke 8. 10; 10. 22). She knows for certain that this position is her Master's. Following him, she declares: "I cannot do anything of my own impulse; I decide as I am bidden to decide, and my decision is never unjust, because I am consulting the will of him who sent me, not my own" (John 5. 30). To those who will not accept her decisions she also declares: "Why is it that you cannot understand the language I talk? It is because you have no ear for the message I bring. You belong to your father, the devil, and are eager to gratify the appetites which are your father's" (John 8. 43–44).

What then must we be or have if we are to be able to listen to and understand the Church's language? Is it absolutely essential to be a Catholic and to have the Catholic faith? Not necessarily or exclusively, at least to begin with. Christ can bring every honest and sincere soul to recognize his voice in the authoritative teaching of his Church, according to his own promise: "I have other sheep too, which do not belong to this fold: I must bring them in too: they will listen to my voice; so there will be one fold and one shepherd" (John 10. 16). In fact, as St John comments regarding the soul of good will and in good faith: "Whereas the man whose life is true comes to the light so that his deeds may be seen for what they are, deeds done in God" (John 3. 21).

That is why, in Pius XI's Encyclical *Casti Connubii* on Christian Marriage, there appears this statement, which is surprising at first sight to non-Catholics: [2]

For Christ himself made the Church the teacher of truth *in those things which also concern the right regulation of moral conduct even though some knowledge of the same is not beyond human reason.*

For just as God, *in the case of the natural truths of religion and morals,* added revelation to the light of reason so that what is right and true "in the present state also of the human race may be known readily with real certainty without any admixture of error",[3] so for the same purpose He has constituted the Church the guardian and the teacher of *the whole* of the truth concerning *religion* and *moral conduct.*

Wherefore let the faithful also be on their guard against the overrated independence of private judgment and that false *autonomy* of human reason.

For it is quite foreign to everyone bearing the name of Christian to trust his own mental powers with such pride as to agree only with those things which he can examine from their inner nature, and to imagine that the Church, sent by God to teach and guide all nations, is not conversant with present affairs and circumstances; or even that they must obey only in those matters which she has decreed by solemn definition as though her other decisions might be presumed to be false or putting forward insufficient motive for truth and honesty.

But everyone can see to how many fallacies an avenue would be opened and how many errors would become mixed with the truth *if it were left solely to the light of reason of each to find out* (the divine laws respecting marriage) *or if it were to be discovered by the private interpretation of the truth which is revealed.*

And if this is applicable to many other truths of the moral order, we must all the more pay attention to those things, which

[2] Pius XI, *Casti Connubii*, Encyclical on Christian Marriage, 31 Dec 1920, *Acta Apostolicae Sedis,* 1930, vol. XXII, No. 13, pp. 539–92. (The passages quoted here from this Encyclical are taken from the translation issued by the Catholic Truth Society, (1936, pp. 51, 52, 53.—Translator's note.)

[3] This quotation, included in the text of *Casti Connubii,* is an extract from a declaration of the Vatican Council, Sess. III, ch. II, concerning the proofs of the existence of God.

appertain to marriage where the inordinate desire for pleasure can attack frail human nature and easily deceive it and lead it astray. This is all the more true of the observance of the divine law, which demands sometimes hard and repeated sacrifices, for which, as experience points out, a weak man can find so many excuses for avoiding the fulfilment of the divine law.[4]

The general survey in the first part of this book will have already given the reader some idea of the extent to which those left to "the false autonomy of human reason" or "to the overrated independence of private judgment" deviate from the genuine demands of conjugal morality as the Catholic Church formulates and defines them. They either exaggerate or minimize these demands. The Malthusians, for instance, minimize the moral requirements of man's personal nature whilst Gandhi, on the other hand, makes too much of these requirements when he considers the intention to procreate as the only moral purpose of the partners' physical union or when he gives to the male seed a kind of absolute quasi-divine value.

The aim of this Third Part will therefore be to present the position of the Catholic Church and to stress the cogency of its claims, the conditions under which they have to be put into practice and the character of a "sign" which the Church has to assume in the contemporary world. With this object in view, there will be five chapters dealing with:

1. The basic natural values and the supernatural truths which the Church proposes to safeguard in taking up her position.

2. The doctrinal position of the Church, formulated as objectively and positively as possible.

3. The soundness of this doctrine as supported by certain philosophical reflections on human nature and its values.

4. The conditions in which the doctrine is to be applied in the lives of the faithful.

5. The part the Church expects her children to play in the contemporary world in this particular sphere of married fertility. They are to be a "sign" and a "witness", and this "sign" and this "witness" must be present both at the level of those who govern and at the level of those under their authority.

[4] The italics in these quotations are those of Fr Lestapis. (Translator's note.)

Chapter VIII

THE BASIC NATURAL VALUES AND THE SUPERNATURAL TRUTHS WHICH MUST BE SAFEGUARDED

" God," says Pius XI in *Casti Connubii*, "has constituted the Church the *guardian* and the *teacher* of the whole of the truth concerning religion and moral conduct." [1] Hence in the sphere of the married vocation the Church feels herself responsible at one and the same time:

(1)—for the safeguarding of the basic natural values involved, values whose discovery "is not beyond human reason", values which are generally obvious to all sincere persons of good will;

(2)—for the safeguarding of the supernatural truths in this sphere which have been revealed by God in the Old Testament and by Christ in the New.

I. *BASIC NATURAL VALUES*

PRESENT CONDITIONS WHICH MAKE THEM
DIFFICULT TO IDENTIFY

It is certain that, in the world today, people's minds are often confused to an unparalleled extent and that the best among them lose courage when they see case after case where things go wrong. This doubtless excuses many who no longer dare to give a positive opinion about anything nor to resist the temptation to adopt an attitude of scepticism when they continually come into contact with the problem of evil.

Thus it is true that many unforeseen and unexpected births often give rise to situations from which there is no issue, when for instance families are badly housed in unhealthy dwellings, when they are ill-equipped and have inadequate means, or when sickness appears to be

[1] *Casti Connubii*, C.T.S., p. 52.

permanently present. How under such circumstances can a new birth be cheerfully accepted?

It is true that, in the cities, large families are hard to bring up and that the obstacles are insurmountable particularly in the case of those whose income is merely the pay packet of a skilled worker. And how much more so in the case of a labourer!

Again, it is true that advancement in the social scale seems a matter of chance for parents who are willing to bring more than three children into the world.

It is true that man, whose dignity lies in his power of foresight and his ability to plan his life and give it a guiding principle, seems to be acting against the logic of his own nature when he leaves to the hazards of chance the task of regulating his fertility and of bringing children into existence.

It is true, as one of the best contemporary observers has written, that "the essential characteristic of our time is not atomic energy, television, Communism, radar, but the fall in the death rate. This is a fact of immense significance, revolutionary, pregnant with consequences. It began (and this is no mere coincidence) just before 1789 and has now spread throughout the whole world." [2]

Although death no longer thins the ranks of those under seventeen years of age and, even if it still lurks in the neighbourhood of the cradle, only succeeds in carrying off 10 to 30 per thousand newborn children every year, it is none the less true that society has to provide food for all these additional mouths. This means that full employment is absolutely essential and that production must always be on the increase and always outdistance consumption. Otherwise inflation reappears with its train of crises and destitution.

It is true that the over-population of underdeveloped countries causes a vicious circle from which nations cannot emerge without outside help.

It is true that the small family, if not the one-child family, gives the impression of enjoying more enviable conditions than the large family.

It is true that the bringing of children into the world is not the sole purpose of marriage nor the sole aim of married love.

It is true that modern man owes much of his greatness to the techniques which he has been able to invent in order to make his work easier.

[2] A. Sauvy.

It is true that in certain spheres, quality may sometimes compensate for quantity.

It is true that nobody can be expected to achieve the impossible, it is true, etc. . . .

But is it not also true that, for every man of common sense, there are natural basic values which must be safeguarded at all costs or else society will grow debased and descend the path that leads to vice and anarchy?

It is true, for instance, that man owes it to himself to preserve human love from all the deviations and perversions which threaten his nature and sex. It is true that humanity must protect this love from organized greed and lucre which are ceaselessly seeking to exploit it.

Thus society must protect married love against spurious imitations. It must not allow it to be subverted by invading, active forces such as venereal lust, donjuanism, libidinous lasciviousness, the white slave traffic and the rest. Misplaced indulgence in this respect would be the worst enemy of sound toleration.

The truth is that all that is most authentic in human love needs to be preserved by social action from the audacious pretensions of vice, which is always ready to play the rôle of a victim of the intolerance and the intransigence of public or religious authorities.

THE PRESERVATION OF MUTUAL DIGNITY IN LOVE

Human love is of its nature *reciprocal*, it involves, that is, a mutual respect, a mutual recognition of equal dignity.[3]

Love is a dialogue between two persons, two subjects. Neither has the right to treat the other as an object for his own satisfaction. "I love you, I adore you" is meant to signify: "I prefer you to myself, I want you for yourself, for your own good, for your own sake, as a person with your own vocation, with a destiny whose secret is known only to your Creator and to yourself."

But too often nature and sexuality seek merely to find some kind

[3] G. Madinier, *Conscience et Amour*, Alcan, 1938. By the same author: "Famille et intimité," in *Pour la Vie*, No. 3, Jan.–April 1946, pp. 15–25; Jean Lacroix, *Force et faiblesse de la Famille*, ch. II, "L'Aveu, fondement de l'Etre familial," Ed. du Seuil, 1948. Martin Buber, *Je et Tu*, Aubier, 1933; (English translation from the original German by Ronald Gregor Smith, *I and Thou*, Clark, Edinburgh, reprinted 1952); M. Nédoncelle, *Vers une philosophie de l'amour et de la personne*, second edition, Aubier, 1957.

of personal satisfaction in love, merely to appease a selfish desire, a voracious appetite. Under the pretext of pacifying the appetite of a sexuality which is still excessively introverted, they cause fixations or even emotional regressions towards that infantile or youthful voracity of appetite which is so opposed to the genuine maturity of the sexual instinct. Sexual crimes bear witness to the existence of these perversions.

Doubtless the border-line between the tolerance which society must show and culpable complicity, is not very clear. But it is certain that those who traffic in vice are on the watch and always ready to take advantage of the slightest opportunity which the indulgence of the authorities indirectly affords them.

This indicates how men of good will owe it to themselves to be on their guard so as to preserve authentic love from its spurious counterfeits or misinterpretations. The stupidity, vulgarity, gluttony and intemperance of sex-appeal should neither stifle nor distort the voice of genuine love.

Unfortunately it is always easier to conjure up, even for some artistic purpose, the perversions of nature, than to suggest the authenticity of truth. The reign of the spirit and the realm of chastity are more difficult to present in all their serene beauty than a tragic "Season in Hell"[4] or a moonstruck journey through the rivieras of vice.

THE PRESERVATION OF LOVE'S WILL TO CREATE

It is in the interests of humanity today not only to safeguard the values of mutual relationship and dignity but also to ensure that love's will to create is protected.[5]

It is true that neither the mutual relationship of two conscious persons nor the dialogue between a man and a woman who respect one another and treat one another as equals can, of themselves, give love its complete fulfilment.

Love only reaches its true dimension when the mutual personal relationship and the dialogue between man and woman go beyond

---

[4] The title of one of Rimbaud's works is "Une saison en enfer" (Translator's note).

[5] Gabriel Marcel, *Homo Viator*, ch. IV, "Le Vœu créateur comme essence de la Paternité," Aubier, 1944; S. de Lestapis, *Amour et Institution familiale*, ch. IV, "Solitude à deux ou Vœu créateur," Spes, 1947.

themselves in a common effort of self-renunciation for the sake of a third person. Love is only perfected when THOU AND I, that is, "both of us", can now identify ourselves objectively with HIM, HER, THEM, our child, our children.

"For, beyond selfish and sensual satisfaction, beyond even the fathomless being of the person loved which is outside the grasp of the person who loves, the will is busy at the work shared by the forces that are theirs and those of their incarnate love; it shapes the visible and real image of their twofold and unique life, the expression of what in each of them seems inexpressible and inaccessible." [6]

If married love should eventually lose this dimension or even underrate its value, the situation would be extremely grave for the spiritual, emotional, creative and self-transcending potential of humanity.[7]

A sterile population is a population that has grown prematurely old. A country where the only child is the rule is a land of men of private means or of civil servants. It has ceased to believe and to use its imagination. There is a risk that the only values it quotes may be the dividend coupon and unearned income.

There is no doubt that the day must inevitably come when each couple finally reaches the last stage of its life, the stage at which old age moves inexorably on its way. But what a difference it makes for the married love of these ageing husbands and wives if, as they look back over the past, they can congratulate themselves on having generously sown the seeds of life and tended them in a spirit of sacrifice, or if, on the other hand, they silently regret and reproach one another for having in practice repressed life and made it sterile for fear of taking risks or from a dread of discomfort.

In former times, when civilization was rural, nature could not claim any great merit for feeling and expressing spontaneously this creative will of love. It was written into the biology of the human couple and was easily transposed from this plane onto that of psychology and spirituality. Rural civilizations are in themselves civilizations that favour and encourage fertile love.

[6] Maurice Blondel, *L'Action*, 1893, pp. 257-8.
[7] A. Sauvy, *Théorie générale de la Population*, t. II, ch. III, "L'homme éternel oublié"; Robert Debré and A. Sauvy, *Des Français pour la France*, p. 115. "Malthusianism is a way of thinking, feeling, reacting to a situation. It is a concept of existence, but a precarious one doomed to be destroyed by its own inner logic. It is in fact a deliberate advance towards death." See also A. M. Henry, O.P., *Morale et vie conjugale*, Ed. du Cerf, 1957, pp. 156-8.

But when the exodus from the countryside drives hungry and poverty-stricken populations to the cities to seek work for which they will receive wages, when this exodus forces them to concentrate in factory workshops and shanty towns, how can nature still find it easy to manifest her will to create? The situation forces men rather to consider this will as a temptation they must resist.

To bring children into the world only to lose them at once, as was so often the case in the nineteenth century, or to procreate them and then only to be able to offer them a miserable disease-ridden existence, means that morbid anxiety swoops down upon the family transported from the countryside, and inevitably paralyses the creative impulse of love within it.

It is in just such circumstances that all men of goodwill owe it to themselves to protect the authentic nature of love and its vital forces.

What advantage indeed is it to a nation to see the spirit of sterility increase among its people? Among populations where love reaches the stage at which it hedges itself round with every kind of precaution, and so becomes as infertile as possible, can we normally expect to find the reflexes and reactions which make nations young and dynamic?

Once more we ask—should we not all pool our resources in order to protect the human couple, the foundation of society and the nucleus of public opinion, against the spirit of sterility? Should we not all unite to show special favour to those whose creative impulse gives expression to the vital power of love?

Instead of it seeming strange and odd voluntarily to have a family of five or six children, this way of life should rather be considered as an ideal, an aim to be pursued as far as possible and, where the public authorities are concerned, an attitude to be encouraged by social legislation as well as by the provision of housing really adequate for these families, and a sufficient income to meet their responsibilities.

Fortunately, since the second world war, an upsurge of vitality has suddenly become manifest in many populations which were recently still affected by the spirit of sterility. But this spontaneous upsurge needs to be sustained by careful thought. It deserves to be justified by the more realistic views of political economy and sociology. Otherwise it will only be a flash in the pan with no future worth the name.[8]

[8] *Renouveau des idées sur la famille*, I.N.E.D., 1954.

THE PRESERVATION OF THE MEANING OF FATHERHOOD

Other values are involved besides those of love which we have just reviewed. No one calls these values into question, at least when they are explicitly formulated, but it is a fact that they are rarely mentioned or given expression in artistic form on the stage or the cinema screen. I refer to the values which Fatherhood and Motherhood represent in this industrial and atomic age.

Let there be no misunderstanding, there is no intention of preaching a return to a patriarchy or a matriarchy. Those days are done and rightly so. Whether we like it or not, the human person has emerged from the group and the awareness of individual vocation takes precedence over the collective consciousness of the tribe, the lineage and even the social class.

What is at issue is the irreplaceable value of the presence at the child's side and the intelligent help of his father and mother at the time when he makes his first steps in the world, that is, from the moment of birth to the age of thirteen.[9]

In fact, nothing better has been found "to set up" a child in life than his father and mother, a father who is genuinely virile and a mother who is genuinely a woman. For before the child enters "social life" at school, in youth movements, military service, it is essential that he should have been given the experience of knowing that his own personality is considered and felt to be a subject in its own right with which relations are established within a warm and generous fellowship of love. The child needs close individual and personal relationships before it requires social security.

Here again everybody agrees that the deficiencies, incompetence, and above all the negligence of fathers and mothers are the cause of neuroses in childhood, juvenile delinquency and, later, produce pseudo-adults, the sexually retarded, the social misfits.

Therefore, it is surely high time, in certain countries, to stop perpetually baiting the father by representing him as a fool or an incompetent or—a little more kindly—as an individual whose task it

[9] Dr Maurice Porot, *L'enfant et les relations familiales*, Collection Paideia, P.U.F., 1954, Part 3, "Le Père, l'autorité"; Dr J. Dublineau, "Attitude du Père dans la famille," *Ecole des Parents*, Feb. 1951; Paul Osterrieth, *L'Enfant et la Famille*, Collection A la découverte de l'enfant, Editions du Scarabée, 1957, ch. VI, "Le rôle paternel," pp. 112–33; *Anneau d'Or*, special number, "Le Père," numbers 9–10, June 1946.

is to bring home money and to make love in the evening, although mostly at inopportune times.

It is surely desirable that in literature, films, magazines and on television, the magnificent part played by the father should have its values fully restored to it, for the father is a man ready to take risks over his future plans and prospects and yet, at the same time, is prudent and realistic in carrying them out.

Is there a finer sight than a father whose moral authority eventually earns and polarizes the enthusiastic admiration of his sons, instead of arresting or shattering it? To exercise authority, as the word indicates, is first and foremost to encourage growth, just as the exercise of magnanimity means to encourage a sense of greatness.

We agree that life in cities and in industry, since it keeps the father away from his children, makes it more difficult for him to encourage their growth in this manner than was formerly the case in the way of life of the agriculturalist and the farmer.

Nevertheless there are still many opportunities for the father to talk to his sons and daughters, to awaken their curiosity, to reveal to them the secrets of modern inventions and techniques. It is for him to arrange to give his children a few moments of his spare time on Sundays or during the holidays. A father who has really grasped the meaning of fatherhood, that is, the significance of the moral authority which the child needs if it is to feel basically secure and to face the future with confidence, will succeed in one way or another in finding opportunities to fulfil his mission towards his children.

Unfortunately in this respect also fatherhood has been stricken with a kind of wasting disease. Too many fathers have in fact come to the point at which they surrender their rights, either out of a false sense of shame or because they misunderstand their task, either out of human respect or by frustration due to the fact that their mission has been unjustly taken from them by wives who are too possessive.

And so if society restores its values to the father's function in the family, it will be working to its own advantage. It will have once more at its disposal the "Venturers" it needs if its economy is to expand and its administration to be efficient. It will have within it examples of the true virility which an erotic and effeminate civilization tends of its very nature to diminish and to submerge in the "wide boy" and "guttersnipe" types of the St-Germain wine-cellars and the more disreputable suburbs.

THE PRESERVATION OF THE MEANING OF MOTHERHOOD

The same may be said of motherhood. Motherhood is not over and done with after the confinement or the child's weaning. It has not done its duty when it has found a good day-nursery or a good kindergarten, where mothers may leave for eight hours a day their noisy, boisterous and exhausting youngsters, who after all, so it is said, will be all the better for the company of other children of their own age.

Motherhood is, and should remain for a long period of time, a presence; mother and child should look at each other, smile at each other; the child should learn to know and recognize its mother; there should be silent interchanges and then mother and child should prattle away together. Finally, the time comes for endless confidential talks, for the task of a mother is to awaken the soul of *her* child.

Of course, the task of bringing about this awakening may be handed over to specialists, to qualified technicians, or merely to paid nurses, just as in the near future, perhaps, the pregnancy already begun in one married woman's womb may be transferred by means of a graft to another uterus.

But everyone should see that by dint of continually finding substitutes, motherhood cannot fail to grow atrophied and eventually appear to be only a kind of forced labour (and an unpleasant one at that!) by comparison with other activities which environment, public opinion and custom tend to overvalue more or less artificially.

Why should there be a systematic contempt for the woman who works in her own home? Provided she has a proper place to live in, why should she not show as much initiative, intelligence, organizing ability and care over her appearance as she would in the surroundings of a professional occupation?

Do we really believe that it is of little importance "to ensure that there shall be a permanent home for human beings who, scattered as they are for a part of the day, will meet together at certain times within it"? [1]

Do we really believe it is of little importance to "take a record" of the child, his acts, his life, his behaviour, his conflicts, his work?

---

[1] Dr François Goust, "Aspects psychologiques et sociaux de la Maternité," in *Mère, qui es-tu?* (Study days organized at Unesco headquarters by Le Mouvement Mondial des Mères, 37 rue de Valois, Paris) in *Chronique sociale de France*, May 1956, pp. 15–25. By the same author: *En marche vers l'amour*, Ed. Ouvrières, 1958.

The child unburdens himself without bothering about the factory timetable. When the moment comes for the secret to be told, the father picks up his hat and leaves for the workshop. The mother remains. She sees all the problems of the growing man brought to her. She does her best to understand and solve them. This is enough to fill a lifetime and to enlarge her consciousness till it is as wide as the world. The woman is rather like a hunter on the alert. We never know when a child is going to take us into his confidence, when he is going to open his heart to us . . . But if neither the father nor the mother is there, how can he unburden himself? (Dr Goust).

In short, unless motherhood becomes again the total commitment of the whole of a woman's being to the creative and educative impulse—and this impulse is supported by a corresponding paternal commitment on the part of the father—society is increasingly threatened with the prospect of a growing number of children in revolt against an existence which they have not asked to receive.

The Public Authorities are well aware of this. There is no lack of books on childhood deprived of an educational environment[2] and on juvenile delinquency. How then are we to explain the increase in the incidence of that kind of motherhood which is a genuine cause of pre-delinquency? Obviously, inadequate housing, too frequent pregnancies and, above all, the fact that pregnancy does not attract sufficient financial aid, provide a valid explanation.

But this is not sufficient to account for so many deviations, so much turning away from the vocation to motherhood. Literature and the section of the press which seeks to popularize knowledge have rightly made people aware of the dangers caused by over-protective or over-possessive mothers. We are still waiting for them to make people aware of the danger caused by indifferent, negligent and egoistic mothers.

The vocation to motherhood is more complicated now than it once was. Nobody will deny this. Hence it more easily finds itself consciously torn by conflicting obligations. It must, on the one hand,

[2] J. Bowlby, *Child Care and the Growth of Love,* a summary of a report prepared under the auspices of the World Health Organization, London, Penguin Books, 1953; R. A. Spitz, "Les parents sont-ils nécessaires?" in *Psyché,* April 1959, pp. 692-707; "L'évocation de l'affectivité pendant la première année," in *Sauveguarde,* May 1949, pp. 48-85; O. Philippon, *L'enfance coupable vous accuse, Les causes familiales et sociales de la délinquence juvénile,* Recueil Sirey, 1950.

give the children all the love, security and affection they need, and, on the other, give these same children timely help in discovering and overcoming their infantile tendencies and their lack of maturity.

In this respect, all mothers would do well to set aside times for serious reflection and recollection, alternating with periods of absence from the home and, if necessary, of work outside it. This, it will be said, is a difficult balance to maintain. The intimate values of the home and those of solidarity with other people must be given equal weight and equal care must be taken to keep the home as a warm nest for the children, yet open on to the world.

It will be gathered that all this is scarcely possible unless mothers and fathers try to understand the more complex demands made on them today by comparison with the past, unless they try to help one another in tasks which they share to a greater extent than was formerly the case.

THE PRESERVATION OF THE RELIGIOUS AND
SACRED CHARACTER OF THE FAMILY

We have not gone far enough yet in this survey of the basic values of modern society, values entrusted first and foremost to the care of the family.

We maintain that there is a sense of mystery surrounding people and things, a sense of their sacred character. It is absolutely essential and we normally acquire it in a home where the parents' love is open to receive the values of religion.[3]

In professional and civic life, individual men and women are inevitably prone to adopt a free-thinking attitude. The high degree of technicality in work and its increasing rationalization end by affecting the mind and, unless we are very careful, atrophy that sixth sense with which man is endowed—the sense of the Divine, the sense of the things that are God's. No doubt, even in modern civilization, religious society, with its liturgical fellowship of adora-

---

[3] Gabriel Marcel, *Homo Viator*, Chapter III, "The Mystery of the Family"; Gabriel Madinier, "Nature et mystère de la famille," in *Semaine sociale de Bordeaux*, 1957, pp. 185–204; J. Guitton, *Essai sur l'amour humain*, Aubier, 1948 (English translation by Melville Chaning-Pearce, Rockliff, London, 1951); Rambaud, *La voie sacrée*, Lardenchet, 1946; G. Thibon, *Ce que Dieu a uni*, Paris, 1945 (English translation, *What God has joined together*, Hollis and Carter, London, and Regnery, Chicago, 1952).

tion and prayer, is present to maintain intact and to encourage the growth of this sixth sense without which worker and citizen are well on the way to becoming more or less automatic machines.

But, in point of fact, this religious society will not strike any answering chord in the citizen or worker of today unless the latter can carry their minds back to a childhood spent in a family where, through contact with parents who were genuine believers, an early and profound religious sense was born.

We certainly do not deny that there may be excellent homes, upright, united, closely-knit, open and welcoming to other people, which yet give evidence of little interest in these things and these religious values.

Such families do exist, especially when the partners have sensed that there exists in their married life a factor in some sort contained in their love and yet transcending it. In such homes there is a pervading and lofty sense of duty. It is all the more urgent in that it does not seem to be imposed from without but is freely accepted by conscience.

These homes are in fact religious, even if they do not admit the fact. They possess and foster this sixth sense, this awareness of the existence of an ideal worthy to be pursued, a standard of conduct worthy of respect. They are afraid perhaps or feel uneasy if they have to make an explicit reference to the absolute will of a personal God. Why is this? It is impossible to say *a priori* or in general terms. Each man's conscience, indeed, has its own existential history, which may have been affected by a trauma in early life or by a shock —resulting from an apparently insignificant incident which in fact was of the first importance, a scandal, a blow, a rejection—which, with the passage of time, has become all the more impossible to overcome since it occurred in the personal unconscious.

How fortunate then is the little child who, from his parents' arms, has been gently led into this world of religious mystery, not to be confused with the realm of the marvellous or with that of superstition any more than beauty is to be identified with the gaudy or knowledge with undigested information.

When the children in a family realize as a result of their living experience that the love of their parents for them is fed by another love which they can begin to see is primal and superior, then quite naturally they themselves move towards this primal source. Not only do they welcome it, but they see in it the source of their parents' kindness towards them, the source too of the gracious good will which contact with this atmosphere of Love engenders.

Where some Christian homes have been at fault and shown misunderstanding is that they have cultivated a form of legal morality faithful to the letter, rather than this religious sense of mystery, this sense of a primal Love as the source of all other forms of love. Their mistake has been to inculcate a fear—amounting sometimes to sheer panic—of transgressing the laws, rather than an authentic sense of confidence in God, that is, in Love itself.

Hence all decent people agree that the family remains the primal trustee of this sense of what is sacred, the fundamental repository of the religious sense. Without this safe custody and this hidden presence, society runs the risk of confining its aims to the utilitarian, to tangible and material well-being, and so is in danger of going down into the lists where men engage in the fratricidal struggles of the herd.

The principal natural values for which the Catholic Church feels herself responsible are: [4]

—Human love, in all the dignity and equality of its mutual relationships and in the spontaneous outgoing of its creative impulse:

—fatherhood and motherhood and the appreciation of their greatness and nobility;

—the sense of the religious and sacred character of the mystery of the family.

II. *REVEALED SUPERNATURAL TRUTHS*

The Church has also been given the trusteeship of a certain number of supernatural truths revealed by God to Israel in the Old Testament and to the Apostles by Christ in the New. These truths are intended to give to the Church, entrusted with the task of educator of the human race, an exact knowledge of the conditions required for genuine freedom and for progress towards holiness, according to Christ's promise: "If you continue faithful to my word, you are my disciples in earnest; so you will come to know the truth, and the truth will set you free" (John 8. 31–2).

[4] S. de Lestapis, S.J., *La Famille face aux structures actuelles*, F.N.A.C., 1954; Paul Archambault, *Eléments d'une doctrine familiale*, Report presented to the U.N.A.F. on 16 June 1946.

What then are these teachings of the Old and New Testaments, which, if they are adhered to, will help to bring to humanity true freedom in the realm of sexuality and fertility?

TRUTHS REVEALED IN THE OLD TESTAMENT

We may systematize under the form of five fundamental facts the truths relating to the problem of fertility and sexuality in man revealed by God to Israel from the time of her remote origins and continuously brought more and more to light as her sacred history unfolded itself.[5]

1. The creation of the human couple is first of all presented as part of the work of the six days and as its crowning act. The animal species are shown as inferior kingdoms destined to be under man's rule. All these kingdoms, including that of man, receive from Yahweh the command to increase and multiply and fill the earth.

> God said: "Let the earth yield grasses that grow and seed; fruit-trees too, each giving fruit of its own kind, and so propagating itself on earth." And so it was done.... God said: "Let the waters produce moving things that have life in them, and winged things that fly above the earth under the sky's vault." ... He pronounced his blessing on them, "Increase and multiply, and fill the waters of the sea; and let there be abundance of flying things on the earth." ... And God said: "Let the land yield all different kinds of living things, cattle and creeping things and wild beasts of every sort"; and so it was done.... Then God said: "Let us make man, wearing our own image and likeness; let us put him in command of the fishes of the sea, and all that flies through the air, and the cattle, and the whole earth, and all the creeping things that move on earth."

[5] The number of works dealing with the family in the Old and New Testament is rather small:

L'abbé Gelin, "Le mariage d'après l'Ancien Testament," in *Lumière et Vie*, June 1952; "La Famille dans le plan de la sanctification de l'Humanité (La Révélation)," in *Journées d'Etudes de l'Union Nationale des Congrégations d'Action Hospitalière et sociale*, May 1953; "Le passage de la polygamie à la monogamie," in Podechard (Institut Catholique de Lyon), 1945; "De l'Eden à St Paul," in *Echanges*, No. 35, Easter, 1958; S. de Lestapis, "Mystère de la Famille et dessein de Dieu," in *l'Anneau d'Or*, Nos. 33-4, May-Aug. 1950; J. Cantinat, "La Famille d'après la Bible," in *Masses Ouvrières*, Sept. 1957, pp. 3-32; R. P. Th. Chary, O.F.M., *Structures de la Famille dans l'Ancien Testament* (roneotyped); M. Daniel-Rops, "L'amour Humain dans la Bible," in Conferencia, *Les Annales*, 15 April 1949.

So God made man in his own image, made him in the image of God. Man and woman both, he created them.

And God pronounced his blessing on them, "Increase and multiply and fill the earth" (Gen. 1. 11–28).

"And *make it yours*," adds God to the human couple. This is already one way of ordering man to become the *master of all things and of himself.*

Such then is the first truth revealed by God. Man is given by delegation from God, sovereignty over all things, including himself.

2. The second creation narrative brings us another equally fundamental truth. Man is created in God's image not as a solitary being but as a communion of persons. From God, Adam receives Eve, formed from his own flesh and so from his nature and race, to be a companion "a mate of his own kind".[6]

The human couple therefore is not created solely for reproduction purposes, as are the inferior kingdoms. Woman is not just a female of the species. She is created to be man's "opposite number", a "well-matched companion". Hence, when confronted with this new phenomenon, peculiar to the human race, Adam enthusiastically exclaims: "Here, at last, is bone that comes from mine, flesh that comes from mine" (Gen. 2. 23). In Eve he finds not only a *Genitrix*" but also an *"alter Ego"*, with whom personal companionship will now be possible and mutual converse and relations assured.

Such then is the second truth revealed by God. The relationship of man and woman has another meaning. It is a *community* of persons in the greatest possible *intimacy*: "The two became one flesh" (Gen. 2. 24).

3. "Both went naked, Adam and his wife," continues the second creation narrative, "and thought it no shame" (Gen. 2. 25). Sexuality and emotions are under complete control and integrated in perfect freedom. Unfortunately this happy state of equilibrium was not to survive the coming of sin.

By their sin, the two partners desire to be the source of their own union, God's rival, not his image, and so the way lies open to a state of unbalance and death. Work and sexuality, although they do not lose their original meaning which is written into their very nature, take on a new meaning for man and woman. They denote a state of *indigence* and the need of salvation.

[6] The "Bible de Jérusalem" translates "Qui lui soit assortie" (=who shall be matched with him). On the two accounts of the Creation, see Introduction and notes in the *Bible de Jérusalem*, Ed. du Cerf.

Human work will be hard toil and, on occasion, will force man to cry to God for "mercy".

Human sexuality likewise will often be a humiliating experience of lack of control and of that perfect freedom which man of his nature longs to possess. Here too the human couple will be obliged to turn to God and implore his "mercy".

Such then is the third fundamental truth revealed to humanity by God concerning the problem of *grace and the flesh*: the *flesh has lost its original state of equilibrium*. It can only regain it by prayer and penance, by the help of grace asked for and obtained.

4. For, in spite of man's proud claim to be self-sufficient, God will not abandon him to his errors nor to the confusion arising from his mistakes. God will give to his chosen people first a law founded on truth, then the promise of a Saviour.

In the Mosaic Law, the human couple will find the institutional framework by means of which it will be able to regain essential mastery over sexuality, now so full of conflicting tendencies. The Law will not only denounce homosexuality but also fornication and adultery. It will train the mind to seek the ideal of monogamy and, little by little, that of indissolubility.

In about the year 430 B.C., the prophet Malachias protested against the epidemic of divorces and addressed the following hard words to those guilty of such conduct: "Yahweh bears witness to her wrongs, that wife of thy manhood's age, whom now thou spurnest, thy partner, thy covenanted bride! Yet doer of this is the same man as ever, the will of him is unchanged; he asks nothing better, now as before, than to breed a God-fearing race; to that will, men of Juda, keep true. Spurn her not, the wife of thy manhood's age . . ." (Mal. 2. 14–15).

Such then is the fourth revealed truth: the exercise of human sexuality and love is only in keeping with the divine will within *the institution of marriage* leading to monogamy and indissolubility. The union of Tobias and Sara will become the model of wedlock presented to the pious Israelite.

5. Finally, a fifth truth implicit in those we have mentioned will clearly define the blessings of marriage and their respective values. First there is the begetting of *generations to come* and with or without it (when the couple unfortunately remains childless) the *mutual aid* given to one another by the partners.

"And now Adam had knowledge of his wife Eve, and she conceived. She called her child Cain, as if she would say, Cana, I have been enriched by the Lord with a man-child" Gen. 4. 1). The first woman rejoices for, as the *Bible de Jérusalem* comments, from being the servant of her husband, she has become the mother of a man. A play on words connects the name of Cain (*Qain*) with the verb *qana*—to acquire. The child is indeed the great "gain" of the married union.

Yet he is not the only one. The community of the partners is, as we have already seen, another "gain" in the marriage. It will be long before it reveals itself to the heart of man, who is prone unfortunately as the result of sin to adopt an attitude of domination over the female sex (Gen. 3. 16). Childless women will find this out to their cost in those stern ages when the great business of marriage was to provide a house with descendants (Deut. 25. 5–10). Husbands themselves, by an odd reversal of this situation, will complain that their wives are only too inclined to concentrate their energies on bearing children. "Anna," Elcana asked his wife, "what need to weep, what need to deny thyself food? What sorrow weighs on thy heart? Is it not worth the love of ten sons, the love I bear thee?" (1 Kings 1. 8).

It was only in the process of time that marriage revealed itself to the consciousness of the partners as a "community of love". It needed the voice of the prophets and the theme introduced by Osee and so often restated by Jeremias, Ezechiel and the second Isaias, the theme of the covenant of love between Yahweh and Israel. In the Persian period, when the book of Tobias describes the ideal of marriage as then understood by the chosen people in exile, this understanding of "a community of destiny" as one of the great advantages of marriage has become a fact:

> Blessed art thou, oh God of our fathers [cries Tobias]
>> And blessed is thy Name . . .
> It is thou who didst create Adam,
>> It is thou who didst create Eve his wife
> To succour and support him.
>> And from these two the human race was born.
> It is thou who hast said:
>> Man must not remain alone,
>> Let us make for him *a helpmate like to himself!*

F.P.M.P.—5*

And now it is not pleasure
That I seek as I take my kinswoman to wife,
But I take her with a sincere heart.
Deign to have pity on her and on me
And bring us *together* to our old age!

(Tobias 8. 5–9).[7]

The aged Raguel then makes this prayer his own:

Give unto them, oh Master, thy favour and protection,
Grant that they may always live
In joy and grace!

(Tobias 8. 7).

By means of these five fundamental truths, the Old Testament not only preserved among the chosen people the highest values of human love and sexuality, but made Israel ready, in the best of her sons at least, to hear the still loftier teaching of the divine Saviour, according to his promise: "Do not think I have come to set aside the Law and the Prophets: I have not come to set them aside, but to bring them to perfection" (Matt. 5. 17).

TRUTHS REVEALED IN THE NEW TESTAMENT

And the fact is that Jesus, returning to the ideal of monogamous and indissoluble marriage towards which Israel had been moving under the guidance of the prophets and the wise men, not only confirms it, but makes it obligatory from now onward upon all his disciples. The New Covenant will not tolerate any exception, as the Old Alliance had found it possible to do.[8]

Adultery and debauchery are again condemned (Matt. 15. 19) not only when committed in fact but also even in thought (Matt. 5. 28).

The original character of Christ's teaching does not however lie

[7] The English here and in the three lines that follow is the translator's. Mgr Knox's version, a rendering of the Vulgate Text, does not correspond sufficiently with that used by the author and the point of the latter's remarks is therefore largely lost.

[8] On the theology of Christian marriage, see M. A. Genevois, O.P., *Le Mariage selon le dessein de Dieu*, Ed. du Cerf, 1957; A. M. Henry, O.P., "Le Mariage," in *Initiation Théologique*, vol. IV, ch. XIII; and for a thorough study of the subject, *Dictionnaire de Théologie Catholique*, art. "Marriage."

here. In the presence of his disciples, who already find these obligations under the New Covenant somewhat arduous, Jesus gives a warning that there is something still better to be done, that there is a still higher call to be heard. It is true, he adds, that "that conclusion cannot be taken in by everybody, but only by those who have the gift." This call, this "conclusion" are the vocation to *voluntary continence for the sake of the Kingdom of Heaven.* To those willing to follow him and to consecrate themselves exclusively to the Kingdom of Heaven, he issues an invitation to perpetual continence, and he adds this enigmatic phrase—"Take this in, you whose hearts are large enough for it!" (Matt. 19. 12).

"Give me the man who loves," said St Augustine, "for he will understand." He will understand why Christ himself has given us the example of this perpetual continence, why he willed to be born of a Virgin-Mother, why, according to the Gospel, chastity when it issues from love becomes sexuality's supreme virtue. In a word, he will understand the full meaning of the mysterious phrase in Genesis —"Make the earth yours and take command of it". To make the earth ours means not merely to canalize the forces of the cosmos in order to press them into the service of man and to make them contribute to his conquest of liberty, it is also to master in oneself the most legitimate movements of one's being, the inborn instinct to found a family, to find fulfilment in a partner, and this instinct is to be mastered to the point at which God alone is seen as "family" and "partner".

It was to be the task of the apostles guided by divine inspiration to make explicit all that was contained in this teaching. Neither Peter, nor John, nor Paul add anything whatever to the Master's teaching, they only make clear its most profound implications. Christ had promised: "So much converse I have held with you, still at your side. He who is to befriend you, the Holy Spirit, whom the Father will send on my account, will in his turn make everything plain, and recall to your minds everything I have said to you . . . it will be for him to guide you into all truth (John 14, 26; 16. 13).

In fact all Paul had to do was to take as his theme the Covenant as it appears throughout the teaching of the prophets, the great theme of the nuptials of Yahweh and Israel. He was thus able to grasp that it was really in the association between Christ and his Church that this theme acquired its full and final meaning. Although it is true that in the Old Testament this mystery of the marriage of Yahweh and Israel had never been looked upon as the type and model of human marriage, nevertheless it cannot be denied that it had gradually refined the sensibility of devout Jewish couples. It was time then to replace the Yahweh-Israel partnership by the association of Christ with his Church now that the figures were fulfilled in reality. So the apostle of his own accord writes to the Ephesians:

You who are husbands must shew love to your wives, as Christ shewed to the Church. . . .

Wives must obey their husbands as they would obey the Lord.

The man is the head to which the woman's body is united, just as Christ is the head of the Church, he, the Saviour on whom the safety of the body depends.

It is unheard of, that a man should bear ill-will to his own flesh and blood; no, he keeps it fed and warmed.

And so it is with Christ and the Church.

We are limbs of his body.

That is why a man will leave his father and mother and will cling to his wife,

and the two will become one flesh.

Yes, those words are a high mystery:

and I am applying them here to Christ and his Church (Eph. 5. 21–32).

Ever since then, this mystery is the source of the conduct of Christian husband and wives. The mystery of Christ and his Church is not merely intended for them to contemplate, it is above all a union in which they share if they as two Christians have genuinely and really promised to live their whole life together in all its aspects under the aegis of Christ and the Church.

All that remains is to deduce in particular cases the practical conclusions resulting from this great truth which Saint Paul grasped and brought fully to light. A whole theology of Christian marriage is potentially contained in it. It will become apparent as problems present themselves to the conscience of husbands and wives whose marriage is under the aegis of Christ and the Church.

Here by way of example are a few of the corollaries, as we may call them, of this doctrine:

1. *Marriage is good. Consecrated virginity is still better.* Marriage is good, declares Paul writing to his disciple Timothy to put him on his guard against the gnostic heresy. "Such teachers wrongly bid them abstain from marriage, and from certain kinds of food, although

God has made these for the grateful enjoyment of those whom faith has enabled to recognize the truth" (1 Tim. 4. 3).

Nevertheless the way of consecrated virginity is better. It approximates still more closely to the manner in which Christ loved the Church and "gave himself up on its behalf".

I wish you were all in the same state as myself; but each of us has his own endowment from God, one to live in this way, another in that. To the unmarried, and to the widows, I would say that they will do well to remain in the same state as myself, but if they have not the gift of continence, let them marry; better to marry than to feel the heat of passion" . . . (1 Cor. 7. 7–9).

He who is unmarried is concerned with God's claim, asking how he is to please God; whereas the married man is concerned with the world's claim, asking how he is to please his wife; and thus he is at issue with himself. So a woman who is free of wedlock, or a virgin, is concerned with the Lord's claim, intent on holiness, bodily and spiritual; whereas the married woman is concerned with the world's claim, asking how she is to please her husband.

I am thinking of your own interest when I say this. It is not that I would hold you in a leash; I am thinking of what is suitable for you, and how you may best attend on the Lord without distraction (1 Cor. 7. 32–5).[9]

2. When he turns to married Christians, Paul wishes to see them *tend towards a progressive spiritualization of their married love,* even to the furthest limit of perfect continence. Yet he warns them against the illusion of angelism!

As for the questions raised in your letter; a man does well to abstain from all commerce with women (1 Cor. 7. 1). But to avoid the danger of fornication, let every man keep his own wife, and every woman her own husband. Let every man give his wife what is her due, and every woman do the same by her husband; he, not she, claims the right over her body, as she, not he, claims the right over his. Do not starve one another, unless perhaps you do so for a time, by mutual consent, to have more freedom for prayer; come

---

[9] On Virginity, see Dom Olivier Rousseau, *Monachisme et vie religieuse d'après l'ancienne tradition de l'Eglise,* Ed., Chevetogne, 1957, Ch. II, "Virginité et célibat consacré chez les Pères Grecs"; A. Metz, *La consécration des Vierges dans l'Eglise Romaine,* Paris, 1954; Pius XII, Encyclical, *Sacra virginitas,* 25 March 1954. See also Fr Bouyer, *Trône de la Sagesse,* 1958; this book is an essay in Christian anthropology.

together again, or Satan will tempt you, weak as you are. I say this by way of concession; I am not imposing a rule on you (1 Cor. 7. 1–6).

But having said this so as to help them to avoid illusions coming from the devil, Paul cannot do otherwise than remind married people that they are pilgrims on the road to eternity, to the Kingdom of Heaven where, as Christ has said, "When the dead rise again, there is no marrying and giving in marriage; they are as the angels in heaven are" (Matt. 22. 330).

> . . . nothing remains, but for those who have wives to behave as though they had none; those who weep must forget their tears, . . . those who buy must renounce possession; and those who take advantage of what the world offers must not take full advantage of it; the fashion of this world is soon to pass away (1 Cor. 7. 29–31).
>
> Only, brethren, I would say this; the time is drawing to an end (1 Cor. 7. 29).

In short, Paul's reflections suggest that he wished all married people might be able to anticipate of their own free will, and with the desire to go forth to meet Christ at his second coming, that next-world state in which they will be as the angels in heaven.

Nevertheless, once again, as he says, none is to overrate his own strength. Married people may try to practise continence for a time. *if they both agree to do so*, in order to "have more freedom for prayer", that is, in order, by making a sacrifice, to belong to Christ in a more spiritual way. But it will be prudent for them to take up their common life again, so as not to run the risk of illusions and the temptations which accompany them. St Paul, speaking from experience, advises even young widows, who of all people, are best placed to anticipate the future life, that it is often wiser for them to remarry: "So I would have the younger women marry and bear children and have households to manage; then they will give enmity no handle for speaking ill of us" (1 Tim. 5. 14).[1]

3. All this doctrine, in spite of its variations of emphasis, forms a perfectly coherent whole, especially if we take care to remind our-

---

[1] On Chastity and Continence, see Etudes Carmélitaines, *Mystique et continence*, Paris, 1952; Fathers Plus and Rayez in *Dictionnaire de spiritualité*"; P. de Lochet, "Notion positive de Chasteté Conjugale," in *Morale sexuelle et Difficultés contemporaines*, Ed. Familiales de France, pp. 335–6; D. Planque, *La chasteté, vertu positive*, Ed. Centre d'études et de consultations familiales, Brussels, 1957.

selves of *the idea of the Christian's body as St Paul understood it.*
As against libertines who considered fornication was as legitimate a
sexual need as are eating and drinking in the case of the stomach, he
asserts:

> But your bodies are not meant for debauchery (1 Cor. 6. 13).
> They are meant for the Lord. . . . Have you never been told that
> your bodies belong to the body of Christ? And am I to take what
> belongs to Christ and make it one with a harlot? (1 Cor. 6. 15).
> Surely you know that your bodies are the shrines of the Holy
> Spirit, that dwells in you. And he is God's gift to you, so that you
> are no longer your own masters. A great price was paid to ransom
> you; glorify God by making your bodies the shrine of his presence
> (1 Cor. 6. 19–20).

And he naturally concludes:

> As for debauchery, and impurity of every kind . . . there must
> be no whisper of it among you. . . . This you must know well
> enough, that nobody can claim a share in Christ's kingdom, God's
> kingdom, if he is debauched, or impure. . . . (Eph. 5. 3. 5).

Hence the rule is the same for both the unmarried and the
married, with all due allowance made as to the manner in which
each will have to apply it: (*Your bodies*) *are meant for the Lord . . .
you are no longer your own masters*. None is to think that he is the
absolute master of his body as regards the use to which he may put
it. This use must be in keeping with the manner in which we belong
to the Lord. For the married couple it is determined by the mutual
rights and duties marked out for it by the nature of the sexual
function. For the unmarried it means complete abstinence from
what is permitted only to the married.[2]

Such then is the heritage of revealed truths confided by God and
by Christ to the Church, in order to help her to guide mankind without error or any wandering from the right path.

We are now able to have a better understanding of Pius XI's
advice which we previously quoted from *Casti Connubii*:

> Wherefore, let the faithful also be on their guard against the
> overrated independence of private judgment and that false auton-
> omy of human reason.

[2] Abbé Monchanin, "Biologie et morale sexuelle," in *Problèmes de la
sexualité*, Plon, 1943. By the same author, "Sexualité et spiritualité," in
Médecine et sexualité, Spes, pp. 215 and 246. Pius XII, "Le Corps humain," in
the collection *Les enseignements pontificaux*, Desclée & Cie, 1953.

Chapter IX

THE DOCTRINAL POSITION OF THE CATHOLIC CHURCH WITH REGARD TO FERTILITY REGULATION

W E have already noted how the Church, when she speaks to the human race as its teacher, takes her stand straight away in the realms of moral and religious consciousness, and not in that of social psychology. Hence, we ought not to astonish anyone if we say that the Church when confronted with the problem of family planning and that of the spread of contraception, defines her doctrinal position:

(*a*) in the first place at the level of the individual conscience of the married couple who are directly involved in the problem of fertility and its regulation;

(*b*) then and then only at the level of the conscience of those who govern and are responsible for a population, public health and eugenic policy.

We shall explain the Catholic Church's doctrinal position from these same two points of view. A preliminary investigation as to the nature of human morality and its norms is necessary. It will doubtless be remembered that for the Reformed Churches it is faith alone which, in the last analysis, gives any act its moral character. As W. G. Cole has written: "For Protestantism, the individual stands before God in a unique situation, where the divine law can dispense with all rules. . . . The ethic of Protestantism is Christian liberty, where the ethic of Rome is the natural law."

In fact, as we shall see, the ethical system of Catholicism finds the sources and standards of its moral code neither in the sphere of personal choice alone nor in that of the natural order alone, but in the indissoluble union of both. "There can be no doubt that for each individual man, fidelity to himself and to his own vocation is the law, but this vocation is not authentic unless it conforms to the general demands of every human vocation founded, according to metaphysical ethics, on the essential *nature* of man."[1]

---

[1] Rev. Fr Brisbois, S.J., "Une morale d'aujourd'hui," in *Nouvelle Revue Théologique*, July-Aug. 1951, p. 711. See below Ch. XI, p. 177, note 9.

THE TWO NORMS OF HUMAN MORALITY:
NATURE AND PERSON

Pope Pius XII in his speech to Midwives dealt with married sexuality and fertility, as it is with these that their professional duties are concerned. He began by urging them to distinguish carefully between (*a*) the part played by *nature*, and (*b*) the part played by man as a *person*.

"If," he said, "nature's part and man's are thus clearly defined," if moreover "your professional training and experience enables you to know how both nature and man act, and also to know the rules and the laws to which both are subject, your conscience, enlightened by reason and by faith under the guidance of that authority which God has established, teaches you how far you are allowed to co-operate, and at what stage, on the other hand, you are under a strict obligation to refuse your cooperation."

"*Nature* places at man's disposal the whole chain of causes which will be the source of a new life."

"It falls to *man* to free the vital forces in these causes" or on the contrary to hold them in check.[2]

In other words, *nature* represents the biological, physiological and psychological datum of sexuality as the Creator has organized it in the human race. This nature is a datum that is fundamentally determined in its essential structures and in the direction of its functional processes. Nevertheless human sexuality is more flexible and more adaptable than sexuality in the animal kingdom where, to take one example alone, it is often subject to the regular recurrence of the rutting season.

Man on the other hand is a free person with a supernatural destiny to be fulfilled in the thousand and one daily obligations of our life in time. Man represents the power to make a choice, that is, to determine consciously and of his own free will how he will decide to act, and this in view of a good end that has been willed for its own sake.

Nature is what it is, as God has made it. From this point of view,

---

[2] "Allocutio iis quae interfuerunt Conventui Unionis Catholicae inter Obstetrices (29 Octobris 1951)," *Acta Apostolicae Sedis* 1951, vol. XLIII, No. 17-18, pp. 835-60, Italian text.

sexuality is a dynamic force which has its own meaning and its own well-defined objectives.

But man is free only to liberate the vital forces of this dynamic system or, on the other hand, to leave it to lie dormant. We have in mind at this point genital sexuality alone. "To nature pertains the development of the living force, leading to its completion. Once man has fulfilled his part and set in motion the marvellous evolution of life, it is his duty to respect religiously its progress and the same duty forbids him either to halt the course of nature or to prevent its natural development."

This preliminary assertion which we have borrowed from Pope Pius XII is justified by the respect which the Church professes *a priori* for the order of Creation, when the latter is in direct relation with the very being of the human person.

"Hence," said the Sovereign Pontiff, "whoever approaches this cradle of the formation of [human] life and plays a part there, in one way or another, should know the order the Creator lays down to be followed and the laws that rule this order. . . . This order founded by a supreme intellect is directed to the end designed by the Creator." [3] Man has not the right to "distort it" or to disturb it according to his own good pleasure. This natural order which is so intimately related to the very constitution of the personality must be respected and maintained in its entirety. Later we shall return to this fundamental principle in connection with sterilization.

In order to avoid confusion regarding the order of nature, we wish to make it clear once more at this point that we do not in any way automatically sin against "the order established by the supreme Mind" when, in our applied sciences, for instance, we proceed to disintegrate the atom or attempt to produce a temperature of absolute zero, etc. We do not sin against this order when we dissect living things or introduce changes into them by artificial means or even produce monstrous forms of life, provided always that the individual thing affected is not a "being-in-itself" (*Dasein*). The interventions of science applied *"in-vivo"* are justified on the grounds that they may serve man by helping him to realize his spiritual destiny. They are part of that process of "making the earth ours" which was confided to man by the Creator himself.

But it is a very different matter when nature and personality bring into existence the *"human composite"* of an individual *sub-*

---

[3] "Address to Catholic Midwives," nn. 3–4, in *Marriage and the Moral Law*, C.T.S., pp. 5–6.

ject. Any intervention which would then be likely to disturb nature becomes an attack upon personality. In this case the order of nature must be respected in its entirety.

In a speech to the doctors present at the Third World Conference on Fertility and Sterility (1956), Pius XII was still more decisive on this point:

> It is obvious that the scientist and the doctor, when they are dealing with a problem that comes within their special sphere, have the right to concentrate their attention on those elements in it which are specifically scientific and to solve the problem in relation to these data alone. But when we are confronted with practical applications, it is impossible to avoid taking into account the repercussions of the methods suggested on the human *person* and his destiny. The greatness of the human act lies precisely in the fact that it transcends the moment of time at which it takes place and, by involving the whole direction of a man's life, brings it to the point at which it has to take up its position in regard to the absolute. If this is true of everyday activities, how much more so is it of an act which involves not only the mutual love of husband and wife, but also their future and that of their descendants.[4]

I. THE REGULATION OF FERTILITY AS IT AFFECTS THE INDIVIDUAL CONSCIENCE

THE TWO ENDS

". . . the conjugal act is destined primarily by nature for the begetting of children . . ." declares *Casti Connubii*.[5] But nature has also given it the further though secondary capacity to produce the conditions favourable to the establishment of the community of man and wife with its essential aims of unity, indissolubility and order in their mutual love. "For," declares *Casti Connubii*, "in matrimony as well as in the use of the matrimonial rights there are also secondary ends, such as mutual aid, the cultivating of mutual love, and the quieting

[4] Pius XII's "Speech to the Third World Conference on Fertility and Sterility," Doc. Cat. 1956 (10.6.56), col. 746.
[5] *Casti Connubii*, C.T.S., p. 26.

of concupiscence." [6] This then is the fundamental affirmation known as the doctrine of the *two ends of marriage* (the two ends that govern the sexual relations of husband and wife), on which rests the whole doctrinal position of the Church in regard to the regulation of fertility.

THESE TWO ENDS ARE CLOSELY UNITED

When we examine the dynamism of the sexual function and analyse the end to which its processes lead, we see that its two capacities are intimately associated. It is obvious that human sexuality is fundamentally directed towards procreation, and no less fundamentally towards the mutual development of the personalities of husband and wife through the total gift of self which each makes to the other and which is signified by their union.

However, in contrast to the state of affairs in the animal kingdom, human nature, which has no rutting season, allows this union to take place and to keep its secondary capacity, even when fertility is biologically impossible. This, we may say in passing, shows that God does not intend fertility to be necessarily the only aim the union of husband and wife has in view.

THE HIERARCHICAL ORDER OF THE TWO ENDS

This close association of the two ends in the natural order of human sexuality nevertheless has its own hierarchical order, a scale of vales we would do well to note. "Just as it can be said that all eyes are intended and constructed to see, even though in abnormal cases because of particular internal or external conditions, they can never be capable of giving sight," [7] so in the same way we should be able to say that the sexual function is intended to allow husband and wife to procreate even though in many cases, as the result of special internal or external conditions, it may never be able to lead to conception. It is none the less certain that a blind eye still has an aesthetic function of considerable value in the field of human relations, but we shall not on this account invert the order of the factors involved, by setting

---

[6] *Casti Connubii*, C.T.S., p. 28.
[7] "Address to Catholic Midwives", n. 47, *op cit.*, p. 23.

the aesthetic function above the visual. So too with sexuality, which although impeded in its procreative function continues to have a "relational" function of considerable value in married life. But all the same, we cannot invert the order of the factors involved and say that sexuality is only intended for procreation accidentally or secondarily.

In any case the Catholic Church is adamant on this point. Pius XII in his "Address to Catholic Midwives" declares without any possibility of evasion:

> It was precisely for the purpose of putting an end to all uncertainty and wanderings away from the truth, which were threatening to spread mistaken ideas about the order of precedence in the purposes of marriage and the relationship between them, that We ourselves, some years ago (10th March 1944), drew up a statement placing them in their right order. We called attention to what the *very internal structure of their natural disposition* [sexuality] discloses.[8]

The Pope adds:

> We drew attention . . . to what is the heritage of Christian tradition, to what the Sovereign Pontiffs have repeatedly taught, and to what was afterwards definitely stated in the Code of Canon Law (Canon 1013, §1). Futhermore, a little while afterwards, to put an end to conflicting opinions, the Holy See, by a public Decree, proclaimed that the appeal of certain modern writers who deny that the procreation and education of the child is the primary end of marriage, or teach that the secondary ends are not essentially subordinate to the primary end, but rather are of equal value and are independent of it, cannot be admitted.[9] (Sacred Congregation of the Holy Office, April 1, 1944.)

THE ORDER OF VALUES AS IT AFFECTS THE
INTENTION OF HUSBAND AND WIFE

The order of the two ends revealed by the objective structure of human sexuality must, as we saw in our introduction, be accepted and respected as "an order inherent in creation" established by a

---

[8] *Ibid.*, n. 48, p. 23.   [9] *Ibid.*

supreme Mind "and directed to an end will by the Creator". Hence the order of ends and the hierarchy which it naturally reveals must give to the different values arising from married sexuality their own true order. The Pope therefore says:

> The truth is that marriage, as a natural institution, is not ordered by the will of the Creator towards personal perfection of the husband and wife as its *primary end,* but to the procreation and education of a new life [the procreation and education of the child as a human person]. The other ends of marriage, although part of nature's plan, are not of the same importance as the first. Still less are they superior. On the contrary they are essentially subordinate to it. This principle holds good for all marriages, even if they are unfruitful.[2]

> [Therefore] tell the fiancée or the young wife who comes to discuss with you the values of married life, that these personal values relating to the body, sense or spirit, are really good and true, but that the Creator has put them in the second place in the scale of values, and not in the first.[3]

"But," it may be objected by some, "two people do not marry so as to bring up children, they marry because they are in love and want to be happy by living to the full their life together." This is in fact possible, even normal. Nature's order of intention (*finis operis*) only becomes the order of values for those who are her agents (*finis operantis*) little by little as the result of reflection, and without reflection, let it be said, man does not reach the fullness of personal life but remains half-way between childhood and adult status.

Therefore it is not at all abnormal for many engaged couples to think first and foremost of having a pleasant home and an attractive, enriching life together. But if the thought of bringing children into the world and rearing them should not seem to them the proper fulfilment of their life together, above all if they put off this task till a much later date, treating the prospect as an eventuality which though doubtless inevitable is something of a nuisance and all but undesirable, then there can be no doubt that their attitude would be the characteristic sign of a lack of maturity in their love.

In fact engaged couples should not delay too long in bringing their

[2] "Address to Catholic Midwives", n. 47, *op. cit.,* pp. 22–3.
[3] *Ibid.,* n. 54, p. 25.

love and their mutual delight in one another's company face to face with this question of the child they are to bring into the world. Their ability to do this will even be a test of maturity for both of them and of the degree of self-giving which their sexuality and their affections have reached.

There can be no doubt that we have the right to marry "in order to be happy", but we should bear in mind that it is still more true that we marry in order to bring children into the world, a certain number of children whom we wish to educate to manhood. As long as husband and wife have not yet come to the point when they say in all sincerity to one another "That is first and foremost what marriage is", there will still be something infantile and frail in their union, which may break down under the strain of their first clashes and their first disappointments.

In our days when sexuality is constantly regressing to an adolescent stage, we must insist on this point in our conversations with young people. We must show them—and this is not so very difficult —that to create is a great thing, that there is no finer work, none more worthy of admiration than the formation of a human person. To bring out all the potentialities of character, temperament, mind, imagination and heart which a child in its infancy bears within him, is the most wonderful thing in the world!

The Pope asked:

Does this mean a denial or diminishing of what is good and right in the personal values which result from marriage and from the marriage act? Certainly not. . . .[4] All this is true and willed by God; but it must not be disjoined from the primary function of marriage, that is, from the duty to the new life [that of the child]. Not only the exterior common life, but also all the personal wealth, the qualities of mind and spirit, and finally all that there is more truly spiritual and profound in married love as such, has been placed by the will of nature and the Creator *at the service of the offspring*. Of its nature, perfect married life means also the complete self-sacrifice of the parents on behalf of their children, and love of husband and wife in its strength and tenderness is an essential need for the most earnest care for the child and the guarantee that this care will be taken.[5]

---

[4] *Ibid.*, n. 49, p. 23.
[5] *Ibid.*, n. 50, p. 24.

THE TWO ENDS IN PRACTICE

So far we have considered the problem of sexuality and fertility only from an *abstract* point of view—the order of the two ends and of the values and intentions it implies and presupposes. It is now time to consider how, in the realm of *concrete practice,* a couple should or can propose to regulate its own fertility.

The first question that comes to mind is this—Are husbands and wives who have had to find in the natural and functional order of sexuality the norm by which they are to make their value-judgments (what is the primary end of marriage, the principal value of married life?) under a similar obligation to take the spontaneous urges of their sexuality as the norm which is to regulate their actual, real fertility in the concrete? In other words, is fertility delivered over to the caprice of instinct, the fertility which the Creator has willed should be normal in the human race? Some have gone so far as to think so and have conferred on this type of fertility the doubtful name of "natural fertility", whereas its real name ought to be "instinctual fertility". The Church thinks quite differently. Instinctual action has never been given any kind of regulating task in the sphere of human acts by the Catholic tradition. On the contrary, this tradition has always assigned this regulative role to reason illuminated by faith and inspired by love and prudence.

Pius XII reminded us of this at the beginning of his "Address to Catholic Midwives":

> [As far as human sexuality is concerned] it is not a question of physical or of biological laws which are automatically obeyed by agents not endowed with reason, or of blind forces, but it is a question of laws, the execution and the effect of which are confided to the voluntary and free cooperation of man.[6]

Hence in the realm of mankind, the practical regulation of sexuality and fertility depends on liberty or in other words on a decision taken after due deliberation by responsible husbands and wives, a decision inspired by the supreme law of all human activity—justice and love towards God and our neighbour.

[6] "Address to Catholic Midwives", n. 3, *op. cit.,* p. 5.

THE NORMS BY WHICH FERTILITY IS REGULATED

1. Justice[7] places on free human beings who are living in the married state a primary obligation from which only "serious motives, grave reasons" that do not depend on the free choice of the interested parties, can dispense. This is *the obligation* of providing in so far as they are able, *for the continuation of the human race.* The reason for this is that, in Pius XII's own words:

> The marriage contract, which gives the spouses the right to satisfy the inclinations of nature, established them in a state of life, the married state . . .[8] [Now this] state of life, while conferring certain rights, at the same time imposes the accomplishment of a positive work which belongs to the very state of wedlock [namely, to provide for the continuation of the human race].[9]

It follows that, to enter into the married state, *to make constant use of the right it confers* and which is only lawful within the limits of this state, and yet to avoid always and of set purpose without a serious motive its principal obligation, would be a sin against the very meaning of married life,[1] an act of injustice towards the human race which has claims upon the partners.[2]

When insisting on this, the Pope had in mind not only contraceptive couples but even those who, although they use only the methods known as "natural", reach a point at which they have "the habitual intention to avoid the fruitfulness of the union, while at the same time continuing fully to satisfy sensual intent." [3]

2. So much for the obligation in justice towards the human race which limits the freedom of husband and wife. It remains to determine *the extent* to which they are under this obligation.

At this point, the virtues of love and prudence provide the regulative norms. The law of love itself demands of each married couple the largest possible number of children whom—when all has been considered in the light of the virtue of prudence—they are able not only to bring into the world under reasonable conditions but also

---

[7] Although Pius XII does not mention justice, paragraphs 34 and 35 of his "Address to Catholic Midwives" suggest that he had it in mind, since the human race has certain "claims" on married couples.

[8] "Address to Catholic Midwives", n. 35, *op. cit.*, p. 18.

[9] *Ibid.*, n. 34, p. 18.   [1] *Ibid.*, n. 35, p. 18.   [2] *Ibid.*, n. 34, p. 18.

[3] *Ibid.*, n. 36, p. 19.

to educate in a fitting manner. The home itself is the only judge of the extent to which it should reach this degree of fertility.

As a general rule, the number cannot be fixed in advance. "Normally it is some months after each birth that husband and wife reconsider the problem together. They must do so in a spirit of loyalty to their consciences and to God, without claiming that they are making decisions which are to be valid in perpetuity." [4]

Thus the question of the regulation of fertility is normally approached by an initial decision of husband and wife in regard to the reasonable *spacing* of births. The day eventually comes when, no less reasonably, they must envisage a definite *limitation* of the size of their family, it being understood however that any unexpected pregnancy will be accepted as a providential gift and lovingly accepted as such.

The motives which should inspire love and prudence in determining the degree of regulation desirable, normally come under the following heads:

—the mother's health,
—the health of the future child,
—financial and housing problems,
—education,
—domestic harmony.

If, as the proverb says, "Charity begins at home", it is also true that charity, once it has done its duty to those nearest to us, must then go out towards those furthest removed from us. We may therefore say that charity towards one's own country—which would find it in its own immediate interest either to increase or to slow down the growth of its population—must be taken into consideration. A nation can indirectly institute a population policy through this free decision of husbands and wives.

THE CHOICE OF THE MEANS

When husbands and wives have valid reasons for postponing births until a later date or even for fixing a definite limit, they then face the question of the choice of means. In this chapter we shall state purely and simply the Church's law and leave our commentary on the reasons underlying it for a subsequent chapter.

[4] P. MacAvoy, S.J., *Pour mieux aimer*, Collection "Foyers," Editions B.P., 1959, pp. 40-2.

Although this law was brought to the knowledge of the faithful principally in *Casti Connubii* (1930), it does not date from the promulgation of that Encyclical. It is already clearly formulated in the works of St Augustine who, in his interpretation of a passage from the Bible, writes: "Intercourse even with one's legitimate wife is unlawful and wicked where the conception of offspring is prevented. Onan, the son of Judah, did this and the Lord killed him for it." [5]

Pius XI quotes this text and continues:

> Since, therefore, openly departing from the uninterrupted Christian tradition some recently have judged it possible solemnly to declare another doctrine regarding this question, the Catholic Church, to whom God has entrusted the defence of the integrity and purity of morals, standing erect in the midst of the moral ruin which surrounds her, in order that she may preserve the chastity of the nuptial union from being defiled by this foul stain, raises her voice in token of her divine ambassadorship and through Our mouth proclaims anew: any use whatsoever of matrimony exercised in such a way that the act is deliberately frustrated in its natural power to generate life is an offence against the law of God and of nature, and those who indulge in such are branded with the guilt of a grave sin. [6]

Pius XII in his "Address to Catholic Midwives" (1951) also declares:

> Our Predecessor, Pius XI, in his Encyclical *Casti Connubii,* December 31st, 1930, solemnly proclaimed anew the fundamental law governing the marital act and conjugal relations; he said that any attempt on the part of the husband and wife to deprive this act of its inherent force or to impede the procreation of a new life, either in the performance of the act itself, or in the course of the development of its natural consequences, is immoral, and furthermore, no alleged "indication" or need can convert an intrinsically immoral act into a moral and lawful one.
>
> This precept is as valid today as it was yesterday, and it will be

---

[5] St Augustine, *De Conjug. Adult.,* L. II, No. 12; cf. Gen. 38. 8–10; S. Poenitent., 3 April, 3 June, 1916, quoted in *Casti Connubii,* p. 26, C.T.S.
[6] *Casti Connubii,* C.T.S., pp. 26 and 27.

the same tomorrow and always, because it does not imply a precept of human law but is the expression of a law which is natural and divine.[7]

Consequently every *contraceptive method* of spacing or limiting births is condemned by these declarations as we shall show more explicitly in the next chapter.

To those who wish to fall back on a *sterilization operation in order to achieve the same result*, Pius XI and Pius XII declared:

> Direct sterilization—that is, the sterilization which aims, either as a means or as an end in itself, to render child-bearing impossible —is a grave violation of the moral law, and therefore unlawful.[8]
> ... private individuals have no other power over the members of their bodies than that which pertains to their natural ends; and they are not free to destroy or mutilate their members, or in any other way render themselves unfit for their natural functions, except when no other provision can be made for the good of the whole body ... (as) Christian doctrine establishes and the light of human reason makes most clear.[9]

These principles [added Pius XII in a speech to the members of the International Congress of Haematology (12 September 1958] make it also possible to solve a problem which is much discussed today among doctors and moralists—is it permissible to prevent ovulation by means of pills which are used as remedies for excessive reactions of the uterus or the female organs, although this drug by preventing ovulation also makes pregnancy impossible?

If [said the Holy Father] the sterilization in question is *indirect* that is, if it is not, by definition, desired for its own sake, but is only accepted as one of the effects of the remedy which has to be used because of a disease of the uterus or the female organs, then this sterilization is permissible according to the general principle of actions with a double effect.

---

[7] "Address to Catholic Midwives," nn. 24–5, *op. cit.,* p. 15. Reaffirmation of the condemnation of "contraceptives" by Pius XII at the International Congress of Haematology (12 Sept. 1958 in D.C. 1958, No. 1287, c. 1244–5).

[8] "Address to Catholic Midwives", n. 27, *op. cit.,* p. 16.

[9] *Casti Connubii,* C.T.S., pp. 33–4. Pius XII made clear what was to be understood by the principle of totality and denounced certain abuses arising from a misunderstanding of this principle, in his speech to the 26th Congress of Urology, 8 Oct, 1953. Ed. *Casti Connubii,* Action Populaire, pp. 164–6.

But if the sterilization is *direct,* that is, if ovulation is deliberately stopped "so as to preserve the uterus and the female organs from a pregnancy which they are unable to tolerate", it is unlawful and, as the Pope makes clear, "Certain moralists claim that it is lawful to take drugs with this end in view (to prevent conception by preventing ovulation) but they are wrong." [1]

The only means recognized and approved by the Church for spacing births or for their permanent limitation, is abstinence from sexual intercourse on the part of husband and wife, in other words, continence. This continence is called *total* if husband and wife mutually agree to renounce absolutely all sexual intercourse. It is known as *prolonged* when such total abstinence is to last for a reasonably long period, and *periodic* under the conditions we are now about to describe.

PERIODIC CONTINENCE AND THE CONDITIONS
UNDER WHICH IT IS LAWFUL

We first recall what Pius XI had already laid down in *Casti Connubii*:

> Nor are those considered as acting against nature who in the married state use their right in the proper manner although on account of natural reasons either of time or of certain defects, new life cannot be brought forth. For in matrimony as well as in the use of matrimonial rights there are also secondary ends . . . which husband and wife are not forbidden to consider so long as they are subordinated to the primary end and so long as the intrinsic nature of the act is preserved.[2]

"If married people use their matrimonial rights even during the time of natural sterility, there is nothing to be said against it," Pius XII explained to the midwives:

> By so doing, they do not in any way prevent or prejudice the consummation of the natural act and its further natural consequences. It is precisely in this that the application of the theory we are discussing [consisting as it does in confining conjugal relations to these sterile days] is essentially distinct from the abuse of it already mentioned, which consists of a perversion of the act itself.[3]

---

[1] Pius XII to the International Congress of Haematology, 12 Sept. 1958. Doc. Cath. 1958, No. 1287, c. 1244.
[2] *Casti Connubii*, C.T.S., p. 28.
[3] "Address to Catholic Midwives," n. 31, *op. cit.,* p. 17.

The theory alluded to by the Pope is based on the fact that the Creator has willed that the female organs should rest for some eight or ten days after the work of ovulation in order to allow these organs to renew themselves and so to become once more ready to give life. To make it a rule to abstain from all inseminatory sexual relations on the days when the process of ovulation is in preparation or in progress, and to confine this type of relationship to the days which are certainly infertile[4] is what is known as the *method of periodic continence.*

The lawfulness of this method of spacing or even of limiting births is recognized by the Church "according as to whether or not the intention to keep constantly to these periods is based on sufficient and reliable moral grounds." [5] This is the sole condition since the method itself does not in any way interfere with nature and does not cause disorder in any of its structures or its dynamism. There is no blockage as in contraception, no mutilation as in sterilization.

Pius XII told the *Fronte della Famiglia* a month after his address to the midwives:

> This is why in our last allocution on conjugal morality We affirmed the legitimacy and at the same time defined the limits— and they are, in fact, very wide limits—of a form of *birth regulation* which, in contrast to what is known as "birth control" is compatible with God's law. It is even to be hoped (although in this matter the Church naturally trusts the judgment of medical science) that doctors will succeed in providing this lawful method with a sufficiently reliable basis, and the most recent information appears to confirm this hope.[6]

It is therefore obvious from this final wish of the Pope's that the "reliability" of a method does not itself contradict the principle of the regulation of fertility approved by the Church. On the contrary, regulation consists, as the word itself indicates, in foreseeing with the greatest possible degree of certainty those periods at which husband and wife will fulfil their "obligation of placing themselves

[4] Contrary to what is too often said in popular pamphlets on the so-called "Rhythm" method, the only period in the woman's monthly cycle, normally to be considered as infertile, is the period of 8 to 10 days after ovulation.

[5] "Address to Catholic Midwives", n. 33, *op. cit.,* p. 18. Pius XII reiterated this teaching in his speech to the International Congress of Haematology (12 Sept. 1958), D.C., 1958, No. 1287, c. 1245.

[6] Pius XII to the *Fronte della Famiglia*, 26 Nov. 1951, Ed. *Casti connubii,* Action Populaire, p. 170.

at the service of motherhood" and the periods during which for valid reasons they will avoid this obligation whilst continuing to practise intercourse in those ways which the resources of nature place at their disposal.[7]

It only remains to be said that the regulation approved by the Church presupposes a special divine power infused by charity into the whole psychic organism of husband and wife. This power is known as the "virtue (dynamism) of chastity".

THE VIRTUE OF CHASTITY

Whilst the contemporary world preaches that "eroticism" is a force that leads to the growth and development of the couple, and under the name of "perfect marriage"[8] teaches a refined cultivation of mutual pleasure in the marriage act, the Catholic Church declares:

"Make it clear that nature has undoubtedly given the instinctive desire for pleasure and sanctioned it in lawful wedlock, not as an end in itself, but in the service of life," [9] of family life which makes continual demands on the devotion of the married couple. "Consequently, the husband and wife do no wrong in seeking out and enjoying this pleasure. They are accepting what the Creator intended for them." [1]

Some would like to maintain that happiness in married life is in direct ratio to the mutual enjoyment of marital relations. This is not so. On the contrary, happiness in married life is in direct ratio to the respect the husband and wife have for each other, even in the intimate act of marriage. Not that they should regard what nature offers them and God has given them as immoral, and refuse it, but because the respect and mutual esteem which arise from it, are one of the strongest elements of a love which is all the more pure because it is the more tender.[2]

---

[7] Cf. *infra* pp. 148, note 4, 160, note 7, 210, note 3.

[8] *Casti Connubii*, C.T.S., pp. 54 and 55. There is an allusion here to Dr Th. H. Van de Velde's book, *Ideal Marriage*, which has been placed on the Index.

[9] "Address to Catholic Midwives," n. 67, *op. cit.*, p. 29.

[1] *Ibid.*, n. 59, p. 26.

[2] *Ibid.*, n. 66, p. 28.

It is precisely with this special *pleasure in love and affection* that chastity permeates married love and even sexuality. And so much so that whilst sexual cupidity is overcome, love does not grow less but, on the contrary, increases.

SUMMARY OF THE CATHOLIC CHURCH'S POSITION

If we had to define the Catholic Church's position in one sentence, we should choose the following from the "Address to Catholic Midwives":

If the exclusive aim of nature, or at least its primary aim, had been the mutual giving and possessing of husband and wife in joy and delight; if nature had arranged that act only to make their personal experience [as husband and wife] happy in the highest possible degree, and not as an incentive in the service of life [to procreate and then educate], then the Creator would have made use of another plan in the formation and constitution of the natural act.

(In other words, the structure and dynamism of this act would not have been those of a process of insemination.)

Instead, the act is completely subordinate and ordered to the great and unique law *generatio et educatio prolis* (the generating and educating of children), that is, to the fulfilment of the primary end of marriage as the origin and source of life.[3]

As G. Thibon has written: "The proof of our love for one another lies in the love we share for another person." Only a love which always desires to create can renew the joy of mutual possession. And it is also true that only a deep mutual love can meet all the demands of a will to create which is willing to assume to the full its duties as an educative force.

[3] *Ibid.*, n. 62, p. 27.

II. *THE REGULATION OF FERTILITY AS IT AFFECTS THE CONSCIENCES OF THOSE IN PUBLIC AUTHORITY*

The Catholic Church obviously speaks in the first place to the consciences of individuals responsible for their own personal and family life. But she does not neglect the consciences of those who govern and are responsible for the temporal and, indirectly, the eternal life of their subjects. She lays upon them the obligation of finding solutions for the problems of population, health and euge- nics, compatible with the moral norms governing birth regulation as we have stated them above.

The most recent teaching of the Roman *magisterium* in this sphere can be grouped round two great principles:

1. *No policy which attacks life and the normal means by which it is transmitted can be tolerated.*

2. *What is essential is a policy of international solidarity.*

THERE MUST BE NO POLICY WHICH ATTACKS LIFE . . .

Already in *Casti Connubii* Pius XI had warned public authorities against the temptation to resort to sterilization policies under the pretext of a national eugenic movement. He wrote:

Public magistrates have no direct power over the bodies of their subjects; therefore, where no crime has taken place and there is no cause present for grave punishment, they can never directly harm, or tamper with the integrity of the body, either for the reasons of eugenics or for any other reason.[4]

Pius XII, in his message to the 26th Italian Social Week, restated this teaching and made it more precise by extending it to all *contra- ceptive policies.*

No solution to demographic problems can be considered just and genuine, if it does not take into account, as it should, the sacred and unassailable value of human life, or forgets to respect in any way the norms which govern its proper transmission. It is therefore a crime—that cannot be justified for reasons of State

[4] *Casti Connubii*, C.T.S., p. 33.

or on the pretext of eugenics or economics—to attack life on its way from the parents to the cradle. We must include under the term "attack" not only the direct murder of the innocent child, but also all fraudulent interference with the intentions of nature which, as such, are the expression of the Creator's will. . . .

Therefore efforts to re-establish the balance between the means of subsistence and the increase in population must not be directed towards a violation of the laws of life nor towards the retrenchment of the human family's natural momentum.[5]

"Overpopulation is not a valid reason for propagating the unlawful practices of birth control."[6]

A POLICY OF INTERNATIONAL SOLIDARITY

To quote Pius XII again:

It would be more rational and more useful for modern society to apply itself with greater resolution and on a world-wide scale to reforming its own conduct by eliminating the causes of famine in "depressed" or overpopulated areas, by more actively utilizing our modern discoveries for peaceful purposes, by adopting a more open policy of collaboration and exchange and a more broad-minded, less nationalistic economy; above all, by resisting the suggestions of egoism with charity, those of avarice with a more concrete application of the principles of justice.[7]

More recently John XXIII said:

Unfortunately the problem of hunger is still a grave one for a large section of mankind . . . The wealth yielded by the earth must be placed at the disposal of all men as God's command and justice both demand. Let us improve the methods of distribution of the good things of this world, let us throw down the barriers of egoism and self-interest, let us study the most appropriate way to help the underdeveloped areas, let us endeavour to win from the earth

---

[5] Letter of Mgr Montini to the 26th Italian Social Week, Doc. Cath., 1953, col. 1556–7.
[6] Pius XII to the Italian members of the Large Families Associations, 20 Jan. 1958, Doc. Cath., 16 Feb. 1958, col. 203.
[7] Pius XII to the Large Families Associations, Doc. Cath., 1958, col. 203.

the incalculable resources that still lie hidden within it and which it can provide for the benefit of all.[8]

On the other hand, the Catholic Church warns us against the tendency to regard increase in population as the greatest evil threatening humanity and which "leads to the belief that the only solution lies in birth limitation".[9] The letter concludes:

Even if this or that region has an excessive population, it would be wrong to blame natural laws for the present difficulties when it is obvious that these are due to the lack of solidarity between men and nations.[1]

The overpopulation in question is a pretext to justify the avarice and egoism either of those nations who fear that the expansion of others will threaten their own political hegemony and lower their own standard of living, or of individuals, especially the more wealthy, who prefer to enjoy a greater quantity of earthly goods rather than win the glory and merit of bringing new lives into the world.

There can be no doubt that the problem of the world's overpopulation has arisen and remains unsolved not because of inertia on the part of Providence or any flaw in its plans, but because of disorder in man—especially his egoism and avarice. Overpopulation is partly a real contemporary fact and partly an irrational fear of some catastrophe hanging over modern society.[2]

According to circumstances, the teaching of the Popes has gone into greater detail concerning the economic and demographic objectives to be proposed to the community of nations. It is above all a question "of bringing about a more systematic *circulation* of peoples, capital and material goods, a more equitable *distribution* of goods".[3] But it is also a question of "exploiting the resources of nature in an increasingly rational way".[4]

---

[8] John XXIII, Speech to the Consistory, 14 Dec. 1959, Doc. Cath., 3 Jan. 1960.
[9] Mgr Montini's letter, *op. cit.*, col. 1555.
[1] Mgr Montini's letter, *op. cit.*, col. 1557.
[2] Pius XII to the Large Families Associations, *op. cit.*, col. 203.
[3] Mgr Montini's letter, *op. cit.*, col. 1556–7.
[4] Pius XII to the members of the F.A.O., 23 Nov. 1953, Doc. Cath. 1954, c. 503–4.

In 1953 the Pope said to the members of the F.A.O.:

> Efforts will doubtless be made to channel towards the under-
> nourished peoples, who represent 70% of the world's population,
> the excess products of more favoured countries, by making certain
> that the latter have stable markets. But what is far more urgent
> is to see that *production is increased* in the very places where
> scarcity makes itself felt.[5]

There follows a whole plan for the organization and improvement
of agricultural production. In 1955 the Sovereign Pontiff returned
to the same subject and congratulated the F.A.O. on its work for
the preservation of the soil and of forests, together with its "researches, which, with many others, have gone into the possibility of
using seaweed as human food, although the exploitation of these
resources seems up to the present to be difficult to realize".[6]
But all these admirable efforts will stand a chance of success only
if the different States endeavour to enlighten public opinion among
their peoples "by awakening in a large number of individuals a
sense of collective responsibility and so initiate enlightened and
generous schemes of assistance".[7]

A man who wishes to safeguard the fertility of his own land
must interest himself in what is happening far beyond its boundaries. Indeed, *the nations favoured by nature* or by the progress
of civilization run the risk of experiencing one day a rude awakening if they do not take the trouble here and now to ensure that
those less fortunate than themselves are given the means to achieve
a standard of life worthy of men and a chance to further their
own development.[8]

Yet, at the same time, *these less fortunate nations* must be persuaded to agree on their part to make better use of their own natural
resources. This aim, Pius XII noted,

> certainly raises unusual difficulties of which the most hard to
> overcome will be the creation of social conditions that will induce
> the workers, whom you will help and advise, to acquire a liking

[5] Pius XII to the F.A.O., *ibid.*
[6] Pius XII to the F.A.O., 10 Nov. 1955, Doc. Cath., 1955, c. 1488–91.
[7] Pius XII to the F.A.O., 10 Nov. 1955, *op. cit.*, c. 1491.
[8] Pius XII to the F.A.O., 10 Nov. 1955, *op. cit.*, c. 1490–1.

for their task, to interest themselves in it and to exploit to the full the resources provided for them. It is useless of course to send experts to teach the new methods and to perfect mechanical equipment if the human conditions in which men live prevent them from obtaining from their labour the fruits they have a right to expect.[9]

To arouse interest and personal initiative, to show that the good of the community will not be brought about at the expense of the good of the individual but for his benefit, to take care that this should in fact be the case—all this is certainly of primary importance if success is to be achieved.[1]

The Catholic Church also asks that to the different measures enumerated above should be added an effort "to encourage *migration* to areas which have not yet been sufficiently developed. This would ease the heavy burden of unemployment." There are few problems to which Pius XII returned more insistently. He formulated the conditions necessary for a successful settling of individuals and their families in countries which accept immigrants and the conditions required if these immigrants are to receive a proper welcome from the resident population.[2]

To sum up the doctrinal position of the Catholic Church as regards population increases in the modern world and inadequate adjustments in the spheres of economics and food supplies—

In a reformed social order founded on moral principles, there is no room for narrow egoistic calculation whose object is to acquire for oneself the economic sources of the raw materials in common use and in such a way that the nations least favoured by nature cannot obtain them.

It therefore follows that an adequate study of the relations between density of population and the means of subsistence should tend to develop on a world-wide scale. The problem with which it deals can only be solved at the same level by the active solidarity of all the nations so that, once the artificial barriers that divide them are destroyed, there may result a more regular circulation of peoples, capital and material goods.

[9] Pius XII to the F.A.O., 10 Nov. 1955, *op. cit.*, c. 1491.
[1] *Ibid.*
[2] Pius XII to the B.I.T., 25 March 1949, D.C., 1949, c. 455. To the 31st Canadian Social Week, Sept. 1954; to the International Catholic Migration Mission (5 June 1951).

Through this subordination of the national economic welfare of particular nations to the common good of the society of States, frontiers will cease to be dikes that separate, they will become bridges which unite, and material goods will thus be able to fulfil their natural function of satisfying the needs of all.[3]

[3] Mgr Montini's letter, *op. cit.*, col. 1556.

Chapter X

THE RATIONAL BASIS OF THE CHURCH'S POSITION

Now that we have pointed out the natural and supernatural values of marriage, love and sexuality which the Church wishes to safeguard, now too that we have described the doctrinal position of Catholicism in regard to fertility regulation, this attitude must be justified by reason enlightened by faith. The essence of the argument lies in showing the balance and harmony that exist between the various statements of the *magisterium* and in revealing also the order of values and the hierarchy of the factors involved.

Man's life spans what Pascal called the three orders—the order of biological nature, the order of personality and liberty, and finally the order of participation in the mystery of the Godhead. On these three planes man's life moves in a rhythm which leads him beyond himself so that he may enter into relationship with a person other than himself, and in communion with this other person, discover himself anew in a third.[1]

THE LEVEL OF BIOLOGICAL NATURE

At the level of biological nature, the sexual function has the task of regulating the vital rhythm destined to ensure reproduction. Sexuality is present in man, as in the rest of the higher animal species, according to a pattern which links the dimorphous factors to those of copulation and the latter to those of reproduction.

Sexual Factors

1. Factors based on differentiation: sexual dimorphism.
2. Conjunctive factors: sexual intercourse.
3. Creative factors: reproduction, upbringing.

What remains exclusively instinctive in the animal species assumes in the human race a psychic character, which, while making the

[1] S. de Lestapis, S.J., "Sexualité et valeurs de la personne," in *l'Anneau d'Or*, No. 43, Jan., Feb. 1952, pp. 14–21. By the same author: *Les vraies valeurs de la vie conjugale (discours du S. Père Pie XII aux sages-femmes)*, note (35), pp. 62–5.

sexual mechanisms more flexible, leaves them unaltered in their essence. Sexuality, for instance, establishes in the whole psycho-somatic human organism a kind of stimulus characteristic of each sex and capable of continually increasing the whole masculine and feminine potential. Genetic sexuality (chromosomal) clearly and unmistakably differentiates the whole cellular system of man and woman. Physiological and anatomical sexuality normally complete the dimorphic constitution of the human race. Although it cannot be said that man and woman form two different "species", it is abso-lutely essential to recognize that they form two distinct types. There is negative proof of this in the fact that castration, by removing the power to reproduce, lowers to a certain extent the vital tone even of the intellectual and social faculties. It would seem that nature has arranged that the arousing of genetic sensitivity should serve, through the mediation of the brain, as a stimulus and a "hormone" for a great many psychic characteristics.[2]

There is another negative proof—people suffering from what are known as "the intersexual states" are manifestly unstable even in the realm of personality. The unity of the living creature demands that this should be so. There is no realm, no organ, no cell which is beyond the power and influence of sexuality. This fact we may recognize as an advantage, as a value which moreover is the basis of the order of differentiation, of the opposite characteristics of man and woman. Each sex, because it is in contrast with the other, becomes aware of itself and of its own definition.

But sexuality goes further than this. It establishes in the individual "a permanent impulse which, when sufficiently exteriorized in normal behaviour leads in the adult to the desire, then to the possi-bility, of copulation. This impulse in the individual . . . determines a specific sensual pleasure known as genital pleasure."[3] This is another value of an order apparently superior to the first. The copu-lation relationship or the possibility of copulation indeed accounts for the existence of dimorphism which is not sufficiently self-ex-planatory. It also facilitates hormonal interactions of benefit to both sexes.[4]

The process however is not fully complete unless reproduction

---

[2] Jean Guitton, *Essay on Human Love*, London, Rockliff, 1951.

[3] A. Hesnard, *Traité de sexologie*, p. 431; *Cahiers Laënnec*, "Les états intersexuels," 1947.

[4] Dr M. Dugast Rouillé, *Etude médicale sur la physiologie de l'acte sexuel, ou conditions de l'Eupareunie,* Ed. du Levain, 1959, Ch. III, para 4; "Impul-sions sexuelles et échanges hormonaux," pp. 99–111, 191–3.

results. It is towards this that sexuality tends from the outset, and from which it receives its own true, final and specific value. By comparison with the value represented by the production of a new being, the development of individuals brought about by the diffusion of their sexuality throughout their organism and even by the fact of copulation, remains in fact of secondary importance. Dimorphism and copulation are only, in a final analysis, the necessary preliminaries needed for the end in view which is written into the very development of the natural function, that is, reproduction.[5]

THE LEVEL OF PERSONALITY AND CONSCIOUSNESS

If we now move to the plane of personality or, more concretely, of consciousness, we see that men and women are called upon to reach a relational state of knowledge and love specifically reserved to beings endowed with spiritual characteristics. We note too that this relational order, this intersubjectivity will develop with a rhythm remarkably like that of sexuality itself, but operating, as it were, an octave higher.[6]

[5] Paul Chauchard, *La vie sexuelle*, in the series "Que sais-je?" P.U.F., 1957: "Animal sexual life is an automatic system whose object is fertilization and which limits sexual activity to the time when it is likely to prove useful for this purpose" (p. 38).

[6] The celebrated ethnologist Malinowski, in his book *Sex and Repression in Savage Society* (Kegan Paul, French, Trubner, 1927) compares sexual relations amongst animals with those amongst men and women. He makes the following observations:
What does the absence of rut in man signify? (p. 198). . . . Instead of an automatic physiological mechanism, we have a complicated arrangement into which artificial elements are introduced (p. 196). The modes of behaviour associated with sex interest are determined in man only as regards their ends: man must mate selectively. . . . On the other hand, the release of the impulse, the inducement to courtship, the motives for a definite selection are dictated by cultural arrangements. These arrangements have to follow certain lines parallel to the lines of natural endowment in the animal. There must be an element of selection, there must be taboos which prevent sex from constantly interfering in ordinary life (p. 200).
Instead of the precise instinctive determinants, we have cultural elements which shape the innate tendencies. All this implies a deep change in the relation between instinct and physiological process and the modification of which they are capable. This change we have termed the "plasticity of instincts" (p. 226). . . . As we know, all these cultural co-determinants closely follow the general course imposed by nature on animal behaviour. . . . *Thus culture does not lead man into any direction divergent from the course of nature* . . . p. 227). ". . . Custom law, moral law, ritual and religious value enter into all the stages of love-making and parenthood. But the main line of their action invariably runs parallel to that of animal instincts. *The chain of responses which regulate animal mating constitute a prototype of the gradual unfolding and ripening of man's cultural attitude*" (p. 228). (Italics are Fr Lestapis's.)

F.P.M.P.—6*

Love and its Values

1. Its value in the field of differentiation: the autonomy of the person.

2. Its value as a unitive force: the mutual conscious relationship.

3. Its value as a creative force: the creative will of the partners.

It is of the nature of personality to begin by establishing itself in an absolutely singular, original and distinct way. This is its first "value". Animals are interchangeable, persons are not. There is more in this than biological dimorphism, there is the autonomy which constitutes the "ego".

But there is more in personality than this. Although autonomous it is essentially altruistic, that is, it is orientated towards the "other". "Solipsism" (or an exclusive absorption with self) is absurd and self-contradictory, for personality is "reciprocal", that is, it wants the "other" both for the "other's" sake and for its own. The mutual relationship of conscious persons brings with it both the enrichment of the self by the "other" and the self's desire to forward the development of the "other". This is a second value. It is not superior to the former one (personal differentiation) but it helps to make it complete, yet only imperfectly if the relationship goes no further than this.

For mutual relationship in its turn must avoid becoming bogged down in a "dual solipsism". There is nothing more dubious than this dual solipsism, nothing more unstable, more regressive for, in the full sense of the word, there are in it *two contrary forces* at work, "You-for-me" and "I-for-you". Suppose, for example, that "You-for-me" becomes the rule of life for a given couple. Immediately there is conflict. One of the two strives to use the other in his own interests. Mutual love then regresses towards a form of servitude. Or again, the "You-for-me" attitude may tolerate neither victor nor vanquished and so breaks down. Divorce follows and each lives only for self; love is dead.

Suppose, on the contrary, that in the interplay of personalities "I-for-you" is the rule and inspiration of the relationship. Then, by the same token, the latter turns from an unstable "dual solipsism" and suddenly bursts its bonds. By virtue of its inner dynamic force in which the order of nature and the order of personality move along parallel lines, the mutual relationship spontaneously expresses its own inherent desire, as though it would thus testify with all its being to the fact that "You-for-me" and "I-for-you" are no longer sufficient. The rule must be "Both-of-us-for-another".

Should not the mutual joy each feels in the other and in his or her love become a kind of self-subsisting common denominator of whom it may be said "We are he"? And "he" is love's third and supreme value.

So the mutual relationship has suddenly discovered that it is spiritually pregnant with all those "others" whom, unbeknown to itself, it bears within its womb. Mutual spiritual relationship can no more be satisfied with its essential unity than can sexual copulation with its momentary union. The logic of the situation makes it feel that it is transcended by an immanent creative impulse.

Maurice Blondel has written:

> The miracle of generation provides a factual indication of what should be and is the fundamental wish of those who hope to find in their unstable unity a moment of rest, satisfaction and fulfilment. When we pursue an aim that inspires our love, it is not so much the aim that is loved as the fruit with which our aim, made fertile by our love, will enrich those who spend themselves on its behalf. Thus our will seems ever to transcend itself, as though new waves issuing from the centre are ceaselessly thrusting forward ever widening circles of action, of an action that seems at every moment to be the final perfection of a new world.[7]

Thus, at the levels of nature and of personality, of sexuality and of love, there is the one single mysterious plan of God whereby he wills to make his rational creatures in their turn creators of persons.

This is because in the sphere of those relations which, according to the Creator's plan, are to exist between human persons, it is for the active work of generation alone to reveal the full meaning of the unity of love. It is the task of this creative work and of the children to which it gives birth to open the way for the altruism of mutual love to become an altruism of still wider scope, and this too

[7] Maurice Blondel, *L'Action*, 1893, p. 254. See also our essay *Amour et Institution Familiale*, Spes, 1947, pp. 133–5.

is according to God's plan.[8] It is only the enthusiastic welcome given to a third person as a gift from God, which, in the final analysis, can change the "closed" and self-sufficient love of husband and wife into a love that is willing to be used and that lies open to God's good pleasure, into a love linked with God, a religious love. Without this "open" character and this transcendence permanently maintained in mutual love and in its natural substratum, sexuality, married love cannot claim to be made in God's image.

[8] G. Madinier in particular has well analysed the false stability of a wedded love closed in upon itself. "We all know that love may draw a circle around man and wife. To make this clear we will take as an example a couple who have succeeded in becoming a We-community closed in on itself, full of affection and well-being but in which the gift of life is cautiously measured out. Both husband and wife subordinate their individual convenience to that of the We-community and this is doubtless proof of their mutual devotion. Yet in so far as the We-community serves them rather than they serve it, this reciprocal egoism is, as we realize, based to that extent on pleasure. Each, though perhaps without realizing it, treats the other as a means and, in our view, they do not form a genuine unity. And this is because authentic love, as we have said, is the love of being . . . This love desires the enrichment and perfection of the other person, desires it to possess all the being of which it is capable, to develop its own freedom and its own creative powers. Thus each of the married partners enriches the other by giving children to him or to her. The other partner is loved and desired as a (creative) *subject*. The resultant unity is a unity of subjects in their own right and is defined by the dialogue between, and the mutual relationship of persons who are present to each other, and by the inner union of their personalities. Love will not become the force that generates being and the unity of the inner heart of two personalities if it seeks a shared pleasure and a reciprocal egoism. Pleasure is the bearer of solitude, it leaves us to ourselves. The point to grasp is that two beings who want to be one in the depths of their souls, and even in their freedom, will never achieve this except by sharing in a common activity. It is into activity that I enter as a subject in my own right and so can be one with another as a subject in his or her own right. This fact needs to be carefully studied. There is communion through an activity but an activity that transcends the subjects who share in it. If there is to be a true intimate relationship, each must come into contact with the very ground of the other's existence. *There is no truly intimate relationship without our giving ourselves together to something transcendent which in me is something more than my own personal self.* In the first place this will be the natural (if we may use the expression) transcendent reality of the home which husband and wife are in the process of founding and which they wish to be fertile. . . . But it will also be . . . the idea which in their view justifies life, gives it its value and its meaning. *We must not be surprised if there can be no truly intimate relationship except through our united gift of self to another person since—we repeat—our being is not a thing, but an activity, and because activities are linked with one another by coalescing around the impulse which actuates them and the end which determines the direction in which they move.* It is by giving themselves to a work undertaken in common—in so far as this work is fundamentally that of a Love which transcends them both—that husband and wife become one" (G. Madinier, "Spiritualité et biologie dans le mariage," in *Limitation des naissances et conscience chrétienne*, Ed. Familiales de France, 1950, pp. 199-201.

Married love can only truly give birth to a person if it is moved from within by "a creative will (*vœu créateur*)", that is, by the sense "of participation in a work of life, infinitely beyond him and yet requiring his contribution as an essential element which nothing can replace." With Gabriel Marcel, we hold that the man who desires to have a child to take his place, or to compensate him one day for his own personal disappointments, automatically cuts himself off from the whole realm of transcendence, for this child is for him only one factor, or, as we may say, a trump card in the closed system which the father forms with himself. The situation changes from the moment when he has truly understood that what he has received is in reality nothing but the reflection, the analogue of a creative gift which in itself cannot belong to him. I can no more give existence to someone else "than I can to myself". The creative will inherent in married love . . . "negatively signifies that our child no more belongs to us than we do to ourselves and that accordingly he is not there for our sake, nor, to go a degree further, is he there for his own sake either. . . . It would indeed be contradictory on my part to admit for him what I deny for myself."

The creative will issuing spontaneously from the mutual love of husband and wife is nothing other than a *fiat*, the ardent "Yes" with which we accept a vocation, a call reaching us from beyond ourselves. "This means that the *vœu*, far from being reduced to a mere wish, has the character of an engagement and a decision. But this engagement or this decision is not made simply within my own being, something transcendent is involved, however indistinct my consciousness of it may as yet be."[9]

This amounts to saying that the married union is procreative only under the sign, implicitly at least, of the transcendent Author of all existence. In the final analysis, the creative will may be defined in relation to the eternal subsistent being of God and in terms of his presence in which we actively share. It is by plunging its roots into God's eternity that the will of husband and wife takes shape and comprehends itself as a hope going beyond all ambition and all personal claims. Love does not produce the child, it expresses the wish to have the child and this means that husband and wife undertake to place all their powers at the service of a possibility which already compels them to recognize its eternal values.

[9] Marcel, *Homo viator, op. cit.*, pp. 118–20.

THE LEVEL OF OUR PARTICIPATION
IN THE MYSTERY OF GOD

The relational order established between human persons by love is but the shadow of that transcendent order which God himself is, for "God", as St John tells us, "*is* love". Further, the human relational order is a participation in the divine order at least for those who "are born of God" by faith, for those who are connected to that divine current of love that comes down from heaven to earth through Jesus Christ.

So that man may be in his image and likeness, God makes him, at the creature level, a trinitarian being. Contrary to the suppositions of agnostic positivism, which is unable to unravel its own metaphysical implications, there is reason to think that the relations between the Divine Persons are in no way the product of a kind of sublimation of human relationships. The exact opposite is true. It is human relationships which, in the course of history, have discovered their own transcendent laws, under the active influence of the revelation through Christianity of the most intimate relations existing in the heart of the Godhead. And revelation teaches us that God is a Trinity of Love.

The Mystery of God

1. God is Three Persons—the mystery of differentiation.

2. God is a Father generating his Son, who is his perfect reflection and image—the mystery of *mutual relationship*.

3. God is the Father and Son from whom proceeds the Spirit in a "spiration" which is uncreated, eternal, inseparable from the generation of the Word—the mystery of *fecundity*.

As Richard of Saint-Victor wrote:

In paternal and filial love, I begin by distinguishing two contrary currents, but in this quest for someone to love I see only one single, unique current flowing towards one single, identical goal. It is as though two powerful waves rushing with full force towards one another, should meet, lose themselves in one another and then hurl themselves from their sea-bed in one immense column.[1]

[1] Richard of Saint-Victor, *De Trinitate*, P.L. 196, Lib. III, no. 19. Cf. Th. de Régnon, S.J., *Etudes de théologie positive sur la Sainte Trinité*, vol. II, pp. 291–332.

Fr Devaux comments:

And so we arrive at a paradox. God, the most absolute of all beings, is reduced, if we may use the term, to a Trinity of pure relations, and Being is none other than the gift of itself. The fact that man is created in the image of God implies first and foremost that he is able to give himself and demands the presence of a partner with whom he may enter into relationship.[2]

This also implies that from this mutual relationship and from this mutual union, others can issue (proceed).

The human race, in so far as it is made up of individuals who are also persons, is called upon to organize itself into a society of persons, into a community of those who share the same destiny, which in the end is identical with the very Life of God himself. Hence, besides the natural duty which the human species has to live and to reproduce itself, it is also obliged in conscience, by virtue of the fact that it is made in the image of God, to live its life in a pattern of relationship whose model is to be found in God, the Trinity of Persons. With this end in view it has received the gratuitous gift of the indwelling within it of the Divine Persons, according to Christ's words: "If a man has any love for me, he will be true to my word; and then he will win my Father's love, and we will both come to him, and make our continual abode with him" (John 14. 23).

And so the three Divine Persons will imprint upon the Christian, who has been regenerated by God's free gift, the pattern of their most intimate relationships. Human personal relationships will become supernaturalized. Human love and friendship will be impregnated with divine charity. Social relations in general and those of the married and of the family community in particular will be given a new value, the very value of the Divine Life itself. As St Paul declares: "And therefore, henceforward, we do not think of anybody in a merely human fashion . . . when a man becomes a new creature in Christ, his old life has disappeared, everything has become new about him" (2 Cor. 5. 16–17).

[2] Éloi Devaux, "Le paradoxe de l'amour," quoted in *L'Anneau d'Or*, "Mystère et Mystique du mariage," Nos. 51-2 (May, Aug. 1953), p. 215.

THE THREE PLANES ARE IN HARMONY: THE
LAW OF CHRISTIAN ANTHROPOLOGY

So stands revealed the wonderful scale of Being, beginning at the lower level of the creature and its functional nature, rising to the level of personality and the human community and then to the level of the Creator and the mystery of his Divine Relationships which, moreover, are communicated to man. So there is made manifest on each occasion, and at each plane of being, a dynamic force and a hierarchy of analogical values, rising from individuality and autonomy to union and mutual relationship, then from union and mutual relationship to the will by which a third person is created, and to permanent devotion towards him.

Thus in the secret places of the most profound mysteries we find the prototype of that vital rhythm which leads from singleness of individuality to differentiation in communion, from the mutual relationship of husband and wife to their final fruitfulness.

Such then is the wonderful order of creation and it has been raised to still greater heights by the Incarnation which redeems us. It is not for man to change this order, to overthrow it or reverse it at his pleasure. In whatever realm—that of spirituality, that of the organism of the psyche, that of sexuality, the human race is bound to keep to the objective norms with which it is equipped by this general pattern of being. The flesh must be for the spirit, the spirit for the Mystery of God, and this cannot be so except we preserve the hierarchy of factors or values in each of these three orders.

We delude ourselves if we claim to remain in friendship with God, to share in him by grace, whilst at the same time we disturb the order of human relations by lying or theft. In a similar way, we also delude ourselves if we claim to derive an authentic personal enrichment by disturbing the natural order of sexuality and by preventing the genital function from doing its work, and this in the interests of the inherent pleasure of intercourse. Husband and wife delude themselves yet more if they claim that by acting in this way they can still please God. No, the three orders must remain in harmony with each other so that the hierarchal integration of human activities aimed at by Christian anthropology may be made possible. Christian anthropology, which was defined long ago by St Irenaeus in the second century, demands that the "human composite" should achieve its ultimate destiny by respecting at each stage

—body, psyche, spirit (pneuma)—the movement of the *ek-stasis,* that is, the gift of self (and not the absorption of self) which maintains the balance of our nature.

It is by their common will to devote themselves generously to their children that husband and wife will most certainly discover the secret of living their married life together in harmony. On the other hand, if they take an opposite course they often delude themselves, for by seeking above all else conjugal and sexual adjustment, the partners run the risk of introducing into their attitude of mind and their behaviour a principle of egocentricity, even of egoism, which threatens the spontaneity of love and devotion which the good of the child demands. And so we have no hesitation in insisting that the values which dominate the whole issue are, beyond all doubt, the *creative will,* and *the care given to the upbringing* of the children.

But we must bear in mind that these supreme and primal values, if they are to be what Nature and Grace expect them to be, are not intended to suppress but, on the contrary, to presuppose the values we call secondary, that is, the mutual understanding between, and the personal development of husband and wife. These secondary values offer in fact the best conditions for bringing into play those that are primary. This is abundantly proved as a result of recent progress in the sciences of child and educational psychology. When husband and wife do not genuinely love one another, or do not try to further one another's personal development, the upbringing of the children is seldom a success.[3] This is a negative proof that enables us to understand more clearly that the married union is *for the sake* of the child. "The child is father of the man", it has been said, to show to what extent care for the child changes a man for the better and brings him fulfilment by calling upon him constantly to transcend himself. We might also say: "the creative will which gives life to the child is the father of married love" and by this we should mean that husband and wife only love one another genuinely and as they ought, if they help each other to be loving and disinterested parents.

There is an ancient axiom in Aristotelian philosophy which states that the final cause—generally revealed by the last of its effects to appear—is the primary determinant of a whole process. Thus, for instance, it is the grape, which comes last, that shows what the vine is ultimately for, although the leaves, necessary as they are for the rest of the process of growth, are the first to appear. We are thus

[3] Dr François Goust, "L'amour peut-il survivre au mariage?" Conférence au Centre Catholique d'Education familiale, 1959.

justified in saying that it is the final cause which really gives the primary reason for a process. It is very curious that this remains true, even when this final end is not fulfilled because of some accident or irrational intervention. When Christ cursed the barren fig tree, it was because a fig tree, even when barren, is still a fig tree, created to bear figs. When a man born blind deplores the fact that he cannot see, it is because he assumes that every eye, even his own, is made to see. But to conclude, as some do, that because there are, unfortunately, childless couples, love and sexuality are orientated to a final end other than the child, is a very odd misconception. It is as though a blind man imagined that because he cannot see, his eye is made first and foremost to weep or to give correct proportions to the face.

Pius XII said:

> If the exclusive aim of nature, or at least its primary aim, had been the mutual giving and possessing of husband and wife in joy and delight; if nature had arranged that act only to make their personal experience [as husband and wife] happy in the highest possible degree, and not as an incentive in the service of life [to procreate and then to educate], then the Creator would have made use of another plan in the formation and constitution of the natural act.[4]

The sexual act would not have been essentially an act of insemination, if fertility had not been its ultimate, that is, its fundamental purpose, rather than the mutual development of husband and wife alone. It is, in fact, from an objective observation of the process and genesis of a human act, that Reason can identify the final purpose of this act, and conclude that the previous phases are subordinate to it.

In reality, human sexuality, since it is both biological and psychological, is entirely subordinated to and orientated towards the will which is immanent within it, the will to bring forth a new personal life. And this is its own supreme value. As figs are not a supplementary "bonus" or a "bounty" given to a fig tree which is considered as destined to exercise only the chlorophyllian function through its leaves, so too the child is not merely a supplementary "bonus" or a "bounty" attached to a function which is considered as destined to be only the sexual activity of husband and wife.

[4] Pius XII, "Address to Catholic Midwives," n. 62, *op. cit.*, p. 27.

Hence it is outrageous to write that the sexual relationship and marriage can claim validity *apart from procreation.* If we think for a moment, this is as outrageous as to write that the function of the organs of taste and salivation can claim validity *apart from mastication.* Because a dog whose stomach has been amputated still continues to salivate, this is no reason for stating that salivation has nothing to do with the assimilation of food or, still less, that it is not subordinated to it.

Some may reply that, in the course of evolution, functions may change their purpose.[5] An example is the tongue, whose primary object in the animal kingdom is deglutition, but which, as the result of the cultural evolution of mankind, has succeeded in adding to its purely biological objective a new, relational purpose—speech, the exchange of ideas. Man may indeed use his tongue for this relational purpose without at the same time bothering to try to make it fulfil its biological purpose—deglutition. Similarly, why should not the married couple have the right to use the sexual function in order "to express themselves" and "to get to know one another" without bothering about the biological purpose—procreation?

It is perfectly true that the tongue may be used alternatively for deglutition and for speech. But this is because nature herself has completely separated the two mechanisms. This is not the case with sexuality in its inseminatory function, for—and once more nature and its objective structures are the reason and make the fact clear to us—the two purposes are of their nature inseparable. It is a fact that it is always simultaneously and in one and the same process—except at the times when the woman is naturally infertile—that nature makes the sexual relationship on the one hand a possible opportunity for spiritual communion and physical adjustment between husband and wife, and on the other, the necessary condition for an eventual pregnancy.

It is therefore impossible to state that the mechanism of the sexual function is,[6] like the tongue, naturally organized to serve two equal and equivalent purposes alternatively and separately, namely, procreation and the expression of married intimacy. There is one natural exception however. During the infertile days following

[5] See above pp. 25–6.

[6] Obviously we are only considering here the mechanism of the sexual function *in the light of its complete development which is destined to culminate in orgasm in the case of both husband and wife.* We are not considering at all those loving intimacies between them which may involve sexuality, but which, on principle, are not permitted by them to lead to intercourse itself.

menstruation or during the sterile period that succeeds the meno-
pause, the act of insemination no longer encounters the conditions
which, in the course of nature, are necessary for a pregnancy to
ensue.[7]

Intellectual reflection on the pattern inherent in the objective
structures of love and sexuality therefore confirms and justifies, from
a rational standpoint, the position of the Catholic Church in regard
to the ends of marriage, their inseparability and their hierarchical
order.[8] The difficulties to which the Church's position gives rise
seem rather to be due to her intransigence when it comes to the
concrete choice of the means of regulating sexuality and births.

[7] The above analysis is clearly valid only in the case of sexual activity that
is *inseminatory* intercourse. It is obvious that the position is quite different
—and even by definition—as far as *coitus reservatus* is concerned if, as some
sexologists increasingly tend to think, its purpose is to make possible between
husband and wife hormonal interactions beneficial to their health, and the
practice of psychosomatic control, which is advantageous for both their
spiritual stability and their ideal of chastity. Cf. below pp. 169–70.

[8] L. Lochet, "Le mariage chrétien, les fins du mariage," in *Nouvelle Revue
Théologique*, May and June 1951; A. M. Genevois, O.P., *Le mariage, dessein
de Dieu*, ch. VI. Le petit prince, pp. 95–109.

Chapter XI

THE RATIONAL BASIS OF THE
CHURCH'S POSITION (CONTD)

THE LIMITATION OF BIRTHS AND HOW
IT IS TO BE ACHIEVED

Our study, on the previous pages, of the behaviour which respect for the order of values imposes, should have made it obvious that it is not possible, in any way whatsoever, to speak of an *absolute* and *a priori* right possessed by man to limit the number of his children. Men and women have not the right, for instance, to marry on the express condition that they will not bring children into the world, although they intend to enjoy all that married life offers them. This way of entering into the marriage contract, far from corresponding to the order of values in the realm of love, is rather, its complete reversal.[1]

Husbands and wives have only a *relative* right in this matter of the limitation of births. It depends, that is, on circumstances and situations. Every couple owes it, we repeat, to God, the creator of human love and sexuality, to itself, to the community, to procreate those children whom it will be able to bring up and to prepare adequately for life. There is an optimum number for each family and each family alone can judge what it is. Both the temporal and the spiritual values must be taken into account at one and the same time, and a way be found to keep the right balance between them. Too much material comfort runs the risk of demoralizing a family whose size is deliberately restricted. Too many insurmount-

[1] We quote again from G. Madinier, "Spiritualité et biologie dans le mariage," in *Limitation des naissances et conscience chrétienne*, p. 203: "By reminding us that the child is the primary asset in marriage, tradition puts the married union in the context of the community. It invites the *union of the two persons* constantly to avoid slipping back, as it is so easy to do, and not to degenerate into a twofold egoism. Tradition makes us understand that this union between two persons will not be a genuine union of soul and will, an inner union, unless it becomes a joyful activity as much as, and still more than a passive pleasure. Finally, tradition, where it leads husband and wife towards the child, shows them that they cannot create, but only make it possible for the child to receive the gift of life, and that *a genuinely unifying activity is one that places us at the disposal of that higher activity through which we allow Creative Activity to work in us.*"

able difficulties run the risk of handicapping the children in their development where the family, because of lack of foresight, is too large.

These are not new ideas. Long ago the book of Ecclesiasticus drew the attention of husbands and wives in the second century B.C. to their duty as educators when properly understood, and showed that it is to be preferred to fertility when the latter results from mere lack of care.[2]

In any case, husbands and wives are to make up their minds about the circumstances which affect their primordial duty to bear children, in the light of their love, their love for the human race, for the land in which they live, for their own home, their children and one another, and this with all due natural and supernatural prudence. In this considered and deliberate love lies the one and only foundation for a Christian regulation of births. All reasons other than those of love—egoism, inertia, the desire for comfort, calculated interests, etc.—give no right to a restriction nor to a limiting of births. If the primary and supreme values of marriage and sexuality were the intimacy and the personal development of husband and wife, *apart from procreation*, the priority of mutual relationship over the creative will and devotion to the children might perhaps confer an absolute and *a priori* right to restrict the number of births. But we have seen that if this is the view we take, we are no longer in line with the traditional thought of the Catholic Church.

Yet some will argue that in the past, even the past of Christian civilization, the values of sexuality were seen and prized not so much as leading to an intimate relationship and to the fulfilment of the human person but as being pleasures easy to come by and able to give individual instincts an easy outlet. And so the Catholic Church may well have been right to consider pleasure and sensual satisfaction as of less account than reproduction. But now that the modern world has discovered the "We-community" of husband and wife, and sees in it a value superior to the reproductive instinct, the traditional positions have been overthrown.[3]

---

[2] "A brood of disloyal sons, let not thy eye dwell on these with pleasure! the fear of God lacking, let not the multitude of them be thy consolation. Not on such lives as these set thy hopes, little regard have thou for such doings as theirs; better one man who fears God than a thousand who grow up rebellious; better die childless than have rebels to succeed thee" (Ecclus. 16. 1–4.)

[3] As we have seen, this is the argument used by Sherwin Bailey, *supra*, ch. III, Opinions of Protestant theologians, pp. 25–6, and by the preparatory report for the Lambeth 1958 Conference under the title: "The Family in Contemporary Society," London, S.P.C.K. 1958, pp. 137–47, especially p. 146.

It is, in fact, not impossible that, for reasons of a contingent
nature, certain more personal aspects of married sexuality did not
impinge to any great extent upon the awareness of a civilization
that was less sensitive than our own to the subjective side of the
question.[4] It is equally certain that a perfectly justifiable modesty
often degenerated into an unjustifiable prudery and so did not always
have the courage to face and to elucidate the true values of sexuality. However, there is no need for us to be angry with the Church
on this account. She may be excused on the grounds that she exists
in time and needs time if she is to free herself sufficiently from sociological conditioning and triumph over it.[5]

But there is no point in exaggerating. Even though we admit that
many more personal aspects of the sexual function have come to

[4] It is certain that, had it not been for the Jansenist crisis, Catholic spirituality would have been more influenced than it was by St Francis de Sales and
his optimism in regard to the values of married life. Cf. *Saint François et ses
amitiés*, by Henry Couannier.

[5] St Augustine is often accused of having imprinted for ever on the tradition
of the Latin Church a certain suspicion of the values of the flesh. Some even
go so far as to talk of a "Manichean dualism" which his theology is supposed to have instilled into the Catholic tradition. This accusation errs by
excess and also has its origin in bad feeling. If we re-read his *De bono
conjugali*, his *De continentia*, his *De sancta virginitate*, his *De bono viduitatis*,
his *De conjugiis adulterinis*, all of which are now available to the modern
reader in the excellent editions of the Bibliothèque Augustinienne (Desclée et
de Brouwer, Paris, 1re série: Opuscules II, Problèmes moraux, III L'ascétisme
chrétien, 1937-9), we shall realize how much such judgments need revising.
"It would be wise for us to consider that among the good things which God
has bestowed upon us, some are desirable for their own sakes, such as
wisdom, health, friendship, whilst others are necessary but in view of another
purpose, such as knowledge, eating, drinking, sleep, marriage and married
intercourse (concubitus). Among these latter, some, like knowledge, are
necessary if we are to acquire wisdom, others, like eating, drinking, sleep
are needed for the preservation of health, *others again, like marriage and
married intercourse, for the maintenance of friendship*. In fact, it is from
these last good gifts that the propagation of the human race derives and in
this, friendly relations hold a most important place" (*De Bono conjugali*,
IX, 9). It is true however that for St Augustine the "pleasures of the flesh" if
we take too great a delight in them keep us far removed from "the pleasures
of the spirit". But he understands these pleasures of the "flesh" in the
Pauline sense of "this flesh of sin". He says: "I summarize the work of
continence by telling you to take care to restrain (*coercere*) and to heal
(*sanare*) all the pleasures of concupiscence (*delectationes concupiscentiae*)
which stand in the way of wisdom and its delights (*delectationi sapientiae*).
Such is the work of continence. *There is no doubt therefore that those who
limit it to the domination of bodily pleasures alone confine it within
boundaries that are too narrow*. Those who do not add the words 'of the
body' but who say that it is for continence to control pleasure or passion
in general, are nearer the truth. Vicious passion is not only an affair of the
body but of the soul as well" (*De continentia*, XIII, 28).

light only recently, yet it is wrong to think or to say that sexuality was, in the past, completely misunderstood as far as the part it plays in helping and unifying the human community is concerned. The Catholic Church has at all times seen in it, in her opposition to the Encratite heresies[6] and to Luther—up to a point—the existence of true values and these she has even taught are the secondary ends of marriage.

It is important moveover to note that when the Church speaks of the primary end, she uses the word "procreation", not the word "reproduction". These two terms are not in fact identical. Animals reproduce their species. Only man procreates. Animals are at the mercy of instinct and do not know that they are involved in a process with an end other than themselves. However instinctively a man acts, he is not ignorant of this fact. Even if he does not think of it as he indulges in pleasure, he knows very well that procreation is possible and that procreation gives birth to a person. If he is a Christian, he believes that he may eventually become the father of a child of God. Further, in recognizing procreation *and* upbringing as the supreme values in marriage, the Church has indirectly consecrated the personal, human, relational aspect of married love. And this has made it all the more easy for her to recognize in the mutual aid and the mutual development which the partners are to provide for and foster in each other, the value attaching to a genuine "end" of marriage.

In *Casti Connubii,* Pius XI states:

> For in matrimony as well as in the use of the matrimonial rights there are also secondary ends, such as mutual aid, the cultivating of mutual love, and the quieting of concupiscence which husband and wife are not forbidden to consider so long as they are subordinated to the primary end and so long as the intrinsic nature of the act is preserved.[7]

In other words, to those married people who wish above all to use the sexual function because of its genuine power to further the harmony of their married life, their fellowship in love, good understanding, joy, self-assurance etc., the Sovereign Pontiff points out once more that all this is good on condition that it does not become

---

[6] Re these Encratite, Catharian and other heresies, see: *Etudes Carmélitaines, Mystique et Continence,* Part III, pp. 117–70 (Paris, 1952).

[7] *Casti Connubii,* n. 60, pp. 67–8.

a withdrawal into oneself, an absolute end. It must remain open, ready to be used for the greater development of their devotion to others and especially to the upbringing of their children.

If, on the other hand, this quest for mutual development is continually and directly pursued and so eventually and progressively obscures what properly belongs to the primary end of marriage, then respect for the order of the factors inherent in sexuality and for the values of love will disappear.

But supposing that a man and wife who, fully complying with the conditions we have enumerated above, judge that they would do well to postpone the next pregnancy for a year or two or even to have no more children at all, we now ask what means are at their disposal today if this result is to be achieved.[8]

LIMITATION OF BIRTHS AND THE CHOICE OF MEANS

From the point of view of results only and apart from all considerations of the morality of the various means or of the varying degrees of immorality in some of them, the choice lies between the following methods:

—complete abstinence from intercourse during the period they have in mind,

—abstinence from intercourse during the fertile days in this same period (this is the method known as periodic continence),

—withdrawal before the completion of the act (*coitus interruptus*),

—abortion,

—sterilization, and finally,

—the use of contraceptives.

[8] A large number of books on this subject have been written over the past thirty years. The following works will be found useful:

Limitation des Naissances et conscience chrétienne; especially Dr Barbe's article, "La continence périodique," pp. 223–50; which covers a great deal more ground than the title would suggest. Editions Familiales de France, 1950.

Fr A. Snoeck, S.J., "Fécondation inhibée et morale catholique et devoir de fecondité," *Nouvelle Revue Théologique*, July–Aug. 1953, Nov. 1953.

F. Dantec, *Foyers Rayonnants*, vol. I, "Guide moral de l'amour chrétien" (Quimper, 1952).

Foyer Fécond. Editions des Feuilles familiales, Brussels, 1952. Fr MacAvoy, S.J., *Pour mieux aimer*, Ed. B.P., 1959.

We purposely mention only a few of the books available. We shall refer later to others when dealing with specific questions.

Before we discuss each of these methods, we begin by asserting —and it is obvious enough—that these various means of spacing or limiting births have not all the same value, nor are they all equally effective.

COMPLETE ABSTINENCE AND PERIODIC CONTINENCE

Complete abstinence, which is obviously the most effective way of limiting births, is not without drawbacks for many temperaments. Except in the case of couples whose love has progressively deepened their unity in every aspect of their life, and is of such a character that it can compensate for the desires of the flesh and sublimate them in a union of the heart, physical union generally remains essential.

St Paul himself seems to have advised against complete abstinence as a presumptuous undertaking, and to have preferred periodic continence. "Do not starve one another, unless perhaps you do so for a time, by mutual consent, to have more freedom for prayer; come together again, or Satan will tempt you, weak as you are" (1 Cor. 7. 5).

Man, said Pascal, is neither an angel nor a beast, but it often happens that a man who tries to play the angel acts like a beast. In any case, this complete abstinence presupposes a genuine harmony of wills and minds, a constant habit of tackling problems together and of continually infusing a spirit of love and affection into the simplest and most ordinary acts of everyday life. It also demands great confidence in divine grace and a genuine attraction to prayer.

Whatever truth there may be in these observations, it is not so very rare to find couples who have lived for several years without any sexual intercourse whatsoever and who have considered this period as a source of great grace in their lives.[9]

After complete abstinence, the simplest and, from the objective point of view, the most natural method is the one known as *periodic*

[9] E. Rolland, "La continence ascétique," in *Limitation des naissances et conscience chrétienne*, pp. 315–34; Dr Barbe, "Humanisme et Chasteté," in *Etudes Carmélitaines, Ma joie terrestre où donc es-tu?* Desclée, 1947, pp. 141–68; Abbé Marc Oraison, "Vie spirituelle, Raison, Instinct dans la conduite conjugale," in *Chronique sociale* 1957, No. 4, July, pp. 323–35.

continence.[1] It also consists like the previous method in an effort to prevent a future pregnancy by a genuine attempt to live continently or, as we prefer to say, chastely, during the fertile periods in the woman's monthly cycle. We emphasize that it is chastity which is involved, that is, a common effort progressively to spiritualize the flesh. Periodic continence when genuinely understood and practised leads to a better grasp of the requirements of chastity in regard to those slight, instinctive indulgences which it is only too easy to allow the eyes and the imagination in the course of the day. These little sacrifices offered to God in a spirit of love and with the desire to merit the grace of a continence which both husband and wife may find less difficult, increase the joy and affection of those who are already in love with one another. It will be all the easier for them since their nerves are calm and they are not fettered or inhibited by any excessive sense of frustration. These efforts to be temperate and

[1] Periodic Continence. Here again there is an abundant literature. It will help to make matters clearer if we divide it into two categories: (*a*) books dealing with the moral aspect; (*b*) books dealing with the medical aspect:

(*a*) The moral aspect (cf. previous note and add the following): *Cahiers Laënnec, Fécondité et continence périodique,* Fr E. Tesson, *Fécondité dirigée et morale chrétienne,* 1954, No. 4, Dec., pp. 35–44; Duval-Aumont, *Le problème de la natalité au foyer,* Casterman, IIe Partie, "Pages de spiritualité"; *Notes de Pastorale Familiale,* No. 30, April 1956 ("Education positive de la continence"), Ed. Feuilles familiales; Fr Tesson, S.J., "La Limitation des naissances et la morale," in *Pastorale familiale,* Congrès de l'Union des Oeuvres de Rennes, 1949, pp. 124–33.

(*b*) The medical aspect: Dr Chartier, "Fécondité et continence périodique, données médicales," in *Cahiers Laënnec,* 1954, No. 4, pp. 2–34. This article has been condensed and made available to the general public in the book already mentioned *Pour mieux aimer,* by J. MacAvoy, pp. 167–83; Dr Barbe, "La continence périodique," in *Limitation des naissances et conscience chrétienne,* pp. 223–50; Dr A. Krempel, *La continence périodique,* Ed. Salvator, 1954 (translated from the German 1937 edition), a work of the highest importance for Ogino's statistical method; Dr H. Knaus, *Fécondité périodique et Procréation volontaire,* Ed. Expansion scientifique française, 1955 (with a calendar); there is an Afterword by Fr Miller, S.J., and the author writes, "On the 7 November I became convinced that this interpretation of the Pope's speeches (on the lawful regulation of births) was in keeping with their obvious sense, when at a private audience at Castel Gandolfo my hopes were fulfilled and I was able to see with my own eyes and hear with my own ears the Holy Father acknowledge the value of my scientific works and give his blessing to both them and their author" (p. 53); Dr John R. Cavanagh, M.D., has drawn up a bibliography of works published all over the world (1952–7), on the question of ovulation and the woman's menstrual rhythm (Nov. 1957), obtainable from the author, 1703 Rhode Island, Washington, D.C., U.S.A.; Paul Vincent, "Statistiques relatives à l'ovulation, à la menstruation et à la grossesse," in *Actes de la 29e session de l'institut international de la statistique.* This article has been republished under the title, "Données biométriques sur la conception et la grossesse," in *Population,* 1956, No. 1, pp. 59–83. The author calls attention to variations in the period after ovulation.

chaste, which the partners make together for love of God and his Spirit present in each of them, may sometimes help to give a new value—even at the level of the senses—to the marriage act, which may well have tended to become commonplace under the corroding influence of habit and opportunity.

Yet, by its very definition, periodic continence presupposes that there are still a number of occasions each month, when genuine, loving intercourse continues to take place and when the language of physical contact continues to help husband and wife to perfect their knowledge of each other and the mutual self-giving which they as well as their home and family need.

And so the *"arsis"* of spiritual self-control during the periods of continence and the *"thesis"* of self-giving at the time of bodily union, constitute a rhythm that makes it possible for husband and wife to regulate births in a way that satisfies both the essential demands of the flesh and the deeper claims of the spirit.

It would be naïve to pretend that this is easy. It would be false to say that it is impossible. The truth is that the difficulties and obstacles periodic continence encounters are for the most part due to bad living conditions—housing, health—and to an almost total lack of preparation before and after marriage. A more regular, more peaceful life, one more in keeping with the demands of human nature—and those who live in the country often lead such a life— does much to make the efforts demanded of husband and wife easier.

It is true that others find it particularly difficult to forgo intercourse on the days when many women feel a natural desire for it. Some observers have even used this fact as an argument against periodic continence on the grounds that it is a method which does not respect nature and even goes counter to it.

Even if the fact were verified—and it is not a universal phenomenon[2]—it is incorrect to use the expression "counter to nature" in

[2] Dr Abraham Stone writes as follows in this connection: "The studies of Havelock Ellis, Marie Stopes, Katherine Davis, etc., tend to prove that there is first an increase and then a decrease of sexual desire during the menstrual month. Our own studies in a large number of cases have also shown that there is a fairly pronounced rhythm of sexual desire in very many women. Most of them state that their erotic desires increase before their monthly periods, and more often, at the end of these and during the days that follow. Yet, in the case of this second period, the recrudescence of desire might well be due to the habitual practice of continence during the week of menstruation. Stopes declares that she has observed this desire in the middle of the menstrual month. There are obviously differences in the cycle of desire and each woman is herself better able than anyone else to identify her own particular rhythm" in *L'éducation du couple*, Denoël, 1953, p. 278. The same author in a more recent work (*The Premarital Consultation*, p. 26) writes: "Most women have stronger sex feelings either before, or, more usually, just after the menstrual period."

the strict sense. It is precisely one of the characteristics of human sexuality, in contrast to the sexuality of many of the higher animals, that it is not subject to a rutting season.[3] If however certain women continue to experience a natural desire which is more in evidence on the days when fertility is possible, we should perhaps see in this one more confirmation of the order of values in sexuality and love as we have analysed them above. It is the longing for, the instinct of, motherhood which bears witness to the primacy of the latter even in the need for physical union which husband and wife experience. Where a woman suffers because she has to restrain her desire for motherhood, a thoughtful husband will help her by joining with her in transferring this parental sense and this generous creative will to the children they already have. Certain couples may even find it to their advantage during the fertile period to make use— after giving it a trial—of the intercourse known as *copula reservata* with the self-control it makes possible. They will realize that, as far as they are concerned, it is a psychological and physiological factor contributing to their hormonal and conjugal stability. Experience will have taught them that there can be an invigorating joy for husbands and wives who genuinely desire to be continent and who, in the intercourse which this form of union offers, are content to keep their emotions on the level of a loving, tender and sensitive affection. They purposely prevent them from reaching the point where nature automatically releases the full sexual mechanism whose action is obviously directed solely to inseminatory intercourse.[4]

[3] See on this subject the very interesting and significant remarks of Dr Chauchard in *La maîtrise sexuelle*, Ed. du Levain, Paris, 1959, ch. I, "Originalité sexuelle de l'homme," pp. 15–23.

[4] Fr Carpentier ("Un problème pastoral difficile," in *Nouvelle Revue théologique*, Nov. 1959, p. 930) says much the same: "Then there is the practice of *copula reservata* which, provided the obvious precautions are taken, avoids conception and, if there is a serious and sufficient reason for it, does not contravene the divine law, but on the express condition that its object and intention is a *less passionate union of husband and wife*." It is clear from what we have just said that the *copula reservata* is not of itself a method for preventing pregnancy or spacing births. Nor is it "a feat which increases the possibilities of sensual experience". It is and it must be, in the words of one of the great specialists in neurophysiology, Dr Paul Chauchard, a form of "sexual control", "an ascesis which, by ridding the sexual act of its animal automatism and so giving it a fully human dimension at the cost of renouncing the extremes of pleasure, brings in its train both peace and joy" (*La maîtrise sexuelle*, Ed. du Levain, 1958, p. 58). So the two serious ambiguities which were due to the lack of scientific foundations in the early literature on the subject (1950) now disappear. It is understandable that, in a matter of such consequence, the Church should be cautious and order the withdrawal from circulation of this empirical and ambiguous literature, whilst insisting that its place should be taken by studies of genuine scientific

CONTRACEPTIVE METHODS

Compared with the methods we have just reviewed, those we have now to mention and to reject are in a different category altogether. They do not, as we shall show, respect the natural requirements of the sexual function nor the essential characteristics of its development.[5]

value. It is easy to appreciate the wisdom of the Holy Office's *Monitum* of 13 June 1952 (Doc. Cath., No. 1136, c. 1556). An understanding of it presupposes that we make the same diligent effort to grasp its meaning as was put into its composition. It appeared a few months after the publication of an article by a theologian who gave it as his personal opinion that the *copula reservata* was not "in accordance with nature" (*Angelicum*, 1951), and it was confirmed by a speech of Cardinal Ottaviani (Doc. Cath., No. 1318, c. 1572–73). The *Monitum*'s first purpose is to insist that the question remains an open one. But, as in any matter requiring elucidation by specialists, the immediate rule must be discretion and prudence as far as the general public is concerned. And this is the *Monitum*'s second aim. In his commentary upon it (*Nouvelle Revue théologique*, Nov. 1952, pp. 974–80), Fr Carpentier wrote: "It will be noticed that the Holy Office, in the terms it has used, has not intended to state, even implicitly, that the *copula reservata* is of itself—and therefore always—when practised deliberately, even a venial sin. The formula employed in fact leaves the question open." However, as in the case of all actions that are in themselves either good or indifferent, the Church fears that a wrong use of the *copula reservata* might distort its meaning and value (*corruptio optimi, pessima*), and so at first insists, if not on absolute abstention, at least on caution, moderation, temperance. Before it has been scientifically demonstrated that the *copula reservata* may, under conditions which will be laid down, lessen tension between husbands and wives and even give greater value and depth to married life, the Church is anxious that all doubt should be carefully dispelled. A third difficulty can be added to those we have already mentioned—the illusion, to quote again from Fr Carpentier, "that it is possible to hope we can rescue (married couples) solely by means of a natural solution, when what is needed is rather an emphasis on nature as wounded" and also "an insistence on the need for the self-abnegation demanded of us by revelation" (*op. cit.*, p. 998). We refer the reader to what we said above (pp. 138–40) on the dangers of this kind of "naturalism" and also of "hedonism". In any case it is desirable that sexological studies, conducted with all the necessary care, should eventually give a complete answer to this question. We have already available the articles by P. Chauchard, "Les voies nouvelles de la psychophysiologie," *Revue des questions scientifiques*, 20 Jan. 1955, pp. 110–18; "Aspects neurophysiologiques des conduites humaines," *Revue des questions scientifiques*, 20 Jan. 1958, p. 127.

[5] On contraceptive methods and their history throughout the ages, see Norman Himes, *Medical History of Contraception*, Baltimore, The Williams & Wilkins Company, 1936.

On the use of contraceptives today: A. Stone and L. Levine, *Premarital Consultation*, Ed. Grune & Stratton, New York, 1956; by the same authors: "Present Day Family Planning Techniques," in *Comptes rendus du Congrès Mondial de la Population*, t. I, pp. 1001–12; Dr Lagroua Weill-Hallé, *La liberté de la conception à l'étranger, étude clinique des méthodes anticonceptionelles et recherches expérimentales*, Libr. Maloine, 1958.

Coitus interruptus, although it seems to provide husbands and wives with the means of implementing their decision to avoid a pregnancy—there are, however, plenty of "accidents" in this connection[6]—does not satisfy the genuine need of husband and wife for union. On all counts, it is a piece of trickery. It is false to nature and to the manner in which nature's sexual characteristics find their expression in the marriage act, it falsifies the hope shared by both husband and wife that, as the Biblical phrase puts it, they will "know" one another. Bernard Shaw used a stinging word to describe this interrupted form of sexual intercourse. He called it "mutual masturbation". It is more likely that it is only a masturbatory act for the male partner in the majority of cases. It is not rare to find that the wife merely allows this perversion of the natural order to take place against her own will and thus submits to, rather than co-operates in, this piece of trickery.

In any case the wife in particular is not deceived. She knows that intercourse thus interrupted silences the genuine language of love. More often than not, it leaves an impression of frustration, and there is the fear that the husband may withdraw too late. Sometimes even, the wife feels that she is simply being refused and rejected. Hence although claiming to satisfy the needs of the sexual function, *coitus interruptus* gives it a meaning that goes counter to what nature has intended, counter to union, identity, harmony in joy and a loving contentment.

Since this "piece of trickery" achieves nothing real or true on the human and personal plane, it is easy to see why ingenious efforts have been made to discover other methods of limiting births while preserving a more complete union and a genuine insemination of the woman's body.

These other methods have the generic name of "contraceptives". They owe their name to the fact that their purpose is to prevent the normal result of the act of insemination, that is, pregnancy, whilst allowing bodily union. In reality, three objectively distinct and separate methods are currently included under this one term, perhaps in order to produce greater confusion in people's minds. The process of insemination can be frustrated in three ways according to whether the method chosen (*a*) is used to nullify immediately the result—impregnation—at the precise moment it has been

[6] Dr Lagroua Weill-Hallé, *op. cit.,* "Contre-indications du coït interrompu," p. 22: "C.I. in many cases proves unreliable as a method of preventing pregnancy."

achieved; (*b*) is used just before the process begins so as to render it ineffective; (*c*) is used during the act itself to prevent one of its effects.

ABORTION PROCEDURES

(*a*) In the first case, we are really faced with an attempt at abortion. In fact, the action which the substance placed in the female sexual organs[7] or absorbed by them (Sannyal quinol or antimetabolic preparations) is intended to effect, consists in preventing the embedding and nidification of the *fertilized* ovum in the uterine membrane. Every fertilized ovum is the identical embryo which nine months later will be the newborn child. To interfere with a fertilized ovum which, although only a few minutes or a few hours old, is already in possession of its own principle of growth, is to interfere with a living creature which is already someone other than its mother. And this is what is known as procured abortion. We are all aware of what morals have to say about this procedure. The word "contraception" used to describe it in the case in question may of course conceal the reality involved, but it cannot change the facts.

STERILIZATION PROCEDURES

The second type of interference takes place even before actual coitus. It aims at preventing the formation or the movement of either the male or the female reproductive cells. Thus spermicidal jellies are placed in the female ducts to destroy the male germs before they can reach the Fallopian tubes. Or the woman takes certain progesterone products during the follicular phase of her cycle (just after the end of menstruation) in order to prevent ovulation and to make her sterile during intercourse.[8]

In regard to this sterilizing procedure (operating physiologically of course and not by means of a surgical sterilization) husband and wife are both subject to the same traditional moral principles.

---

[7] We shall not deal here with preparations used to kill the germ in the male seed before it can reach the ovum.

[8] Dr Jean Sutter, "La limitation des naissances en France, Annexe II, Etat des recherches actuelles sur la reproduction," in *Population*, 1956, No. 2, p. 233; "A la recherche de la 'pilule stérilisante'," in *Population*, 1957, No. 3, pp. 495–6; Dr R. de Guchteneere, "Les inhibiteurs de l'ovulation," in *St-Luc Médical*, 1959.

The principles which deal with the sterilization of an organ or of a function essential for the existence of the individual or the species are perhaps less well known than the moral teaching of the Church on procured abortion. Pius XI and Pius XII, however, continuing a long series of declarations on the part of the *magisterium,* restated them several times.

In *Casti Connubii,* Pius XI insisted:

> Furthermore, Christian doctrine establishes, and the light of human reason makes it most clear, that private individuals have no other power over the members of their bodies than that which pertains to their natural ends; and they are not free to destroy or mutilate their members, or in any other way render themselves unfit for their natural functions, except when no other provision can be made for the good of the whole body.[9]

A distinction must therefore be made between direct and indirect sterilization. Pius XII, referring to his speech to the midwives, insists:

> By direct sterilization, we intended to refer to the procedure adopted by those who propose, either as an end or a means, to make procreation impossible. But we did not intend that this term should be applied to every procedure which in actual fact makes procreation impossible. It is true that man does not always intend the results of his acts, even if he has foreseen them. Thus, for instance, the removal of diseased ovaries will have the inevitable effect of making procreation impossible, but this impossibility may not have been deliberately intended, either as an end or a means ... These same principles make it possible to solve a problem which is much discussed today among doctors and moralists— is it permissible to prevent ovulation by means of pills which are used as remedies for excessive reactions of the uterus or the female organs, although this drug by preventing ovulation also makes pregnancy impossible?[1]

[9] *Casti Connubii,* C.T.S., pp. 33–4. See Ch. Tiberghien, *Eugénisme, stérilisation,* Ed. A.M.C. 1934 and Dr E. Mayaud, *Le Problème de la stérilisation humaine, La société a-t-elle le droit de stériliser les individus?* (Paris, Jouve 1934).
[1] Pius XII to the International Congress of Haematology, 12 Sept. 1958, D.C. 1958, No. 1287, p. 1244.

The Pope then makes the distinction—in a passage we have already quoted[2]—between direct sterilization which is always illicit and indirect sterilization "which is permissible according to the general principle of actions with a double effect". This distinction, moreover, as the Pope pointed out, can be arrived at by reason alone.

Unfortunately at the time when technical advance is as rapid and as extraordinary as it is today, even "the light of Reason" seems to be obscured by it. Accustomed as he is to transforming nature and even the constitution of matter itself, man comes to a point at which, he forgets that what he has a perfect right to effect in the objective world of *things* that belong to kingdoms inferior to his own, he has not the right to do it to *himself*.[3] To take concrete examples, man has the right to make a lightning conductor to protect himself against lightning, he has the right to alter the course of a river in order to irrigate fields or to construct a dam, he has the right to experiment on guinea-pigs even though this may produce terrible deformities, organic atrophy and the rest, in these animals. The whole world has been given to man by the Creator and man has sovereign powers he may use for any end which is of service to himself, provided that, in so doing, and in the course of these activities, his own stature increases and moves nearer to man's ideal and end, which is God. "Everything is for you," says St Paul to mankind, "but you (are) for Christ, and Christ for God" (1 Cor. 3. 23).

But in relation to himself, man is no longer in possession of sovereign powers. He does not belong to himself. If he must, as the saying goes, be master of himself, be in control of himself, this is a proof that this obligation derives from a moral duty to respect the welfare of others. A tenant-farmer or a manager hold their land or their premises as beneficial occupants not as owners. The same is true of man in regard to this existence which he has received and has not given to himself, in regard to this body and its functions, these physical, psychical and other faculties, which he is called upon to

---

[2] See above, Chapter IX, p. 136. See also on sterilization pills: Rev William J. Gibbons, S.J., and Thomas K. Burch, "Physiologic Control of Fertility, Process and Morality," in *The American Ecclesiastical Review*, No. 4, April 1958, pp. 246–77. See below pp. 270–2.

[3] Dr J. Sutter says (*L'Eugénique*, p. 141): "It is difficult to arrive at a reasonable estimate of the total number of sterilizations (carried out by the Third Reich). On the basis of the Baden and Würtemberg records, they may easily be estimated at more than 600,000, on the strength of the Kiel records, at more than 300,000." See also: F. Bayle, *Croix gammée contre caducée*, Imprimerie Nationale, 1950, and Hedwig Conrad-Martius, *Utopien der Menschen-züchtung*, Ed. Keesel, Munich, 1951.

manage and for which he is responsible so that they may function in the best possible way.

It is true that man always has the right to improve not only his lot, but even the operation of his activities, functions and organs provided he accepts and makes his own the direction and purpose nature has imprinted upon them. Medical science, hygiene and all therapeutics are founded on this very principle. Some of our contemporaries would like to go further and refashion for other ends and purposes organs and functions given to man by nature. On this point, the Church's teaching is categorical and cannot change. It rests—and we have just vindicated the principle on which it is based—on the character itself of the human person, created a composite of nature and mind, and whose whole substantial identity, though transcending the categories of time and space, yet depends on a certain kind of organization, a given objective structure. To interfere with this substantial identity, even indirectly through its functional nature with a view to transforming man into another type of composite or a composite with another ultimate purpose, is to open the door on to an unknown world, is to plunge ourselves into a future of pure relativism . . . We shall return to this point in a later chapter.

CONTRACEPTIVE METHODS PROPERLY SO-CALLED

(c) There remains a third way in which a deliberate attempt is made to prevent pregnancy and the beginning of a new life. As we have said, it achieves its purpose by blocking or stopping the passage of the male cells towards those of the female. There is no need to go into uninteresting and useless details. The effect is produced with the aid of protective appliances in the case of the man and in that of the woman by occlusive procedures mechanical (the diaphragm) or organic (phosphorated or sulphonated hesperidine).[4] This procedure alone strictly deserves the name "contraception" by contrast with sterilization and abortion.

"Contraception" in fact means: an obstacle to, a blockage, a damming-up of the normal progress of the marriage act. The principal effect of the husband's act of insemination, that is, the complete impregnation of the woman, must at all costs be prevented.

[4] Hesperidine insulates the female cells and the spermatozoa are no longer able to enter them.

Only a relatively superficial effect—male and female orgasms—is to remain and these should eventually become simultaneous.

In contraceptive intercourse, the woman no doubt accepts the pleasure she experiences when her husband is united to her, but she refuses to allow herself to be totally possessed, entered, transformed by his substance. So there results an emotive psychological dissociation in the woman. She accepts her husband but refuses his substance. On the other hand, the wife who only desires intercourse according to the natural order of things, both on fertile and infertile days, wants to be entirely receptive, is ready for any change that may take place in her. For her, the act of insemination has its full meaning as a way by which her husband's love and his very substance passes into her secret and innermost depths. It is only in this authentic context, as nature has intended it, that orgasm in the woman has its true sense, that of joy and pleasure not only in welcoming her husband but also in assimilating his substance and in being herself transformed by it.

How disintegrating from the psychological point of view must be the dissociation between what the wife accepts from her husband and what she refuses, between what she loves in him and what she hates! For exaggerated though the expression may sound, the husband's seed is really an object of fear. It is refused, even hated. If only orgasm could take place without it! It is easy to understand that already in this dubious and divided state of mind there is all that is required to produce psychological unbalance and to favour the growth of those neurotic tendencies that are never completely absent in any human being.[5] There is, at least, all that is needed to encourage the development of frigidity in the woman, and this, as we know, is seldom due to purely physiological causes.[6]

Meanwhile, what can the contraceptive husband pride himself on having given to his wife? Something of himself to assimilate, or has he merely made a pretence of giving her this? Here again there is a lack of authenticity, an element of deceit which has intruded itself into his psychology. He too bears a grudge against nature, nature which must be caught by the throat and muzzled, since it does not automatically do what we wish it to do.

Hence the Church's condemnation of contraceptive practices is

[5] Dr Barbe, *Les conséquences pathologiques des pratiques anti-conceptionelles*, Maloine, 1937; Dr Mertens de Wilmars, *Psychopathologie de l'anticonception*, Lethielleux, 1955.
[6] *Cahiers Laënnec*, 195, "L'anaphrodisie féminine."

absolute, unqualified, unconditional. This is because "since the conjugal act is destined primarily by nature for the begetting of children, those who in exercising it deliberately frustrate its natural power and purpose, sin against nature and commit a deed which is shameful and intrinsically vicious". For "no reason, however grave, may be put forward by which anything intrinsically against nature may become conformable to nature and morally good".[7] Hence, as Pius XII put it, "No alleged 'indication' or need can convert an intrinsically immoral act into a moral and lawful one". "This precept is as valid today as it was yesterday, and it will be the same tomorrow and always, because it does not imply a precept of human law but is the expression of a law which is natural and divine,"[8] written definitively into the very structure of the sexual function.

THE CHURCH AND THE NATURAL ORDER: DOES SHE RESPECT IT OR TREAT IT AS A FETISH?

It may seem amazing that the Church should have shown such intransigence in defence of such an apparently minor point as the preservation of the integrity of one phase, a fundamental one it is true, of the sexual function. It may be even more astonishing to think that the Church should have concerned herself with what appears to be the most vulnerable and unimportant aspect—the preservation of a functional process—of a problem so vast, so crucial, so complex as that of the limitation of births, a problem which involves at one and the same time, the policy of States (eugenic, social and public health policies), the improvement of the status of women, the education of the young, even peace and war.[9]

[7] *Casti Connubii*, C.T.S., p. 26.
[8] Pius XII, "Address to Catholic Midwives," nn. 24–5, *op. cit.*, p. 15.
[9] In the human sphere "respect for nature" will always be seen as the primary condition of a respect for personality and for the relations between persons by means of which human personality grows and becomes mature. To act towards nature in any other way, that is, to claim that we can "act personally" (*actus humanus*) without bothering to conform to the obvious demands of nature, is to imply an ethical system which has recently been given the name of "situational morality". By emphasizing in a situation the personal element which *enters into our involvement, situational morality reaches the point at which it fails to lay sufficient stress on our awareness of law and of universality.* This tendency arises from a philosophy which refuses to recognize in each human being, and in each of the particular situations he experiences, the universal structures of an essence. According to this philosophy it is false to assert that essence has its own absolutely unique and particular existence. Neither "from this point of view, can the general moral law be understood as a declaration having genuine value for any man in the

Certain people, therefore, will not fail to remark that by adopting such positions, the Church goes so far as to sacrifice the spirit to the letter, liberty to law, personality to nature, the individual to the collectivity. That this may appear to be the case, and that often—accidentally or on occasion—law and morals may, in the case of the man who wishes to observe them strictly, offer the danger and risk of legalism and formalism, we shall all agree, particularly after our Lord's words to the Pharisees and the epistles of St Paul to the Romans and Galatians. We shall go into this matter more thoroughly in a later chapter, but before we do so, we must point out here and now that to set the letter against the spirit, law against charity, nature against personality, as certain people do, on *a priori* grounds and with no possibility of reconciling them, is to run straight into sophistry.

Fr K. Rahner has some wise observations[1] which we are restating when we say we cannot utter too strong a warning against the false solutions of "situational ethics", according to which "it is not what we do that matters, but only our intention. If this is good, the rest is of no account before conscience and before God. The moral demands specifically defined by the Christian revelation are reduced to a purely formal duty to be true to our own conscience and courageous in obeying it . . . The knowledge of the individual subject is no longer to take as its norm the essential and objective structure of things . . . Conscience is no longer the voice and the mediator of an obligatory norm which, in principle, makes an objective understanding possible between men. It is, so to speak, itself our lawgiver.

concrete in such and such a unique situation. The sophism is obvious. Since a general law is incapable of apprehending the *totality* of a concrete situation, it is wrongly argued that the situation itself cannot come within the scope of this law," J. Fuchs, S.J., "Morale théologique et morale de situation," in *Nouvelle Revue Théologique*, Dec. 1954, p. 1075. Pius XII denounced this situational ethics ("Speech to the World Federation of Young Women's Organizations," 18 April 1952, D.C. No. 1121, col. 592). An instruction of the Holy Office returned to this important subject in 1956 (2 Feb. 1956, *Acta Apostolicae Sedis*, 1956, pp. 144-5). See also the pertinent citicism of M. Gusdorf's Ethics by Fr P. E. Brisbois, S.J., "Une morale d'aujourd'hui, in *Nouvelle Revue Théologique*, July-Aug. 1951, pp. 710-11: "No doubt there are personal values which each man must adopt for himself, but which will only be authentic if they conform to the essential conditions of all true human values, of all genuine human fulfilment. *Each man's own law (no doubt) is fidelity to himself, to his own vocation, but this vocation is only authentic if it conforms to the general demands of every human vocation, founded, according to metaphysical morality, on man's essential nature."

[1] K. Rahner, *Dangers dans le Catholicisme d'aujourd'hui*, Desclée, 1959, pp. 68-70.

Its verdicts admit of no appeal. On each occasion, they are an-
nounced in an original and inscrutable way, and each particular
verdict is only valid in one unique case."

Such a view forgets that the spirit has the amazing faculty of
being able to make its gentle way into the letter, transfigure it and
give it life. And so by what right can the human person seek to by-
pass the law in the name of the spirit and of liberty?[2] Or by what
right can it attempt to alter nature and its demands? Christ when
speaking of the Law said that, far from doing violence to it, he had
come, on the contrary, to ratify it by giving to it the fullness of its
meaning.

In conclusion: the Catholic Church, faced with the possibility of
birth limitation, teaches that there is, in principle, a right, or better,
a duty, to practise a form of birth regulation based on careful
thought, provided that this regulation is inspired solely by motives
of genuine charity, and that it respects the order of values inherent
in the sexual function and also the pattern of its structural factors.

[2] The "personal" aspect of sin has been more emphasized of recent years,
and this is all to the good. Nevertheless, we must not lose sight of its aspect
as an act that *breaks the law.* "We might say that, from a practical standpoint,
I am lacking in love for a person, but from the point of view of a specific
definition, my sin is always a transgression of a law. This is due to the
structure of the human being, who is nature and person in a unity that cannot
be destroyed. It is also due to the nature of a free act whose specific definition
is always distinct from the act in the concrete. . . . So we may keep to the
definition of sin in relation to the eternal law even under the Christian dis-
pensation. The new Law, like the natural and the written law, is contained
within the eternal Law. Sin in the concrete is always an insult to God as a
Person, but in the strictly formal sense, it is a *privation* and hence can only
be measured in terms of an order, that Divine order of which created natures
are the reflections." Cf. Geffre, "Péché, loi et personne," in *Supplément à la
Vie spirituelle*, 1958, No. 45, pp. 151 and 153. See also L. Vereecke, "L'obligation morale selon Guillaume d'Ockham," in *Supplément à la Vie spirituelle*,
1958, No. 45, pp. 123-4. The analogy between Ockham's nominalism and
modern existentialism is remarkable. On the possibility of the coexistence of
Law and Grace and the fact that one even implies the existence of the other
in the ethics of marriage, cf. G. Martelet, S.J., "L'Eglise, la Loi et la Grâce,"
in *Christus*, No. 18, April 1958, pp. 205-16.

Chapter XII

BIRTH CONTROL OR BIRTH REGULATION?

Now that we have stated the doctrine of the Catholic Church and the reasons which justify it, we must return to an expression we have constantly used, that is, *birth regulation*, an expression coined by Pius XII:

> We have affirmed the legitimacy and at the same time defined the limits—and they are, in fact, very wide limits—of a form of *birth regulation* which, in contrast to what is known as "birth control", is compatible with God's law.[1]

As we see, birth regulation is as different from birth control as is moral behaviour from unlawful conduct. Doubtless words indicate whatever we intend them to express and so there is always something arbitrary about them. But the two terms in question will henceforward signify two different doctrines. It may therefore be useful to try to determine why the Church feels that the new expression *regulation* is more in keeping with her "mind" than that of "birth control", already used by, and so marked with the stamp of, the reformed Churches.

There are, we believe, five reasons:

1. Regulation can be contrasted with control in the same way as a code of conduct with a technique.

2. Regulation tends to stress the priority of quality in the moral sphere; control lays greater emphasis on the quantitative aspect.

3. Regulation implies an art; control involves an artifice.

4. Regulation leads the way to an "open" universe; control organizes a universe that is "closed".

5. Regulation and the spiritual life are compatible; control, on principle, takes no account of spirituality.

---

[1] Pius XII to the *Fronte della Famiglia*, 26 Nov. 1951, D.C. 1951, c. 1543, *in fine* of *Casti Connubii*, Ed. Action Populaire, 1955, p. 170.

THE REASONS FOR A CHOICE BETWEEN
REGULATION AND CONTROL

1. In our opinion, regulation can be contrasted with control in the same way as a code of conduct with a *technique*. The term "birth regulation" implies management, control of sexuality through *natural self-mastery*, an ascendancy resulting from an effectively balanced personality, whilst contraceptive birth control implies first and foremost the use and successful operation of a *technique of substitution*, mechanical or chemical, which may well conceal a chronic lack of balance.

In fact, birth regulation presupposes in any case complete or temporary continence, periodic or lasting for a considerable time, practised by mutual agreement between husband and wife and organized in accordance with nature and the actual characteristics of the female organism.

Hence the whole process indicates on the one hand that natural birth regulation bases its code of conduct on the actual structure of female sexuality (with its "work" cycle—ovulation—lasting some 18 days and demanding a corresponding cycle of "rest and recovery" of from 8 to 10 days immediately before menstruation) and, on the other hand, that regulation imposes this standard female pattern on male sexuality by calling on it to confine its inseminatory activity to the days when the female organs are at rest, and this out of respect and love for its partner.[2]

Contraceptive birth control, on the contrary, disregards nature's directions and overrides them. It thinks it can get along perfectly

[2] No one will be surprised that it should be the female organs and their need for rest which set the pattern of married intercourse during the period when husband and wife propose to postpone the next pregnancy. The needs of the wife should in this case take precedence over those of the husband, or at least, the needs of the wife should help the husband to advance to a state in which his love will subordinate his personal pleasure to the needs of his wife. Moreover, it seems that in this way the balance disturbed by sin is restored, since the man agrees not to lord it on principle over his wife (Gen. 3. 16: "and thou shalt be subject to thy husband; he shall be thy lord") but, on the contrary, to treat her as a genuine companion, an "*alter ego*".

well without nature and do better than she does. It probably thinks
it can act like God but without him (Gen. 3. 5).[3]

2. Birth regulation offers the same kind of contrast with birth
control as does priority given to *quality* by contrast with *quantity*.

As regulation necessarily presupposes periodic abstinence, the
intention of husbands and wives, who look to nature for the norm
of their behaviour, will lead them to desire this pleasure less frequently and to hope that it will signify all the more clearly their
total, mutual self-giving in that it is the sequel to a period of sacrifice which they have both agreed to undergo.

So true is this, that when we use the word "temperance" to indicate one way in which this regulation of births is achieved, we must
not think only of a decrease in the number of times intercourse
takes place. "Should we not think still more of the self-mastery
which husband and wife must acquire during intercourse itself so
that the latter may be a spiritualizing force and rich in the values
of the soul?"[4]

Contraceptive control, on the other hand, seems to stake everything first and foremost on the number of sexual relations, considered
on principle as possible at all times. Of itself contraception does not
appear to ask instinctive sexuality for any disciplinary or ascetic
effort. It therefore does not seem capable of giving to the couple, in
addition to sensual pleasure, either the enriching joy of the effort
towards self-mastery or the spiritual reward of a personal and
mutually agreed control over instinct.

[3] It is this proud pretension of technics to dispense with all effort to link
itself to spiritual values, which Pius XII has called the "self-sufficiency" of
technics. "There is no denying that technical progress comes from God and
so can and must lead us back to God. It often happens, in fact, that the
believer, as he admires the conquests of technics and uses them in order to
deepen his knowledge of creation and of the forces of nature . . . feels
drawn to adore the Author of all these good things which he admires and
uses. . . . Yet it seems that this same technics which has in our century
reached the height of its splendour and its maximum output, becomes, in the
actual play of circumstances, a grave spiritual danger. *It seems to instil into
modern man, prostrate* before its altar, a sense of *self-sufficiency* and satisfaction in regard to his limitless desire for knowledge and power. . . . It follows
that technics is considered to possess an autonomy beyond the bounds of
possibility, and this autonomy is transformed, in the minds of certain people,
into an erroneous idea of life and of the universe, an idea known as the
technical spirit." (Pius XII, "Christmas Message," 1953. See also "Christmas
Message," 1955). See our article, "La Régulation des naissances peut-elle être
une technique?" in *Revue de l'Action Populaire*, No. 132, Nov. 1959, pp.
1092–1105.

[4] Abbé de Locht, *Le prêtre éducateur des adultes*, Ed. Feuilles Familiales,
1956, p. 105.

3. Again, birth regulation is opposed to contraceptive control as *art* is to *artifice*. Contraception, in fact, presents itself simply as a "prescription", an "appliance", to use the term popular in Anglo-Saxon countries. From the point of view of this artificial technique, a woman who is "fitted" (with an appliance) is essentially different from a woman who is not so "fitted".[5] And so the supposed mutual self-giving relation between husband and wife surely runs the grave risk of sinking to the level of a reciprocal technique or more often a technique directed exclusively to giving the husband satisfaction.

On the contrary, since, as we have already said, birth regulation is not a technique but a form of control, it presupposes a whole pattern of life. It demands a genuine education. This is why it is in the sphere of art and not that of artifice. It makes us free of the profound joys of art, joys, let it be noted, not merely pleasures. This distinction we owe to Bergson. Pleasure is only an artifice Nature has devised to ensure that living creatures hand on the gift of life. It does not point out the direction in which life is to move. But joy always shows that life has succeeded, has gained ground, has won a victory: "Every great Joy sounds a note of triumph".

And we here are considering one of the most difficult triumphs man can win—the taming not only of strange and external cosmic powers, but of those obscure and secret forces which from the depths of his own being are always attempting to invade and overwhelm his freedom.

From the point of view of birth regulation, the couple have no choice. They must grow, discipline themselves, triumph over the humiliating exploitation of their liberty. In practice, the contraceptive couple pay no heed whatever to these realities. This is why birth regulation again stands out in contrast to birth control.

4. Birth regulation leads the way to the kingdom of the "open" universe. Birth control immures us in the "closed" universe.

"Open" and "closed" are Bergsonian categories that have become

[5] It is particularly heart-breaking to find among persons who have the best of intentions regarding preparation for marriage in Protestant and Anglo-Saxon countries, a *spiritual blindness* which causes them no longer to see any harm in this "fitting of appliances" in the case of young women, still virgins, before their marriage! A marriage guidance review, in other respects of high standing, does not hesitate to explain how a doctor—a Marriage Guidance Counsellor whom a girl about to be married will see before her wedding in order to be "fitted" (i.e. with a vaginal diaphragm of the right size)—will show her how to deflower herself if no other method is available; Rosalie Taylor, Medical Officer to the L.C.C. Family Planning Clinic, "The Pre-marital Consultation," in *Marriage Guidance,* a monthly bulletin on Marriage and the Family (National Marriage Guidance Council, London), Feb. 1956, pp. 8–10.

well-known since the publication of *Les Deux Sources*. "Closed" morality is that in which behaviour remains imprisoned in a static world that revolves on its own axis and never emerges on to a higher level. "Open" morality is the exact opposite. It is the kingdom of vital energy, it is the acquisition of a dynamic force, a victorious advance towards its own appointed end. Those who take up their abode in a "closed" well-being—which they imagine will be permanent—run a very great risk of finally succumbing to boredom and of sinking into an empty, isolated existence. Those, on the contrary, who open their hearts to a self-transcending vocation, find joy in progress and discovery. Whilst in the "closed" world we cease to move or we merely mark time, in the "open" world we go forward and upward.

Those husbands and wives who, without losing heart, aim in their mutual love at achieving true chastity are well aware of this. All progress in this field is immediately felt as a victory whose fruits cannot be lost even if sometimes less successful periods follow and cast a shadow over it. Their joy in fact consists in realizing that the demands of instinct are not suppressed nor allowed to regress, but rather that there is an increasing integration (increasing because more subject to reason) of the vehement movements of the flesh under the dynamic control of the spirit. The chastity which they achieve is nothing other than the movement of desire spontaneously entering into union with the order of reason.[6] Chastity is the spiritualization of the flesh which does not cease thereby to be flesh nor to express itself in its own language. The presence of this chastity inculcates a supreme form of art under whose guidance the flesh no longer tends to speak out of its turn or without rhyme or reason. It has a better understanding of its own real task which is to intensify at the proper time and with its own specific accents, the fundamental, true dialogue between persons who genuinely love one another.

> The spiritualization of married love does not ordinarily consist in making it disincarnate (that is, in separating it from its roots in the flesh) but in intensifying the deep, spiritual aspects of bodily union, in impregnating this union more and more with the values of the soul . . . for chastity is more immediately a virtue of the positive practical order than a virtue whose essence lies in abstention.[7]

[6] A. M. Henry, O.P., *Morale et vie conjugale*, Ed. du Cerf, 1957, p. 103.
[7] Abbé de Lochet, *op. cit.*, p. 105.

This fact leads to the discovery of a final contrast between birth regulation and birth control:

5. Birth regulation is, of its nature *compatible with the spiritual life*: birth control, in practice, takes no account of this life.

In the chapter dealing with the position of the reformed Churches, we referred to the strong terms in which the religious authorities asked their people not to treat contraception as an occasion for licence. As the British Council of Churches declared in 1945:

> On one point Christian thought is unanimous in its understanding of the bearing of Christian principle upon the practice of contraception. It is that the use of contraceptive methods is to be cut out and condemned entirely wherever it is merely an expression of the desire for pleasure without responsibility, for that strikes at the very root of personality.
>
> This principle clearly rules out the employment of contraceptive methods to enable sexual union to take place outside marriage. It also provides a criterion for judging their use within marriage itself. Apart from such responsible standards the practice of contraception would stand on the same level with other and uglier perversions of sexuality.[8]

We have duly noted this declaration and the good intentions it presupposes, yet none the less, we insist that contraceptive techniques are bound by definition to separate pleasure from all responsibility. Of itself their use does not ask for any such spiritual effort as that demanded by the practice of continence. They are supposed to act automatically. There would be little harm in this if such techniques were in keeping with nature's wishes, dynamic forces and structures. After all, a pair of glasses, a hearing-aid act automatically enough and require no spiritual effort if they are to bring about the good result we expect of them. But, if we look a little more closely into the matter, we find that the comparison is not valid. Spectacles or hearing-aids only correct the sense organs in the line of their own dynamic movement, they help these organs to achieve their purpose. The comparison could, if necessary, be taken further although at the risk of bordering on the absurd. What should we think of a sighted person with black eyes who, in order to have blue eyes to charm a lover or a mistress, has his or her natural eyes

[8] *Home and Family Life* (S.C.M. Press), London, 1943, Chapter IV, "The Christian Understanding of Marriage and the Family," Section 5, "Problems for Christian Solution: Contraception," pp. 41-2.

removed and replaced by others made of glass and of a colour he chooses? This would be obvious madness. The primary purpose would be sacrificed in the interests of the secondary end, organic vision in the interests of aesthetics. There is surely a similar state of affairs in the case of the contraceptive couple who use a technique that cuts across the fundamental meaning and direction of the sexual function, and gives preference to sensual excitement which normally signifies that this function has successfully completed its operation.

Whether we like it or not, contraceptive methods are null and void, they are incompatible with the dynamic movement of the human spirit. Above all they are directly opposed to the supernatural inspirations of the Holy Spirit. "Grieve not the Holy Spirit", said St Paul to the first Christians. This means: do not grieve the Holy Spirit by living in a manner diametrically opposed to his purposes and his inner guidance.

No doubt, "freedom claimed you when you were called", as St Paul said to the Galatians, "only, do not let this freedom give a foothold to corrupt nature. . . . Let me say this; learn to live and move in the spirit; then there is no danger of your giving way to the impulses of corrupt nature. The impulses of nature and the impulses of the spirit are at war with one another; either is clean contrary to the other. . . . It is easy to see what effects proceed from corrupt nature; they are such things as adultery, impurity, incontinence, luxury, idolatry, witchcraft, etc. I warn you, as I have warned you before, that those who live in such a way will not inherit God's kingdom" (Gal. 5. 13–21).

BIRTH REGULATION : A WAY OF SANCTITY

Birth regulation through continence, on the contrary, satisfies the demand that flesh should be subordinate to spirit. It alone has any right to count on the strength and grace of the Holy Spirit. It alone gives true spiritual joy.

There is no lack of evidence in proof of this. One couple states:

> After seventeen years of married life, we may say that we are grateful to periodic continence for having helped us to live our wedded life in a more human and more Christian way. We used this method from the first months of our life together. In fact, we thought it would be advisable, after the birth of our first child, to have our children at the rate of one every two years. The

experiment was a complete success and it seems to have been a good thing for both mother and children, and so for father as well! Once we had made this reasonable choice for the good of our family circle, we did all we could to see that our sexual relations were not under the sway of chance, instinct and passion but ruled by reason and love.

Thanks to periodic continence, we were able first of all to make suitable preparations for the conception of each of our six children. Since we were almost certain that our sexual relations would be fertile, we did our best to place ourselves in the best possible conditions both physical and moral. We can say with conviction that we really wanted each of our children and that we tried to give them what was best in ourselves at the moment they were conceived.

And the method also made it possible for us to "regularize" our sexual relations. By confining these to the sterile periods (except when we deliberately chose to conceive), we had to prescribe periods of continence for ourselves or rather nature herself prescribed them for us and we accepted the consequences. And so we arranged to make the times when we were doing work which absorbed all our attention coincide with the fertile periods. In this way, we never had the impression that continence required an extraordinary effort of will or that it ran the risk of causing tension between us.

Some people have told us that this regimentation of sexual relations seems to them to go counter to the spontaneous impulses of love. We would point out to them that genuine love can be quite at home with reason, but that too often passion masquerades under the name of love. Surely love does not require that we should be guided by a chance meeting or by what we happen to read! On the contrary, do we not degrade and cheapen it when we allow caprice to rule it? Once we accept the fact that reason is our guide, especially as regards the needs and desires of our bodily life, there seems no point in making an exception for sexual life.

We would add that when sexual relations are contained in this way, they take on all their value and charm. Those who agree to live continently for a few days each month, find far more satisfaction in these relations than those who give way to all their passing whims. Above all, the type of asceticism demanded by periodic continence gives them a far more secure moral strength, not only as regards sexual ethics, but in the whole field of the moral life. It obliges them, in fact, to follow a "rule of life" which they accept for the sake of a greater good, namely the harmonious development of the family community. If they are to succeed, husband and wife must obviously keep a watchful eye on all the influences which might hinder them from carrying out their resolution, such things, for instance, as plays, books, etc. And this vigilance is itself a factor in moral progress. We can therefore acknowledge the help which periodic continence has given us in living a more Christian life from the first day of our marriage.[9]

We are inevitably reminded by testimony of this kind of St Paul's words to the Ephesians:

> You who are husbands must shew love to your wives, as Christ shewed love to the Church.... And that is how husband ought to love wife, as if she were his own body.... It is unheard of, that a man should bear ill-will to his own flesh and blood; no, he keeps it fed and warmed; and so it is with Christ and his Church.... He would hallow it, purify it . . . he would summon it into his own presence, the Church in all its beauty, no stain, no wrinkle, no such disfigurement; it was to be holy, it was to be spotless (Eph. 5. 25–9).

A couple claiming to follow this ideal with the help of contraceptive procedures would be labouring under a delusion. The reverse is true in the case of the Christian couple who accept the Church's teaching on birth regulation and do their best to model their conduct on this teaching. Such a couple places itself genuinely under the direct authority of the Holy Spirit in accordance with Christ's words to the Apostles: "Who hears you, hears me, who despises you, despises me."

We may go even further and say that this readiness to learn from the Church and the Holy Spirit will lead the couple to make remarkable discoveries along the way of Divine and human love. Christ will help husband and wife to understand the Mystery of his own Love. He will give them a share, not only in the life to come, but already in this world, in the bridal feast of the Lamb. He will assist them to mount step by step the path that leads to that sanctity which they will reach together. We are far beyond the mere pass-

[9] *Notes de Pastorale familiale,* No. 30 (April 1956), Ed. Centre des Feuilles. Familiales, Brussels.

ing dream of temporal well-being and comfort envisaged by the advocates of birth control.

We now understand why the Church cannot bring herself to watch the married state debase itself, nor to see it sink into the stagnation of the flesh, instead of seeking here and now "Things no eye has seen, no ear has heard, no human heart conceived, the welcome God has prepared for those who love him" (1 Cor. 2. 9).

BIRTH REGULATION AND SPIRITUAL LIFE.

FURTHER EVIDENCE

In fact, many days of recollection for married couples, many "Family Group Meetings" would bring more enlightenment and more graces if they urged Christian husbands and wives to meditate on and to study the nature of Faith. Everyone would then undoubtedly understand better that joy and happiness are not to be found by remaining outside the scope of the moral Law but rather by going through and beyond it, in the light and warmth which the Holy Spirit pours out upon men, as St Paul says. "But you live the life of the spirit, not the life of nature; that is, if the Spirit of God dwells in you" (Rom. 8. 9). "And if the spirit of him who raised up Jesus from the dead dwells in you, he who raised up Jesus Christ from the dead will give life to your perishable bodies too, for the sake of his Spirit who dwells in you" (Rom. 8. 11). This promise is valid not only for the future life but already on this side of the grave, since there is a progressive healing of the concupiscence that issues from sin. Is not this one of the purposes of the sacrament of matrimony? "The Spirit comes to the aid of our weakness ... the Spirit himself intercedes for us, with groans beyond all utterance" (Rom. 8. 26).

Speaking of the effort towards chastity and continence presupposed by a decision to postpone a pregnancy or to keep the size of the family in future as it is at present, a husband and wife made the following observations: [1]

There is a difference (between this problem) and other problems and trials. To point out what this difference is, we may take as an

---

[1] On the efforts required of a Christian couple when it contemplates for health reasons a limitation of the number of births, see Claude Serviès, *La Chair et la grace*, Spes, 1948. This book by the mother of a large family is full of sound teaching and judicious advice.

example the death of a child. This is a terrible tragedy in a home and God calls on us to accept it as something he relentlessly demands of us. And this acceptance in its profoundest sense can be left to the work of time: "Give him 'to me, let your faith in my Love go even to that length . . ." When the child has died, we can already say in some sort of way: "Yes, I accept", whilst we put off until later a consent inspired by love, for there is no immediate need, imposed from without, to make this leap forward. Once we have made our act of acceptance, there is apparently nothing we have to change in our life. Doubtless, there is an inner, vital need but that is a drama which refuses to be expressed in an outward act. To delay answering "Yes" is not a sin in the context of daily life, it is simply and solely an inner drama (apart of course from such consequences as are possible in human experience, for instance, nervous depression, the sense of the futility of living, etc.).

Another example is the separation forced on husband and wife— and it may last for months or years—for professional reasons, or by war or sickness. Here too there is, in most cases, no outward choice to be made. We have no choice at all. We must at all costs organize our lives according to this edict of God's will that has been imposed upon us and we must try to accept it with the maximum of inner consent. Although it is true that this acceptance completely changes our inner life, yet it does not demand normally any outward action on our part.

CONTINENCE AND ABSOLUTE FAITH IN CHRIST

But chastity,[2] or rather continence, if it is an urgent call from God, is also, in the concrete, a work to be undertaken, a plan that has to be carried out. It is quite possible to postpone this task or even to evade it both inwardly and outwardly. It is a problem akin to that of poverty which we constantly hesitate to choose deliberately since it too, as we feel, involves a complete acceptance. We cannot hope to make such an acceptance by any merely formal consent. It can only be the result of *faith* and *love*.

The concrete problem is then this: Do I love Christ enough to believe that he can achieve his work of love in me, in us? Even

[2] On married chastity, see the next chapter and the bibliography on p. 208, note 6.

if it seems madness from the human standpoint, beyond the power of nature, dangerous for our family life, can I nevertheless trust sufficiently in Christ to make the attempt with his help? or rather to allow him to make this attempt in me? Am I ready to offer him my being as an extension of his human nature? If I am, I still have to ask myself whether I love him enough to love what he wills. As in all the acts life demands, there is a tremendous gap between accepting God's will and loving it. Unless I love his will, continence is impossible.

And yet, if we throw ourselves into Christ's arms, chastity will gradually become possible. It will issue from the dialogue we have begun with him, a dialogue which involves on our part a spirit of generosity, but also lapses, sufferings, doubts, moments of weariness. Let us make no mistake about it, if this decision brings both darkness and light alternately, *it ultimately gives us the certainty that we are living with Christ in the truth*, even if there are moments of weakness, even if sometimes we sin.

And so we eventually cease to worry very much about these lapses, when we have chosen Christ. We do not think God is very angry with us if we sometimes happen to go beyond the lawful bounds through some sudden impulse or because of our weakness. The only thing to do is to ask at once for forgiveness, for if we return to him and to our dialogue with him, he is always ready to receive us, is kind, welcoming, our friend.[3]

Finally, our salvation lies, as always, in absolute faith in, and adoration of, the Mystery of Christ *living* in us, Christ loving us. This sentence contains everything, absolutely everything.

We are members of his Body and he lives in our souls. So for us the real problem of the Christian is: Who shall live in me? Christ or myself? If Christ, then he will live his own life in me and he will bring me the solutions to my problems.

[3] On this spirituality of confidence in God, as the clearest sign of "a firm purpose", see the excellent article by Fr Carpentier, "Lumières de la charité sur un problème pastoral difficile" in *Nouvelle Revue Théologique*, Nov. 1959, p. 939. "Knowing as he does the facts of the Redemption, the Christian is aware that his life is one of continual progress, and a striving towards a nobler love. He is aware that, if he is willing, *this struggle will not, by God's grace, be interrupted by his falls (even if frequent)* into sin, even over a long period (we shall have something later to say on hope and success). He is aware from actual experience of the true conditions under which he may receive absolution and he has no fear that it will be refused" . . . For, "What, in the last analysis is the Christian's *firm purpose*? It is a sincere prayer, repeated even after numerous evidences of weakness, a prayer by which we humbly ask, and with the desire that our prayer be answered, for the grace not to fall again" (p. 940).

Is everything within his power or are there things he cannot do? Does he or does he not love us? We must go blindly forward, as we do in the case of the Eucharist. If we wait until we understand the Eucharist before we communicate, we may have to wait a long time. Its truth will become evident not through logic, but through God's grace. God's *living* grace. And the principal advantage is the *inrush of light* into the soul, the realization of the truth of the words: "Christ lives in us." All else flows from, and is given life by, this fact.

"Is it not just a matter of allowing Christ to continue in us his redemptive work?" one couple asks:

No doubt the gradual application to our souls of Christ's redemptive act affects every phase of our lives. This is especially true of continence since body and soul are both involved and continence is not bodily abstinence alone. Christ lives in us. This is an inexhaustible truth. He completes his Passion in us, in us he continues to save the world, first ourselves and then other people. It is certain that by that sacrifice which is at the heart of human love, he saves our wedded love. But far more than this is involved. He saves his Mystical Body. He incorporates us into himself and into the universe in all aspects of our nature that are within the scope of his redemption. And so when we allow him to live within us as our redeemer, our love goes out to him, we make an act of faith, we fulfil an obligation in justice. And all this is a vital necessity for the Christian. To consent to be a Christian, is to know we shall be crucified, torn by conflict. We shall always find ourselves in uncomfortable situations. Life will hang us on the Cross. In the death of a little child, in separation, temptation, continence, etc., we are given Christ Crucified.... But it is God who gives us the Christ whom we receive.

The problem is obviously not for the individual alone, since there are two of us and matters are very different when one of the partners has not "wagered" on God.[4] But when both partners have invited Christ into their home and in their own poor way receive him there as God by making every effort to love him, then the problem has a well-defined character.

If we consider this problem under all its human aspects, or what

[4] There is an allusion here to Pascal's doctrine of the "wager", a quasi-mathematical apologetic defence of the arguments for the existence and providence of God and for the future life.—Translator's note.

appear to be such, if we say to ourselves: "Is it really important? Am I bound to fail? Shall I destroy our love? Supposing I am forcing my wife to be unfaithful or turning her into a neurotic, supposing I am making my husband a victim of repressions, supposing the atmosphere in the family becomes electric and family life unbearable, etc. . . ." there will be no end to it and we may go round and round indefinitely and never dare to make a start. But if, by God's grace, we genuinely love our partner, we cannot possibly go wrong and little by little the answers to all these questions will be found.

CONTINENCE AND SUPERNATURAL FAITH
IN ONE'S PARTNER

Hence the problem of trust not only makes us face the question of our love for God, it also drives us to the heart and the very essence of human love. It forces us, as it did in our relations to God, to make up our minds where we shall stand and to respond in exactly the same way—by faith and love. "Do I love my wife enough to believe in her? Do I love God in my husband enough to have confidence in them both? Do I love God living in my partner enough not only to leave God free to do as he wills, but also to do all I can to help my husband's love for him to increase?"

"Do I love my husband enough to make God's life in him the object of all my effort and action? Is it my wife's soul that I love? Is it the divine life which I love for her sake?" If I can answer "Yes," then we must walk in God's footsteps, we must make our leap forward in Faith. The growth of mutual love and the relations it creates in the souls of the partners then become God's task. It is for us to stand aside and to be content to love.

A constant care and zeal for the coming of God's kingdom in our partner increase our human love to an incredible extent. Respect for the body, which is both the dwelling-place of purity and the means by which genuine love expresses itself when the period of continence is over; our esteem for our partner as the dwelling-place of God and as cooperating with him, affection, trust, gentleness, simplicity, humility during moments of weakness, all these bring us closer together. One great benefit among the rest is the fact that continence *develops* love for the body and for the marriage act since by protecting and enriching the soul, it makes us *ready* to love the flesh of husband or wife and, in all simplicity, happy to give and to receive sexual fulfilment. Our efforts for the benefit of the other's soul are continued in our efforts for the benefit of his or her body and impurity is seen to be senseless.

From this point of view sexual relations produce remarkable fruit. "Husbands and wives who, after months of continence, can once more experience their mutual love in the deliberate conception of a child and with the sense that they are collaborating in a divine task, live through hours whose depths and intimacy are a wonderful source of joy, and the memory of which is a constant spur to their love."

CONTINENCE AND THE GROWTH OF WEDDED LOVE

Further, this experience will do away with a problem which might sometimes cause suffering: "Should I be first and foremost a husband or wife, or a father or mother?" The child is our love made life. He is the product of a husband who has a respect for love and of a wife whom love has made fertile. A new knowledge of the meaning of marriage has come to them both and he is, as it were, entirely moulded by it. He is its fruit so he too is dearly loved. The older children who were not conceived like him at a given, chosen moment, but whom their parents were eager to have in the early days of their marriage, will also benefit by this fresh mutual fervour in their parents' hearts.

And so riches pour into a daily existence under the seal of continence, bodily union—and the love of God.

This is how "birth regulation" works. It brings with it not only the solution to the crucial question of fertility limitation, but still more the secret of human love and personal self-mastery.

"When one uses contraceptives," a husband once admitted, "one has the impression of being controlled by, rather than of being in control of, a technique."

But "regulation", depending on married chastity and continence, gives, on the contrary, a supreme sense of freedom to the consciousness of the partners. Freedom brings joy in its train, and joy makes love perfect.

Chapter XIII

PREPARATION FOR BIRTH REGULATION AND ITS PRACTICE

THE HEROISM OF THE FAMILY IN THE MODERN WORLD

NOBODY will deny that the Catholic Church's doctrine on birth regulation is noble and uplifting. It shows optimism concerning the possibilities of human nature when helped by divine grace. Some will be tempted to consider this optimism exaggerated. "This is all very fine, too fine even for the bulk of mankind," certain people will object, "under the conditions of modern life, it is impossible in practice. The Church asks of a human race, whose aspirations are none too lofty and whose resolution is weak, conduct which presupposes heroism."

Indeed, the Church speaking through the late Sovereign Pontiff, Pius XII, has on several occasions recognized that, in the contemporary world, vast numbers of men "cannot lead an upright, honourable and happy wedded life except by overcoming very formidable difficulties".[1] "Lack of understanding, callousness, ill-will on the part of others," he explains, "make life hard and all but unbearable for the heroes who do their duty in marriage. In fact, only a genuine heroism sustained by Divine Grace can preserve in the hearts of husbands and wives the desire to experience the joys of a large family."[2]

Indeed, we see families over which hovers, like an ominous spectre, the danger that the source of their whole income may dry up if employment should suddenly cease. For others, this uncertainty as regards their wages is complicated by the fact that these are inadequate and to such an extent that they do not allow them to buy enough clothes nor even a sufficient amount of food to prevent illness. This state of affairs grows still worse when they are forced to live in a small number of unfurnished rooms lacking

[1] Speech of Pius XII, 2 Nov. 1956.
[2] Pius XII to the Sacred College, 2 June 1947, D.C., 22 June 1947, c. 773.

all the modest comforts that make life less difficult. . . . But the saddest sight of all is that of families that are completely destitute, families in direst poverty, where the father has no work, where the mother sees her children grow weak and yet is unable to do anything for them. Day by day there is not enough to eat, not enough to wear, and woe to all of them when sickness enters this cave that does duty for a human habitation! [3]

What a humiliation it is for the world to have fallen so low, to a social condition so opposed to nature! [4]

Therefore the Church calls all true Christians, all men of good-will, to a genuine crusade of charity, to work for the transformation of social conditions so that families can live in conditions more worthy of human beings, "in face of such urgent need, the social order must be improved". [5] No one has done more than Pius XII to urge our world to provide healthy accommodation for families and to organize a system of social security genuinely at the service of men and their families. No one has given more encouragement to families to organize themselves into "a solid front aware of its strength", and able "to make its voice heard in the affairs of every nation, every form of society, to such effect that the family may never have to suffer at their hands, but, on the contrary, be benefited by them to the greatest possible extent". But once she has made all this clear, the Church remains inflexible in her doctrinal position: "Man, born as he is to attain to temporal and eternal happiness, cannot attain to either except by fulfilling those duties which are of obligation, and by obeying the law of God."

On the day following the proclamation of the doctrine of the Assumption, Pius XII made this clear:

Even when we want to come to the aid of men in the difficult crises of married life . . . we cannot appeal to the gift of freedom which God has granted us, in order to insist that we are dispensed from adhering to the divine order. . . . We may never take this road since to do so is criminal and disastrous. . . . It is therefore a pernicious thing, both for the Church and for civil society, that shepherds of souls, in their teaching and in everyday life, should habitually and deliberately keep silent, whatever the circumstances may be. Excuses are sought in the privation and poverty that

[3] Pius XII, "Christmas Message," 1952.
[4] Pius XII to the Sacred College, 2 June 1947.   [5] Pius XII, 2 Nov. 1950.

ordinarily make the family's position difficult. Our fatherly heart regrets and deplores this, but we are forbidden to turn away from the firm and stable order established by God. May it never be weakened anywhere!

Even when it is improved and relieved of its excessive and unduly crippling burdens, the social order will not prevent the conflict between flesh and spirit from continuing. When we are faced with the problem of the dilemma between wedded chastity as the Church has defined it and the solutions proposed by modern civilization, there is no way of escape.

But who will deny that this wedded chastity, if we are better prepared for it by more realistic and positive methods of education, is to that extent made more easy for couples who show goodwill?

Are we not justified in complaining of the fact that certain past generations of parents and Catholic educators have sometimes confined their teaching too exclusively to the promulgation of the law, and this is in its most negative form: "You must not do this or that"? We expected them to set our feet firmly on the way of positive perfection, and to emphasize in their teaching that we should trust in God's help, and work for his greater glory.

We must not generalize too quickly in lodging this complaint. We should think rather of the formation which has been given for a long time past by youth movements, beginning with the Wolf Cub's motto "I will do my best" and ending with that of the Jéciste (a member of the Jeunesse Etudiante Chrétienne, the Young Christian Students): "The Jéciste belongs not to himself, but to God for the sake of his brethren."

Even in the sphere of sexual and matrimonial morals, we have only to re-read the Encyclical *Casti Connubii* from beginning to end —and particularly the magnificent third section, which has been the real cause of the revival of family spirituality in the contemporary world.[6] We find in it the main lines of a method of preparation for marriage and for that control of fertility which is in accordance with the Christian faith. There is "*a gap to be filled here,*" as Mgr

[6] *Casti Connubii*, "How to remedy the Evil," C.T.S., pp. 57–64. On the revival of family life and spirituality brought about by *Casti Connubii*, see our article: "Histoire d'un renouveau familial," in *Revue d'Action Populaire*, No. 93, Dec. 1955, pp. 1229–36, and Jacques Starck, "Dans cette vallée de larmes, un peu de paradis, le vingt-cinquième anniversaire de l'encyclique *Casti Connubii*," in *Etudes*, 1955, pp. 290–302, and less recently, Jacques Leclerq, "Où en est la question familiale?" in *Etudes*, Dec, 1949, pp. 357–69.

Suenens forcefully remarks. "We must train men to master sexuality, for there lies the true key to a human and Christian solution of the problem of love." [7]

THE MAIN LINES OF A METHOD OF PREPARATION FOR MARRIAGE

PERILS TO BE AVOIDED

The basis of a happy wedlock, and the ruin of an unhappy one," says Pius XI in *Casti Connubii*, "is prepared and set in the souls of boys and girls during the period of childhood and adolescence." [8]

Christian generations in the past seem to have misunderstood or to have only partly understood this truth. Much evidence is available from adolescents and young people, who have been left to discover by themselves what, after the religious life, is the most important thing in the world, namely the discovery of genuine human love and its emotional and sexual implications. [9]

One adolescent writes:

How are we to make our parents see that this matter of love, which they think is so remote from our thoughts and about which they never speak to us, is one of the chief things that occupy our minds, perhaps the principal one, after that of our life at school?

As many do not dare to put their questions, young people live in a state of real confusion in this connection. "We are left 'to sink or swim' "—the phrase just hits it off—"in the false and complicated conjectures our imaginations suggest to us. We float about and live in a kind of inner state of agitation."

And so there is a waste of nervous energy and who knows what unconscious upheavals! And especially if, on top of it all, there is a predominantly negative religious education, for which chastity is merely the outcome of the struggle against temptations.

---

[7] Mgr L. J. Suenens, Auxiliary Bishop of Malines, *Un problème crucial: Amour et Maîtrise de soi*, Desclée, 1960, pp. 59–65.

[8] *Casti Connubii*, C.T.S., p. 57. On preparation for marriage, see Pius XII, "Allocution sur l'éducation des adultes"; 19 March 1953, "aux aumôniers de la J.A.C.," 8 Sept. 1953.—Cardinal Feltin, Archbishop of Paris, "La fidélité conjugale."

[9] Pierre Chambre, *Les jeunes devant l'éducation sexuelle*, with evidence supplied by several hundred adolescents. Ed. Néret, 1958. This book is of capital importance and should enlighten very many parents who still hesitate to do their duty by educating their children in the problems of sexuality.

When we try to put ourselves in the children's place by making use of the observations of child specialists or the testimony of young people themselves, we cannot possibly fail to discover the unhappy consequences for their active life, of the silence of adults on such important problems.

And if we asked husbands and wives to tell us about the lack of information or the uncertainties which have been the cause of so many mistakes in their married life, we should hear an equally large number of complaints. There would be those who, in the quite recent past, accepted the assurance that if they had remained chaste until the time of their marriage, they would then have "the right to do just what they like". There would be those who were told by a father or mother that they ought to have "experiences" so as to "get to know" women better before meeting the woman who was to be their wife. As for young women, they would have an equal right to complain. Until quite recently, they were kept completely ignorant and so ran the risk of innocently accepting the worst kind of conduct from their husbands from the wedding night onwards. Or else, as soon as they were married, they took fright—quite wrongly—at the mere requirements of nature. How many blunders, misunderstandings, false starts could have been avoided had they been given suitable information and education regarding their emotions and sexuality!

At present, silence and ignorance are more rare, although we must not jump to hasty general conclusions . . . since people now fall into other and no less harmful excesses.

In the nineteenth century no woman could mention sexual questions without being aware that she was one of the "emancipated" sort. Women's books were all silent on this point. Sexual sensibility was undoubtedly dormant or repressed. The opposite is the case today. All the magazines discuss this subject and try to persuade us that the sexual awakening of the woman is the one essential for a happy married life and responsible for all the qualities of a good wife and mother. Frigidity on the woman's part may certainly cause serious disturbances, but we observe today that obsession with sex, anxiety over the awakening of the woman's senses and her sexual satisfaction, become in their turn the starting point of other disturbances and other misunderstandings. Some women become mesmerized by the idea that they are not receiving their due in marriage and that the latter therefore cannot last. They read magazines which suggest that they should blame their husbands for this state of affairs. They look elsewhere for further explanations and sometimes for other partners, in order to prove to themselves that they are capable of sexual satisfaction.[1]

And so humanity falls out of the frying-pan into the fire. Yet the Church keeps watch and tries to draw fruitful lessons from this spasmodic movement. Anxious as she is to preserve those basic values of which we spoke earlier, she endeavours with each generation to perfect the education of the young by means of her own experience. She rightly thinks that certain requirements can be more easily accepted by the coming generation if they are known in time, and if the best way to meet them is clearly taught. And so we are able to give a detailed account in the following pages of her programme of education and preparation for a genuinely human and spiritual mastery of fertility, and birth regulation will be only one of its aspects.

INITIATION OF CHILDREN INTO THE
MYSTERY OF LIFE

1. This education begins by initiating children into the mystery of life.[2] A mother who answers her young children's questions simply and sensibly, when they talk to her about the birth of babies, is a woman who already and without knowing it is preparing her children for the discovery of more important truths and for the kind of preparation that is more immediately connected with marriage. In the same way, it is a happy father who has the courage to explain to his boys how Providence has decreed that children should be born of the love of their parents, and how, with this end in mind, it has wonderfully organized the bodily structure of husband and wife so that their love may achieve a union of the greatest intimacy in which the husband's embrace makes his wife fertile. If they impart secrets such as these to their sons, fathers will receive from the latter in exchange an abundance of trust and grati-

[1] Dr J. Bouttonier-Favez, "Vie sexuelle et vie à deux," in *Ecole des Parents*, Nov. 1953, p. 36.
[2] Pierre Chambre, *Les jeunes devant l'éducation sexuelle*, Néret, 1958. See the detailed bibliography, pp. 145–7.

tude that seems beyond belief. There is no better means of working for the stability of a boy's character and towards developing his respect for chastity than a conversation of this kind with his father.

THE FAMILY ATMOSPHERE AS A FACTOR MAKING
FOR STABILITY OF CHARACTER

2. The creation of a healthy atmosphere in a family where love rules and in which husband and wife have learned to appreciate the meaning and value of chastity, is, in its own special way, one element in the process of preparation. We all know what a mark is left on us by the attitude of our parents towards each other and towards ourselves from the earliest days of our childhood. If parents could only realize to what extent they are responsible for the future psychological balance of those they have brought into the world, they would control themselves far more than they actually do.[3]

This is the case with mothers who refuse to accept their role as women. They repudiate their feminine nature, which they experience as something intolerably inferior. Far from filling them with joy, motherhood seems to them a kind of degradation. Hence it will be very difficult for them to accept their child and to love it; they will generally refuse it their affection or else, by a process of compensation, become over-protective. Since they play a part in family life that is neither one thing nor the other or else is undisguisedly masculine, they prevent the father from playing his own specific part. In any case, they have mostly chosen a weak and submissive husband with few manly traits and they dominate him without any difficulty. Under such conditions the frame of reference which the family provides for the children is completely distorted. The daughter will identify herself with a viriloid feminine model always claiming the privileges of the male, whilst the son will refuse to identify himself with a masculine model which he sees is constantly belittled.[4]

The exact opposite will be the case with the family in which each parent has succeeded in accepting his or her own sex and in de-

[3] Dr Nodet, *Conflits familiaux et psychologie profonde*, in *Pastorale familiale*, Congrès de l'Union des Oeuvres, Rennes, 1949, pp. 134-46; Dr Maurice Porot, *L'enfant et les relations familiales*, P.U.F., 1954.

[4] Dr Paul Osterrieth, *L'enfant et la famille*, Editions du Scarabée, p. 108.

siring that each partner should be complementary to the other. In such a family, stability will be the rule and the children will benefit by it in their own journey towards maturity.

THE EDUCATION OF THE GROWING CHILD

3. When the period of adolescence arrives, it still falls to the parents, if they are to be genuine educators, to put before the young people an ideal of self-transcendence instead of trying constantly to prevent a son or daughter from growing out of their more childish attitudes.[5] Further, the child likes to strive towards an ideal, when he feels he has the backing of his educators or of a youth movement for which he has an affection. This is the place to mention the self-respect, the "hygiene", of chastity which a young man or a young woman want to learn. Nothing will contribute more towards achieving it than their parents' obvious trust in them. To make this trust plain is a more difficult task than people usually think. The adolescent feels a natural desire to move away from his family circle. He is stubborn and touchy. His parents no longer know "how to handle him". Above all, he tends to remain shut up in himself. He is not so communicative as he was. He keeps his emotions hidden under a mask of indifference, sometimes even of cynicism. The art of the educator will then consist in the ability to share the interests of this unstable adolescent and to assure him that he can succeed—and the lad has far graver doubts on this point than he is willing to admit.

THE DISCOVERY OF THE OTHER SEX

4. Eventually the time comes when the psychology of the other sex has to be discovered. How many misunderstandings would be avoided if, in the family, each of the partners took the trouble to reflect upon, and above all, to ask, what "love"—a word they both use but in a different sense—means for the other! In fact psychologists say that emotional maturity begins when each sex admits and accepts the sexuality of the other as complementary to his or her

[5] Jean Rimaud, *L'éducation, direction de la croissance*, Aubier, 1946, especially Book III, ch. 3-5: "Direction du jeune et du grand adolescent. Notes sur la première étape de l'adolescence des filles. Pendant la seconde étape"; *Cahiers Laënnec*, "Direction et problèmes de l'adolescent," 1946.

own.[6] Women are often surprised at the two aspects that mostly characterize male sexuality. Unless they have learned to accept the inevitable, they will revolt against the fact that they seem to be the object of desire rather than of genuine love. Maturity will come when the woman, although refusing to make herself cheap on his account, yet admits that this dual aspect may be excused or rather justified by the natural temperament of her partner.

At the opposite end of the scale, the young man has to reach a better understanding of the woman's diffused sexuality, slow to be aroused and something of a mystery to women themselves. He must understand how rich her nature is although so different from his own. But a man will not be brought to admit this unless he is humble, unless he is willing to listen, to recognize how ignorant he is and to try to overcome ignorance by finding out the facts.[7]

EMOTIONAL AND SEXUAL DISCIPLINE

5. Youth is the time when instincts should become mature. Instincts which are egocentric at birth have gradually to be centred on others. With the married relationship in mind, the young man ought little by little to come to see it much more as an opportunity to give joy to his partner rather than to seek pleasure for himself. So many misunderstandings arise from a failure to understand this. Frigidity on the woman's part is never or almost never the result of physiological abnormality. Three-quarters of the time it is caused by a lack of psychological understanding on the part of the husband who has been given inadequate information on the emotive reactions of women.

But this maturity is only achieved at a cost. The young man has to agree to discipline himself, to sacrifice his fickle passions. He has to learn not to seek pleasure at the expense of, or even with the willing consent of young women. He has to accept all this not be-

---

[6] Dr André Berge, "Que recherche-t-on dans le mariage? La vie du couple," in *Ecole des Parents,* "La préparation au mariage," Nov. 1953 pp. 18–21.

[7] Dr Jouvenroux, *A la découverte de l'amour,* Ed. Ouvrières, 1942. P. Dufoyer, *Le Mariage (livre du jeune homme), Le Mariage (livre de la jeune fille),* Casterman, second edition, 1957. Myriam Dominique, *Quand l'amour s'éveille,* Ed. Ouvrières; Fabienne Van Roye, *Toi qui deviens femme déjà,* Casterman, 1950; Jacqueline Martin, *Soif,* Ed. Mappus, Le Puy, 1954. This book, written by the mother of a family, makes it quite clear what the woman expects and what the man does *not* expect it will be his duty to give her.

cause of any categorical imperative urging him to indulge a will to power, but as the highest manifestation of courtesy towards the other sex, and he will think of sexual union with the other sex solely in the person of his future wife whom he already loves by anticipation.[8]

The same is true of the young woman. She will accept the fact that she is attractive but will behave discreetly and carefully out of respect and love for the other sex to which her future husband belongs.

At this stage—at least in the case of girls between fourteen and sixteen—family education should see to it that the mother provides a fairly complete body of information on the monthly cycle of fertility; she should already have in mind the birth regulation whose norms, as we have said, are found in the actual structure of nature.[9] Experience proves that as far as the education given hitherto is concerned, not one young girl in ten knows how to note exactly the regular sequence of her fertile and sterile cycles or has observed that nature does not always follow a strict pattern in this repect. Is it so difficult or so odd that a mother should help her child to grow in the knowledge of herself and her physiology, by explaining to her at this early stage that there is nothing unimportant or of little account when we are dealing with a love that desires to be chaste, that there is no genuine love, no constant devotion without discipline and asceticism?

Nature has made the female organism fragile. In marriage, as we have seen, this organism will have to regulate and temper the physical expression of the love of husband and wife in relation to its own needs and requirements as regards fertility and periods of rest. Sexuality is not in any sense, as the contemporary world would have us believe, a form of play provided for the couple by nature to be indulged in for their amusement and at their own good pleasure. It is something far more important.

Sexuality is the means given by nature to a man and woman whereby they may express their greatest creative potentialities, that within them which will most ennoble them—the gift of self, and devotion to one another.

[8] Dr Carnot, *Au service de l'amour*, Ed. Beaulieu, 1938; L. Husson, *Eléments de morale sexuelle*, Aubier. This is an excellent book by a master in a grammar school. It aims to lead to emotional and moral maturity by way of reflection, Dr Biot, *Éducation de l'amour*, Plon, 1951. This book is written at a very high moral level and suitable only for more mature minds.

[9] Claire Souvenance, *Construire un foyer (le livre de la fiancée)*, Éd. Mappus, 1949. Dr Holt, La fertilité cyclique de la femme.—Méthode facile de régler les naissances par la mesure de la température basale.—Vigot, 1959.

THE CHOICE OF A PARTNER : THE ENGAGEMENT

6. The choice of a partner is one of the most important acts in life. Upon it depends the happy development of the married union. Some choices are made as the result of family pressure. Others, on the contrary, are determined by aggressive reactions against the parents. There are cases of love at first sight. There are decisions taken after long and mature deliberation. The issues have been carefully weighed and the choice made in all humility and with trust in God and his Providence.

"Let, then, those who are about to enter on married life, approach that state well disposed and well prepared, so that they will be able as far as they can to help each other in sustaining the vicissitudes of life," declared Pius XI.[1]

Before the engagement takes place, the period during which the young people begin to keep company will provide the first topics for them to think about—the family and the social circle, the kind of education each has received, temperament, character, tastes, inclinations, tendencies, etc. There is all the more chance that the life they are to lead together will be solidly based if both of them become convinced that marriage is a religious act, an act which includes the whole of existence and affects it at every point. Their love is mature if it is able to gather into itself all the aspects both pleasant and unpleasant of their life together.[2]

The period of the engagement proper is the best time of all for the two young people to begin to face all the great problems of family life. They should know that the Church's most difficult demands as regards married life stand a chance of solution only if they are discussed during the engagement period. To think that "marriage will put everything right" is an illusion. Engaged couples ought to discuss together questions that might later cause clashes or mutual misunderstanding. Such problems are—the size of the family, the

---

[1] *Casti Connubii,* C.T.S., p. 58.
[2] Abbé Godin, *Le Christ dans les fiançailles,* Ed. Ouvrières, 1941; J. Maillet, *Lettres à sa fiancée,* Ed. du Feu Nouveau; *Anneau d'or,* "Ce que doivent savoir le fiancés"; A. d'Heilly, "Fiançailles chrétiennes," Nos. 21-2, May-Aug. 1948, pp. 251-83; P. Dufoyer, *Pour toi, jeune fiancé et jeune mari—Pour toi, jeune fiancée et jeune épouse,* Casterman, 1955; P. Michel, *Construire un foyer,* Ed. Mappas: S. de Lestapis, "Les retraites de fiancés en France," in *Revue de l'Action Populaire,* No. 77, April 1954; by the same author, "La préparation du mariage à Chicago," in *Revue de l'Action Populaire,* No. 105, Feb. 1957.

possibility of having four, five or six children, what spacing is desirable, what trials are to be expected, what likelihood there will be of the need for more or less lengthy periods of continence.

Engaged couples may be surprised to learn that the first months or years of married life will very probably bring the greatest number of difficulties. "Forewarned is forearmed" says the proverb. Engaged couples should know that after their initial difficulties, others will appear towards the seventh or eighth year of marriage. When three or four children have been born, the problem of future births begins to present itself. No couple can avoid this question and it is no use keeping it out of sight before marriage. The Church herself considers that a morally prudent attitude of mind will inevitably have it in view from the very beginning in the case of couples entering the married state after due deliberation.[3] This does not mean that we are given a special gift of state to enable us to solve the problem eight years in advance nor does it mean that we are obliged to delay the first birth. But it is already a great step forward if we have given the matter some thought.

How many future husbands have considered the possibility that their wives may fall ill and remain ill perhaps for a long time? How many have faced the fact that continence may be necessary for a month or for a period of years? No doubt there is no point in scaring those who make up their mind to marry. Nevertheless they must be realists if they want their undertaking to prosper and to last.

A priest who had, on one occasion, to preach a retreat to engaged couples asked some working-class husbands and wives what they thought he ought to tell these young people. He had not long to wait for the answer: "Tell them that it won't be anything like they expected." Not that this way of putting it means that disappointment is inevitable. It implies that the unexpected is inseparable from a vocation in which the risk that love may die has to be taken into consideration.

[3] Fr P. MacAvoy, S.J., *Pour mieux aimer,* Ed. B.P., 1960, p. 40.

A RIGHT ATTITUDE OF MIND AND MODERATION
DURING THE EARLY DAYS OF MARRIAGE

7. Husbands and wives should also see that in the first days of their married life they practise the moderation which is in keeping with the expression of their mutual love. As Pius XI advised:

> Let husband and wife resolve . . . to use the rights given them by marriage in a way that will be always Christian and sacred, more especially in the first years of wedlock, so that should there be need of continency afterwards, custom will have made it easier for each to preserve it.[4]

Doctors are unanimous in recognizing that habits easily become tyrannical when reason has kept an inadequate check on them. Sexuality may be compared to a piece of material which we must be careful not to crease. There is always, no doubt, during the early days of marriage, a certain amount of over-excitement in the enjoyment of the pleasures of the body. There is nothing wrong in this and no reason to be scrupulous about it, especially if the wish to have a child—and this is normally the case—soon begins to appear.

The birth of the first child should not be delayed, unless there are serious reasons, connected in most cases with the problem of inadequate accommodation or insufficient financial resources. Far from threatening the happy relations between the young husband and wife, the coming of the first child, on the contrary, will strengthen and hallow them.

If they wish to postpone the birth for longer than a year, and for no other reason than to be able to enjoy more freedom and leisure together, they run the risk of making a false start. We have said often enough that married love which fails to go forward spontaneously towards the complete maturity which is represented and implied by giving birth to a child is a love still weighed down by self-centredness of an infantile or juvenile character. It is far better to agree together to make every effort to pass beyond rather than to remain permanently at this transitional stage.[5]

[4] *Casti Connubii*, C.T.S., p. 36.
[5] Marc Oraison, *Man and Wife*, Chapter 8, "Marriage an Education."

SPACING OF SUBSEQUENT PREGNANCIES

8. Finally, it is essential that before marriage the future partners should be sufficiently acquainted with the grave problem of the spacing of births. Under modern conditions of life, we strongly advise that everything possible should be done to space the children, whom their mothers will have to bring up and rear, at intervals of about 18 months or 2 years. On this point, the Church's teaching is becoming more and more clear and precise. As we have said, there is only one lawful method—prolonged and periodic continence.

The word "continence" however, does not fully convey the reality it represents. The word is too negative and does not adequately suggest the positive aspect of the virtue of chastity.[6] In actual fact, chastity, we may say, is simply charity enveloping instinct and giving it its true scope. A husband very much in love with his wife and, at the same time, full of consideration for her, was able to say, during the periods when they had recognized that it was necessary for births to be spaced: "I love you too much, my dear, to desire you for the time being." The ability to say this presupposes a self-mastery beyond the power of the will, however active. More is necessary—the grace and adaptability which divine charity alone can infuse into the soul.

At this point, we might well bear in mind the whole spirituality which is necessary during this period when births have to be spaced. It is a spirituality of activities undertaken in common, a better organized participation in the liturgy, a more frequent reception of the sacraments. St Paul speaks of "having more freedom for prayer".

And so, if these spiritual conditions are fulfilled, the natural

[6] Marc Oraison, "Signification chrétienne de la famille," in *Orientations de pastorale familiale,* Ed. Familiales de France, pp. 79–98. "Chastity is an affair of the *spirit* and not merely a matter of organized birth limitation. It seems to me that this is not stressed often enough or strongly enough. Yet the Church's traditional teaching on this point is sufficiently clear." See also Fr Gilleman, S.J., *The Primacy of Charity in Moral Theology,* London, Burns & Oates, and Westminster, Maryland, Newman Press, 1959, p. 320; D. Planque, *La chasteté conjugale, vertu positive, Etude de pastorale,* Ed. Feuilles Familiales, Brussels, 1957. There is much food for thought in these pages. On the relations between married chastity and virginity, see *below,* pp. 283–5, and Fr Antoine, S.J., "L'Eglise et le Birth Control," in *Revue de l'Action Populaire,* 116, March 1958. *Etudes Carmélitaines, Mystique et Continence,* 1952; Mgr Garrone, "Charité conjugale et charité virginale," in *Vie Spirituelle,* June 1947, pp. 734–47; Fr Héris, "L'amour virginal," in *Vie Spirituelle,* Jan. 1951, pp. 45–69.

method of birth spacing will fall into place. Whether continence is to be practised over a long space of time or only periodically, it will in any case require the kind of effort which the partners, in their love for one another, have agreed to make together. It will require much charity, mutual understanding, mutual encouragement.

The couple would be well advised at this stage to ask for information either from a Marriage Guidance Centre [7] or from an *experienced* doctor, concerning what is known as the temperature method.[8] As we said above, the girl whose mother has been able to educate her in these matters is already sufficiently prepared to be able to make a fresh series of observations, during the four or five months of her engagement, and this will demand of her a new ascetic effort. But there is nothing she would not do so that the home she is to found may grow and flourish in the true joy of chastity.

It is an undoubted fact that the more accurately and exactly the future wife is able to diagnose her period every month and even perhaps the actual day when ovulation begins, the more natural and easy will be the regulation of births when it becomes necessary. And why should it not be possible in the near future, if the appropriate training is given, to establish a coenesthetic diagnosis of ovulation? [9] In this age of Pavlovian medicine, of which, for the masses, painless childbirth is the most practical example—and it is possible because of a more accurate identification of certain "conditioned reflexes"—it is rather the use in and out of season of mechanical and chemical contraceptives which ought to be considered as an aberration and an outdated notion.[1]

[7] Dr Billiard-Duchesne, "Le problème de la planification des naissances, aspect médical et moral," in *Pages documentaires de l' U.C.S.S.*, 1957, "Problèmes de déontologie," pp. 17–32 and especially p. 26.

[8] Claude Souvenance, *Construire un foyer*, Ed. Mappus, J. MacAvoy, *op. cit.*, pp. 167–83; on the "cervical test" perfected by Dr Doyle, a Boston (U.S.A.) Catholic doctor, see Dr R. de Guchteneere, "Un nouveau test d'ovulation," in *St-Luc médical* (Brussels), 1958, No. 6, pp. 462–6; for further information, *Chromotesteur Doyle*, Dynam-Institut, 27, rue D'Astorg, Paris, 8e.

[9] "According to the Japanese doctor, Hisao Ito, 40% of nurses and 70% of women doctors and students amongst whom he conducted an inquiry, were able by careful self-observation to predict the date of the onset of menstruation." (Quoted by Koller, *Zentralbl. für Gynak.*, p. 2644). "Dr Holt even goes so far as to assert that a long period of study in this connection has convinced him that every woman should be capable of detemining the precise time of her ovulation by means of one or other of the phenomena that accompany it" (*Een Ovulationssyndrom*, Nederl, Tijdschr. Geneesk, 1937, pp. 1902, seq.); Dr. A. Krempel, *La continence périodique*, Salvator, 1954, p. 116, Dr Holt, *La fertilité cyclique de la femme*, Vigot, 1959, pp. 47–53.

[1] Dr Chauchard, *La maîtrise sexuelle*, Ed., du Levain, 1959, pp. 55–6.

SELF-MASTERY IN THE MAN, AND MARRIED LIFE

9. The young man too would profit by learning from some authoritative source that reflexes can be trained, that there are psychological, spiritual and physiological conditions which make sexual mastery and sexual hygiene possible.[2] Past generations had no knowledge of the considerable powers human nature and its psychological factors possess over the obscure forces of instinct. The Orientals have more experience than ourselves of such possibilities. It might well be most useful for the man to learn gradually how to achieve this self-mastery, for love of the woman he respects. All self-mastery, whether in the realm of the mind, of the will or of the body, cannot fail to serve the cause of genuine love and sexual adjustment in marriage. In fact it makes even the *temptation* to practise onanism loathsome. It humanizes sexual intercourse and gives an increasingly monogamous direction to the desires that lead to it.[3] With training such as this, the husband will be better equipped than his elders were when he begins his married life, especially if to this form of asceticism he has been able to add that of faith and love. In any case, for fiancés who have received this kind of formation, "voluntary motherhood and fatherhood" have a far truer meaning than for the contraceptive couple. Painless childbirth, made possible by the use of conditioned reflexes in place of anaesthetic and analgesic methods, has increased the mother's sense of joy by making her aware that she is, in a manner of speaking, doubly creative. In a similar way, natural control of sexuality and natural fertility regulation should make her more keenly and more joyfully aware that she has deliberately chosen to have this child.

Further, engaged couples should know that another difficult bend in the road awaits them during the period following the birth of their first two children. The husband has been put to the test since he has been obliged to practise a praiseworthy continence. He cannot but feel anxious to express his love for and his gratitude towards the wife who has made him a father. Yet the very understandable ideal of pregnancy spacing will now demand a greater effort still.[4]

[2] Dr J. Vermeire, *Hygiène sexuelle*, Ed. de Vroente, 1959 (Ed. Fleurus).
[3] Dr P. Chauchard, *L'Equilibre sexuel, pp.* 53–6; Mgr Suenens, *op. cit.*, pp. 80–1 and 92–4; see above, p. 160, note 7, and pp. 169–70.
[4] It is a fact that his presence during the confinement of the woman he loves gives to the marriage act, hitherto still too superficial and carnal, the added values of a more realistic and deeper love.

He will find considerable help in making this effort if the mother feeds the baby herself. Ovulation normally ceases during the lactation cycles for the first four months. If it does not in any given case, it is permissible for the doctor to compensate for the hormonal deficiency and so rectify the anomaly which is responsible for this state of affairs. At least, this is the opinion of theologians who have seriously considered the question.[5]

HUSBANDS AND WIVES BUT PARENTS TOO

10. It is obviously impossible before marriage to cover all the ground and foresee all the eventualities. Even if everything it is desirable they should know has come to light, the engaged couple will not really understand its full meaning until they have lived out its implications. Hence the Biblical phrase "The two become one flesh" can only yield its meaning gradually. Marriage should make it possible for husband and wife to be *two* and to be *one* alternatively and also at one and the same time. This dialectic agrees perfectly with that recommended by St Paul in the text we have already quoted: "Do not starve one another, unless perhaps you do so for a time, by mutual consent, to have more freedom for prayer; come together again, or Satan will tempt you, weak as you are."

Love requires that husband and wife should sometimes be two, it equally requires that they should sometimes be one. Each must, at the appropriate time, be able to turn in his or her own way towards his or her own task: prayer, the duties of their state, their mission as educators of their children. At other times, they should both unite and share one another's being and life. As parents, they will more often act separately in parallel and complementary ways. As husband and wife, they will more often be "one" with each other and for each other's sakes.

If they are too intent on their task as parents, their love suffers as much as if they were too intent on their relations as husband and wife. The happy mean is a mutual interdependence between the "We-community" of husband and wife and the "We-community" of parenthood. The latter expresses outwardly what the former carries in its heart. The former integrates into itself the values the latter brings to it.

[5] Dr R. de Guchteneere, "Les inhibiteurs de l'ovulation," in *St-Luc médical*, 1959, No. 1, pp. 18–22; L. Janssens, *Éphemerides Theologiae Lovanienses*, April 1958.

And so, some—not without a touch of humour—strongly advise husbands and wives to go on treating one another as though they were perpetual fiancés, each seeking always to give pleasure to the other. But it is just as proper to insist that they should also both forget one another and think of others, their children in particular. "Lovers," it is said, "have the whole world to themselves." It is, in fact, a good thing for husband and wife to behave deliberately from time to time as if this were so, by having a kind of miniature second honeymoon.[6] But once their union has been strengthened anew, it must be shared, it must increase and multiply.[7]

IN THE HOLY SPIRIT AND THE CHURCH

11. Who then can give to married love this dauntless vitality, this mastery of, and victory over the lower forces? Who can guarantee it that vital rhythm of give and take without which it inevitably becomes atrophied?

The Church replies: the Holy Spirit, the Spirit of love proceeding from the Father and the Son and communicated to us for this express purpose in the sacrament of matrimony. "Without me, you can do nothing," said Christ. "But where two or three are gathered in my name, I am in their midst." These are profound truths and husbands and wives are constantly made aware how true they are as the years of their married life slip by.

It is desirable therefore that a retreat for engaged couples should already have steered the still inexperienced and over-confident love of the fiancés in this direction. During the course of its existence, married love needs to be very humble. It is only thus even that it can increase.[8]

Hence to conclude this rapid survey of the factors that make for the stability and deepening of true Christian love, we must underline the importance for married life of those family groups and apostolic activities organized either by a parish or a Catholic Action movement. We cannot insist too much on the fact that divine love, by entrusting its own great designs to human love, gives to the latter

[6] Abbé Joseph Templier, "L'amour partagé," collection *Mon village,* M.F.R., Paris, 1956, Ch. IX, "Recommencer le voyage de noces," pp. 63–5.
[7] Abbé Joseph Templier, *L'amour multiplié,* M.F.R., 1958.
[8] Abbé H. Caffarel, *Propos sur l'amour et la grâce,* Ed. du Feu Nouveau, Paris, "La chair et l'esprit," pp. 18–31.

its genuine dimensions. And the converse is true. We cannot insist too much on the fact that the true home should be able through its integrating power daily to enlarge the inner consciousness of man, tempted as he is always is to be wholly absorbed in external activities. As René Bazin has written:

> When a man comes home after a day's work or a day's leisure, he almost always brings with him an idea, an image, an example, a project, which are occupying his mind. If he has a wife of genuine moral quality, it is from her that he expects to receive the solution, even though he often does not recognize the fact.

It may be objected that we have gone beyond our brief—"Preparation for a human and personal control of fertility". We do not think so, for what we wanted to show was that birth regulation is only one aspect of the control of love itself, under the influence of grace and of the Holy Spirit, and in the community environment of the Church.

With the help of this preparation both remote and immediate, the regulation advocated by the Church no longer seems impossible. On the contrary, it is all of one piece with the fundamental requirements of human nature, it corresponds with the profound dynamic forces of the emotions and of sexuality in both men and women.

Where contraceptive methods only succeed in masking examples of bogus stability, the practice of continence, when foreseen and prepared for by suitable training, leads to an authentic stabilization of the sexual function.

Birth regulation makes men and women adults. Contraception keeps them adolescent. Regulation ennobles human effort. Contraception declares it redundant and eventually deprives it of all value.

Pius XII in his Allocution to the Midwives said:

> Do not be disturbed when, in the practice of your profession and in your apostolate, you hear this clamour about impossibility. . . . It is obvious that he who does not want to master himself will not be able to do so; and he who thinks he can master himself, relying solely on his own powers and not sincerely and perseveringly seeking divine aid will be miserably deceived.

But the man who trusts in God will not be deceived. And the Pope adds:

F.P.M.P.—8*

In confirmation of this argument, we have the doctrine of the Council of Trent which, in the chapter on the necessary and possible observance of the Commandments, referring to a passage in the works of Augustine, teaches: "God does not command what is impossible, but when he commands, he commands, he warns you to do what you can and to ask his aid for what is beyond your powers, and he gives his help to make that possible for you." [9]

This then, in the final analysis, is the source of Catholic optimism: "God does not demand the impossible".

[9] Pius XII to the Midwives, nn. 41, 40, *op. cit.*, pp. 18–19.

Part Four

The Mission of Catholics in the World

INTRODUCTORY NOTE

IN marked contrast to the civil authorities' usual method of procedure, the Church's approach to human problems, both social and political, and her search for their solutions, is always, as we have seen, concerned in the first place with their innermost realities and the point at which they open on to the supernatural. If this truth has been kept in mind by the reader as he has scanned the preceding pages, he will not have been surprised that, in dealing with the whole immense question of family and world fertility, Catholicism has given priority to the point of view that is concerned with the moral conscience of husbands and wives, and with its enlightenment and formation.

It now remains for us to show that, after she has spoken to the conscience of husbands and wives, who are primarily responsible for the creative forces of nature, the Church has also a body of teaching directed to the conscience of her children in their capacity as citizens or members of governments.

The Catholic Church reminds her sons and daughters as *citizens* of a temporal society and members of the community of Nations which is struggling to be born, that they have an essential part to play, a duty to do—they are to be a "sign to the world", the leaven in the lump.

The Church reminds those of her children who share with others the *responsibilities of public office*, that they have an obligation to provide for the common good of nations and peoples, and by methods most fitted to safeguard the health, vitality and the morals of these nations and peoples. "Even when there is not unanimous agreement among all the citizens on the principles and the criteria of morality, it is still lawful and indispensable for the State in its laws to impose certain rules of conduct considered indispensable if a minimum of public order and peace is to be maintained."[1]

[1] Fr Riquet, S.J., Foreword on birth control in *Saint Luc, Evangile et médecine,* Dec. 1957, p. 347: "The problem of the morality or immorality of contraceptive methods is of primary interest to the individual conscience. It is bound up with a certain concept of man, of nature, and of the relation of both to God. The principles and arguments a Christian, or a man who believes in spiritual values, finds valid, are not necessarily so to a materialist atheist nor even to a certain type of existentialist. It follows that there exists a real difficulty in discussion between men in good faith, but who base their arguments on very different criteria. If we want to find arguments that are equally valid for a Marxist and a Christian, we run the risk of finally convincing neither. On the contrary, we may well arouse distrust or scepticism in

218   *The Mission of Catholics in the World*

The following two chapters will therefore analyse:
—on the one hand, this *"Mission to be a sign to the world"* transmitted by Christ and the Church to the Catholic faithful in so far as they are members of a temporal society:
—on the other hand, *the aims to be pursued in the matter of population policy* by men in power who are anxious to act in accordance with Catholic ideals and principles especially when dealing with underdeveloped countries whose birth-rate is high.

both. This is particularly the case when we claim to justify a moral condemnation of contraceptive practices by instancing their ill-effects either on the physical and mental health of individuals, or on the future population problems of the nation. Such considerations are certainly not unimportant, but they cannot provide the basis for an absolute *moral* standard. Respect for nature and for its ultimate purposes only constitutes a rule of morality in so far as man discerns beyond nature, the certain fact of God's will. If a man excludes God from the universe and refuses to recognize that mankind is subordinated to a transcendent order, then our demands may well seem to him always excessive or arbitrary. It is important not to forget this."

Chapter XIV

THE PROPHETIC ASPECT OF THE
MISSION "TO BE A SIGN IN THE WORLD"

"YOU ARE THE SALT OF THE EARTH"

THERE is a phrase in the Gospel which explains why the Catholic Church so often gives the impression of being intransigent in moral matters: "You are the salt of the earth," our Lord told his disciples, "if salt loses its taste, what is there left to give taste to it? There is no more to be done with it, but throw it out of doors for men to tread it under foot" (Matt. 5. 13).

The Church has taken this declaration quite seriously. Out of love for her Lord, she wants her children really to be the salt of the earth, the leaven in the lump, the light on the lampstand. Every Christian has the duty of witnessing to the truth, to be a "sign" to the world.

The Church, in fact, is a voice among men, calling them to holiness. We have only to remember the Sermon on the Mount. Our Lord did not then teach two religions, one for the *élite* and the other —a second-rate affair—for the common run of mortals! He did the exact opposite. Christ honoured humanity by believing that it was capable as a whole of reaching the highest summits: "But you are to be perfect, as your heavenly Father is perfect."

In all spheres of morality, the Church desires to be, in her children, the ideal constantly there for us to see. She should be the city set on a hill which none can avoid noticing, and this is not the case with a little township hidden in its rich valley.

When he speaks of our love for our enemies or of virginity, Christ teaches us what, as a general rule, the pagans could not find out by themselves. Moreover the history of the Church confirms this law. When the apostles had to teach chastity and virginity to the pagans of Corinth, Athens or Rome, the attempt was pure madness in the eyes of human wisdom. But the Church has not betrayed her Lord. She has resolutely undertaken this task of calling men to sanctity. And the facts have proved her right.

Under the mysterious influence of grace, and with the air of martyrdom, the miracle happened and Christianity was able to set right what was wrong. Virginity blossomed on the ruins of that ancient world of putrefaction and decay. Chastity overcame the licentiousness of Greeks, Romans and Barbarians.[1]

There is also the negative proof. Wherever the Catholic Church has disappeared or at least hardly exists any longer, there follows a considerable lowering of standards, in the spheres of both faith and morals, and on a par with that produced by atheism or laicism. Everything seems to show that the Reformed Churches are not able of themselves constantly to raise the souls of men towards sanctity,[2] even in spite of declarations inspired by the very highest ideals.

On the other hand, in countries predominantly Protestant, but where a strong Catholic minority is on the increase, a kind of friendly rivalry establishes itself among the various religious bodies and this prevents their followers from too rapid a descent towards facile solutions. At least when these religious bodies tolerate such facile solutions out of "pity for the masses" they continue to recognize that the solutions which the Catholic Church has traditionally made of obligation for her faithful are still valid for an *élite*.[3]

THE CATHOLIC SECTOR IS OF SERVICE TO HUMANITY

Even if we set aside revealed truth and the command given by our Saviour to his disciples: "You, therefore, must go out, making disciples of all nations, . . . teaching them to observe all the commandments which I have given you", the existence of the Catholic sector in the world is, merely from the sociological standpoint, an inestimable boon to humanity.

[1] André Baudrillart, *Moeurs païennes, moeurs chrétiennes*, Vol. I, "La famille dans l'antiquité et aux premiers siècles du christianisme," pp. 53–8, 99–109, Bloud et Gay, 1929.

[2] H. Engelmann and G. Philipson, *Scandinavie*, Les Presses d'Ile-de-France, 1957, pp. 95–105: "Licence ou liberté?" Eva Freden, "Le malaise suédois," in *Le Monde*, 15 Feb. 1957; by the same author: "Les bagarres du 1er janvier témoignent du désarroi moral des jeunes Suédois," in *Le Monde*, 5 Jan. 1957. See also *Réalités*, Feb. 1957. E. Mounier, "Notes scandinaves," *Esprit*, Feb. 1950.

[3] Dr Frank Lorimer, Jean Bourgeois-Pichat, Dudley Kirk, "An Inquiry concerning some ethical Principles relating to Human Reproduction," in *Social Compass*, IV, Nos. 5–6, pp. 201–12, The Hague.

The latter, in fact, because it has at its service a Catholic Church which has always been absolutely opposed and will remain opposed to any legalization of what it considers intrinsically evil—for instance, divorce, euthanasia, direct abortion, contraception—is constantly being warned against unexpected and unfortunate developments.

The world will always have to stand in fear of the sorcerer's apprentice's dangerous undertaking, it will always have to mistrust false prophets. The Catholic Church, by forbidding her children ever to go beyond the moral barriers which nature itself points out to her, protects the world from the immense peril of relativism.[4]

Catholicism will, it is true, always play the ungrateful role which older and more experienced persons are criticized for assuming, when she shows herself opposed to rash enterprises. But genuine science also issues her warnings and pleads with us to be sensible. Not long ago, Jean Rostand warned his audiences and his readers, intoxicated by the power of applied biology in our own times:

I must admit that there are moments when I wonder whether man will always be able to accept the new picture of himself which science offers him, whether he will go on indefinitely adapting himself to his increasing knowledge, whether he will be able to assimilate all his inventions without endangering his emotional balance. It may well be that the progress of biology will lead us along paths too remote from what is human and where our deepest needs are too often thwarted. May it not be that by mishandling nature, we are going to create a climate for men in which they will not be able to breathe? Just as there are limits in radioactivity beyond which we must not go, so too, in the spiritual and moral order, there are perhaps mysterious frontiers which must not be crossed if we are not to bring the human animal to a state of confusion and solitude.[5]

[4] As a humorist has said, it is sometimes a good thing to change the bath water, but we must be careful not to empty out the baby with the bath.

[5] Jean Rostand, "Pour une morale biologique," in *Demain*, No. 98, 30 Oct. 1957, p. 24. These pages are reprinted in *Bestiaires d'amour*, Lardenchet; see also by the same author an earlier work: *Peut-on modifier l'homme?*, Gallimard, 1956, pp. 142 etc.; *Semaine sociale de Montpellier, Les découvertes biologiques et la médecine sociale au service de l'homme*, especially Mgr Tiberghien, "L'action de l'homme sur la vie humaine," pp. 175–91, and L. Beirnaert, S.J., "La personne devant les techniques psychologiques," pp. 193-208.

The history of humanity is already full of such cases. The race, tempted as it is to seek salvation by the "broad way that leads to perdition", has been forced, after certain ill-starred experiments, to turn back and enter once more by the "narrow gate and onto the strait path" which, according to the Gospel, "lead to Life". "And few they are," adds St Matthew, it is true, "who find it." And in fact, who today dares, apart from the handful of Catholics gathered round their pontifical *magisterium*, sound a warning to our human race tempted as it is to rush lightheartedly along the way of family planning and its contraceptive techniques?

Yet, examples are not wanting in the past, when the reservations of the Catholic Church have most certainly been of service to the cause of humanity on the verge of entering a blind-alley. Present-day scientific history surely owes something to the Church's opposition to the modernist conception of history, and the history of religions has also its debts to Catholic exegesis with its refusal to yield to the temptations of syncretism.

Do not even medicine and biology owe something to Catholicism for its desperate opposition to therapeutic abortion? Would the progress of medicine in accordance with its own inner law, which insists that it should protect life, be the same in an atmosphere of surrender? No doubt, it will be always difficult to assess the respective share of influence of each of the different factors involved. This analytical problem does not do away with the fact itself that Catholicism has such an influence.

Who can say that the resistance offered today by the Catholic Church to the inauguration of a contraceptive civilization may not be of immense help to humanity in the near future, in all the strength of its new discoveries and its new processes of production and distribution of wealth? Is it not better to entertain greater hopes of what can be accomplished by man's genius rather than to "dwarf" man down to the level of his own avarice? Although it is unwise to attempt rash schemes, both in the world of the mind and in that of life itself, it is none the less true that man is a composite creature of matter and spirit in whom the flame of genius must remain supreme. Otherwise the existence of the human race as a specific kingdom in the realm of the spirit is no longer possible. Materialism, even in its dialectical form, must mend its ways and correct its errors or it will experience, in this respect, some very rude awakenings.

FRUITFUL TENSIONS : USEFUL DISCUSSIONS

In addition to the possibility that humanity may have these indispensable second thoughts and abandon its errors, it must be pointed out that the opposition raised by the Catholic attitude in the debate on the planning of births is unquestionably fruitful. It is so, not only for other people to whom it suggests that the problem should be re-examined, but also for Catholic thought itself.

It cannot be denied that tension and even discussion between those who are convinced of the possibility of contraceptive birth control on the one hand, and, on the other, those who give a reasoned allegiance to the Catholic position, have forced us to go more deeply into the moral question and to perfect our methods of research in the psychosomatic field.

It is almost certain that, had it not been for discussions of this sort, the assertion, contained implicitly in *Casti Connubii* (1930), that birth regulation is possible, would not have been made so unequivocally by Pius XII in his Address to the Midwives (Oct. 1951) and in that of November of the same year, addressed to the *Fronte della Famiglia*. The term—birth regulation—found for the first time in the Allocution of November 1951—seems to have been invented only as a last resort and in order to cut short the disputes over the interpretation of, and the defamatory campaigns occasioned by, his previous speech to the midwives.

"The hope" expressed by the Sovereign Pontiff, that medical science "would succeed in giving to this method (known as the use of the infertile periods) a sufficiently sure basis", obviously proves not only that the Roman *magisterium* "looks with sympathy and understanding on the real difficulties of married life in our times", but also that it encourages scientific research.

In 1954 Pius XII in his speech to the demographers said: [6]

The science of population is young, but it is of the first importance, because it is directly concerned with human life and can

---

[6] Pius XII to the members of the World Population Conference, Rome, Sept. 1954, D.C., c. 1446. See also the courageous words of Mgr Suenens to the First Catholic World Health Congress: "We have no right to ask men to observe the law without doing at the same time all in our power to make obedience possible." D.C., No. 1289, c. 1175, 14 Sept. 1958, and his commentary in his book published later *Un problème crucial: Amour et Maîtrise de soi*, Desclée, 1960; Part II: "Que faire?"; Ch. X, "Le rôle du médecin," Ch. XI, "Le rôle des universitaires et des chercheurs," pp. 143–80.

throw light on some of the most serious individual and social problems. The Church is not ignorant of these problems. She is not indifferent to the agonizing difficulties they present, as is shown by many documents recently issued by the Holy See concerning family life, national economics, the relations between nations, some of whom are provided with an abundance of wealth, whilst others remain in a tragic situation.

But the Church has always sought to set the problems of population in their proper perspective, that of a personal, moral destiny which, by courageous and even daring action in this world of time, is to find its fulfilment in the eternal possession of God.

That is why we cannot but rejoice at the light which your labours,[7] and those of all sincere demographers, bring to our knowledge of the laws and the values that condition the evolution of populations. That is also why we urge Catholics to take an active share in the researches and efforts which are being made in this sphere. But we hope that at the same time they will remain faithful to Christian doctrine and in communion with so many men and women who, enlightened by reason and upheld by a legitimate trust in Providence, yet fully conscious of the difficulties they are facing and of their duties towards the community, respect the creative will that is found at the very heart of love and of life.

As can be seen, the Church's attitude is not only encouraging, but plainly positive. Whilst maintaining her fundamental God-given attitude, she also tries to preserve the essential truth in the teaching of her opponents. The birth control controversy is no exception to this general law.

In point of fact, all the discussions that have taken place over the last thirty years have not been without their value in helping the Catholic view to establish distinctions, that may seem subtle to the average person, but which bear fruit in the field of sociology, distinctions between birth control in the backward-looking, Malthusian spirit, and birth regulation which is genuinely compatible with the will to create.

The same is true of the distinction between technical control,

---

[7] An allusion to the Proceedings of the World Population Conference, 31 Aug.–10 Sept. 1954. See S. de Lestapis, S.J., "La science démographique fait le point," in *Revue d'Action Populaire*, Sept.–Oct. 1954, pp. 785–8 and in *La Croix*, 2 Oct. 1954, "La terre pourra-t-elle nourrir indéfiniment tous les hommes?"

which is only an artificial and mechanical impediment to life's processes, and a human regulation of procreation, which desires above all to be a form of self-mastery that respects the sexual function, its structures and its laws.

The very expressions "birth control" and "self control" of themselves help us to realize the distance which separates an attitude in which the subject treats himself as an object, and a type of behaviour by which, on the contrary, he develops his personality. To treat procreation as a mere *objective* problem to be solved and as though it has not profound relations with the subjects it involves, is a process which, in the final analysis, treats persons as things and degrades the human personality.

But on the contrary, to treat this act of procreation as a "personal mystery" that is, to use an expression of Gabriel Marcel's, as an existential problem which comes to grips with its own data, this surely is to ask husbands and wives, in their rôle as procreators, to adopt an attitude which is, in practice, sacred and religious. Does this not increase the stature of man in his dignity as a spiritual being and in the very act which his sexual nature calls on him to perform?[8]

Are not all these results, enriching natural philosophy and psychology, essentially due to Catholic thought acting under the very stimulus itself of discussion and controversy?

On the other hand, for the advocates of contraception, one of the most valuable fruits of these discussions seems to be this new piece of evidence: "birth limitation can only be successfully achieved in well-developed countries. Hence the need for a policy of investment in underdeveloped countries."[9]

This sociological discovery, whilst not directly due to the controversy between Catholics and non-Catholics, nevertheless is to some extent illuminated by it. If we wish to teach the man who follows his instincts to regulate and modify the obscure vital forces within him, we must first of all appeal to him to make a creative effort, we must do something to help him reach a higher social and cultural level. In a word, we must lead him to a more complete self-mastery!

---

[8] J. Vialatoux, *Le peuplement humain,* Vol. I, pp. 141–6.
[9] A. Sauvy, *Express,* 4 Nov. 1955. See below *Conclusions,* pp. 270–1.

THE CATHOLIC POSITION AND THE POPULATION PROBLEM

Whatever may be the truth concerning this estimate of the help brought to humanity by Catholics and their doctrine, the sociological demographer still has one serious difficulty in regard to the Catholic position. Let us suppose, he says, that the birth regulation envisaged by Catholicism becomes a reality for the majority of the world's population groups; far from solving the problem, this state of affairs will aggravate it still further. Fertility will not diminish. At times, it might even increase.

It is a fact that husbands and wives who, courageously and for love of one another, decide to regulate births on the basis of periodic continence, often continue to have families of from four to six children. If families of this size became general in an Asiatic population, the present increase in the birth rate would not appreciably decrease, whilst in a European population, it would rise considerably.

This being so, we shall be told, how can you still seriously turn to this birth regulation envisaged by the Catholic Church and claim to find in it, even in conjunction with an economic effort to achieve better distribution and higher production, the solution to the present population problems?

Precisely, we shall reply, it is because of this inertia among the masses which you are the first to recognize, that the Church's views, which you declare are Utopian, acquire their full meaning and value. Is it not at a time when the masses are sorely tempted to allow themselves to be carried thoughtlessly away into the dangerous experiments of erotic and Malthusian individualism or of an anti-personalist planning of births, that the Church should insist still more upon urging her children to practise the heroism demanded by a deliberate and altruistic regulation of births? And even if the resultant fertility should exceed to some small extent, as is suggested, what is needed for an optimum average increase in the immediate future, we should be only more convinced of the long-term cogency of this appeal.

As we have already said, fundamental demographic phenomena are slow to develop. When a country has entered a period in which the number of old people increases, more than a century is needed to rectify matters after the nation has become aware of the problem. What will Japan be like in 1990? Where will it find sufficient numbers of young people to counterbalance its population of elderly inhabitants?[1] And who will people the Sahara, if North Africa experiences a fall in the birth rate or, what is more, a wave of immorality hitherto unknown?

In the rising birth rate which France experienced in 1942 and the United States after the second world war, the rôle of catalyser played by a minority group of deliberately large Catholic families was certainly not without importance. The establishing of family groups and communities, the rise of family movements, all or almost all of Catholic origin, have powerfully influenced the present family revival.[2] This is not a fact easy to prove statistically. In any case it is conspicuous by its absence in the Scandinavian nations where the Catholic Church as a sociological factor is non-existent. We have said often enough that civilizations which no longer believe in creative love and in life are on the road to death. The time is perhaps not too far distant when we shall begin to wonder what will remain of nations which are now satiated and satisfied. Technics will not be of much avail when that day comes.

In a human race which is a mystery to itself, it is not the so-called rational, nor above all, the rationalist solutions which are the most certain, even if they appear to have all the evidence on their side. History and sociology are there to bear witness.

Bergson, in his *Deux Sources de la morale et de la religion*, gave this warning in no uncertain terms. Faced with the danger of overpopulation, he recognized the need for a deliberate "intervention on man's part". You will not avoid regimentation (an ugly word, but it expresses clearly what it signifies, since it arrogantly adds something to "rule" and "regulation"), and Bergson quotes examples: the distribution of raw materials, the limitation of rights, legislative action in various countries, etc. But once this is admitted, "what would happen if our standard of living became more austere?" the philosopher asks. "Mysticism is undoubtedly at the origin of great moral changes. Humanity doubtless seems as far from it as ever. But who knows?[3] Once the hero launches his appeal, we shall

---

[1] "The ageing of the Japanese population will bring about profound changes in all its institutions and give rise to problems hitherto unknown. . . . At some time or other, a considerable upward movement of the birth rate will be necessary and this will bring new burdens and be unwelcome to, and misunderstood by, the population."—A. Sauvy, *De Malthus à Mao Tse-Toung*, Ed. Denoël, 1958, p. 240.

[2] S. De Lestapis, S.J., "Les Mouvements familiaux dans le monde," in *Cahiers de pastorale familiale*, 1957, No. 4, pp. 41–5.

[3] H. Bergson, *Les deux sources de la morale et de la religion*, Alcan, pp. 313–14.

not all follow him but we shall all feel we ought to, and we shall know the path to take and shall widen it if we pass along it . . . It only needs a genius to arise and he will draw after him a human race whose body will already have achieved immense growth and whose soul he will transfigure." [4]

"This mystical movement," observes Bergson, "will want to make humanity a new species or rather deliver it from its status as a species, as a static collectivity."

"If a gleam of light should reach us from that unknown world, from that 'beyond' . . . what a transformation would follow," he continues, "in a human race accustomed, whatever it may say, to accept as really existing only what it can see and touch!"

And he concludes:

The truth is, that if we were certain, absolutely certain of survival, we should be able to think of nothing else. Pleasures would remain, but would be dull and colourless because their intensity arose only from the attention we gave to them. They would grow pale like the light of our electric bulbs in the morning sunshine. Pleasure would be eclipsed by joy. The simplicity of a life which a widespread mystical intuition would propagate throughout the world would indeed be joy. Or again our joy would be that which would automatically follow a vision of the beyond in the context of a broader scientific experience. [5]

The Christian faith gives us what the philosopher dreamed of. And divine grace makes it live in us. Christ is that tangible light coming to us from the unknown world. The Catholic Church is that mystical movement which wants to make humanity a new species.

And so, in a world like ours, in which sin will continue to be at work until the end of time, the so-called world problem of fertility awaits its solution above all from the example of heroes and saints living, to the full and without any compromise, the life of faith in the higher values, in the highest values of Christian Love. The world, in its uncertainty, waits for Catholics to show it a more vital faith in the values of existence, a more spiritual mastery of fertility through continence, an ardent search for the help that a

[4] H. Bergson, *op. cit.*, p. 338.
[5] H. Bergson, *op. cit.*, pp. 342–3. For similar points of view in the writings of Père Teilhard de Chardin, see Claude Cuénot, *Pierre Teilhard de Chardin,* Ed. Plon, 1958, pp. 45, 52.

deeper science of man could provide, and finally, a struggle for a more just distribution of wealth and of men upon this planet.

The world needs above all else families which will prove to it that the conflicts between flesh and spirit can never be resolved by the repression or the watering down of the demands of the spirit. No doubt, it is only too ready to say that all this is too good to be true, too far above us to be possible . . .

But we, for our part, believe. We believe in freedom restored in us by Christ. We believe in the power of love delivered by grace, in its power to triumph over the dark spectres of cupidity, avarice and concupiscence. We believe in the education of the masses, not in their brutalization. We believe that in time, with the help of experience, science and grace, humanity, first in its *élites*, then more and more in its vast multitudes, will pass beyond the temptation of family planning and its contraceptive techniques and will turn towards the only form of birth regulation worthy of it, namely the personal and natural mastery of fertility.

The Pavlovian era of conditioned reflexes upon which we have entered may doubtless lead to still greater evils, by giving the powers of this world the means of producing men who are mere robots. But it may also place the obscure forces of nature more surely at the service of that mastery which we can achieve through the spirit and through grace.

Chapter XV

CATHOLICS AND THEIR MISSION AS PROMOTERS OF POPULATION POLICIES IN UNDERDEVELOPED COUNTRIES

THE PROPHETIC VOCATION AND THE POLITICAL MISSION

As members of the temporal order, Catholics receive from their baptism and their incorporation into the Church the mission to be "a sign to the world". Their vocation is genuinely prophetic and often makes them "a sign which men will will refuse to recognize". Its purpose is to remind the human race, constantly tempted to forget it, that it has here below no abiding city, but is always moving towards "a new heaven and a new earth", where "there is no marrying or giving in marriage".[1]

Yet even though it is only a "passing city", the temporal order has to ensure conditions indispensable for the security and peace which man needs in order to accomplish his journey in the society of others.

Catholics have no right, under pretext of their obligation to prepare the world principally for its final passage out of this life, to remain disinterested in the present and its organization, in social and economic progress. On the contrary, they must bring their power and resources to bear on the building up of the temporal order. Their prophetic vocation as "a sign to the world", far from dispensing Catholics from a political mission, invites them to undertake it.[2]

[1] Apoc. 21. 1–4, 2 Peter 3. 13, Matt. 22. 30.

[2] "There is one way of acting that is 'out of the question', that of the deserter, the man who has been well called 'a voluntary exile in his own country' (*émigré de l'intérieur*). It is the withdrawal from active life of the sullen or disappointed man, who, because he is dissatisfied or discouraged, makes no use of his qualities and energies, shares in none of the activities of his country or his time, but goes apart—like the Greek Achilles in his tent, near the fast-moving ships, far from battle—whilst the destinies of his motherland are at stake. Less worthy still is withdrawal due to passive and idle indifference. And worse than bad temper, disappointment and discouragement would be an attitude of unconcern in the presence of the disasters into which his own brothers, his own people are on the point of falling. This attitude would seek in vain to hide itself under the mask of neutrality. It is in no way neutral. Whether we like it or not, it is a form of collusion. *Any man who lives on the wealth of Christian thought does not allow himself to be downcast or dis-*

If our eternal home is a life of charity and a community of love and if already in this life we must anticipate the relationships of the world to come, it follows that there is a still more urgent duty to establish the temporal order on the foundation of brotherly relations and on social stability based on justice and charity.

It is precisely at this point that the great difficulties inherent in a rational system of world population present themselves: what is the best geographical distribution of populations, the best method for the mutual exchange of wealth, the best way to provide all with sufficent food, etc.?

Among all these problems, one of the most crucial in our times is that of the prolific African, Asiatic and American nations. They are also those least well equipped as regards capital and industries.

We have already outlined (Ch. IX) the Church's doctrinal position on this point as it affects these peoples. We have even indicated the basic principles which should determine, at government level, the obligations of the various nations towards the underdeveloped peoples.[3]

It now remains for us to come down from the sphere of principles to that of practical application. What concrete policy does Catholicism offer to the responsible authorities in a prolific and underdeveloped nation if it is true that Catholicism is opposed on principle to any policy of family planning achieved by means of contraceptive techniques?

Catholicism cannot remain silent or without a positive solution on this point or it runs the risk of seeing those who understand only the language of facts call its whole doctrinal position into question once again.

The problem we have therefore to study now as we draw towards the close of this book, is the following:

What objectives must be pursued in regard to population policy by civil authorities who are anxious to act in accordance with Catholic ideals and principles, especially when dealing with underdeveloped countries whose birth rate is high?

couraged by human events of whatever kind. He courageously turns his eyes towards all that has stood the test and which is still so great and so worthy of his attention. . . . *Your mission, therefore, is far from being a negative one.* It presupposes in you much study, much work, much self-denial, and above all, much love. In spite of the rapid evolution of our times, it has not lost its value, it has not reached its goal."—Pius XII to the Roman aristocracy, D.C., 16 Feb. 1946, pp. 194–7.

[3] Cf. above, pp. 141–6.

ON WHAT SCALE SHOULD THE PROBLEM OF
OVERPOPULATION BE EXAMINED?

In the West at least, everybody knows the rate at which the world's population is growing. There is a birth every second. At the end of every day, there are 100,000 new human beings. At the end of every year, there are 40 million extra inhabitants on the globe! When we look back over the past, we find that it was only after several thousand years that the earth's population rose to 500 million. This figure was apparently reached at about the year 1650. Only two centuries were needed to reach the 1,000 million mark, 100 years for the second 1,000 million and less than 35 years for the third, which will be reached in 1961–1962 or thereabouts.[4]

The average annual population increase, which was 0.30% between 1650 and 1750, is now 1·7%. This rate shows that the figure has doubled during the last 40 years. Magazines which trade in sensationalism take the trouble to calculate how long it will be, under present conditions, before each human being has even less than a metre of ground under his feet. We are told that we shall have to wait for about 600 years!

All this is true in the same way as abstractions and averages are true. But nothing justifies us in viewing—if we wish to be scientific —the problem of the future existence of humanity on a world-wide scale.[5] The phenomenon known as "population explosion" must be analysed at the level of continents or better still at the level of the great homogeneous regional groupings. At this level it is possible to have an exact idea of what is taking place and to foresee to some extent what will happen between now and the year 2000. Central America, for instance, with 21 million inhabitants in 1950 will have four times that number. But Northern and Western Europe with 120 millions will only have increased by 35%.

And so the real problem is seen to be the following: there are zones with a rapid population increase which are at the same time

---

[4] *The Future Growth of World Population*, New York, United Nations, 1958—ST/SO A, Series A/28; See our article: "Crise de surpopulation mondiale?" in *Revue de l'Action Populaire*, No. 127, April 1959. See Appendix XI, p. 448.

[5] A. Sauvy, *Théorie Générale de la Population*, t. II, pp. 185–6; "Le faux problème de la surpopulation," in *Population*, 1949, No. 3; Frank Lorimer, *Culture and Human Fertility*, a Study of the Relation of Cultural Conditions to Fertility in Non-Industrial and Transitional Societies, Unesco, 1954.

economically depressed areas. It is among them that the great struggle between economic necessity and population is enacted, with their birth rate of 30 to 50 per thousand combined with a death rate which has fallen to 15 or even 10 per thousand, whilst the national income is less than 100 dollars per individual inhabitant! On the other hand, there are zones where the population figures are by no means excessive and where the economy is steadily expanding. Such zones do not present any immediate problem.

Instead therefore of formulating the problem in the terms used by the Reader's Digest, we should do well to set it in its true scientific context. There is no threat of overpopulation, but there are *distorted and dangerously irregular developments.*

The real question then is—what measures are to be agreed upon on a world-wide scale, to help those countries in which there is such a tragic discrepancy between a feverish increase in population and a deplorable economic, social and cultural inertia? How are they to be helped to discover and to accept more stable conditions, similar in all probability to those of the other nations we have mentioned?

Obviously there is no simple answer. There are so many relevant factors and divergent interests involved. Within the limits of this book, we are forced to simplify what ought to be studied in minute detail and to list the various factors and values, in the interests of clarity, under three main headings—*economic, demographic and social and cultural.* We must add that nations at present underdeveloped cannot overcome their difficulties singlehanded. They need the cooperation of the wealthier nations.

We shall therefore deal in turn with the objectives that a population policy should normally adopt in its attempts to contain these distorted and irregular developments:

—economic objectives,
—demographic objectives,
—social and cultural objectives,
—the objectives of international cooperation.[6]

[6] An abundant literature has appeared over the past five years on the state of underdevelopment in a great number of countries and on the means calculated to overcome their difficulties. It is impossible to give here an exhaustive bibliography on so complex a problem. We refer the reader to the *Encyclopédie Française,* Vol. XI, "La Vie internationale, Eléments bibliographiques," pp. 11, B-1-8. However we list the few books below either because they have become classics or because they approximate to our own point of view:

(a) *The world economic situation.*

W. S. Woytinsky, *World Population and World Population Trends and*

I. ECONOMIC OBJECTIVES

Countries economically underdeveloped with a marked tendency towards a rising birth-rate and predominantly agricultural, labour under a handicap too obvious to need emphasizing. Thus the remarkable effort towards agricultural development in Mexico over a period of thirty years has produced an annual increase in food resources of 4%, only to find that this progress is for all practical purposes wiped out by the annual increase in population, which at the present moment is 3·5%. In the space of thirty years this nation has more than doubled its population. Its food resources have only advanced by 80%. To improve on this, Mexico would have required still more modern techniques capable of bringing about a more rapid increase in agricultural productivity.

The same is true of India, whose population has, since 1921, increased at an annual rate of approximately 1·25%. This increase is principally due to a marked lowering of the death rate. The present rate of (net) formation of capital is equal to 5% of the net national income. If we assume that the ratio of capital to production is as 4 is to 1, then we can see that the income per head has, at the most, remained constant.

Other examples could be quoted in the case of populations such as those of Malaya, Burma, Ceylon, those in the Far East or in

Outlook, New York, 1953; Chardonnet, *L'économie mondiale au milieu du XXe siècle*, Hachette, 1951.

(b) *Economic progress and growth.*

Radnar Nurske, *Problems of Capital Formation in Underdeveloped Countries*, Oxford, 1953; W. Arthur Lewis, *The Theory of Economic Growth*, Allen, London, 1955; Alfred Bonné, *Studies in Economic Development with special reference to Conditions in the Underdeveloped Areas of Western Asia and India*, Routledge, London, 1957; *Le Tiers Monde. Sous-développement et développement*, ouvrage réalise sous la direction de Georges Balandier, Cahier No. 27 de l'I.N.E.D., Paris, 1956; *Processus et problèmes de l'industrialisation des pays sous-développés*, O.N.U., 1955; Jacob Oser, *Must Men Starve?; The Malthusian Controversy*, J. Cape, London, 1956; Raymond Barre, *Le développement économique, Analyse et politique*, Ed. I.S.E.A., 1958; André Piatier, "Inégalités démographiques et économiques," in *Encyclopédie Française*, t. XI, pp. 11–12–16–11. 18–4.

(c) *International efforts.*

"L'assistance technique aux pays insuffisament développés," 3 fasc. Direction de la Documentation, Paris, 1955; see also: Secrétariat Social d'Alger: *L'Algérie surpeuplée, orientations pour une politique de population*, 1958, 5 rue Horace-Vernet, Alger; L. Lebret, *Suicide ou survie de l'Occident*, Ed. Ouvrières, 1958.

Latin and Central America with the West Indies and various South American republics.[7]

Certain American demographers have drawn up tables in which the world's regions are classified (very schematically, it is true!) as underdeveloped and developed areas, and we are invited to compare the respective population increases over a period of forty years.[8]

In view of such facts, we are surely tempted to conclude that, with rates of population increase on this scale, the countries that are economically underdeveloped are forever doomed, unless their economic output is speeded up to an extraordinary degree.

The first condition required, if there is to be such a speeding up, is the formulation of a Plan which will offer certain choices and demand very detailed studies of the production and productivity possibilities.

There are at least four main choices which the authors of the Plan will have to decide upon: investment or consumption, agriculture or industry, heavy equipment or light equipment, home production or imports.[9]

This is not the place to discuss these choices especially since to do so would be pointless unless we were dealing with one specific country. It will be enough for us to make a kind of panoramic sur-

[7] At the same time care must always be taken not to assume as a matter of principle that two countries geographically contiguous are bound to share the same fate. In proof of this, see G. Etienne, "Tendances et rythms d'expansion en Asie," in *Politique étrangère,* 1958, No. 6, pp. 570–613, and *De Caboul à Pékin,* Ed. Dunod, 1959.

[8] Kingsley Davis, "Recent Population Trends in the New World: an Overall View," in *The Annals of the American Academy of Political and Social Science,* Philadelphia, March, 1958, p. 3, according to the data in the Demographic Year Book, 1956, and "The Future Growth of World Population" in *Population Studies,* U.N., 1958, No. 28.

Underdeveloped Areas *Rate of Increase 1920–60*		*Developed Areas* *Rate of Increase 1920–60*	
	%		%
Latin America	126·3	Australia, New Zealand	92·4
Asia (except Japan)	68·4	Japan	71·7
Africa	67·6	North America	68·4
Pacific Islands	63·6	U.S.S.R.	36·1
Southern Europe	42·6	N.W. and Central Europe	23·3
Average	70·5	Average	41·1

[9] Jacques Méraud, "Remèdes aux disparités de niveaux de vie," in *Revue de l'Action Populaire,* No. 102, Nov. 1956, pp. 1054–56. Colin Clark, "Population et niveaux de vie," *Revue Internationale du Travail,* Aug. 1953, pp. 103–4.

vey of the economic measures that have to be envisaged if a hitherto backward region is to be developed[1]:

(*a*) an increased area to be cultivated (dams, irrigation schemes, drainage, etc.); (*b*) an increased output of home-grown foods; (*c*) increase in the quantity of livestock and its produce; (*d*) development of the fishing industry and fish-breeding; (*e*) development of industries, by a gradual transformation of the structures of industry (crafts, small industries, trading estates) rather than by too violent and complete a change (e.g. heavy industries); (*f*) the setting up of home markets made practicable by an increased purchasing power spread as widely as possible through measures for providing grants in aid and for increasing or even redistributing incomes; (*g*) the gradual institution of a savings system with a view to long and short term investments and aimed at precluding the wastage resulting from the consumption of luxury goods by a wealthy minority outside the control of the taxation authorities; (*h*) a re-planning of the national territory through a better distribution of the active sectors of the population (plans for industrialization, the development of the sources of energy, town planning, etc.).[2]

[1] *Analyses and Prospection of Economic Development*, I, "An Introduction to the Technique of Programming," N.Y.—U.N., 1955. *Measures to be taken for the Economic Development of Countries insufficiently Developed*, Report of a group of experts appointed by the Secretary-General of the U.N. Organization (known as the Report of the Five Experts), New York, 1951, 112 pp.

[2] *Méthodes et problèmes de l'industrialisation des pays sous-développés*, United Nations, 1955, "Coefficient d'absorption de la population par l'industrie en divers pays," p. 163; A. Sauvy, "Développement économique et répartition de la population," in *Revue d'Economie politique*, Paris, 1956, pp. 372–96; with A. Piatier ("Inégalités démographiques et économiques," in *Encyclopédie Française*, t. XI, 1958, pp. 11, 16–15) we underline the following facts: "But development is not merely a question of productivity, of output, of adaptation to modern production tools. Too many plans concentrate on dotting an area all over with new units of production. What must above all be brought about is a functional differentiation of activity, the creation of a coordinated whole. An agglomeration of people in an underdeveloped country is like a proliferation of undifferentiated cells. Social services, medical, cultural, legal, administrative, commercial organizations are non-existent, and there is a mere juxtaposition of persons and families. Just as it is necessary to pass from this 'agglomeration' to the functional town, so too it is necessary to pass from the nation as a humdrum collection of individuals scarcely distinct from one another, as we have seen, to a nation with a solidly built national structure. Not only must there be different productive activities (agriculture, industry, commerce, transport)—Egypt with a population a third of that of France has 15 times fewer workmen, and if we turn to a still more differentiated function, the tourist industry, Egypt has 85 times less hotel accommodation—but also differentiated activities of a general nature, cultural, administrative or political. This is a necessary condition for continuity of

Some idea of the effort needed to achieve these objectives and in the first place, those concerned with the food supply, may be given by merely reproducing the annual returns of the F.A.O. for the whole world. Taking as their basis (index figure 100) the average agricultural production for the years 1934–38, these returns show the index number 110 for the period 1949–1953 and for the period 1957–58 the index number is 131. This brings, for this latter period, the food production of the world to an index number of 101 per head. This is slightly above that of the pre-war period. Nevertheless it conceals—and we must not forget it—serious differences in the levels of food increases. Still, in comparison with pre-war figures, North America shows a food production index of 115 per head, Western Europe 109, Africa 107, whilst Latin America shows a decline with an index number of 97, as does the Far East with 91. So there are countries where the situation is frankly not so good as in 1938.[3]

What is to be done? In the first place, there must be a reduction in the wastage of foodstuffs. This reaches figures that are staggering. We may also note the great improvement that may be made in

effort. An excellent example is provided by the collection of statistics in certain undeveloped countries. Most of these countries attempted a few years ago to form a group to undertake this work for the first time. But as the movement could not be kept in being, statistical information has deteriorated, since those who specialized in this field have been caught up in official political or administrative activities and the 'younger men' have not taken their places. *Any plan which concerns itself solely with quantitative aims in production, and fails to consider this many-sided problem of the creation of a genuine national economic unity with its networks and its centres of power, is doomed to failure.* It is not enough to produce wealth by means of a type of production known as Western, it is necessary also to see that this wealth circulates and penetrates into all the particular groups. Otherwise families and villages will remain in their separate compartments and continue to live on their own products, whilst the new income will be absorbed as though into some vast sponge, by the charges of the usurers and the manœuvres of the hoarders. Man-power will be available but useless because it is untrained. Work will be done in an irregular fashion since more pay will be an incitement to rest rather than to a heightened effort. Over and above the necessities, demand will be for imported consumer goods rather than for capital equipment. The stimulus of investment which Westerners estimate in terms of an electric multiplier will not materialize since investment will 'leak' into closed monetary circuits, etc. In other words, all the apparatus of the modern economist's analysis will remain 'up in the air' and the parameters and variables of his equations will be as little to the point as the idea of unemployment which we were criticizing a moment ago."

[3] F.A.O., "La situation mondiale de l'Alimentation et de l'Agriculture," 1958; M. Guerrin, *Humanité et subsistances,* Ed., Dunod, Geneva, 1958; L. Estrangin, "Agriculture et pays sous-développés," in *Semaine Sociale d'Angers,* 1959; N. Drogat, *Economie rurale et nourriture des hommes,* Spes. 1957.

food production by the modernization of the methods of cultivation. Thus Japan, by force of circumstances, has been obliged to exact the maximum from her soil. She succeeds in producing from it every day products equivalent to 13,200 calories per acre, whilst Western Europe only produces 7,500 calories, the United States 4,500 and India 2,500. It is true that in 1953–54 Japan gave her soil 57 kg of fertilizers per acre per year, Europe 23, the United States 12 and India 0·3 kg.[4]

For her part, India, between 1951 and 1956, thanks it is true to exceptional atmospheric conditions, increased her basic food production by 20%, whilst her population during the same period only increased by 10%. Responsible economists think there is no reason why, between now and 1981, India should not succeed in doubling her food resources.[5]

Much more could be said on the problem of food and of hunger, beginning with the possibilities, at present unforeseeable, to which the discovery of photosynthesis and its application to agriculture might lead, and ending with some thoughts on the nature of "hunger" and how it can be evaluated in terms of "standards".[6]

The improvement of living standards however must not be confused with the increase in food production. It depends largely on the development of industries which are progressively less primary in nature.[7]

What seems to be an overpopulation crisis may, in the final analysis, be no more than a crisis due to insufficient industrialization. Japan used to be a flagrant example of this. It is true that industrialization implies the opening of new markets and the granting of

[4] Harrison Brown, "Life in the Americas during the next Century," in *The Annals of the American Academy of Political and Social Science*, March 1958, p. 12.

[5] Gilbert Etienne, "La population de l'Inde. Perspectives démographiques et alimentaires," in *Population*, 1957, No. 4, pp. 661–78: rice, for instance, which covered an area of 30 million hectares in 1956, would show—if it can be cultivated by Japanese methods—a yield of 1,200 kg per hectare, which means that there would be more than 30 million extra tons of rice in ten to fifteen years time. (The English equivalent of 30,000,000 French "tonnes" is 29,464,336 tons. Translator's note.) See also Ansley, J. Coale and Edgar M. Hoover, "Prospects for the Population Growth and their Implications for the Economic Development in India, 1956–1986" (mimeograph), Office of Population Research, Princeton University, 1956, printed edition, 1958.

[6] Dr A. Trémolières, "Remarques sur le problème de la sous-alimentation et du sous-développment," in *St-Luc*, March 1959, pp. 99–115, and *Revue de l'Action Populaire*, March 1950.

[7] See above, p. 236, note 1, A. Piatier's remarks.

considerable credits. But this leads on to considerations involving international cooperation, and these will be found at the end of this chapter.

II. *DEMOGRAPHIC OBJECTIVES*

As we have said, there can be no improvement in the standard of living of a nation, without a general production plan and a rational organization of markets, in a word, without carefully studied and carefully controlled economic management.

But there is another fact which directly determines the standard of living, namely the demographic factor, the rate of growth of the population. This varies considerably from nation to nation. It depends on several elements which may be found in different combinations. Before launching out into any particular population policy, the head of State in an underdeveloped nation should isolate the different factors which affect demographic development. He ought especially to identify the type of structure his own country presents.[8]

DETERMINING FACTORS IN DEMOGRAPHIC DEVELOPMENT

The *rate of increase in a population* depends, in the first place, immediately and directly on three demographic factors: the *death rate*, the *marriage rate* and the *fertility rate*. We will leave aside migration whose influence is infinitesimal in the case of the great masses of population in the so-called underdeveloped countries.

Thus, in proportion as the death rate decreases, which means that medical science and social hygiene gradually raise the age at which death takes place, a population is increased by the number of individuals whom this longer span of life maintains in existence. Since it raises the average of the population, the lowering of the death rate tends to add to this population an "old guard" that in the past was negligible.

But before becoming an "old guard", the individuals who are

[8] Pierre George, *Introduction à l'étude géographique de la population du monde*, 1951, and especially Louis Henry, *Caractéristiques démographiques des pays sous-développés, natalité, nuptialité, fécondité*; Roland Pressat, "Mortalité," in *"Le Tiers Monde," Sous-développement et développement*, ouvrage réalisé sous la direction de Georges Balandier, I.N.E.D., Cahier No 27, Paris, 1956; Warren S. Thompson, *Population and Progress in the Far East*, Chicago Press, 1959.

rescued from death while they are still relatively young pass through the adult stage. A larger adult population will have, as we shall see later, a happy influence on the economic future of the nation if this population can be fully employed.[9]

But disregarding for the moment this question of the economic activity of the population, we must note that these young adults rescued from death in infancy or during childhood see several paths open to them: a more or less early marriage according to the habits and customs of the country under consideration, or celibacy. Celibacy will have its effect on the demographic movement, but it is obviously marriage which has the more active influence because of its fertility.

The *marriage rate* of a population may be more or less high. Marriage may also take place more or less early in life. Adults, men and women, may marry, preferably, and on an average, at 15 or 22 or 25 or 30 years of age, and this cannot fail to influence the question of fertility. It has in fact now been proved that, if no method of voluntary restriction of births is used, a marriage is all the more fertile if it has been contracted by younger people. This is the case at least as far as the woman is concerned. The marriage age of the mother, together with the marriage rate, is one of the most important natural factors in fertility and its rise and fall. Biological and natural sterility among women has hardly any effect as it only affects from 3 to 4% of the female population at the age of twenty.[1]

Finally, together with the death and marriage rates and even to a greater extent than these, *fertility* is the factor most directly responsible for increases in population. Indeed a country's increase in

[9] But we must not extrapolate purely and simply our schemes of full emploment in the Western sense to countries which are not sufficiently equipped. A. Piatier has the following to say on this point: "The 'transposition' to underdeveloped countries of the purely Anglo-Saxon vision or more correctly the Keynesian vision of the world (is) as ridiculous as a boxing bout for old ladies or pipes for children in arms. It is not because in undeveloped countries, only from 4 to 15% of the population of working age belong to the wage-earning class that the other inhabitants are unemployed. They *do not work* and that is quite another thing. They are found as hangers-on of agricultural or craft production units, or else they do non-productive 'jobs'. Egypt has a surplus of active persons engaged in agricultural production of at least 5 millions (the country has 20 million inhabitants). Unemployment is everywhere and yet it is nowhere. And it is certainly easier to open employment bureaux than to change a mentality, to create a will to work and to alter people's habits of life." *op. cit., Encyclopédie Française,* pp. 11, 16–12.
[1] Louis Henry, "Caractéristiques démographiques des pays sous-développés," in *Le Tiers Monde,* p. 152.

population depends on the number of new citizens that married couples are willing to give it.[2]

In other words, according as these three factors combine—and they can be measured by what are known as the death, marriage and birth rates—so we are dealing with rather different types of population increase, as we shall now see.[3]

VARIOUS TYPES OF POPULATION INCREASE

The Population Department of the United Nations has identified five principal types of situation throughout the world in regard to population. They are based on the present difference between the death and birth rates. The marriage rate was not taken into account and this is a pity, because, if it had been included, it would be possible to come to much closer grips with the principle underlying population increase. Using this classification, we shall therefore say that there is:

1. A *pre-modern* type of population increase, involving a high fertility rate and also a high death rate at an early age. For instance, we may have a birth rate of from 40 to 50 per thousand and a death rate of 35 per thousand, which gives a very variable and unpredictable population increase of from 0·5 to 1·5%

2a. A type in which the *death rate is beginning to fall*, that is, an appreciable decrease is beginning to make itself felt but it still leaves

---

[2] There has been much discussion concerning the *fertility potentiality*, i.e. the probability of conception and live birth per unit of time (excluding pregnancy and the period of temporary normal or pathological sterility immediately following confinement) in various races and populations whether undernourished or not. L. Henry comes to this conclusion: "Finally, no data allow us to assert that the legitimate fertility of present underdeveloped populations is very much greater than that of former European populations. It even seems probable that, in quite a large number of cases, this legitimate fertility is lower than that commonly found in Europe in former times. Nevertheless the birth rate is higher because the marriage rate is higher and marriage takes place earlier than in Europe" (p. 158). "As for J. de Castro's thesis, according to which a lack of food and a shortage of proteins—and both are common in underdeveloped countries—are a cause of a high birth-rate, there is no evidence to support it, since medical knowledge does not allow us to consider a lack of proteins as a contributory factor. Further the reciprocal relation between the birth rate and the percentage of proteins in food—and it is on this that de Castro relies—is easily explained. Birth limitation is less frequent in underdeveloped countries which are those that consume the smallest quantity of proteins" (p. 159).

[3] *Perspectives de l'évolution démographique du monde*, Mme I. B. Taeuber's Report to the 14th session of the World Population Conference, in *Proceedings of the World Population Conference*, 1954, *General Report*, 1956, pp. 75–6 (in the French edition).

the death rate high, e.g. 25 per thousand. There will be a medium sized population increase of about 1·5%.

2b. A type in which there is a *very considerable fall in the death rate* which is low—9 to 15 per thousand, with a stationary and high rate of fertility—40 per thousand. The population increase will be very considerable, it will be in the region of from 2·5 to 3·1%.

3. A *transitional* type in which, whilst the death rate remains low, the fertility rate will begin to decline. The birth rate will be around 25 per thousand. Population increase will begin to slow down, it will be in the region of from 1·5 to 1%.

4. A *modern* type. Death and birth rates will be very low and population increase almost insignificant—0·5%.

These various types of population are not abstract concepts the demographer has been pleased to invent, they correspond to four movements, four situations, four cross-sections in the historical demographic movement of the most advanced nations. It is a fact that the Western European populations who admit that they now belong to type 4, belonged to the first type two or three centuries ago.

Within the framework of these five categories, it is now possible to classify as follows the various population groups of the world:

1. *Pre-modern*: region—Central Africa. Population: 140 millions.

2a. *The death rate is beginning to fall*: regions—North Africa and Asia, excluding Japan. Population: 1,280 millions (52% of the world's total population).

2b. *A very considerable fall in the death rate*: regions—South Africa, Central and tropical South America. Population: 149 millions.

3. *Transitional*: regions—the temperate zone of South America, Japan, the U.S.S.R. and the Balkan Peninsula. Population: 359 millions (15%).

4. *Modern*: regions—North America, the major part of Europe, Australia and New Zealand. Population: 523 millions (21%).

Unclassified: regions—the Pacific Islands. Population: 2·8 millions.

POPULATION TYPES ACCORDING TO THE DISTRIBUTION OF THEIR SOCIAL AND PROFESSIONAL SECTORS

This list of nations itself suggests another classification based on professional and social characteristics. The well-known economist,

Colin Clark, has drawn up a classification of this sort. Among the professional and social activities of an active population he distinguishes three reasonably well-defined types: Primary activities—agriculture, hunting, fishing. Secondary activities—the mining and building industries, those concerned with production and the supply of power. Third order activities: administration, distribution, services, liberal professions, etc.

According to the proportions in which an active population is divided into these three sectors of activity, the nations of the world can be once again classified into four types. These incidentally almost overlap the types of population increase previously analysed:

1. The *agricultural* type has more than 70% of its active population working in the primary sector. Broadly speaking Asia, Africa, Tropical America and, in Europe, the Mediterranean States belong to this type.

2. *The agricultural* type *with a subordinate industrial activity* whose primary sector provides employment for no more than 50% of the active population. In this category come—the most advanced States of South America, the Union of South Africa, Japan, Iran and Iraq.

3. The *industrial* type. The active population is divided equally or almost so among the three sectors, each employing from 30 to 35%. This type is very characteristic of Western and Northern Europe.

4. Finally the type where *industry predominates*, and in which the third sector is particularly well represented (50 to 57%). To this type belong the U.S.A., Australia and New Zealand.

The populations which rightly interest economists and demographers are those of types 1 and 2.[4] If we accept the hypothesis according to which all the areas of the world, as far as population growth is concerned, pass progressively from the pre-modern agricultural type to the modern in which industry predominates, the

[4] *The Future Growth of World Population*, U.N., 1958, ch. IV, "Theoretical and Practical Uses of transitional Population Models," pp. 39–51, and Appendix C, "Detailed Tables of Future Population Estimates for the World, Continents, Regions and Countries"; Table I (A), "1950–1975 on high and low assumptions"; Table I (B), "1975–2000 on three assumptions"; Table II, "Countries 1955–1975, medium assumption". See also, Louis Henry and Roland Pressat, "Perspectives de population dans les pays sous-développés," in *Le Tiers Monde*, pp. 189–213, especially p. 205 (Table); and our article, "Vers une crise de surpopulation mondiale? Prévisions et réactions," in *Revue de l'Action Populaire*, No. 127, April 1959.

populations whose rate of increase is of type 2 will experience a still more rapid population increase. It is now 1·3% and is on the point of becoming 2·3% and even more.

And so a modern State is faced with this problem—how is the historical evolutionary movement to be speeded up sufficiently for a type 2 population (agricultural with a subordinate industrial activity and the beginnings of a lower death rate to pass to type 3 (the industrial type with a slowing down of fertility) or even to type 4 (the type in which industry is predominant and which has a very slow rate of population increase—0·5 to 1%)?

In theory every modern State has at its disposal three methods of control which it can operate as it wishes—health and death rate, marriage rate and fertility. With the most modern medical and biological techniques and with the psychological techniques of propaganda and publicity, it can pride itself on its ability to shape its population as it wills. This at least is what it understands the language of birth control experts and public opinion sociologists to imply.

ACTION IN THE SPHERE OF HEALTH AND THE DEATH RATE

The common reaction towards underdeveloped regions—at least in the case of Western man more or less tainted with Malthusianism —is to deplore the fact that the birth-rate is too high. Yet India by comparison with the economically dominant nations is handicapped not so much because she has too great a child population as because she fails to rear her children to an adult age at which they are able to work, and even where she does this, is unable to offer them a better type of employment.[5]

If we suppose for the moment that in addition to the potential wealth at her command, India could be sure of obtaining on the one hand the necessary investment of capital and, on the other, technical assistance in all its possible forms, would not her great handicap then be that her population is too young? Expectation of life in India at birth is 33 years instead of 60 or even 70 as in Europe.

[5] See the two reports prepared by the Population section of U.N., for the World Population Conference 1954, session No. 16: "Composition par âge et effectif de la main-d'oeuvre; les facteurs de variation de la population active," in *Comptes rendus du Congrès Mondial de la Population*, t. III, pp. 571–96 and 597–613.

If we wish to revive this nation, the remedy is surely to prolong the span of existence of the children who are born, not to reduce fertility. Some may think that when a fire is on the point of going out, it is because there are too many logs of wood to kindle. But others, no less wisely, may think that there is not enough draught in the air-shaft.

When we compare the activity rates of the population in the various nations of the world, we come to the conclusion that low rates are a sign of underdevelopment or else on the contrary of over-equipment. Thus the Asiatic masses have only one third of their population engaged in skilled and professional work: India—39·5%, Burma—36·9%, Malaya—39%, Pakistan—30·7%. The European nations have about half of their populations so engaged: France (1954)—45·6%, Germany—45·4%, Switzerland—45·7%, United Kingdom—46·2%, Sweden—44·1%. In an expanding economy, these rates could be increased with advantage. The standard of living of the population would be all the better for it. If France, for instance, succeeded in abolishing her excessive male adult death rate, due to the scourge of alcohol, there would be the equivalent of a sudden immigration into the country of some hundred thousand workers, and this would be a valuable factor in her economic development.[6]

When aeroplanes began to spray D.D.T. in Sardinia and Greece and so destroyed the cause of malaria, they brought back strong arms to fallow land and doubled human productivity.

When in Canada, thanks to a sound age structure, 100 adults have to support only 49 young persons under 20 years of age and only 12 old men over 60, it is obvious that death does not decimate the rising generation. There are sufficient numbers of adults to undertake every kind of activity and responsibility.

But when in India there are 64 young persons and 10 old men to be supported by every 100 adults, the rising generation never succeeds in providing a full complement of adults. Half of the Indian population dies before the age of 31.

It is easy therefore to see that action in the sphere of health and

---

[6] Abnormal male deaths cost France each year from 30,000 to 60,000 men between the ages of 20 and 60, i.e. productive adults. 51,000 extra men (and this is what France would gain were her death rate that of Great Britain), would represent labour assets amounting to 637,000 years of work and 522,000 years of retirement, i.e. a net gain of 115,000 years of work. S. Ledermann, "La mortalité des adultes en France," *Population*, 1946, p. 674. See below, Appendix IV, p. 295.

F.P.M.P.—9*

the death rate in an underdeveloped population may, by prolonging life, bring new blood to this particular nation under certain economic conditions. The effect upon work would be good, especially if there were also, as we shall repeat later, motivations on a national scale capable of inspiring the masses.

What techniques has a head of State at his disposal if he is to bring his influence to bear on health and the death rate? Obviously, hygiene and medicine. According to Dr Pampana, the cost per inhabitant of the fight against malaria in various countries varies from 4c5 in Baluchistan to 1·02 dollars in British Guiana. According to L. Andarelli, the cost in Algeria was 86·85 francs.[7]

Besides these methods, improved housing is an invaluable factor in the promotion of good health. A scheme of family allowances linked to housing and rent might be envisaged on the model of our French housing grants. These allowances would indirectly have a useful social and cultural effect as far as fertility is concerned. If we are to teach a man who lives by his instincts to govern the dark vital forces within him, we must first of all provide him with a certain framework of existence in which it will be possible for him to improve his standard of living. Only then in fact will he discover the value of that life which it is in his power to hand on. An experienced wife, who has discovered how interesting and happy a task it is to care thoroughly and work hard for her child, will come to an agreement with her husband to delay for a while the birth of the next baby. Of itself, such a decision is certainly patient of more than one interpretation, but why should it not be inspired—especially in more favourable surroundings—by a more personal sense of what human existence means? Married couples are not affected only by arguments based on self-interest, they are well able to respond to good educative influences when these are available.[8]

ACTION IN REGARD TO THE MARRIAGE RATE

It has been shown that to raise *the age at which women marry*— and in Asia they marry very young—would, if it could be done, of itself bring about a substantial decrease in fertility. It is well known as a result of the detailed inquiries of J. N. Sinha at Bangalore

---

[7] A. Sauvy, *Théorie générale de la Population*, t. II, p. 219.
[8] A. Sauvy, *op. cit.*, p. 226. See below—Social and cultural objectives.

(1951), that in this town marriages of over fifteen years' duration [9] produced an average of 6·4 children per family when the mother had married before the age of 14, 6 children when she had married between 14 and 17, 5·3 children when she had married between 18 and 21 and 3·5 children when she had married after the age of 21. In a word, if the marriage age of young women is raised by 8 years India might succeed in reducing her fertility rate by 30%.[1] But we must not delude ourselves as to the difficulty of putting such measures into practice. There have already been laws on the subject but they are hardly ever applied.[2] The average age of girls at marriage has only changed from 12·77 years in 1891–1901 to 14·51 in 1941–51.[3] In this respect, modern India is still far behind even the recent averages of age at marriage in the case of girls in Christian countries: Canada—21·09 years: U.S.A.—20·37: Bolivia 21·28: Austria—23·99: France—22·60: Norway—24·35: Ireland—26·52.

Another appreciable difference between the civilization of the Far East and Christian civilizations is the extremely small incidence of *female celibacy* in the former—only 4%, whereas in Europe it is 10%. If we examine the historical situation in our Christian civilization, we shall see that in Sweden in 1750, 73% of the girls between 20 and 24, and in France in 1851, 69·5% were still unmarried. On the contrary, in India in 1931 and in the island of Ceylon in 1946, the girls between 20 and 24 were all, or almost all, married except 4·5% in India and 29·5% in Ceylon who had remained single.[4]

[9] This figure has to be taken into account since many marriages of young girls less than 14 years old are terminated by the death of the young mother in childbirth and so reduce the birth rate for families in which the woman's age at marriage is so low. The latter fact contradicts the generally accepted correlation with fertility considered as inversely proportional to the age of the mother at marriage.

[1] J. N. Sinha, "Fertility and Age at Marriage," in *Bulletin of the International Statistical Institute*, Vol. XXXIII, Part IV (1951), quoted by S. Chandrasekhar, "Fertility Trends in India," in *Comptes rendus du Congrès Mondial de la Population*, session No. 8, vol. I, pp. 831–2.

[2] A. Nevett, S.J., "Accroissement démographique et niveaux de vie," in *Revue Internationale du Travail*, Nov. 1954, p. 484.

[3] S. N. Agarwala, "The Age at Marriage in India," in *Population Index*, April 1957, p. 97.

[4] M. Louis Henry doubts whether fertility will appreciably diminish if the age at marriage is raised in underdeveloped countries: "The raising of the average age of women at marriage from, say 17 to 22, would have less effect than might have been the case in Europe in the past had it been raised from 20 to 25," *Le Tiers Monde*, p. 171 and *ibid.* p. 161. Cf. Appendix V, p. 296.

The truth is that neither Islam nor Hinduism practise religious celibacy consecrated by vows. They have no idea of its powerful influence, which is greater than people think, on the destinies of women and on the maturity of those who marry. Doubtless many prejudices will have to be overcome in India and, above all, many customs changed if later marriage is to become the rule. Yet it is in the best interests of the woman that she should be somewhat older when she marries. She is more mature and better educated after a longer period of study and so proves a more suitable companion in domestic and social life.[5]

But how will these reforms be brought about? By force and collective control as was recently the case in China? Will they be achieved by imitating the West and by the dubious libertarian emancipation of women? Or, on the contrary, must we look to educational and religious efforts for a genuine improvement in the status of the human person?

It is clear that a marriage policy presupposes on the part of the public authorities, choices of a philosophical and religious order.

ACTION AFFECTING FERTILITY

But it is quite obvious that where demographic problems have to be unravelled, State action is expected especially in regard to the nation's fertility.

Faced with such difficulties, the modern State may adopt one of *two* contrary *attitudes*. The *first* is that envisaged by the Marxist totalitarian regimes, for whom there are ultimately no natural structures, rights or requirements. For these ideologies human nature has no essential form but merely the potentialities of a *"homo economicus"* and a *"homo faber"* who can be moulded and transformed at will.

The U.S.S.R. and Soviet China are examples in point. Their scheme is simple. All that has to be done is to induce the population to carry out a reproduction plan at the required time and in the same kind of way as when they are told to carry out a production plan in

[5] K. L. Joshi and P. D. Shukla, *La femme et l'éducation en Inde* (L'éducation des jeunes filles et des femmes en Inde de 1800 à 1947); *La situation actuelle (1949–1950), Unesco*, 1953; Renato Do Rego, *La femme dans l'Inde* (an unpublished thesis), 1957 (Institut Catholique de Paris).

the field of economic enterprise.[6] The formula is already in Engels: "According to the materialist concept of history, the determining factor in history is, in the last analysis, production and the reproduction of life . . . On the one hand, the production of the means of existence, . . . on the other, the production of human beings themselves, the propagation of the human race."

It will be the task of propaganda to create the same "mystique" both for the development of plans for the restriction of human fertility and of those concerned with the expansion of resources. In each case, it will never be consideration for the well-being of the individual or the comfort of the family which will be stressed, but always the building up of socialism, the raising of the economic level of the whole community.

With such objectives and above all with the powerful means of coercion which the totalitarian systems do not hesitate to use, it is quite possible that a nationalist and socialist policy of this kind applied to the planning of fertility may have quite spectacular results of a short-term character. The standard of living in a country hitherto underdeveloped may rise steeply but it will do so at the expense of the nation's respect for personal liberty. Although for a different purpose—birth restriction—Communism will then, like Hitler's eugenic policy, bring about the depersonalization of beings whose task is to hand on the gift of life.

What result may we finally expect from a State-controlled fertility policy? Presumably that which the regime of the Third Reich

[6] E. A. Arab-Ogly, critical commentaries on A. Sauvy's article, "Some Population Problems," which appeared in *Voprosi Filosofi*, 1957, No. 6 (Moscow), translated in *Population*, No. 2 bis, pp. 12–28. "A. Sauvy also gives an inaccurate account," states M. Arab-Ogly, "of the communist view on population problems. Whilst they are logically enough opponents of Malthusianism, the Marxists base their population policy nevertheless on the fact that population growth is not an end in itself, but should be subordinated to the radical interests of the workers, i.e. to the victory of socialism and the rapid progress of the people's material and cultural well-being (see Karl Marx and F. Engels, Oeuvres, t. XXVII, p. 108). It is precisely on this account, as A. Sauvy remarks, that communists in Italy and France have admitted that a certain amount of birth limitation is permissible. The government of the People's China has recognized that it is rational to limit the growth of the population to some extent. And for this reason also the ban on abortion in the U.S.S.R. was lifted in 1955. As J. Fréville writes, the men of the future communist society 'conscious of their aims and masters of their fate, will be able to coordinate size of population with the latter's possibilities and needs. Far from thinking of birth limitation as a means to consolidate the position of the old hierarchy, far from adopting the policy of reaction and imperialism, they will consider this limitation as a factor making for stability in a planned economy'" (J. Fréville, "*L'Epouvantail malthusien*," Paris, 1956, p. 30).

produced. But this prospect is not necessarily immediate. Contraceptive civilization only shows up in its true colours over a long period. This is all the more so here since the acme of mystification would consist in using a technique calculated by its very nature to bring about sterilization yet under cover of an anti-Malthusian campaign.

The *second attitude* which a modern State may adopt presupposes that it is firmly convinced of the absolute existence of a natural law, natural rights, natural structures which are constituents of both the human person and of society in their essential characteristics.

In this case, when faced with a high fertility rate among families, and with the resistance the latter's conservatism sets up against all forms of change, the government will refuse all recourse to physical or moral coercion and will proceed by way of an educational policy. This brings us to the point at which we shall have something to say about the social and cultural objectives in a population policy for underdeveloped countries.

III. *SOCIAL AND CULTURAL OBJECTIVES*

The essence of social and cultural action can be summed up in three aims: [7]

1. To recognize as clearly as possible the source of the resistance offered to a wise policy aimed at slowing down fertility;

2. To identify the dynamic forces latent in the populations in question; to use these forces as a foundation; to cultivate in groups of chosen leaders a disinterested will to create and to work for the advancement of others;

3. To invite religious societies to make an effort to provide education for family life and to form in the people the sense of their responsibilities.

[7] An excellent study by the Secrétariat Social d'Alger on *l'Algérie surpeuplée; Orientations pour une politique de population* (Editions du Secrétariat Social d'Alger, 5 rue Horace-Vernet, Alger) deserves to be quoted here at length. In particular the notion of *seuil à franchir* (the threshold to be crossed) as explained by Fr Sanson gives much food for thought. This concrete example of Algiers shows better than any process of reasoning the capital importance of social and cultural factors (pp. 242–8). See also S. de Lestapis, "Conditions psychologiques de l'abondance dans les populations à fort potentiel d'accroissement démographique," in *Comptes rendus du Congrès Mondial de la Population*, 1954, t. VI, pp. 785–98 and in *Revue d'Action Populaire*, No. 82 (Oct. 1954) and 83 (Nov. 1954).

DETECTING THE SOURCES OF RESISTANCE

The detection of psychological resistances in the sociological field should be undertaken without any kind of prejudice and as objectively as possible by means of inquiries and sample observations.[8] It is absolutely essential that the public authorities should have a real conspectus of the reasons why their peoples remain attached to ancestral habits—early marriages, arranged marriages, preference for male children, belief in the reincarnation of souls, etc.

It is also of primary importance that the transitional stage between the sociological past of a people and the technical, economic and other innovations which the growth of culture will bring to the population, should not give rise to a moral or spiritual regression, or lead to proletarianization or dehumanization.[9]

On the contrary, it is essential that, when the older type of stability has to give way in favour of a better one from a human point of view, the latter should have been adequately envisaged and desired by the whole community or at least by its *élites*. It is a case of "more haste less speed". Even those who are most anxious to spread contraceptive methods in underdeveloped countries are now convinced—to judge by what they write—that no good results are to be expected from "ill-timed forms of propaganda". It is better for the moment, they say, to make people aware of the problem rather than to impose solutions by means of propaganda.

Decisions as to size of family are made by couples for highly personal reasons. The most pervasive influence is undoubtedly the culture in which they live; the traditions which have been handed down, the attitudes of their friends and neighbours. These things are changed by contacts with the outside world and by their local leadership. In isolated and largely illiterate communities, such as those where a large proportion of the world's population are found today, attempts at outside influence are looked upon with

[8] G. Balandier, "Le contexte socio-culturel et le coût social du progrès," in *Le Tiers Monde*, pp. 298–303, and by the same author, *Conséquences sociales du progrès technique dans les pays sous-développés, Tendances actuelles et bibliographie, La Sociologie contemporaine*, 1954–1955, 3,1,75 p; Bert. F. Hoselitz, *Progress of Underdeveloped Areas*, Chicago, 1952.

[9] Frank Lorimer, *Culture and Human Fertility*, Unesco, 1954, especially ch. VI, "The Relation of Cultural Conditions to the Demographic Transition."

suspicion and may harden rather than change existing attitudes. Mass education thrives only on indigenous soil, and must be undertaken by local leadership. The intellectual respectability of ideas, as endorsed by leaders in terms of patriotism and piety, may be of greater importance in determining acceptability in areas of low literacy and education than in a society where more of the people are able to deal with intellectual concepts of their own.[1]

Hence long basic educational work, even if it does not seem to pay off at once, is better than hasty and unacceptable practical methods. Once the incubation period is over, chain reactions begin and we make up for time which had apparently been lost.

Briefly, when public authorities have opted against methods which "do violence to the masses", the only method available is this basic or general education. But we must not be credulous or forget that these authorities must expect to meet many obstacles, not the least among them, the privileges of those who benefit by the order which is destined to disappear, and the opposition of the traditional religious organizations who will be apprehensive of the changes that are likely to come.

What then, we again ask, is to be done and what advice given here and now to those authorities who are fully conscious of the unfavourable demographic situation of their country?

The answer is clear. Caught as it is, between the two rival camps of the economically dominant nations, the one inspired by Marxism and the other by Malthusianism, the "Third World" of the under-developed countries must at all costs discover the latent dynamic forces within itself. No policy can be initiated for the benefit of a given population unless the latter is keenly interested in, and even enthusiastic about the objectives emanating from official sources.[2]

---

[1] *Population: An International Dilemma*, by F. Osborn, *op. cit.*, pp. 62 *et seq*. Even the advocates of birth control for underdeveloped countries do not deny that it is difficult to persuade these populations to accept ideas which will inevitably seem to them "outlandish and foreign". As Louis Henry very rightly notes: *"Ill-timed propaganda on the part of Western peoples in favour of birth control might give rise to general reactions ultimately leading to the opposite result from that intended*, especially if the cultural environment is very different from that of the West, when this action may well be interpreted as an indirect way of weakening or eliminating a culture foreign to the West" (*Le Tiers Monde*, p. 173).

[2] S. H. Frankel, *The Economic Impact on Underdeveloped Countries*, Cambridge, 1953, p. 96; G. Balandier, "Motivations et stimulations économiques dans les pays insuffisament développés," *Bull. Intern. des Sciences sociales*, 1954, VI, No. 3 and in *Le Tiers Monde*, p. 290.

THE DETECTION AND UTILIZATION OF
LATENT DYNAMIC FORCES

It is therefore incumbent on the modern State to bring to light the energizing and creative will in man. It has to recover what runs to waste in an unchecked, uncontrolled traditionalism instead of being transformed into energy for the will, for research and reflection. This project is of the same type—allowance being made for individual liberty—as the recovery of hydraulic power from glaciers and mountains where it runs away in torrents and is lost.

Economists used not to be aware of this. They seemed to expect that a nation's economic activities would begin only as the result of some homogeneous cause such as the law of supply and demand. At present they say the basic effort of nations in a state of demographic crisis should be directed to the psychological plane.

The creation of a psychological atmosphere favourable to economic progress seems to us a preliminary condition for any attempt at technical development. The advance of countries at present under-equipped cannot come about without the enthusiastic support of the native population. This support cannot be given if the spiritual leaders are indifferent, reticent, even hostile to progress and technics. The success of a policy for improving the standard of living of the masses depends largely on the attitude of these spiritual leaders at every level of the hierarchy.[3]

The *Report of the Five Experts*, published by the United Nations in 1951, already underlined the decisive role of a certain desire for progress:

Economic progress only occurs if the atmosphere is favourable to it, if the population is keen on progress and if the social, economic, juridical and political institutions are favourable to progress.... A society will have no desire for progress if it does not realize that progress is possible. Progress only occurs if the population is persuaded that man can dominate nature by a conscious effort.[4]

[3] J. Méraud, "Remèdes aux disparités de niveaux de vie," *Revue de l'Action Populaire*, No. 102, Nov. 1956, p. 1048.
[4] *Mesures à prendre pour le développement économique des pays insuffisament développés*, Rapport d'un groupe d'experts, U.N., 1951.

Among peoples with a very low standard of life, curious though it may be, it is not so much the idea of an improvement in their living conditions which will "arouse and bring to white heat" their dormant energies until it makes of them a great explosive and revolutionary force. The thought that this is so is one of the most obvious misapprehensions of those who believe in "the miracle of contraception" for underdeveloped peoples. No, it is not a crusade for pleasure and comfort which will produce *élites*, still less arouse the conservative masses. Rather than a plan for their well-being, what should be offered to the latter is "a redirection of their own inner dynamic forces", for every nation has its own reasons for existing and for which on occasion it is perfectly willing to lay down its life. But this plan is not possible except through the medium of a "real ideological mobilization".

As L. Wirth expresses it, the underdeveloped countries are not ready to pay for their material progress with the loss of their "soul". They are very probably ready to undertake an effort that may well be superhuman, if they are offered a more authentic, more realistic, fuller and more effective way—as they see it—of reliving their own traditional values and faith. Certain ideologies, such as nationalism or anti-colonial freedom movements, doubtless provide the desired occasion for this psychological shock, which alone can separate the two forces—population and the means of subsistence—hitherto inseparably locked together.

Once this has been achieved, a creative effort should normally follow. In an atmosphere of "liberation" or "progress in building up the nation" methods and projects for a basic education become feasible.[5]

A BASIC EDUCATION

As far as its immediate and visible aims are concerned, basic education sets out to persuade a human group to live a better life by adapting itself more and more to the real facts of its surroundings. Thus farmers living in a group in a village will learn to utilize

[5] G. Balandier, "La mise en rapport des sociétés 'différentes' et le problème du sous-développement," in *Le Tiers Monde*, pp. 119–33. See also the observations of Eugene R. Black, President of the International Bank for Reconstruction and Development, on the output of work asked for and obtained in nationalist Egypt (8 June 1959), in *Population Bulletin*, Aug. 1959, pp. 96–7.

more successfully the resources of the soil and turn them to better account by closer cooperation.[6]

Basic education succeeds in bringing into being, among people attached to their traditions, structural changes which, far from causing any harmful social disorganization, allow them on the contrary, to achieve a better internal cohesion. Far from imposing on them a "foreign civilization", basic education helps indigenous populations to "develop the best elements in their own culture". It rescues them from the torpor of routine and puts their destinies into their own hands.

Such a type of education obviously presupposes educators and leaders of quality. Training colleges will have to be founded and regular courses of instruction organized. The knowledge taught there will have as its aim not so much to set individuals at the head of the communities in question as at their heart.

Within the framework of this kind of basic education, it is no longer impossible to envisage influence being brought to bear on family fertility.[7] And what is more to the point, it is within this framework that it has most chance of success. We have already pointed out how slowly populations are persuaded to accept innovations. This is especially the case where changes have to be introduced gradually. We may well believe that in so private a sphere the aims in view would benefit by merging with the objectives of a family and religious policy that shows a respect for values.

A POLICY OF FAMILY AND RELIGIOUS EDUCATION

A modern State which wishes to avoid the temptation of "a nationalist and State-controlled eugenic policy" has scarcely any other choice, if it is to carry out its demographic policy, but to

[6] S. de Lestapis, "Education de base et pays sous-développés," in *Revue de l'Action Populaire,* No. 87 (April 1955), pp. 451–65; Fr Queguiner, *L'Education de base,* préoccupation catholique et initiatives de l'Unesco, 1955. See the *Revue d'Education de Base,* published quarterly by Unesco, and the two bibliographies on the subject published by the *Revue analytique de l'Education* 1956, No. 7 and 1959, No. 8. The English term which is used to describe the sociological context of basic education is "Community Projects". See the very interesting monograph, *India's Changing Villages,* by C. S. Dube, London, Routledge, 1958, and its bibliography on India.

[7] S. de Lestapis, "Problèmes de Population, Solution à ces problèmes dans les pays neufs," in *Revue de l'Action Populaire,* No. 54 (Dec. 1951): "Education ménagère et familiale, éducation eugénique," 708–11.

appeal to families themselves as well as to the religious societies to which they belong. Action in regard to fertility which on principle is desirous of respecting personal liberty can only be brought to bear on families through the medium of families [8] or of those societies which appeal to their conscience, that is, religious societies.

But, as we have seen, religious bodies are in fact divided on this problem of birth limitation. Some have given up the struggle. Others still hesitate between control or regulation. The position of a man like Gandhi of course is fairly close to that of Catholicism. The ideal of *Brahmacharya* and that of married chastity among Catholics have points in common. Both—to take one example—refuse to sanction contraceptive techniques and envisage recourse to continence alone for the spacing or limitation of births. But, apart from these religions, how many others accept birth control as a necessity and contraceptive methods as a boon!

What therefore is to be the policy of the State in a nation of divided beliefs, whose subjects are members of different religious bodies? The rule for the government to follow in this case is that of the temporal common good. In a democracy this implies the right of the citizen and of particular societies to compete in their efforts to forward human progress, provided that this progress is sought by all concerned in a spirit of justice, charity and truth. Normally, in fact, it is by means of this attempt at a common front based on the higher values that the mistakes, faults and ignorance of individuals and societies stand the greatest chance of being eliminated.

Even without rising to the level of philosophical or theological reflection, the State can observe empirically that there will never be enough persons or families whose life is inspired by a devotion and

---

[8] G. de Beaulieu, "La famille représentatif de la Nation," in *Pour la Vie*, 1945, No. 1; P. Renaudin, "Apport de la Famille dans la Nation," in *Pour la Vie*, 1950, Nos. 39–40; S. de Lestapis, *Au-delà du Marxisme par l'organisation des Familles*, Spes, 1946, "Either the Family will abdicate and accept the diminished and stunted role which the Marxist State will allow it to play, or else the Family will rise up against this excessive State interference and organizing itself spontaneously into a Family Authority declare, 'L'Etat, c'est moi'; I am the State because I bring children into the world, because in the crucible of the home, I forge the persons of the future and prepare man for the social tasks of society" (p. 101). In a pastoral letter on the Family, Cardinal Suhard wrote: "*The new civilization as a whole should—if it wants to be viable—be conceived in relation to the family considered as its basic unit.*" It therefore follows that "the first duty of families is self-awareness, an awareness too of the power they represent in the nation. And this is what the majority of families fail to understand. They are even somewhat suspicious of Family Associations. . . . Families must cast aside their fears and their inertia and acquire an all-conquering mystique of the family" (Card. Suhard, *La famille*, 1946).

a creative will, which are a source of inspiration to others. There will never be too much self-sacrificing and spiritual energy in the nation whose destiny lies in its hands. If the government is sincere and honest, it will be able to classify the various religious bodies according to the moral demands they make upon their members.[9]

When, in civilizations which are contemplating the legalization of birth control or have already legalized it, *Catholics* bear witness to their faith in the ideal of married chastity and in their writings call upon all who want to follow our Lord more closely to adopt it, then they are certainly preserving a tension that is both fertile and of value to civilization. The State has no cause either to subject them to annoyance, to eliminate them or to discredit them in theory or in practice. On the contrary, Bergson, speaking as a sociological philosopher, has shown clearly enough the beneficial effect of the appeal to heroism and sanctity.

If Catholics are of the opinion that they see further and more clearly into the profound requirements of human nature raised by God to the supernatural order, then it is for them to say so and to bear witness to the fact by their lives and their achievements. It is for them to convince the world of this, provided of course that they are given sufficient chance to do so, and that they themselves respect the liberty of others.

These were the conditions which long ago Gamaliel called on the Jewish Sanhedrin to accept: "And my advice is still the same; have nothing to do with these men (Christ's apostles and their disciples), let them be. If this is man's design or man's undertaking, it will be overthrown; if it is God's, you will have no power to overthrow it. You would not be willing to be found fighting against God" (Acts 5. 38–9).

But this raises a serious problem—Catholics ask for *toleration*; ought they to grant it to others, even when they are quite certain

[9] Emmanuel Gounot, "Les impératifs familiaux de toute politique," in *Semaine sociale de Bordeaux*, 1957, pp. 379–97. "Without appealing to any philosophical creed, the experimental wisdom of all time never ceases to repeat: 'Society is worth what the family is worth'. . . . Do not the recent and concordant observations of psychologists, psycho-analysts and doctors show that, contrary to certain opinions or predictions current half a century ago, the stable, united and fertile family, even if very deficient from a technical standpoint, remains for every child the natural framework for his development to manhood, and incomparably the best environment for his physical, emotional, moral and even intellectual growth and for the progressive unfolding of his personality? So much so that it is the family as we have defined it which in fact conditions not only the collective life and the prosperity of society, but also the personal value of each of its future citizens" (p. 383).

that the doctrine opposed to their own leads to an inevitable social evil, which we have called "contraceptive civilization"?

DEMOGRAPHIC POLICY AND TOLERATION

As far as contraception is concerned, it would obviously be desirable that the exigencies of the law should coincide with those moral requirements that are most consistent with the dignity of the human person as well as with the progress of nations. Yet we must not forget the doctrine commonly taught by theologians and notably by St Thomas Aquinas—"human law is not obliged to forbid all the immoral acts from which virtuous people abstain, but only the most heinous, those from which the majority of men are able to abstain, and especially those which harm other people and the repression of which is seen to be indispensable if a human society is to be preserved. Consequently human governments can legitimately refrain from preventing certain blameworthy deeds, for fear they should otherwise hinder the good or incite men to worse crimes" (I. II, q. 96, a. 2).

Politics is the art of the possible and often the art of avoiding what is worse by tolerating a lesser evil.[1]

It is therefore not beyond the bounds of possibility that a government, even a Catholic government, should have to ask itself whether it is preferable to forbid or to close its eyes to a limited diffusion of contraceptive methods. In spite of the fact that objectively error has no rights and even the erring conscience has no right to profess error publicly, the psychological and moral state of society may in certain circumstances demand some toleration in the interests of public order. Pius XII in fact declared in a speech to Italian jurists:

The obligation of repressing moral and religious offences cannot be an ultimate norm of action. It must be subordinated to higher and more generous norms which, in certain circumstances, allow and even perhaps make it obvious that is is better not to prevent error in order to bring about a greater good.[2]

[1] Fr Riquet, S.J., "A propos du birth control," Preface, in *Saint Luc, Bulletin de la société médicale Saint-Luc*, Dec. 1957, pp. 437–8.
[2] Pius XII's speech to Italian jurists, 6 Dec. 1953, D.C. 27 Dec. 1953, col. 1, 604 and commentary by G. Courtade in *Revue de l'Action Populaire*, No. 75, Feb. 1954; see also *Tolérance et Communauté humaine*, Casterman, 1953, and J. Lacroix, *Personne et Amour*, Ed. Seuil, 1955, ch. v, "Verité et charité."

"What is the greater good?" asked Cardinal Lercaro, Archbishop of Bologna, in the course of a lecture on "Religious Tolerance and Intolerance". He answered:

> It is respect for truth and the way the human mind reaches it. None should be forced against his will to accept the Catholic Faith. Respect for truth demands freedom of consent. A truth which is imposed is not accepted as a truth. . . . When truth is imposed, it is because religion is confused with politics. . . . Instead of politics being in practice subordinated to religion as the Christian conscience demands that it should be, we have that inclusion of religion in the area of politics, which is typical of all forms of paganism and is carried to the extreme today in the totalitarian regimes. . . . If this principle is valid for all metaphysical and moral truth, it is *a fortiori* valid for faith and grace.[3]

Underlying this principle, as Mgr Charrière, Bishop of Lausanne, Geneva and Fribourg, also remarks, we discern the parable of the cockle which is not to be removed once it has begun to grow for fear that the wheat might be plucked out at the same time.[4]

But once this point had been made, there can be no question of allowing, under pretext of toleration, a liberty *without limits*. No modern State would agree to do this, not even in the case of such established freedoms in the democracies as freedom of opinion, freedom to form trades unions, religious freedom. Everybody is agreed that public order and public morals imply that there are limits to freedom of speech, freedom of religion and worship. The Catholic Church when she reminds us that there are limits to religious toleration is only insisting on a conviction which everybody holds.

In the case of contraception with which we are dealing here, we can envisage a whole sliding-scale of prohibitions and, to counterbalance it, of activities which are tolerated. The line of demarcation cannot be defined *a priori*. The case is similar to that of a treaty to define a frontier. The contracting parties must discuss the matter and in the present case these are the State and the representatives of the societies involved: families, religious bodies, etc. Sociology and philosophy as well as natural reason and Faith have also their contribution to make.

[3] Card. Lercaro, "Tolérance et intolérance religieuse," D.C., 15 March 1959.
[4] Mgr F. Charrière, "L'Eglise catholique et la tolérance religieuse," lecture given at Basle in Jan. 1957, Imprimerie Saint-Paul, Fribourg.

Humanity however has a suspicion that it does not possess the right to treat itself like livestock whose existence can be technically planned by a breeder without running any risk.[5] And so, in view of the hesitations and uncertainties of its own natural reason, the human race has the right and the duty to ask modern States above all not to let go of the controls in regard to this particular issue, even if propaganda pressure becomes intense. Majorities are not always right. It is therefore the State's duty to make them understand this with the assistance of experienced and far-sighted minorities.[6]

MUTUAL UNDERSTANDING AND EFFORTS
TOWARDS IT. OPEN DISCUSSION

Thus in a study recently published under the signature of demographers of the first rank,[7] and which is a kind of manifesto addressed to men of goodwill with a view to reaching agreement on "some ethical principles relating to human reproduction", the following passage is especially noteworthy:

[5] J. Vialatoux, *Le peuplement humain*, Editions Ouvrières, 1957. "The question of human population is thus (cf. pages 144, 147–8) on the one hand, a moral and philosophical question (it has its aspect of 'mystery'), and on the other, it is a complex of biological, economic, social and political questions (it has its 'problem' aspect) ['mystery' and 'problem' are here used in the sense given them in the philosophy of Gabriel Marcel.—Translator's note]. These two orders are so utterly distinct from one another that we cannot down-grade the first by making it solely a series of 'problems', without completely falsifying its character. . . . To the extent that it is conditioned by its physical and biological nature and exists in the world, *the (human) empirical subject may be one of the 'objects' of science* (and it is under this aspect that 'the sciences of man' will consider him in the initial stages of its work). But—and here lies the difference between man and things outside him or living beings who do not possess personality—in so far as the empirical human subject is also conditioned by its link with the personal, spiritual and transcendental subject, *it is no longer reducible to a pure object*, and 'the sciences of man' which study it cannot be integrated without further ado with the sciences of nature (second meaning of the word 'nature', p. 155). Among all the 'sciences of man', human demography bears irrefutable witness to this truth," pp. 151, 156. See also, *L'Algérie surpeuplée*, Ed. Secrétariat social d'Alger, pp. 167–74.

[6] Cf. the applications of this principle proposed by Norman St John Stevas in his interesting brochure *Birth Control and Public Policy*, Center for the Study of Democratic Institutions, Santa Barbara, California, 1960.

[7] Dr Frank Lorimer, J. Bourgeois-Pichat, Dr Dudley Kirk, "An Inquiry concerning some Ethical Principles relating to Human Reproduction," in *Social Compass*, Vol. IV, Nos. 5–6, pp. 208–11, The Hague, 1957.

Significant progress has been made during the last decade in recognizing the distinction between scientific issues and ethical issues relating to population, in exploring the implications of information about actual conditions, and in the spread of mutual respect, tolerance and courtesy. . . .

We seek here to enlarge the areas of cooperative action. We believe that it is possible, especially in the spheres of scientific inquiry and social action. . . . For example, we affirm that an unprejudiced empirical investigation of the role of the family in various cultures and our own society, provides strong support for the principle that for normal persons parenthood is an essential aspect of marriage. . . .

This does not imply any denial of love as the motivating principle of true marriage, or of the contribution of the spouses to the mutual development of their lives as an essential function of marriage. . . .

And the authors of the manifesto conclude:

We are, therefore, led to the following questions, *Can there not be a more positive emphasis in Catholic teaching on ethical motives and personal responsibility in marriage and the regulation of procreative activity*? If this emphasis has already received full recognition in the learned councils of the Catholic Church, can it not be more effectively implemented in the ministries of parish priests, lay organizations, and educational programmes in various countries?

Finally, we ask, would not such emphasis in Catholic teaching, if consistent with its fundamental principles, in conjunction with greater appreciation by others of the ethical force of its central principle in this field, bring a broader *consensus of value* as a basis for cooperative action among sincere, socially responsible persons nurtured in different traditions? . . .

Might not stronger emphasis in such situations on the positive aspects of creative and responsible living within the family and in other social relations, contribute both to economic progress and to the advancement of religious ideals?[8]

We are of opinion that it would. In particular we believe that if this spirit is the principal source of inspiration in the basic educa-

[8] Commenting on these remarks, Fr C. Mertens ("Problèmes de population et morale," in *Nouvelle Revue Théologique*, Dec. 1959, pp. 1044–5) has very wise recommendations in regard to teaching in seminaries, pastoral care, preaching and the formation of the faithful.

tional centres which family associations or religious societies and parishes can provide for engaged couples, young married people and parents, to help them acquire a better knowledge of their creative and educative work and a better will to do it, then both nation and State cannot fail to benefit considerably. As the sense of their responsibilities grows among married couples, without prejudicing in any way their creative will and devotion, the aims of an economic population policy as set out above will begin to appear less utopian, more realistic. Policy never operates in the abstract. It has to be accepted by a public. In the ordinary course of things these basic educational centres, parochial, family and social, if well run, are bound to contribute to the formation of this receptive environment.

Here we must end the rapid outline we have attempted to draw of the economic, demographic and psychological aims the government of an underdeveloped nation should adopt if it wishes to lead its people out of the impasse caused by an inadequate national income face to face with a considerable population increase. We have pointed out, in passing, the help it must seek from religious bodies in pursuing these educational aims, as well as the spirit of toleration and the firmness of purpose it must display. We must note in conclusion that every State has the right to count on international solidarity and the assistance of the community of nations.

IV. *INTERNATIONAL COOPERATION AND ITS AIMS*

If an undernourished and under-equipped nation is to make a start along the path of progress, a psychological shock is necessary, as we have said, and we have gone into considerable detail as to how a government may set about producing this initial shock. In reality it only stands a chance of occurring if "the community of nations deliberately sets out to help this nation to emerge from the rut into which it has sunk. The intervention of the community of nations is preferable to that of one or two foreign powers which will necessarily create ties of dependence and run the risk of appearing more or less unreliable." [9]

[9] J. Méraud, "Remèdes aux disparités de niveaux de vie," in *Revue de l'Action Populaire*, No. 102, Nov. 1956, p. 1050; J. Parizeau, "Les problèmes de l'aide extérieure," in *Le Tiers Monde*, pp. 331–48; Pierre George, "La transformation des régions sous-développées en économie socialiste," in *Le Tiers Monde*, pp. 349 seq.

The Asiatics, the Africans and even the South Americans cannot avoid wondering how they are to obtain the cooperation of the West and at the same time defend themselves against the West's determination to control them.

The Great Powers are always tempted to "work in their own interests" even when they wear an international label. This at least is what occurred more than once in the past in the days of President Truman and the American aid promised by the Mutual Security Agency. It occurs when offers of help are made to the Arab States by the Soviets. "The two blocs are tempted to consider the underdeveloped countries as a field in which a decisive victory must be won. But these countries are not deceived. They merely do their best to extract the maximum benefit from a contest they feel to be a quarrel that does not concern them, a kind of dispute between 'rich men'."

Nevertheless progress has been made on both sides towards a certain renunciation of imperialistic motives. "Our aim," said Aneurin Bevan, "is more limited, it is a victory over hunger in its most literal, physical sense." Competitive coexistence seems to confirm the possibility that the two blocs are trying to follow the same line in pursuing this more restricted aim.

In actual practice, what can and what should a nation do?[1]

1. At the very least, they should *avoid making large profits at the expense of underdeveloped countries* or squeezing them out of the export markets. The condition of poor countries which export raw materials has too often in the past been used as an opportunity to exploit them by means of contracts giving the lion's share to the other party.

Some economists suggest the creation of an "international organization for buying from and selling to underdeveloped countries," in order to have a better guarantee against this kind of temptation. In the long run, it would be possible by this means to correct the machinery of competition and its tendency to work at the expense of the weaker. "The wealthy nations will help those that are poor by ceasing to impoverish them still further."[2]

[1] P. Laurent, "Comment aider les pays sous-développés?" in *Revue de l'Action Populaire*, No. 110, June 1958, pp. 648-63; Léon H. Janssen, "Duties to Underdeveloped Countries," and the international Symposium following this article in *Social Order*, May 1958, Saint-Louis, U.S.A.; Rev A. Zimmerman, S.V.D., *Overpopulation*, The Catholic University, Washington, 1957.

[2] Jacob Oser, *Must Men Starve?*, ch. IX, "Profits, Wages, Taxes, and Industrialization," pp. 204-11; Léon Tabah, "La population mondiale et les besoins en matières premières," in *Population*, Oct., Dec. 1953.

2. The nations should then *organize philanthropic and free assistance*. Its first and most accessible form is "technical assistance", placing at the disposal of underdeveloped countries experts in very varied spheres—scientific, economic, etc.—until such time as these countries are themselves able to form their own contingent of scientists, teachers and technicians.[3]

3. *International Financial Loans*. These have already been granted by the International Bank for Reconstruction and Development and they ought to be considerably increased by the lowering of the interest rate hitherto charged—4%. If the Point Four Programme has not succeeded, it is because the American Congress did not offer a government guarantee to private investments which might have been made in underdeveloped countries.[4]

4. In the face of the difficulties that arise, some go further and look for the solution of the investment problem in what François Perroux calls a *"gift economy"*, which would be a great advance on capitalism. The wealthy countries would then be quite rightly taxed for the benefit of those that are poor, in the same way as compensation is calculated in family allowances according to the size of the family. Studies have been undertaken in this field. One of the best known is the *Plan of the Five Experts*, drawn up in 1951 for the Department of Economic Questions in the United Nations.[5]

According to this report, an annual investment equal to 20% of the national income of the poor countries of the whole world should

[3] "L'approche actuel au problème du sous-développement. Assistance technique," in *Le Tiers Monde*, p. 65; *L'Assistance technique aux pays insuffisament développés*, 3 fasc., Direction de la Documentation, Paris, 1955; *Documents concernant le développement économique et l'assistance technique aux pays insuffisament développés dans le cadre de l'O.N.U.*, 1 fasc., Direction de la Documentation, Paris, Feb. 1950; le Bureau international du Travail et l'Assistance technique, *Revue du B.I.T.*, Dec. 1952; N. Drogat, *Pays sous-développés et coopération technique*, Spes, 1959.

[4] A. Piatier, "L'Occident devant les pays sous-développés. Une nouvelle politique est-elle possible?" in *Politique Etrangère*, revue du Centre de Politique Etrangère, 54 rue de Varenne, 1958, No. 2, pp. 196–230; cf. our Appendix VI, p. 297 for a statement on the present international effort towards underdeveloped countries in the financial field; cf. our Appendix VII, p. 299 for a view of what this effort might become if a world tax were levied proportional to the income of the economically dominant countries.

[5] *Mesures à prendre pour le développement économique des pays insuffisament développés*, U.N., 1951; *"Paley" Report, or Resources for Freedom*, U.S. Government Printing Office, 1952, vol. II; Léon Tabah, "Le problème Population-Investissement-Niveau de vie dans les pays sous-développés," in *Le Tiers Monde*, pp. 227–88; see A. Piatier's remarks on this article, "Inégalités démographiques," in *Encyclópedie Française*, t. XI, pp. 11, 18–3.

make possible an annual increase of 2·5% in the national income of these countries. To put this in more general terms, to obtain an increase of X% of this national income, it would be necessary to invest 8X% of it, approximately. But it has been pointed out on the strength of available data in the case of certain underdeveloped countries, that the ratio of 1 to 8 between the percentages mentioned above is much higher than it would in reality be, at least for the countries in question. A ratio of 1 to 2·5 would be nearer the truth.

If we accept the ratio of 1 to 2·5, we may conclude that, in order to obtain an annual average increase of 7·2% of the national income of the underdeveloped countries, an increase, that is, which would double it over a period of ten years, it would be sufficient to invest approximately 18% of this national income. (This was equivalent in 1949 to 18 milliard dollars or 5,728 milliard francs). (In the U.S.A. 1,000,000,000 = 1 billion. In the U.K. the billion = a million million.—Translator's Note.)

If we suppose that these underdeveloped countries are able to invest from their own savings 5 milliard dollars per year, foreign aid would have to provide almost 13 milliard dollars, that is, 3% of the annual national income of the wealthy countries. This is on condition that the world population remains stationary. If we suppose the annual increase of this population is 1%, then after a period of six years the national income per head would not have doubled (100%) but all the same it would have increased by 75%.

From a material standpoint an effort of this kind does not seem impossible to realize. The contribution the United States would be asked to make would correspond to about 8% of the total of her investments in 1949, or at the most 10% if it were considered that America should on principle make a larger contribution. In France 3% of the national income represented in 1954, for instance, about 13% of the total income from direct taxation. This, on the average, is what our country has assigned since the last war to the overseas territories of the French Union.[6]

In actual fact, from 1950 to 1955, the 800 million inhabitants of the underdeveloped countries received from the United States and the international organizations only 1,400 milliard francs (5·3 milliard

[6] J. Méraud, *op. cit.*, pp. 1052–3.

dollars).[7] Yet the military expenditure of the U.S.A. amounts to more than 40 milliard dollars per annum.[8]

It may be objected that such a sense of international solidarity is beyond the power of man and that there is good reason to give military "realism" precedence over aid for underdeveloped countries. If this is so, any social ethic is useless. We may as well leave Machiavelli to look after international peace, and rest content with phrases and labels, calling what is in reality only anarchy and the barely concealed jealousies between nations "international order".

In any case, as long as this anarchy and jealousy have made no effectual attempt to mend their ways, "if any given area has an excessive population," as Pius XII said, "it would be wrong to blame natural laws for our present difficulties whilst these clearly arise from a lack of solidarity between men and nations."

5. Finally, international effort should encourage *emigration movements* which would relieve congestion in over-populated countries. Although we cannot count to any great extent on the possibility of emigration from country to country and still less from continent to continent, since great masses of people, who may well reach the million mark, would have to be moved each year, yet we have no right to minimize the interest that all nations should take in a measure of this kind.

In the first place, it would prove that the nations are seeking to form a community even if they have not yet fully succeeded in doing so. And, as we have seen, without this international effort we shall never obtain the funds so urgently necessary for investing in countries in course of development.

Then for islands which have too large a population and are situated near a mainland able to absorb it—and here we are thinking of the West Indies and even perhaps of Japan—it is the most rational of all foreseeable measures. The United States has done much for Puerto Rico by accepting emigrants from that island. Doubtless still more could be done but here the greatest difficulties to be overcome arise from various nationalist prejudices.

It cannot be denied that, in the interests of the common good, each nation has the right to lay down conditions for those immi-

[7] See Appendix VI, p. 297 and VII, p. 299.

[8] For military budgets, see Jacob Oser, *Must Men Starve?*, ch. IV, "War and Hunger," especially pp. 100–10; see also our Appendix VIII, p. 300. The American budget presented to Congress in 1958 included 40·3 billion dollars for armaments, i.e. 47·6 billion for the total defence budget; *U.S. News*, 24 Jan. 1958, pp. 34–5 (Billion on U.S.A. reckoning.—Translator's note).

grating to its territory. Nor is emigration as practised in previous centuries possible in the twentieth. Today migrations have to be organized. They presuppose employment contracts signed before the emigrant leaves home, and when he arrives a welcome for him and his family since family emigration alone is truly human. "This is why there must be no half measures about an organized migration. Unless it can guarantee the migrant living conditions considerably better than those he had before he came, it must make detailed preparations and not bank on the fact that the newcomers will be of inferior type."[9]

But this requirement automatically reduces the possible annual number of immigrants from an over-populated country.

We must therefore be under no illusion regarding the actual total of free immigrants who have succeeded in taking root in another continent since the end of the second war.[1] They amount to hardly more than ten million for the period of fifteen years, whereas the population of India increases annually by five million and that of Japan by almost one million!

We must therefore stop thinking of emigration as an overall cure for underdeveloped and apparently over-populated countries. But at the same time we should not disparage the official or private institutions for the encouragement of emigration. Pius XII showed only too often how interested he was in such organizations.[2] As we said above, these organizations keep alive the international spirit and develop charity between the nations.

[9] A. Sauvy, *Théorie générale de la Population*, ch. XV, "Migrations spatiales," p. 258.

[1] "If we rely principally on the figures recorded and partly also on the numbers as estimated, we find that at least 6,300,000 persons have migrated from one continent to another during the period 1945-52. Out of this total, 4,452,000 have left Europe for other continents and 1,150,000 have come from other continents to Europe. At least 100,000 emigrants have left the Asiatic continent for destinations other than European and 100,000 emigrants from Africa have gone to Asia, most of them to Israel. A certain number of smaller intercontinental movements also figure in the available statistics." "Etude des migrations intercontinentales au cours de la période d'après-guerre," Nations Unies, Division de la Population, in *Comptes rendus du Congrès Mondial de la Population*, Rome, 1954, t. II, p. 291.

[2] See above ch. IX, note 2, p. 145. See also the Three International Congresses organized by the International Catholic Migration Committee, 11 rue Cornavin, Geneva, and the bi-monthly review published by this important organization, *Migration News*; see *Osservatore Romano* (French edition), 26 Aug. 1955, on the Christian conscience and emigration problems.

CONCLUSION

As it faces the crucial problem of the underdeveloped nations, has the human race no solution other than birth limitation and its contraceptive techniques? We no longer have any right to think so now that we have examined the creative resources at the disposal of the community of nations and the potential energy latent in the peoples who seem most fixed in their attachment to tradition. No, we no longer have the right to think so when we are already witnessing, as the result of the sudden explosion of mystical dynamic forces, a reawakening and upsurge of the spirit of sacrifice and devotion which could not have been foreseen only a short time ago.

If to this we add the fact of a progressive mobilization of the educational forces of a nation, beginning with those of the family and religious bodies, it is no longer utopian to hope that a population policy insisting to a greater extent on the responsibility of parents as educators should be understood and eventually succeed in developing also the notion of a more premeditated, more human and more altruistic type of procreation.

If in addition the universal community of nations is willing to organize a policy of genuinely world-wide development with its own fundamental requirements, its own precise aims and its own clearly defined[3] lines of action, it is no longer fanciful to hope that we shall

---

[3] In Nov. and Dec. 1959, a very lively discussion took place in the United States between Catholics and Protestants on the question of aid to underdeveloped countries. Should such aid include as a preliminary clause the need for the countries aided to envisage a policy of birth restriction, or should it not? The Committee appointed to study the question (Study Committee for Military Aid to underdeveloped Countries under the chairmanship of General W. H. Draper) answered in the affirmative, as did also a group from the University of Stanford which was in contact with the Senate Committee for External Affairs. On the contrary, the Catholic Bishops of the United States protested in the opposite sense and denounced the kind of psychological pressure which had been organized for some time previously by the press, T.V., etc., in favour of the Draper point of view. The President of the United States, Eisenhower, when asked for his opinion, declared: "We do not wish to interfere in the internal affairs of any government whatsoever. If they want to do something in this very difficult field, that is their own affair. If they want help, they should apply to specialized groups and not to governments. As long as I am here, the government will have no positive political doctrine connected in any way with birth control. It is no business of ours." (F. Bernard, "L'aide aux pays sous-développés et le contrôle des naissances," in *La Croix*, 12 Jan. 1960 and *Revue de l'Action Populaire*, March 1960, p. 358.)

cut the Gordian knot of insufficient resources face to face with population increases. On the day when military expenditure decreases in favour of genuine investment in the cause of peace, the underdeveloped section of the race will be able to see the dawn of its own day of liberation.

Chapter XVI

CONCLUSIONS

THE TEMPTATION TO ADOPT CONTRACEPTIVE FAMILY PLANNING AS A SOLUTION FOR THE UNDERDEVELOPED COUNTRIES

IN the state in which so many of the countries we call under-developed now find themselves, it is understandable enough that many philanthropic minds spontaneously think of initiating amongst these populations great movements in favour of a contra-ceptive limitation of births.

We might almost say that there are scarcely any books inspired by Anglo-Saxon thought which do not consider Family Planning as the very first measure to be adopted. If we wish to release the machinery of economic demography and prevent it from beating the empty air we must obviously begin by an automatic reduction of its output. Once we have done this, we are told, the rest—that is, the increase of food resources and the raising of standards of living, professional training and the development of culture, savings and investments—will all become possible again.

Unfortunately this reasoning—and this is one among many of its weaknesses—rests on the presupposition that there will be a rapid, almost instantaneous adoption of scientific Family Planning by the populations which are at present underdeveloped. And this is just not true.

Family Planning perfect as it is (?) for the use of advanced societies accustomed to treat technically all kinds of problems, turns out to be, according to the statements of an ever increasing number of serious sociologists, an unmitigated failure among the rural, illiterate and traditionalist masses of our various continents.

SIR SOLLY ZUCKERMAN'S EVIDENCE

Let us quote one of the most recent pieces of evidence on this point. It is provided by a learned professor in the University of

Birmingham, the vice-president of the British Advisory Council on Scientific Policy and president of the National Resources (Technical) Committee, Sir Solly Zuckerman.[1]

Speaking of India and the campaigns initiated in that country in favour of controlled conception, he writes:

> In spite of valiant efforts, the results so far achieved are trivial in relation to the scale of the problem and have hardly begun to make any impact on the general situation. One or two costly and highly publicized experiments designed to spread a knowledge of the so-called rhythm method of control—which is based on the idea that fertility can be controlled by regulating sexual behaviour in accordance with estimates of the likely time of ovulation—proved conspicuous failures, for the simple reason that the individuals concerned were neither literate enough to appreciate what needed to be done nor impressed with the sense that anything needed to be done at all.
>
> The vast mass of India's population are illiterate villagers engaged in peasant farming, and even the inhabitants of most of the larger towns, such as Calcutta, live in squalid, crowded conditions. As one Indian demographer has put it, to an Indian villager the cost of an additional baby is less than the cost of a contraceptive. Even if this were not the case, the prevailing social conditions, such as the low standards of housing and the paucity of educational and medical services, make it almost unthinkable that Western methods of fertility control could be spread fast enough to stem the growth of population over the next decade or so . . .
>
> Yet so far there is no sign that the national campaign for fertility control has made any impact on India's demographic problem. What has become clear in India, as in so many other areas, is not only that there is a direct relation between economic status and the recognition of the need to limit fertility, but also that action based upon a recognition of this need depends on the feasibility of the available techniques of birth control. As has already been said, those that are known today do not satisfy the need even in advanced countries. They are hardly likely to satisfy the far

[1] "The Control of Human Fertility," in *Impact*, Unesco Publication No. 2, pp. 61–78; for similar remarks in the case of Japan, see Rev A. Zimmerman, S.V.D., *Overpopulation*, ch. III, "Whether Birth Control can solve Japan's Problems," pp. 64–72, the Catholic University, Washington, 1957.

greater need which exists in impoverished, overpopulated and illiterate societies.... But in Egypt, as in India, the major difficulties with which the authorities have to contend are, first, the failure of a predominantly peasant population to appreciate the need to limit the size of their families; second, illiteracy and squalor; and third, resignation to a state of poverty which is all that has ever been known.

THE CONTRACEPTIVE PILL

In view of this failure, the author remarks—but without saying whether he is of the same mind—

> What everyone is hoping for, is some discovery that will allow people to control fertility simply, efficiently, harmlessly, reversibly and above all cheaply enough for the method to be within reach of even the poorest countries. The image that has been conjured up is that of an "anti-fertility pill" which can be taken by mouth as and when required. How near are we to discovering a substance which will temporarily and harmlessly inhibit the process of reproduction in the female or the male?

Sir Solly Zuckerman does not venture to answer this question with any certainty—

> A dispassionate appraisal of all this current research inevitably leads to the conclusion that the hopes of finding a simple oral contraceptive that is sure in its action and has no undesirable side-effects are greater today than they were, say, two years ago. Even so, it would be foolhardy to take the view that the problem is likely to be solved in any specified period of time, if indeed ever.[2]

It would be wearisome to follow this author as he goes into detail in his explanations. If we did, we should see that none of the attempts to produce the contraceptive pill with all the necessary provisos has yet satisfied the scientists. The first tests, which were originally considered sufficiently conclusive, have all eventually

[2] Sir S. Zuckerman, *op. cit.,* pp. 77-8.

raised doubts, reservations and, in practice, an insistence on caution.[3]

Thus the concentration of ovarian or testicular hormones needed to block the pituitary and prevent it from secreting its own gonadotrope hormones is generally accompanied by harmful effects on other physiological functions.

Of the 418 women who agreed to take part in the experiment organized by the Puerto Rico Family Planning Association, and who took doses of a substance similar chemically to progesterone, half very soon withdrew from the experiment. Of the rest of the group, some 70 continued the treatment for more than a year.

No pregnancy occurred in these 70 women during the period they took the "pill" according to instructions, nor in a further 130 who persisted with the treatment for a shorter time than a year. Pregnancies were, however, reported as soon as the treatment was stopped. Unfortunately, a number of undesirable side-effects were also recorded, so that for the time being judgment must be reserved both on the report of the trial and on the value of this technique of fertility control.

Other substances were tried, about ten in all, and two of them deserve to be mentioned: the plant *Lithospermum* and *Pisum sativum*. The first had to be abandoned when it was observed that the expectation of life of the animals used in the experiment had been considerably reduced after they had been made to eat one of the varieties of this plant, and other pituitary functions had been seriously disturbed. As for *Pisum sativum*, its effectiveness was not considered adequate, and since it has to be taken at about the time when ovulation is due to begin, it can hardly be considered of any practical use at least in the case of the illiterate population of India.

Efforts have also been made to find a substance capable of directly inhibiting spermatogenesis in the man and the maturation of the ovular cells in the women. In these experiments the difficulty has been that the doses of the products employed (nitrofurazone) necessary to produce the desired effects provoked extremely undesirable disturbances in other physiological functions. The suppression of the

[3] Dr J. Sutter, "A la recherche de la 'pilule' stérilisante," in *Population*, No. 3, pp. 495–504; "If mechanical procedures are relatively less dangerous," declares Prof. Chauchard, whose competence in the neurophysical field is universally acknowledged, "on the other hand, *all the new chemical procedures* are far more perilous: we cannot with impunity disturb the female endocrine system, and the sterilizing products have effects that are not limited to the gametes," Dr. P. Chauchard, *La maîtrise sexuelle*, Ed. du Levain, 1959, pp. 55–6.

seminiferous tubes in the man takes a long time and to reverse the process is a lengthy procedure. Other products are at present being studied with erucic acid as their base. It is too early yet to pass any opinion on these.

No product to be taken by mouth is yet known which is capable of reducing the number of ovular cells in the woman. Exposure to X-rays has this effect. "It may be thought that we have here one way of controlling fertility, but much remains to be done before this is proved."[4]

Other research is studying a pill capable of acting on the uterine mucous membrane and so preventing the embedding of the fertilized ovum or even of inhibiting the growth of the embryo (anti-histamine or anti-metabolic preparations), but this type of pill can no longer be called "contraceptive". Its action plainly induces a type of abortion. In short, not only is the problem of the contraceptive pill unsolved, but its solution seems even further away than ever, for:

> Moreover, even if a "pill" is discovered, it does not mean that it will be used on a wide scale in countries like India or the islands of the Carribean, unless the people concerned, having been made to understand the reasons why they should limit their fertility, link this need directly in their minds with all the other measures aimed at improving their social status and their standards of living. It is a sobering thought that the Japanese national campaign to limit fertility has not yet managed to spread a knowledge of the subject sufficiently widely to prevent people from turning to abortion as the most certain method of fertility control. . . . .[5]

It may even be supposed, in the light of the data indirectly provided by the very considerable proportion of male children in large

[4] We refer the reader to what has already been said in chapter IX, viz., that every sterilizing process is unlawful unless subordinated to the good of the body as a whole. On the sterilizing pill and its unlawfulness, see W. J. Gibbons, S.J., and T. K. Burch, "Physiologic Control of Fertility, Process and Morality," in the *American Ecclesiastical Review*, April 1958. Consult especially in notes 1, p. 246 and 17, p. 254, the bibliographies on research carried out in the U.S.A., on these pills. On this research, see also G. G. Pincus and Rock, "Symposium of Progestational Substances," in the *Annals of the New York Academy of Sciences*, 1958.

[5] Sir S. Zuckerman, *op. cit.*, p. 77. See our Appendices I, p. 289 and IX, p. 303.

families, that the practice of infanticide has not entirely disappeared in remote areas.[6]

And yet Japan is flooded with literature on the subject; has numerous birth control clinics; and has gone to the length of training one instructor in the subject for every 3,000 of the population. Experience in the Caribbean equally emphasizes the enormous difficulties which have to be overcome before any "pill" that may be discovered will break down the barriers of ignorance and apathy.[7]

THERE IS NO "LIGHTNING SOLUTION". A SOCIAL AND CULTURAL REVOLUTION MUST COME FIRST

From these various observations we may conclude that it is certain that contraceptive practices are not a lightning solution and that they cannot be, in spite of appearances to the contrary. Far from making higher standards of well-being possible in the underdeveloped countries, they presuppose that these are already in existence. In any case then, the social and cultural revolution is necessary whether or not it is essential for any underdeveloped country to move towards a reduction of the rate at which its population increases. Hence, however paradoxical it may seem, the factors involved must be reversed and before we talk of fertility control, we must initiate social and cultural changes.[8]

More precisely, it is necessary before all else to make every effort towards helping the underdeveloped masses to acquire an increased psychological and moral awareness, or at least we must help them in this respect while at the same time putting into their hands the tools they need for their economic, social and cultural advancement. Moreover this does not imply that the process should take as much time as has been needed for the emergence of a reflective adult consciousness in the West.

Although centuries of Christian history and of conflicts between

[6] Harno Mizushima, the "Trends of Fertility in Japan," in *Comptes rendus du Congrès Mondial de la Population*, 1954, t. I, pp. 966–7.

[7] Sir S. Zuckerman, *op. cit.*, p. 89. On the Japanese experiment see our Appendix IX. G. Tillion, *L'Algérie en 1957*, IV. The problems of backward peoples can only be solved by a genuine social transformation.

[8] Alex. Greschenkron, "The Progress of Underdeveloped Areas," in *Economic Backwardness in Historical Perspective*, edited by E. Hoselitz, University of Chicago, 1952.

the spiritual and the material orders, between science and faith, between egoism and love, have been necessary to bring families to the point where they define themselves in terms of love and charity and not of egoistic calculation, it is in no way evident that as many struggles and vicissitudes will be necessary in the case of people now under-equipped, technically speaking, but who "have not lost their souls".

THE SOCIAL AND CULTURAL REVOLUTION
AND CATHOLIC MISSIONS

We have only to see how eagerly African or Asiatic populations, once they have come into contact with the Catholic ideal, adopt it in all its rigour and in spite of the few promises and the few material or worldly advantages such acceptance can offer them. The whole history of Catholic Missions during four centuries could be cited in support of this.

It is certainly not because of any pandering to the false demands of the flesh or of sex that the Catholic Missions succeed in less than three generations in raising peoples who but yesterday were un-cultured, illiterate and polygamous, to the highest levels of moral consciousness and to a fully adult sense of responsibility, as is proved today in the case of so many Christian communities in Madagascar, the Cameroons, Vietnam, Polynesia and elsewhere . . .

If the great sociological law binding on all who would bring an influence to bear is, as Basic Education is now rediscovering, that "communities must be taught to work for their own evolution them-selves" and if, "in the final analysis, what is important for this pur-pose is the formation of the leaders of these communities far more than the employment of educators who do not belong to the group in question",[9] can we not see that these are the very principles

[9] M. Pauvert, "La formation du personnel d'Education de base," in *Initiatives, Bulletin de l'Education de base au Cameroun*, No. 2, p. 11, 1953: "Every expert in basic Education should have a solid foundation of teaching experience in a special technical field, personal qualities such as understanding and humility so that he can adapt himself to the mentality of the people with whom he is working and grasp their needs; a certain moral and physical stamina if he is not to find the life too hard for him, and practical experience of work in areas that are insufficiently developed. . . . Even with experts who possess all these qualities, there will still be many problems of adaptation and mutual relationships, and they will be hard to solve." (See also by the same author, *Bulletin d'Education de base,* Unesco, 1953, p. 60.)

which have always governed the founding and the development of Catholic Missions?[1]

Too often unfortunately the rapid advance of peoples who have been won over to Catholicism has been slowed down, if not stopped, by the bad influence of more "civilized" co-religionists who ought to have set them an example. Here again the history of the Spanish Catholic Missions in South America, or that of the Christian communities in tropical and Southern Africa, could provide many instances of this arrested development and these heart-breaking recessions.

On the other hand, where the activities of the clergy, first composed of missionaries, then of natives, are intelligently supported and seconded by the example and zeal of a fervent missionary laity, extraordinary community progress is seen.[2] The Second World Congress of the Lay Apostolate at Rome in 1957, and also Catholic Action sessions in Africa and Asia have provided irrefutable proofs of this: every genuine social and cultural advance in the case of a large mass of people can only be the result of the influence within the mass of *élites* whose psycholgical and moral awareness is perfectly formed and enlightened.

This being so, it is now possible—unless atheistical materialism or positivist and agnostic rationalism interfere—that, as they learn to know our own history with its ins and outs and its blind-alleys, nations today under-equipped may avoid the trials and errors and the mistakes of our own erratic career.

And so, to return to our subject—birth limitation—we may hope that Indians, Mexicans, Africans and others, when better informed on the blind-alleys of contraceptive family planning, will in the near future avoid the grim experiences which the Japanese and the West Indians, under Western Malthusian influence, are now undergoing to their cost.

[1] C. H. Parias. Mgr Bretault tells us: "When we have 500 catechists and pioneer teachers, we shall see no more famine in our villages," in *La France Catholique*, 8 Jan. 1960, p. 7.

[2] Here are some of the societies for lay missionaries: "Ad Lucem," Auxiliaires Féminines Catholiques Internationales, The Grail, Association for International Development (AID), Lay Mission Helpers of Los Angeles, etc. These societies are now federated in the secretariat of the U.C.C.I. (Union catholique de coopération interraciale), Koningslaam, 30, Amsterdam, Holland. See the appeals of Pius XII (*Evangelii praeconis*, 1951) and of John XXIII (*Princeps pastorum*, 1959) for the formation of an apostolic laity in the missions (Doc. Cat. 1959, No. 1318, c. 1547).

THE DANGER OF FACILE SOLUTIONS WHICH ATTRACT
BECAUSE OF THEIR TECHNICAL CHARACTER

We may now leave the underdeveloped areas and return to our own so-called "civilized" countries and ask whether we too have not the right to think that a day will come, and perhaps sooner than we imagine, when contraception will go the way of abortion at the present time. The latter meets with unanimous disapproval from the sciences of man, although it was quite recently tolerated or even approved by certain bogus scientists who claimed they had freed themselves from the superstitions of a medieval theology.

A similar case is that of "tranquillizers" which are now denounced by medical science although only a few years ago, hasty pharmaceutical propaganda on the other side of the Atlantic recommended them to people suffering from worry or anxiety.[3] The attraction of this propaganda lay in its promise of a "chemical peace of mind" which would probably be more certain, less liable to fail, more "automatic", one might almost say, than the other kind, namely the peace of mind gained by spiritual efforts towards psychological and moral awareness.

The propaganda was irresistible. Tempting promises that such and such a pill would ensure "the disappearance of pathological anxiety, morbid fears, nervousness, doubt and their effects on the functioning of various organs, a lucid and tranquil state of mind, restful sleep, a return of confidence in life . . ." and all this "without an exaggerated sense of well-being, without excitement or subsidiary effects such as sleepiness or fatigue, without risk of poisoning or habit formation". Another tranquillizer was loudly praised since it produced "that tranquillity of mind, that sound judgment a man needs if he is to act as he should in all the circumstances of life". These seemed to provide the answer to a universal or at least a widespread problem, for the advertisers recommend the use of tranquillizers to the people of the U.S.A. in circumstances so widely different as "family tensions, illnesses, accidents, weddings, funerals, marriage breakdowns or differences of opinion".[4]

And Dr Escoffier-Lambiotte from whom we have been quoting remarks:

[3] Dr Escoffier-Lambiotte, "De la médecine de l'anxiété au procès des tranquillisants," in *La Nef*, April 1958, pp. 53-7.
[4] Dr Escoffier-Lambiotte, *op. cit.*, p. 57.

In this case we are dealing with a monstrous distortion of the very principles of therapeutics. It is all the more monstrous and dangerous in that these drugs, which are sold relatively cheaply, were until quite recently freely available to the public in all American drugstores and were lauded to the skies by advertisements in English newspapers.

Fortunately the dangers of their improper use are beginning to be denounced on the other side of the Atlantic as cries of alarm are raised by doctors "overwhelmed by the heaviest pressure from industry and public opinion known to history".

Removal of anxiety feelings by chemical means, they point out, would be equivalent in a given society to an act of surrender. It is surely the drama of this individual and collective act of surrender which one of the greatest American psychiatrists has in mind when he considers tranquillizers "the most powerful political weapon humanity has ever possessed".

CALLING THE BLUFF OF WESTERN CIVILIZATION

Why then must a whole sector of our Western civilization continually enter the blind-alley of these solutions which are "simple, short-term and, above all, require no other effort than that demanded by the mere technicalities of their application"?

With such a question in mind, we may be permitted to broaden somewhat the basis of the debate and, using a dialectical process of thought, return to the problem of the underdeveloped countries.

In fact our guilty natural conscience, faced with the indecencies and anomalies of contraceptive practices, seeks to excuse and even to absolve itself by arguing from the existence of *hunger in the world*, and for this we lay the blame on the unduly prolific nations.

For our conscience is guilty not only because it dimly realizes that contraception is a form of egoistic calculation, but also because it is not willing to recognize that our national position is one of privilege. Our privileges ought in fact to lead us to sacrifice some of our affluence in the interests of the "proletarian" nations. But at this point our unconscious cleverly effects a guilt transference.

If there is indeed any sin to be expiated and for which even reparation must be made, we shall think it can only be the sin of improvidence committed by these irresponsible "prolific" peoples.

If only they had reduced their fertility, they would not have to endure their present state of underdevelopment. Is not wealth the reward of virtue, the virtue of prudence in particular?

Thus by comparing itself with others our guilty conscience becomes clear. Further by making itself available to teach others, in the name of prudence, the careful calculations which are the secret of the acquisition of wealth, it achieves an astounding self-transformation and becomes a conscience free of guilt. Fooled by their own interests, the wealthy nations then consider themselves as models to be imitated and in all seriousness offer themselves to others as such. Birth control quite logically partakes of the magical character of the situation and the process of self-deception is complete.

Nor should Marxism above all take it into its head to attempt to call our bluff. If it did, this would be only one more excuse for the dominant nations to wrap themselves in their guiltless consciences and harden their attitude. The deadlock would then be complete and the delusion absolute. If we are determined to continue moving in the direction of the alibi Malthusianism has conveniently provided for us, if we persist in making a good conscience out of a bad one, we cannot hope to be cured of this delusion.

OUR SALVATION—INTERNATIONAL MUTUAL AID

We must look for our salvation in the opposite direction, not, that is, in either a good or a bad conscience, but in the truth, namely, as A. Piatier has written, in "the casting aside of both superiority and inferiority complexes, in passing beyond the methods of competition and struggles between nations, in the attempt to produce a scheme of world organization, in new types of contracts and human relationships, in the elimination of narrow fanaticism and nationalism".

The work has certainly already begun and this is what gives us cause to hope.

Although their results to date have not been spectacular, the measures perfected since the end of the second world war, bear witness to a change—slow but sure—in international relations. The United Nations Organization has perfected a vast programme of Technical Assistance in which the specialized Institutions take part—the International Labour Organization, Unesco, the World Health Organization, the Food and Agriculture Organization, the International Civil Aviation Organization, the World Meteorological Organization, the International Telecommunications Union, the International Bank for Reconstruction and Development, the International Monetary Fund, etc. A Special United Nations Fund for Economic Development was created in 1952 (S.U.N.F.E.D.) with the task of making gifts or loans at a low rate of interest. Finally in 1956, the International Finance Corporation (I.F.C.) was set up to encourage the development of productive private undertakings. When it begins to function it will complete the work of the previously mentioned organizations by mobilizing private capital and making every effort to create conditions favourable to private investment.

In addition to this international effort, individual States have not remained inactive. After the Marshall Plan, the United States launched the Point Four scheme. Great Britain is responsible for the Colombo Plan for South East Asia. France has increased her investments in the countries of the French Union and drawn up a number of plans for development and industrialization. The countries concerned have on their part intensified their efforts in many parts of the world, they have created new industrial corporations (e.g. Latin America, India), they have drawn up long-term plans (India, China, etc.). But here again the fundamental reality runs the risk of being hidden under the sheer multiplicity of events. And this reality is the inadequacy of the means adopted and the insufficient increase in production always outdistanced by the growth in population.

It has been said—and it is true—that France has invested more in the countries of the French Union and made them more gifts than all the international organizations in the rest of the world put together. But even if these investments and gifts were suddenly multiplied by 5 or even 10 the problem would not thereby be solved. In actual practice there are genuine limits to the amount of credits or equipment from abroad which a nation can absorb.[5]

To force the pace would mean resorting to compulsion.... What then is to be done?

[5] A. Piatier, "Inégalités démographiques et économiques, Que pouvons-nous faire? Eléments des solutions proposées," in *Encyclopédie Française*, 1958, XI., pp. 11, 16–11, 12.

WE MUST EDUCATE

We must educate; we must educate public opinion, awaken in it the sense that the nations are interdependent, make it aware of reciprocal obligations, of the need for sacrifice. We must educate the individual, the family, the group. In a word, everywhere and always, we must educate each and all in *the sense of charity* which begins with the nearest of our neighbours, but goes out to the furthest confines of the human community.

It is truly only when the activities undertaken, the sacrifices made, witness to a genuine transformation of people's minds, it is only when a universal charity begins to arouse men far more effectively than can empty phrases, that the question of an eventual slowing down of population increases in certain places can be envisaged without risk of self-deception. It is so easy, as we have seen, to dress up our most secret egoism in the trappings of altruism.

In other words, when everything has been done to stimulate production, to encourage improved productivity and to promote the best all-round distribution of capital and wealth, then will be the time to discuss *in an atmosphere of goodwill and charity* the formidable question of an eventual limitation of human fertility in any given population group.

In this sense the problem is no different from the one husband and wife attempt to face in the context of the genuine material and spiritual interests of their family. We shall therefore end this book with a discussion of their particular problem.

THE HUMAN COUPLE; MARRIED LOVE AND CHARITY

In a Christian home, the genuine love of man and wife urges them, through the universal charity which they receive from Christ, to be as creative as possible.

A mature love—as we have said over and over again—is essentially a "will to create" persons. Husbands and wives who have found fulfilment in their married love spontaneously desire to reveal to one another its splendour and dignity by having as many children as they are able to bring up and train to become persons adequately prepared for life.

This is in fact love's ultimate destination. Any other concept of love is erroneous and sooner or later has to be paid for by disappointment or scepticism, by a lack of energy or by instability, remorse or regret.

Of course two human hearts do not discover this truth all at once. They may be even turned away from it by "earthly voices and earthly food". These are bad counsellors and invite them to turn in upon themselves, instead of turning outwards together in a creative effort.

But it is precisely here that the Catholic Church keeps watch, warning her children against these tempting voices that come from our threefold concupiscence and from the world. Love, Christian love, cannot be made to serve sterility. It cannot divert by artificial means the course of the creative powers it possesses (including those of sexuality) towards disguised forms of sterility.

The love which God gives to it as a model to be imitated is the charity with which Christ loves his Church; this is a love essentially creative and fertile. Indeed, as St Paul tells us, it is "on him all the body depends (that is, the whole family of God's children); it is organized and unified, and achieves its natural growth, building itself up in charity". But this law of growth will one day cease to be: "we shall reach perfect manhood, that maturity which is proportioned to the completed growth of Christ" (Eph. 4. 3–16). Then God will be all in all.

Similarly, it is in accordance with this law of growth that a Christian man and wife move towards their full growth, "the completed growth of Christ". And they do so through the charity which inspires them. And this divine charity urges them, on the one hand, *to increase the visible number of the elect* whom God places in the care of his Church, and on the other, to fulfil and *to transcend themselves by moving* towards that heavenly state which calls them and awaits them and in which "those who are found worthy to attain that other world, and resurrection from the dead, take neither wife nor husband" (Luke 20. 35).

This is equivalent to saying that in this growth of charity, *fertility* and *chastity* require one another, fertility to inscribe its work in history, chastity to go beyond this work and to transfigure it. In fact physical love, however valid it may be, is of its nature called upon to transcend itself and to become progressively more spiritual. The union of the flesh should be the sign—and because of sacramental grace, the efficacious sign—of a love which remains, whereas bodily union will cease. Moreover if both partners eventually identified their love purely and simply with the passing union of their flesh, would they be genuinely in love with one another?

Whether they like it or not, at the heart of their bodily love there is also present what will be its term and yet transcend it, a more spiritual love—*the virginal charity of Christ.*[6] With such a prospect in view, this virginal charity appears as the soul of bodily love and also its final fulfilment, and not—as so many people imagine—its shadow or a pale image of it. Virginal charity is not only a future thing, a term we reach after death. It is *at the very heart* of the history of a couple's married life and it is there to direct it towards its true end. It is the inner force of this life and constantly causes man and wife to transcend it. *Agape* gives *Eros* what it needs if it is to avoid stagnation or even regression.

On both these counts, Christian marriage is a movement towards the fullness of Christ. It cannot consider the joys of the flesh as ends in themselves. These nevertheless find their meaning not only in the creative work to which they bear witness but also in the very movement which leads married love towards its final transcendence —virginal charity. Christian marriage commits those who have chosen this way of life to a double task of fertility and spiritualization.[7]

As has been well said:

And so we can understand why the Church allows the use of the method of periodic continence for regulating fertility. There is no question of the Church considering it as an ideal (a method belongs to the realm of means not ends) or as an infallible prescription for providing a universal answer to all the difficulties of the times. . . . But the Church recognizes that this method, whilst respecting the nature of human sexuality, makes it objectively certain by its insistence on the practice of continence, that "virginity" as we have just described it in the terms used in the writings of St Paul, is present in the marriage. This method, there-

[6] Fr Antoine, S.J., "L'Eglise et le contrôle des naissances," in *Revue de l'Action Populaire*, No. 116, March 1958. "Les fondements évangéliques de la morale sexuelle," p. 265, and especially "Mariage et Virginité," pp. 266-70.

[7] It is abundantly obvious that the first and most immediate purpose of the joys of the flesh is to witness and testify to the creative will of the partners when they decide to bring a child into the world. But this does not mean that these joys do not find their ultimate meaning in the fact that they are directed towards the most spiritual reality in the vocation of the human person—communion in the Spirit.

fore, is in itself capable of being assumed into the Christian's spiritual life and it can direct the marriage—not towards an egoism as sterile spiritually as it is materially—but towards its complete fulfilment which is virginity.[8]

For the same reason the Church will never permit the use of any contraceptive or sterilization methods. These are by definition and by nature "an *a priori* refusal to set any limits to sexual relations" and an *a priori* refusal to subordinate these relations in any way to virginal charity as the final aim of human love.

Such practices give no indication that bodily love goes beyond itself towards spiritual love and, at rock bottom, they fail to recognize the presence of virginity as a final end present in marriage. . . . Further the very notion of artificial techniques to prevent conception, whilst it offers free rein to the bodily manifestations of sexuality, can only be envisaged if the value and superiority of virginity have been disregarded from the outset. Sexuality then appears to have no transcendent object unless it be man himself desiring to be sole master of his own history and bending it to his own ends by means of his techniques. Instead of collaborating with God the Creator to bring the world to its natural fulfilment (and man, made in the image of God, has received from the Creator the power to share in his lordship over the world) technics is now only a demiurgic attempt to be God's equal and by it man, refusing all forms of self-transcendence, imprisons himself in his own history.

A FORWARD, TRANSCENDENT MOVEMENT. THERE IS NO TURNING BACK. A LIMITED OBJECTIVE IS NOT ENOUGH

When Catholicism faces the agonizing problems of the under-developed countries and of married couples in difficulties, it will only solve them by a "forward, transcendent movement". It will not turn back, as fear and egoism would have it do, or be satisfied with a limited objective. In other words, it is by insisting on an increase of *creative* charity that *humanity* will set the great powers and the underdeveloped nations on the road towards a solution. It is only in such a context that the necessary sacrifices will be accepted and the risks be run.

[8] Fr Antoine, *op. cit.*, pp. 271-2.

Similarly it is by insisting on an increase of *creative* spirituality that a *married couple* will reach the best solution to the problem of its stability. Only thus can it succeed in dispelling the mirage which egoism may have fashioned. Only in this context will man and wife be able without harm to themselves to call a temporary halt to their fertility or even, if it is absolutely essential, to impose on it a definite limit.

In any case, the abandonment of a creative spiritual effort will never offer any genuine hope of success.

Technics will never take the place of man.

Above all, the advent of contraception will never usher in the reign of the spirit. Finally, the advent of contraception can never announce, prefigure or prepare for the coming of Christ, who entered this world "that they may have life, and have it more abundantly" (John 10. 10).

IN A WORD...

In a word, *at the level of the race*, the problem of hunger in the world or, to call it by its other name, the problem of the under-developed countries, is fundamentally the problem of a more uni-versal, more authentic CHARITY, a charity which is better able to develop and to organize the common life of nations. Once the better equipped and wealthier nations put themselves at the service of the others, the latter will in their turn become conscious of their own responsibilities and their own destiny. They will acquire a more adult, more moral and more spiritual will to master their own fertility.

In the same way, *at the level of the married couple*, the problem of fertility is fundamentally the same as that of married CHASTITY which is sensed from the outset and is then gradually experienced as the very purpose of love and the explanation of its power to attract.[9]

In practice, at each of these levels, these problems are soluble only through Christ the divine model of universal charity and

[9] We have attempted, with the idea of interdenominational discussion in mind, to summarize in a few pages the position of the Catholic Church in regard to the problem of population and birth limitation in an article entitled "Familles" (*Le Monde*), Sept. 1959; see also Ch. de Locht, "Limitation des naissances et pression démographique," in *Collectanea Mechliniensia*, Nov. 1959 and in *Notes de pastorale, supplément 1959*, No. 7 and No. 8 (Brussels).

virginal chastity; only soluble too in the communitarian spirit of hope and love which the Church spreads abroad through her sacraments and her *magisterium*.

ALL MEN ARE CALLED TO ACCEPT THIS SOLUTION

When faced with so lofty and spiritual a doctrine, some will doubtless say—"This is all very well for those who want to be Christians. That the Church should legislate for them is quite right and proper. But let her distinguish between those who are baptized and those who are not and treat each in a special way and at the same time leave them to be guided by their own consciences."[1]

It is true that every man is responsible before his own conscience and the Church will never bring force of any kind to bear upon anybody. On the other hand, all men, in the Church's view, are without exception redeemed by Christ and are potentially saved by him. And so:

Her only problem is how to preach (this salvation) to them, how to bring them to a knowledge of it and convert them to it. This is why the Church speaks to all those who are not baptized of the universal demands of Christianity, which, it must be insisted, should be carefully distinguished from ecclesiastical laws which only concern those who are baptized. . . . Since the Church knows of only one vocation for all mankind, she does not recognize the existence of two laws, one for non-Christians, the other for Christians. There is only one law, as there is only one God, the Father of all that is and for whom we are made, and one only Lord Jesus Christ, by whom all exists and through whom we go to the Father.[2]

ALL THIS IS FOR A VERY DISTANT FUTURE...

If this is to be in fact the case, it will again be objected, it will only be in a very distant future!

But who ever said that Redemption should be instantaneous and immediate? To those who asked for such a Redemption and who

---

[1] G. Martelet, S.J., "L'Eglise, la Loi et la Grâce," in *Christus*, No. 18, April 1958.

[2] G. Martelet, *op. cit.*, pp. 215–16.

said to Christ: "If thou must needs act thus, show thyself before the world," Jesus only replied with this mysterious sentence in which is hidden the whole economy of Redemption: "My opportunity has not come yet. Your opportunity is always ready to hand" (John 7. 5–6). In other words, for you any solution is good as soon as it seems to give immediate results. Here indeed lies the permanent temptation of History: "If thou art the Son of God, bid these stones turn into loaves of bread." Press on, and the whole world will believe in you! . . .

But no, God has created time as the very condition of our salvation. In time he became incarnate, he has established his Church in time. To time he has given the task of discerning the good from the evil, the wheat from the tares. Above all, he has entrusted our growth to his grace and to time, for:

> He said to them: "The kingdom is like this; it is as if a man should sow a crop in his land, and then go to sleep and wake again, night after night, day after day, while the crop sprouts and grows, without any knowledge of his. So, of its own accord, the ground yields increase, first the blade, then the ear, then the perfect grain in the ear; and when the fruit appears, then it is time for him to put in the sickle, because now the harvest is ripe" (Mark 4. 26–9).

This has always been the case with Redemption. . . .
This has always been the case with man's education and growth to maturity. . . .
This will still be the case in future with the problem of world hunger and birth regulation in the human race. . . .

"Separated from me, you have no power to do anything," said Christ (John 15. 5), "He who does not gather his store with me, scatters abroad" (Matt. 12. 30). "In the world you will only find tribulation; but take courage, I have overcome the world" (John 16. 33).

LEGAL ABORTION IN SWEDEN

The law of 1734 made induced abortion a capital offence. The law of 1890 reduced the penalty for this crime to two years hard labour. In 1921 new legislation reduced the sentence still further. But on 17 June 1938, a law came into being (it has been in force since 1 Jan. 1939) authorizing the termination of pregnancy on medical, public

THE FIGURES FOR LEGAL ABORTIONS IN SWEDEN 1939–1952

Year	Number of births	Number of abortions	Abortion rate per thousand confinements
1939	97,380	439	4·5
1940	95,778	506	5·3
1941	99,727	496	5·0
1942	113,961	568	5·0
1943	125,392	703	5·6
1944	134,991	1,088	8·1
1945	135,573	1,623	12·0
1946	132,597	2,378	17·9
1947	128,779	3,534	27·4
1948	126,683	4,585	36·2
1949	121,272	5,503	45·4
1950	115,414	5,889	51·0
1951	110,027	6,328	57·5
1952	110,100	5,322	48·3

GROUNDS FOR ABORTION

Year	Sickness or Infirmity %	Debility %	Likelihood of debility %	Eugenic Grounds %	Compassionate Grounds %
1940	71·9	3·4	0	23·7	1·0
1941	65·1	1·6	0	33·3	0·0
1942	56·0	2·1	0	40·5	1·4
1943	58·1	2·3	0	38·4	1·2
1944	58·9	2·5	0	37·7	0·9
1945	65·9	5·9	0	27·3	0·9
1946	insufficient data available				
1947	57·2	21·8	2·2	18·2	0·6
1948	45·5	36·8	2·6	14·8	0·3
1949	36·3	47·1	4·4	11·9	0·3
1950	30·2	50·7	9·6	9·2	0·3

health, eugenic and compassionate grounds. In 1946 an amendment added a further reason—the likelihood of "impaired health".

The implemention of this legislation has resulted in a remarkable rise in the number of legal abortions:

It is not impossible that these legal abortions may have slightly reduced the (estimated) figure of 20,000 clandestine procured abortions in 1930 (20% of births). But the most interesting fact is that, according to an inquiry conducted by Dr M. Ekblad among 479 women, it was established that 38% of those who were married became pregnant, though unintentionally, during the twenty-two months following their legal abortion. To all intents and purposes therefore, contraception had been unsuccessful. Hence more certain methods are sought and doctors are clearly advising sterilization.

(Martin Ekblad, *Induced Abortion on Psychiatric Grounds*, Ejnar Munks-gaard, Copenhagen and Stockholm, 1955), pp. 18, 19, 99–102.

STERILIZATION, ABORTION AND CONTRACEPTION IN JAPAN

From 1940 to 1948 Japan was under the law of "National Eugenics" (May 1940). According to the provisions of this law, when a prefect had been informed of a request for a sterilization operation, he had to decide whether he would grant the request, after he had asked for the opinion of the prefectorial Committee of Eugenic Inquiry. A petitioner dissatisfied with the prefect's decision could then appeal to the Minister of Health. This law had little effect in spite of widely publicized warnings of the disasters hereditary diseases might bring in their train.

FIGURES FOR STERILIZATION OPERATIONS PERFORMED AS A RESULT OF THE LAW OF "NATIONAL EUGENICS" (1940) (BOTH SEXES)

Year	Number	Year	Number
1941	94	1945	1
1942	189	1946	59
1943	152	1947	25
1944	18		

This law was annulled and replaced by the "Eugenic Protection Law" (13 July 1948). This law envisages two cases where sterilization may be authorized: (a) when the doctor is of opinion that it is necessary, (b) when the eugenic protection inquiry Committee makes the same decision. Sterilization is obligatory once the inquiry Committee has decided in its favour (this was not the case under the law of "National Eugenics"). This same law of "eugenic protection" contains clauses which make abortion possible on the mere opinion of doctors nominated ad hoc. In fact since May 1953, a doctor no longer needs to ask the Committee of Inquiry for its opinion.

Both for sterilization and for abortion the law envisages as sufficient grounds not only the existence of a hereditary disease in the person in question or in a relative of the person as far as the fourth degree of affinity, but also:

(*a*) for *sterilization*: danger to the life of the mother as a result of pregnancy or confinement, the state of health of a mother of several children when threatened by considerable deterioration at each new confinement.

(*b*) for *abortion*: the danger that the mother's health may be seriously affected for physical or economic reasons by the continuation of the pregnancy or by the confinement. Pregnancy resulting from rape (by force or under threat) or at a time when the woman involved was not in a fit state to resist or refuse.

These "grounds" as a whole are covered by the expression "the protection of the mother"—and a strange form of protection it is.

As a consequence of this legislation, sterilizations in fact became eight times more numerous over a period of six years, and in 90% of the cases the grounds for sterilization are stated to be "the protection of the mother". The same is true of officially notified *abortions*: for every 100 births there are 59 more abortions than there were six years previously.

FIGURES FOR STERILIZATIONS CLASSIFIED ACCORDING TO THEIR GROUNDS AS DEFINED IN THE "EUGENIC PROTECTION LAW" (1948)

Year	Hereditary diseases	Leprosy	Protection of the mother	Total	Mental illness	Overall Total
		Medical decisions (the doctor's opinion)			Decision of the Inquiry Committee	
1949	167	97	5,356	5,620	132	5,752
1950	235	103	10,782	11,130	273	11,403
1951	237	107	15,409	15,753	480	16,233
1952	340	237	21,241	21,818	606	22,424
1953	344	116	31,162	32,622	930	33,552
1954	333	122	36,601	37,056	1,000	38,056
1955 (first six months)	279	64	20,503	20,846	704	21,550

ANNUAL FIGURES FOR ABORTIONS AND PERCENTAGE IN RELATION TO BIRTHS

Year	Number of abortions	Number of births	Percentage of abortions in relation to the number of births
1949	246,104	2,696,638	9·13
1950	489,111	2,337,507	20·92
1951	638,350	2,157,414	29·59
1952	798,193	1,999,488	39·92
1953	1,068,066	1,862,348	57·35
1954	1,143,059	1,765,126	64·76
1955	1,170,143	1,727,040	67·64

REASONS FOR ABORTION (%)

Year	Hereditary diseases	Protection of the mother	Other reasons	Total
1949	1·11	97·95	0·94	100
1950	0·89	98·52	0·59	100
1951	0·50	99·28	0·22	100
1952	0·88	98·63	0·49	100
1953	0·44	99·26	0·30	100
1954	0·25	99·55	0·20	100
1955	0·16	99·66	0·18	100
Jan.–June)				

These figures make it clear that *contraceptive methods have failed*. Although it is true that the use of contraceptives decreased between 1950 and 1955 from 33·6% (per 100 births) to 28·1% in the towns and increased in the country districts from 12·2% to 17·6% (in 1952), at the same time the abortion rate increased from 20·92% to 67·64% (1955).

(Ayanori Okasaki. *Histoire du Japon: L'Economie et la Population*, I.E.N.D. Cahier No. 32, 1958, pp. 153–60).

M. Muramatsu (*Family Planning*, Vol. 7 No. 3, Oct. 1958) gives the number of abortions as 1,200,000 in 1956 and 1,100,000 in 1957.

The figure for legal sterilizations was 215,855 in 1956–7 and 258,205 in 1957–8. (Y. Koya, "Family Planning among Coal Miners in Japan," in *Population Studies*, Nov. 1959, p. 160.)

THE FALL IN THE AMERICAN BIRTH RATE
BETWEEN 1910 AND 1950

Messrs Tietze and Grabill ("Differential Fertility by Duration of Marriage," in *Eugenics Quarterly*, 1957, March, pp. 3–7) have studied the fluctuations of the American birth rate in relation to the different social classes. They conducted their inquiry among families of white women after 10 to 14 years of marriage.

It will be seen from the following table that the birth rate, after a more rapid fall among families in the wealthier social categories, has also risen again in these same classes. The slight increase which began to show itself in 1940 and has become more marked since 1950 seems to indicate that, at least in the social strata in which it is found, birth limitation has reached its maximum:

NUMBER OF CHILDREN BORN TO 1,000 WHITE WOMEN

BY THE END OF 10 TO 14 YEARS OF MARRIAGE

(WOMEN WHO HAVE ONLY MARRIED ONCE AND

WHOSE HUSBANDS WERE PRESENT WHEN THE

DATA WERE COLLECTED)

Husband's profession	Average number of children			Percentage variation	
	1910	1940	1950	1910–1940	1940–1950
The whole sample	3,134	2,183	2,205	−30·3	+ 1·0
Intellectual and liberal professions	2,245	1,649	1,939	−26·5	+17·3
Higher grades	2,496	1,711	1,956	−31·5	+14·3
Black-coated workers	2,289	1,643	1,872	−28·2	+13·9
Lower-paid staff	2,923	2,104	2,163	−28·0	+ 2·8
Skilled workers	3,085	2,326	2,296	−24·6	− 1·3
Unskilled workers	3,431	2,805	2,561	−18·2	− 8·7
Farmers	3,780	2,831	2,662	−25·1	− 6·0
Wife's level of education					
College: 1 year and more		1,634	1,944		+19·0
High School: 4 years		1,767	2,027		+14·7
1 to 3 years		2,110	2,221		+ 5·3
Elementary School:					
7 to 8 years		2,421	2,427		+ 0·2
less than 7 years		3,107	2,928		− 5·4

(Cf. *Population*, 1957, No. 3, p. 518.)

WORKERS AND PRODUCTIVE YEARS

If 1,000 men of the age of twenty all reached the age of sixty, they would represent in any given country 40,000 years of productive work. But this is not the case in any nation. In France only 730 per 1,000 reached the age of sixty before the 1939–45 war. According to its death rate for adult males, every country has at its disposal a greater or lesser number of workers likely to reach the age of sixty.

In relation to this death rate in each nation, it has been possible to calculate the probable age at death, for a man of twenty, that is, the age which an individual aged twenty has a 50% chance of reaching. (In other words, the probable age X is that at which, in the death statistics used, the generation of men now twenty years old will find itself reduced by half).

By working from these two data, it has been possible to calculate the average number of productive years which men of twenty have ahead of them in their respective countries.

Probable age at death, for a man of twenty			*Average number of productive years that may be expected from a man of twenty*	
Period	*Country*	*Males years*	*Country*	*Males years*
1931–1935	Holland	73·6	Holland	37·5
1931–1935	Denmark	72·7	Denmark	37·2
1930–1932	Italy	50·5	Italy	35·7
1930–1932	England	70·0	England	36·3
1928–1932	Belgium	69·5	Belgium	35·5
1933–1937	Switzerland	69·4	Switzerland	36·5
1935–1938	France	66·7	France	34·5
1931–1935	Finland	66·0	Finland	34·0
	Outside Europe			
1931	New Zealand	72·7	New Zealand	37·0
1930–1939	U.S.A. (whites)	69·5	U.S.A. (whites)	36·1
1926–1930	Japan	63·5	Japan	33·2
1931	India	48·7	India	26·5

(*Population,* 1946, pp. 664–6.)

It can therefore be seen that the twenty-year-old Indian worker has on the average only 6·5 productive years ahead of him, whilst the Dutch worker has 17·5, almost three times as many.

CELIBACY AT DIFFERENT PERIODS AND IN DIFFERENT PLACES

The following table gives the percentage of celibates in three definite age groups for two European and three Islamic countries in the Mediterranean basin, India and Ceylon, and two Far-Eastern countries. It will be easy to see how the situation differs according to periods and geographical position:

NUMBER OF CELIBATES OF BOTH SEXES AMONG 100 INDIVIDUALS OF THE SAME AGE GROUP

	Women			Men		
	20–24 years old	30–34 years old	40–54 years old	20–24 years old	30–34 years old	40–54 years old
Sweden 1750	73	26	12·5	84	17·5	6·5
France 1851	69·5	26	16	89·5	32	14·5
Algeria 1948	23	5	2·5	68	18·5	6·5
Tunisia 1946	28·5	7·5	4	73	23·5	8·5
Palestine 1931	30	6	4	75	18·5	6
India 1931	4·5	1·5	1	35	8·5	4·5
Ceylon 1946	29·5	6·5	4	80·5	22·5	9
Formosa 1930	14·5	2	1	52	9·5	4·5
Korea 1930	2·5			33·5	4	1·5

(G. Balandier, "*Le Tiers Monde*," I.N.E.D., p. 161.)

TOTAL AMOUNT OF INVESTMENTS IN THE UNDERDEVELOPED COUNTRIES

The annual sum invested in underdeveloped countries by the nations with a developed economy is estimated at three thousand million dollars. The estimate is broken down in the following table:

1. *International effort.*

(*a*) Over a period of nine years (1947–1956) the International Bank for Reconstruction and Development has lent 1,895 million dollars:

770 to Europe, 380 to non-European developed countries;
750 to underdeveloped countries.

These 750 million dollars (80 per year on an average with a tendency to increase of recent years) have been distributed as follows:

184 to Africa; 382 to Latin America (of which 152 to Brazil, 57 to Colombia, 110 to Mexico); 184 to Asia.

(*b*) Multilateral technical assistance: 29·6 million dollars per year.

2. *National efforts.*

(*a*) Bilateral public investments:
American aid (1955): military aid and aid to relieve distress: 2 million dollars; aid for schemes to remedy the causes of such distress (and this alone concerns us here): 800 million dollars.
British aid: 125 to 140 million dollars.
French aid: 500 million dollars.
Belgian aid (to the Congo): A loan guaranteed by the State: 100 million dollars.
Russian aid: 500 million dollars (?).
(*b*) Private investments (in underdeveloped countries):
U.S.A.: 500 million dollars a year.

Great Britain: 200 to 500 million dollars a year.

France: 100 million dollars a year.

3. *Total amount.*

3 thousand million dollars (2 thousand million of which are public investments and 1 thousand million private investments).

(A. Piatier, "L'Occident devant les pays sous-développés," in *Politique Etrangère*, 1958, No. 2, p. 207.)

HELP ACTUALLY GIVEN TO UNDERDEVELOPED COUNTRIES AS COMPARED WITH WHAT COULD BE DONE IN THIS DIRECTION

If, in order to meet the need of the underdeveloped countries for investment, it were thought desirable to institute a kind of world tax assessed according to the national income of each of the wealthier countries (an *ad valorem* or a graduated tax), we should find that the sums listed below would be required, which, except in the case of France, are much in excess of the help which is actually being provided.

Countries	Actual annual investments[1] (in milliards of dollars)			Estimated world tax (in milliards of dollars)	
	Public	Private	Total	Ad valorem	Graduated
United States	1[2]	0·6	1·6	7·2	8·4
Great Britain	0·1	0·2	0·3	1·1	0·9
France	0·5	0·1	0·6	0·8	0·7
Germany	0·0[3]	0·0	0·0	0·5	0·5
Canada	0·0[3]	0·0	0·0	0·0	0·0
U.S.S.R.[4]					

(N.B. Here again, "milliard" is used because of the confusion over "billion."—Translator.)

(Cf. P. Moussa, *Les chances économiques de la communauté franco-africaine,* Colin, 1957, quoted by P. Laurent, *Revue de l'Action Populaire,* No. 119, June 1958, p. 657.)

[1] These figures correspond on the average to those for the period 1954–6 (actual investments and national income).

[2] This figure takes into account the fact that the greater part of the loans made by the International Bank for Reconstruction and Development is financed by American capital.

[3] The figure 0·0 indicates a sum difficult to calculate with any accuracy. It is certainly considerably less than 100 million dollars (and may well be less than 50 million).

[4] It is difficult to ascertain with any accuracy the actual help provided by the U.S.S.R. Hence it is difficult also to assess the sum the U.S.S.R. should provide for the world tax on the basis of national income.

THE COST OF THE TWO WORLD WARS

The economist, J. Oser (*Must Men Starve?* J. Cape, 1956) has attempted to calculate the amount of expenditure involved in the two great world wars, and to express it in terms of milliards of American dollars.

MILITARY EXPENDITURE, 1914–1954
(*in milliards of dollars*)

Countries	1914–1919	1939–1946	1914–1954
Germany	39·0	272·0	333·2
Argentine		1·6	7·0
Australia	0·2	8·1	15·0
Austria	21·2		22·0
Belgium	3·0	3·2	10·3
Bolivia			0·5
Brazil		1·9	5·8
Bulgaria	1·6		2·2
Burma			0·4
Canada	1·6	19·6	38·1
Ceylon		0·1	0·3
Chile		0·4	1·6
China			25·0 (?)
Colombia		0·2	0·9
Czecho-Slovakia		1·5	5·1
Denmark			1·3
Egypt		0·4	1·5
Finland		2·2	2·5
France	35·3	15·0	104·3
Greece	0·3	0·2	1·8
Guatemala			0·2
Holland	0·8	1·0	8·1
Hungary			0·6
India	0·9	6·7	16·9
Iran		0·2	0·5
Iraq		0·1	0·3
Ireland		0·3	4·3
Indonesia			2·0
Israel			0·3
Italy	13·0	94·0	123·4
Japan	0·7	56·0	64·6
Malaya			0·3
Mexico		0·6	2·0
New Zealand	0·2	2·5	4·3
Norway		0·1	1·5
Pakistan		0·2	0·7
Peru			1·6
Philippines			0·5

MILITARY EXPENDITURE—1914-1954
(in milliards of dollars)

Countries	1914–1919	1939–1946	1914–1954
Poland		2·0	4·7
Portugal		0·4	1·0
Rumania	1·6		2·8
Spain			2·6
Sweden		3·6	7·3
Switzerland		2·1	4·3
Thailand			0·4
Turkey	1·4	2·6	6·1
Union of South Africa	0·2	1·2	2·7
U.S.S.R.	24·4	192·0	379·3
United Kingdom	41·5	128·4	247·1
U.S.A.	30·7	347·1	735·2
Uruguay			0·6
Venezuela		0·1	0·5
Yugoslavia	0·4	0·2	1·8
TOTAL	218·0	1,167·8	2,207·3

(J. Oser, *op. cit.*, pp. 101-2.)

War damage should be added to this expenditure. J. Oser gives the figures for this in the case of certain countries as follows:

WAR DAMAGE, 1914–1918 AND 1939–1945
(in milliards of dollars)

Countries	1914–1918	1939–1945
France	9·5	23
Belgium	6·7	3
Italy	2·6	10
Germany	1·5	50
Great Britain	1·7	6
Russia	1·2	140
Rumania	1·0	etc.
Yugoslavia	1·9 (Serbia)	11
TOTAL	27·8	316·3

If to this expenditure and war damage is added the estimated loss in production due to the shortage of agricultural and industrial labour, we reach the astronomical figure of 2,551·4 milliards of dollars as the cost of the two wars (1914–54).

J. Oser then attempted to show how the equivalent of this sum could be used for peaceful purposes.

If we assume that the 1,700 million people who form the population of underdeveloped countries in Asia, Africa and Latin America, etc., had received 1,000 dollars per head (i.e. the equivalent of the purchasing power per head of population in the U.S.A. in 1937) the total amount of this "grant" would have been 1,760 milliards of dollars.

The remaining 788 million dollars could have provided the underdeveloped nations with as many TVA schemes (the equipping of the Tennessee Valley for dams, factories, irrigation, etc.) at the cost of 3·06 million dollars each, as there are groups of 6 or 7 million persons to be fed in these countries: i.e. 257 TVAs!

(J. Oser, *Must Men Starve?* pp. 103–9.)

of the purchasing power per head of population in the U.S.A. in 1937) the total amount of this "grant" would have been 1,760 milliards of dollars.

The remaining 788 million dollars could have provided the underdeveloped nations with as many TVA schemes (the equipping of the Tennessee Valley for dams, factories, irrigation, etc.) at the cost of 3·06 million dollars each, as there are groups of 6 or 7 million persons to be fed in these countries: i.e. 257 TVAs!

(J. Oser, *Must Men Starve?* pp. 103–9.)

MILITARY EXPENDITURE—1914-1954
(in milliards of dollars)

Countries	1914–1919	1939–1946	1914–1
Poland		2·0	
Portugal		0·4	
Rumania	1·6		
Spain			
Sweden		3·6	
Switzerland		2·1	
Thailand			
Turkey	1·4	2·6	
Union of South Africa	0·2	1·2	
U.S.S.R.	24·4	192·0	
United Kingdom	41·5	128·4	
U.S.A.	30·7	347·1	
Uruguay			
Venezuela		0·1	
Yugoslavia	0·4	0·	
TOTAL	218·0	1,1	

(J. Oser, *op. cit.*, pp. 101-2

War damage should be added to this e
the figures for this in the case of certain

WAR DAMAGE, 1914–1918
(in milliards o

Countries	1914–
France	9·5
Belgium	6·7
Italy	2·
Germany	)
Great Britain	
Russia	
Rumania	
Yugoslavia	

TOTAL

If to this expenditur
loss in production due
labour, we reach th
dollars as the cost

J. Oser then att
could be used fo

If we assume
lation of und
America, etc

F.P.M.P.—

CONTRACEPTION IN JAPAN

The results of a seven-year experiment with 1,161 families

On the 13 July 1948 Japan enacted the "Eugenic Protection Law", as it was called, which recognized contraception as the best method for preventing births. A Population Commission was established and the medical profession invited to share in the Family Planning campaigns.

Dr Koya, former director of the national Public Health Institute at present director of the Japanese School of Medicine in Tokyo, answered the invitation and inaugurated a pilot experimental Family Planning scheme in three Japanese villages.

THE SITE AND THE METHODS USED FOR
THE TRIAL EXPERIMENT

The first village, Kaminfunaka-Mura, is situated in the irrigated region of Kanagawa. It has 370 households. All the mothers have been educated at the elementary school and 25% of them have studied in the secondary school. The second village, Minamoto-Mura, is in the mountains of the Yamanashi district and has 459 households. Most of the women have been educated at the primary school and 14% have studied in the secondary school. Finally, the third village, Fukuura-Mura, is a typical fishing village with 332 households. Only 12% of the women have completed a secondary school course. The standard of living is lower than in the other two villages.

These 1,161 families with a total of 6,936 souls, among whom Dr Koya began his experiment, numbered 1,325 families with 7,133 souls in 1957.

Dr Koya and his team of doctors made it a strict rule during the first year to visit each of the families in the three villages at least once a month, and one doctor stayed for several days at a time in each village to interview the women. In addition to this, in each village a midwife visited the families during the absence of the doctors. The aim was to provide the women with a more precise knowledge of the phenomena of the sexual function and to teach them the various methods of preventing pregnancy. The medical report points out that the first obstacle was the "*Kodakara*" mentality which considers the child as the family's and the nation's greatest "asset".

It was necessary, continues the report, to put forward the advantages of limited families in relation to the new legislation which has introduced equal shares in the family inheritance. It was, so it appears, this "educational" work which made it possible to inaugurate a Family Planning experiment which would last.

Dr Koya reported the results of his experiment in 1951, 1952, 1954, 1955 and finally in 1958.[1] These last results are those summarized here:

THE PROPORTION OF FAMILIES USING CONTRACEPTION

Of the 1,325 families visited in 1957, 570 were still able to have another child, 627 could not (end of the fertile period, sterility, widowhood, divorce) and 126 were unable to for the time being (illness, separation, pregnancy already established).

Of the 570 families in a position to give birth to a child at the time, 429, i.e. 75% were practising contraception, and this included sterilization.

This then was the initial result of the campaign!

Families definitely unable to have a child:	627	
End of the fertile period		388
Sterility		81
Widowhood		147
Divorce		11
Families unable to have a child for the time being:	128	
Pregnancy already established		43
Recent confinement		56
Temporary separation		11
Illness		18
Families able to have a child:	570	
Still wanting to have children		138
Not able to make up their minds, but not using contraception		3
Practising contraception		429
Total of families visited in 1957		1,325

[1] Yoshio Koya, with the assistance of Dr H. Kubo, Dr Shu Yuasa and Dr H. Ogino. "Seven Years of a Family Planning Program in Three Typical Japanese Villages," in the *Milbank Memorial Fund Quarterly*, Oct. 1958, pp. 363–72.

SIZE OF FAMILIES USING CONTRACEPTION

Of the 687 mothers able to have children (to the 570 families mentioned above were added the 128 who at the time of the medical visit were not in a position to give birth to another child; on the other hand, the 11 families temporarily in a state of separation were subtracted from the total number), 46 mothers had had themselves sterilized, and 23 of these had not had their fourth child. The number of families practising contraception increases in proportion as the number of children they already have is greater. Thus after the fourth child, 94% of these families adopt contraception.

Families	*Number of existing children*						
	0	1	2	3	4	5+	*Total*
Number of families	74	146	157	155	96	59	687
Wife sterilized	1	1	8	13	12	11	46
Families practising contraception	2	64	83	110	78	46	383
Percentage of families making use of sterilization or contraception	4%	45%	58%	79%	94%	97%	62%

FALL IN THE BIRTH RATE

The results just quoted only show the condition of the families in relation to the problem of the birth rate after seven years of a campaign in favour of birth control. It may be interesting to follow the trend of the results obtained as the campaign develops further. It should be noticed in particular that the domiciliary visits were made at longer intervals, and of set purpose, during the fourth and fifth years of the campaign, in order to find out whether this would lead to a recovery in the birth rate.

The years in the campaign			*1st*	*2nd*	*3rd*	*4th*	*5th*	*6th*	*7th*
	1948	1949	1950	1951	1952	1953	1954	1955	1956
	1949	1950	1951	1952	1953	1954	1955	1956	1957
Number of families			1,161	1,165	1,160	1,239	1,233	1,259	1,298	1,325
Number of pregnancies	220	200	190	155	126	130	120	119	105
Number of live births	205	185	157	107	101	95	97	100	97
Number of procured abortions	3	12	19	31	20	25	16	10	9
Number of sterilizations	0	0	0	5	16	31	31	40	46
Pregnancy rate (a)	35·6	29·9	28·6	21·0	17·8	18·0	18·2	17·1	15·1

(a) This rate, invented by Stix and Notestein, gives the number of pregnancies per year for 100 families.

In the sixth and seventh years, these visits were renewed and became much more frequent. The question was whether this new effort in the contraceptive campaign would lead to a further reduction in the birth rate. The reduction, which was very marked during the first three years, has varied very little since. It would seem that the birth rate in these three villages has reached its lowest level which is half what it was before the pilot experimental scheme.

It will be seen from the table that there is a constant increase in preventive sterilizations and in the number of procured abortions during the first years. There is an increase in the abortion rate between 1950 (rate = 6 abortions per hundred pregnancies) and 1954 (rate = 19·4%). Then there is a decrease. The 1957 rate (8·7%) is nevertheless higher than that of 1950.

THE PILOT EXPERIMENTAL SCHEME IN ITS
JAPANESE CONTEXT

It is interesting to compare this fall in the birth rate in the three villages in which contraceptive propaganda made a special effort, with that for the rest of the country where birth control campaigns were conducted less systematically.

	1948	1949							
	1949	1950	1st	2nd	3rd	4th	5th	6th	7th
Birth rate Japan	33·5	33·0	28·1	25·3	23·4	21·5	20·0	19·4	18·4
Birth rate Experimental pilot scheme	29·6	26·7	22·6	15·4	14·6	13·7	13·8	14·2	13·6
Sterilization rate Japan	0·07	0·39	0·39	0·65	1·0	1·43	1·92	2·36	2·84
Sterilization rate pilot scheme			0·72	2·3	4·4	4·4	5·6	6·4

These statistics clearly show that the fall in the birth rate was much more marked and much more rapid in the three villages than in the rest of the country. There was also a much greater increase in the number of sterilizations.

THE BIRTH PREVENTION METHODS USED

The report indicates that each family was told of the various methods of birth limitation, with the exception of legal abortion. Each family was encouraged to make its own choice and allowed to change it when it was considered desirable to do so. Expenses incurred in the purchase of contraceptives were reimbursed. Sterilization was only recommended in the case of families with at least four children and in financial distress, or again in cases where there were eugenic grounds for it.

The following table shows the proportional use of the various methods and the preferences shown when changes were made:

Methods for prevention of pregnancy	1951	1957	*Variations*
Occlusive pessary, spermicidal solution	22	1	−21
Jelly + Syringe	20	1	−19
Periodic continence	12	10	− 2
Tablets	0	4	+ 4
Male sheaths	32	38	+ 6
Coitus interruptus	1	8	+ 7
Female diaphragm + Jelly	4	13	+ 9
Male sheaths + Periodic continence	1	12	+11
Sterilization	0	13	+13
Other methods	0	4	+ 4
	100	100	

This table again shows a disturbing increase in the number of sterilizations, and the relatively constant number of those who are only willing to use periodic continence.

To sum up: after a seven years' contraceptive campaign in the three "experimental" Japanese villages, 75% of the families practised birth control. Of the families with 4 children, 94% used contraceptive methods. The number of pregnancies had decreased by 50%, and the annual pregnancy rate for 100 families able to have a child fell from 30% to 15%. The number of sterilizations increased from 0 to 64 per ten thousand inhabitants whilst for Japan as a whole the rate has not yet exceeded 28. And the prophylactic effect of contraception as regards induced abortion (recourse to the facilities for legal abortion provided by the eugenic law was not contemplated in these pilot experimental schemes) does not seem absolutely convincing.[2]

Another inquiry[3] ordered in 1953–4 by the Committee for Maternal Health, and conducted by the Imperial Society for Assistance to Mothers and Children, was to throw light on the question of the

[2] These results should be compared with the remarks of Mayone Stycos on the similar experiment at Puerto Rico: cf. above, p. 60, note 5.
[3] Masabumi Kimura, "Induced Abortions in Japan in 1953–54," in the *Milbank Memorial Fund Quarterly*, April 1959, pp. 154–74.

serious increase of abortion throughout the country. Based on 6,932 questionnaires which were answered by almost 550 doctors who had been called on to perform legalized abortion operations, this study reveals among other things that of 6,174 abortion operations performed in 1953–4, 3,896 were on women resorting to this procedure *for the first time* and 2,278 on women who had already resorted to it previously once, twice, three, four, five or more times. In this latter group of 2,278 women, it is noted that at the time of their first abortion, their average age was 31·1 and the number of their live children 2·6. The other group of 3,896 women, who aborted for the first time in 1953–4, was approximately the same age, 31·4, but had fewer children, 2·4. These figures seem to suggest that the size of the family leads to an earlier recourse to abortion. This interpretation is confirmed by the fact that in the group of "older women" 9·3% were resorting to abortion on the occasion of their *first pregnancy* whilst in the younger group, the proportion was 14·3%. In its commentary on this fact, the inquiry report remarks: "The influence of the recent rapid diffusion of contraception on abortion is suggested by the fact that the average number of living children was greater at each order of abortion for the earlier abortions."

If we understand this aright, it means that, because of contraception and its adoption in practice, a mother resorting to abortion will now have fewer children than would have formerly been the case. Moreover the much higher number of women aborting for the first time in 1953–4 (the fifth year since contraception was legalized in Japan) namely 3,896, when compared with the 2,278 women who had had at least one abortion during the fifteen preceding years (the total abortion figure for these 2,278 is 3,417) does not prove, to say the least, that legalized contraception has a prophylactic effect as regards abortion.

THE ABORTION RATE

Dr Koya's experiment in a mining district, to which we referred on pages 53 and 54 but without information as to its final results, can now, after five years of work, provide authoritative proof in the matter of the abortion rate. We wrote that it seemed likely that the abortion rate would increase although the actual number of abortions would show a decrease because of the widespread diffusion of contraception. As will be seen from the table below, this is precisely the case.

ABORTION RATE IN A MINING AREA TRAINED IN THE PRACTICE OF CONTRACEPTION AT JOBAN, JAPAN

	Before the experiment	Since the adoption of contraception				
	1952 1953	1953 1954	1954 1955	1955 1956	1956 1957	1957 1958
Number of families	716	697	696	675	638	590
Number of pregnancies	208	177	105	88	78	53
Number of births	130	77	53	32	32	17
Birth rate (per thousand)	33·5	20·8	14·4	9·6	9·7	5·4
Number of procured abortions	63	91	49	46	37	28
Abortion rate	30%	51%	47%	52%	47%	52·8%

This shows that the rate, from the time the experiment began to the time when it ended five years later, increased from 30% to 52·8%. In other words, before contraception was propagated, less than one-third of the pregnancies were interrupted by procured abortion. Five years later more than half of the pregnancies were terminated by a procured abortion. When asked for what reasons they had asked for abortion to be procured, 17 of the women in question (i.e. 60%) stated that some mistake connected with contraception had brought on an unexpected and undesirable pregnancy. Seven others said that they had wanted a baby but had been led to change their minds during the pregnancy. Finally two of the women aborted twice in the same year (1957–8), doubtless because this seemed the easiest way out.

STERILIZATION

In the experiment conducted by Dr Koya with which we have just dealt, it is possible to trace an increase in the incidence of sterilization similar to that noted previously in the experiment with the three villages chosen for the pilot scheme.

F.P.M.P—11*

INCREASE IN THE INCIDENCE OF STERILIZATION

Number of sterilizations	1952–3	1953–4	1954–5	1955–6	1956–7	1957–8
Joban mining area	17	29	48	52	69	56(a)
Pilot villages	16	31	31	40	46	
Japan as a whole	55,812	88,364	126,420	169,675	213,855	258,205

(a) Fall due to the fact that a number of sterilized persons had left the mines.

Of the 56 sterilization operations in 1957–8 at Joban, 20 (i.e. 35%) were performed for economic reasons, 24 for therapeutic reasons and 12 on other grounds.

(Yoshio Koya, "Five-Year Experiment on Family Planning among Coal Miners in Joban, Japan," in *Population Studies*, Nov. 1959, pp. 157–63.

APPENDIX X

THE EVOLUTION OF FERTILITY IN
FRENCH FAMILIES 1937–1957

It is well known that the French birth rate declined between the
two wars and recovered after the second. After the gradual decrease
in the number of births, which fell to 620,000 in 1936–8, came the
gap caused by the war years and the period of the occupation. The
figures reached their minimum at 520,000 in 1941. After the liberation came the bulge in the birth rate. The numbers went as high
as approximately 860,000 in 1947–9. After a fairly rapid fall
(1950–3), the number of births has remained stable for some years
at a little above 800,000. These wide fluctuations, for which the
structure of the age "pyramid" and the war are principally responsible, conceal the really important phenomenon: the behaviour
patterns of husbands and wives. Variations in this field are of fundamental importance for the future of the population, although they
are slower and less apparent than those in the number of births.

From 1944 onward, it had been recognized that a change in these
patterns had taken place, probably about the year 1941, perhaps
even earlier. Since then, demographers have perfected their statistical tables and their analyses and can measure the intrinsic characteristics of fertility apart from disturbances due to the war. They
have also increased their efforts to furnish similar data for the period
between the wars in spite of the defective statistics of that time. We
shall outline in brief the current conclusions of these studies:

—the gross rate of reproduction, the classical index of fertility,
rose from 109 in 1931 (approximately) to 130 in 1955, i.e. there was
an increase of 19%.[1]

—the new tables drawn up since 1943 make it possible to observe
the issue (the cumulative number of births) of the marriages which
took place during each calendar year. According to the observations
to date, the behaviour pattern of husbands and wives during the
more recent period is remarkably uniform: the average number
of children for marriages of equal duration remains practically con-

---

[1] The net reproduction rate, which also takes into account the fall in the
death rate between the two periods, rose from 91 to 124 (+36%).

stant.[2] The extrapolation by various methods of the figures for the oldest group (people who married in 1943) whose marriages had already lasted for 14 years, brings the average number of children per marriage to at least 2·35.[3] This characteristic of the new regime should be compared with the average number of children per marriage in 1925.

(The average number of births in question is that for which a husband and wife are responsible when considered at the time of their marriage and whatever their subsequent history may be, i.e. whether they remain together until the woman has passed beyond the period of physiological fertility or whether the union is broken by death or divorce, which was the determining factor in the fertility of marriages in the pre-war period.) It is estimated at 1·98. If therefore the issue of the marriages taking place after the second war is compared with that of the inter-war period, the increase is in the region of 20%.

—a study of the figures for the frequency of families with 1, 2 . . . children reveals that there has not been a uniform increase, as the following estimates show:

WOMEN MARRIED BEFORE THE AGE OF 50

Probability	Between the two wars	After the second war	Variation
of 1 child	0·795	0·810	2%
of 2 children in families which already have 1	0·664	0·807	22%
of 3 children in families which already have 2	0·587	0·624	6%
of 4 children in families which already have 3	0·587	0·574	− 2%
of 5 children in families which already have 4	0·577	0·577	
of 6 children in families which already have 5	0·571	0·578	1%
of 7 children in families which already have 6	0·583	0·577	− 1%

The proportion of childless families has not fallen to any great extent (20·5% to 19%). The most important fact is the 1·5 increase in the probability of a second child in families where there is only

[2] Apart from certain exceptions which can be explained by the phenomena of choice at the time of marriage. For instance, the women who married in 1944, in spite of the upheavals due to the battle of France and the Liberation of a great part of the national territory, have a higher fertility rate.

[3] Maurice Febvay, Head of the Demographic Statistical Department at the Institut National de la Statistique et des Études Economiques, *Niveau et évolution de la fécondité par catégorie socio-professionelle en France,* International Population Conference, Vienna 1959, No. 63, pp. 1-2.

one, whilst the probability in the case of families with two children has only advanced by 6% and in that of families with 3 or more there has been no change in the pattern. In other words, families with at least two children have increased in number by +24% but their distribution according to size (2, 3 . . . children) is much the same as before the war.

FORECASTS OF WORLD POPULATION
BETWEEN 1950 AND 2000

On three occasions over a period of eight years, the United Nations have undertaken to work out figures for the estimated world population between now and the end of the twentieth century. Tables I and II summarize these calculations.

Table 1

WORLD POPULATION IN 1950 AND 1980 (IN MILLIONS)

Years		*According to the methods used for estimating and predicting in*		
		1951	1954	1957
1950		2,406	2,454	2,500
1980 forecast	minimum	2,976 ⎱ ± 660	3,295	3,850
	maximum	3,636 ⎰	3,990 ± 695	4,280 ± 430

The estimated margin of +660 million future inhabitants of the globe in 1980 is now reduced to +430, i.e. the present figures for the population of Europe excluding the U.S.S.R.

Table 2

WORLD POPULATION IN THE YEAR 2000 (IN MILLIONS)

Forecasts	*According to the methods used in predicting in 1957*		
Minimum	4,880 ⎱ (*a*)		⎱
Average	6,280 ⎰ ± 1,400 ⎱ ± 620	⎰	± 2,020
Maximum	6,900		⎰

(*a*) Approximation margins in millions.

In the long run, these approximation margins become considerable. We find 1 milliard 400 millions between the minimum and the average evaluation. This is equivalent to the population of the globe in 1890, and 2 milliards 20 millions between the minimum and maximum estimate (i.e. the total for the whole human race in 1940).

In an effort to differentiate between masses of population, the

United Nations have taken eighteen regions sufficiently homogeneous in various ways and have tried to discover how each of them is likely to develop. Table III sets out in descending scale the different developments in these regions; they vary from a maximum increase of 432% in Central America to an increase of only 135% in Western Europe.[1]

Table 3

PRESENT POPULATION OF THE WORLD DIVIDED INTO 19
REGIONS, AND THE ESTIMATED INCREASES IN THESE
REGIONS BETWEEN 1950 AND 1975

HOMOGENEOUS REGIONS	POPULATION IN 1950 (IN MILLIONS)	ESTIMATED INCREASES (%) FOR 1950–1975	POPULATION IN 2000 (INDEX 100 IN 1950)
Central America	21	92–108	432
Tropical South America	50·6	78–93	402
North Africa	29	65–79	344
South Africa	8·7	62–76	339
South-West Asia	45·9	69–83	325
Pacific Islands	2·2	71	297
Caribbean	10·5	54–66	294
South-East Asia	118	51–64	291
Far East (excluding Japan)	453	49–61	286
Central Southern Asia	343	46–58	281
Central Africa	109	42–62	227
U.S.S.R.	163	47–52	209
South America, temperate zone	17·2	49–53	205
Australia, New Zealand	7·4	52–57	204
North America	126	38–43	186
Japan and the Ryukyu Islands	59·7	32–40	183
Southern Europe	105	20–26	156
Central Europe	117	18–22	143
Northern and Western Europe	120	12–16	135

If we now rearrange these masses taking into account not only their more or less rapid population increase but also the area of the territory they occupy and therefore their density of population per square kilometre, we eventually have a classification of the world's population in four major groups, each of which may well offer the greatest possible similarity in regard to the problems they will have to solve (cf. Table 4):

1. Low density, moderate increase.
2. High density, moderate increase.

[1] *The Future Growth of World Population*, ibid., p. 26, Table 9.

3. Low density, rapid increase.
4. High density, rapid increase.[2]

Table 4

DISTRIBUTION OF WORLD POPULATION IN 1950 AND
2000 IN RELATION TO INCREASE IN DENSITY
PER SQUARE KILOMETRE

	1950			2000		
	In millions	*%*	*Density per square kilometre*	*In millions*	*%*	*Density per square kilometre*
Total population	2,497	100	18	6,269	100	46
1. Low density, *moderate increase.* (N. America; S. America, temperate zone; U.S.S.R.; Australia; New Zealand)	386	15·5	6·9	786	12·3	46
2. High density, *moderate increase.* (Europe, excluding U.S.S.R.; Japan)	477	19·1	90	721	11·5	136
3. Low density, *rapid increase.* (Africa; Central America; S.W. Asia; Tropical S. America; Pacific Islands)	384	15·4	7·3	1,220	19·5	23
4. High density, *rapid increase.* (Caribbean; Central S. Asia; S. E. Asia; Far East excl. Japan)	1,250	50·1	58	3,560	56·8	166

This is probably the most reliable table we have for the future of the world's population because it shows *the great groups whose immediate future seems quite certain* (Groups 1 and 2) *and those, on the contrary, whose future remains doubtful* (Groups 3 and 4). The areas covered by the first two groups will experience only moderate increases and all the more so since in 1950 some of these areas had a greater density of population. Thus in the year 2000 for 100 souls in 1950 they will have 175. Their population figures will, it is true, be only 23·8% of the total population at that date whilst at present, these same areas still contain 34·6% of the world's population. On the other hand, the areas covered by Groups 3 and 4 will advance from 100 to 292 in the year 2000 and will then account for 76·3% of the human race!

[2] *World Population Situation and Prospects*, Population Commission, Tenth Session, E/CN/9/147, 22 Dec. 1958 (Roneotyped), p. 4.

INDEX